EARLY COMMON PETITIONS IN THE ENGLISH PARLIAMENT,
*c.*1290–*c.*1420

To Anthony

with my best wishes

W. Mark Ormrod

EARLY COMMON PETITIONS IN THE ENGLISH PARLIAMENT,
*c.*1290–*c.*1420

edited by
W. MARK ORMROD, HELEN KILLICK,
and PHIL BRADFORD

CAMDEN FIFTH SERIES
Volume 52

CAMBRIDGE
UNIVERSITY PRESS

FOR THE ROYAL HISTORICAL SOCIETY
University College London, Gower Street, London WC1 6BT
2017

Published by the Press Syndicate of the University of Cambridge
University Printing House, Shaftesbury Road, Cambridge CB2 8BS, United Kingdom
1 Liberty Plaza, Floor 20, New York, NY 10006, USA
477 Williamstown Road, Port Melbourne, VIC 3207, Australia
C/Orense, 4, Planta 13, 28020 Madrid, Spain
Lower Ground Floor, Nautica Building, The Water Club,
Beach Road, Granger Bay, 8005 Cape Town, South Africa

© Royal Historical Society 2017

First published 2017

A catalogue record for this book is available from the British Library

ISBN 9781108419673 hardback

SUBSCRIPTIONS. The serial publications of the Royal Historical Society, *Royal Historical Society Transactions* (ISSN 0080-4401) and Camden Fifth Series (ISSN 0960-1163) volumes, may be purchased together on annual subscription. The 2017 subscription price, which includes print and electronic access (but not VAT), is £185 (US $309 in the USA, Canada, and Mexico) and includes Camden Fifth Series, volumes 52 and 53 and Transactions Sixth Series, volume 27 (published in December). The electronic-only price available to institutional subscribes is £155 (US $259 in the USA, Canada, and Mexico). Japanese prices are available from Kinokuniya Company Ltd, P.O. Box 55, Chitose, Tokyo 156, Japan. EU subscribers (outside the UK) who are not registered for VAT should add VAT at their country's rate. VAT registered subscribers should provide their VAT registration number. Prices include delivery by air.

Subscription orders, which must be accompanied by payment, may be sent to a bookseller, subscription agent, or direct to the publisher: Cambridge University Press, University Printing House, Shaftesbury Road, Cambridge CB2 8BS, UK; or in the USA, Canada, and Mexico: Cambridge University Press, Journals Fulfillment Department, 1 Liberty Plaza, Floor 20, New York, NY 10006, USA.

SINGLE VOLUMES AND BACK VOLUMES. A list of Royal Historical Society volumes available from Cambridge University Press may be obtained from the Humanities Marketing Department at the address above.

Printed in the UK by Bell & Bain Ltd.

CONTENTS

PREFACE		vii
INTRODUCTION		1
I	MINISTERS AND OFFICIALS	19
II	CHURCH AND RELIGION	47
III	LIBERTIES, FRANCHISES, AND RIGHTS	67
IV	CRIME, DEBT, AND THE LAW	97
V	MERCHANTS, TRADE, AND FINANCE	129
VI	WAR, RESISTANCE, AND REVOLT	165
VII	MULTIPLE PETITIONS	191
APPENDIX: CHRONOLOGICAL LIST OF KNOWN COMMON PETITIONS, 1290–1340		273
BIBLIOGRAPHY		283
INDEX		297

PREFACE

This collection of early common petitions in the English parliament has been some years in the making, and we owe thanks to a number of organizations and individuals who have made it possible to bring it to fruition. The original identification of the relevant body of material in the National Archives was completed for Mark Ormrod by Dr Lisa Haworth Liddy under a small grant from the Department of History, University of York; this work was supplemented by further identifications and the creation of critical editions of documents, undertaken by Mark Ormrod and Helen Killick, and funded by the Andrew W. Mellon Foundation; we are grateful to Professor Alexandra Gillespie and Professor James Ginther, the Principal Investigators on these projects, for their interest, commitment, and support, and to Dr Kitrina Bevan, Dr Gwilym Dodd, Dr Holly James-Maddocks, Professor Linne Mooney, Professor Anthony Musson and Dr Matthew Phillips, who participated in workshops arising from these grants and have given freely of their knowledge in the making of this edition. Phil Bradford joined the editorial team at a later stage to assist particularly with the historical notes. We are especially grateful to Dr Shelagh Sneddon for her expert assistance in the reading and interpretation of some problematic documents, and to Dr Gwilym Dodd for giving so freely of his expert knowledge of petitioning in the medieval English parliament. Throughout, Caroline Kennan's assistance in managing grants, organizing editorial meetings and co-ordinating text files has been invaluable. We acknowledge the considerable assistance and support that we have received from the National Archives over a sustained period, and especially the former and current staff, Dr Nick Barratt, Dr David Crook, Dr Sean Cunningham, and Dr Paul Dryburgh. We are very grateful to Miranda Bethell for her expert advice and copy-editing, and to the team at Cambridge University Press, particularly Melanie Howe and Daniel Pearce, for a very efficient production process. Finally, the intellectual stimulation and practical support of the Department of History and the Centre for Medieval Studies at the University of York have been crucial to the successful outcome of this project.

INTRODUCTION

1. The common petition in parliament

The opening decades of the twenty-first century have seen a notable revival of interest in the records of the medieval English parliament. In 2004–2005 a team of scholars funded by the Leverhulme Trust and led by Chris Given-Wilson published *The Parliament Rolls of Medieval England* (*PROME*), a new electronic and print edition, with full translation, of the extant parliament rolls for the reigns of Edward I to Henry VII. Because *PROME* focuses on those aspects of parliamentary business that were committed to permanent record on the parliament rolls, it does not consider systematically the other available records associated with the medieval parliament. In particular, it does not reproduce the substantial numbers of unenrolled petitions submitted in parliament that were printed in the eighteenth-century edition of the rolls, *Rotuli Parliamentorum* (*RP*), though it does include introductory materials and appendices providing summaries and transcripts of these and other ancillary documents. In order to address the petitioning side of parliamentary business, in 2003–2007 a research team funded by the Arts & Humanities Research Council and led by W. Mark Ormrod and Gwilym Dodd produced detailed summaries and indexes of the contents of the series SC 8 ('Ancient Petitions') at The National Archives (TNA); these data, along with linked digital images of the relevant documents, are available via TNA's main online catalogue, Discovery. Together, these resources have helped to spark a new body of scholarship on the records and process of petitioning in parliament, and in the process created a new appreciation of the range and scale of parliamentary business over the later thirteenth and fourteenth centuries (*Petitions Religious Houses*; Brand 2004b; Given-Wilson 2004; Ormrod 2004; Bradford 2007; Dodd 2007; Ormrod 2008a; Ormrod 2008b; Brand 2009; Ormrod 2009a; Dodd 2009; Bevan 2013; Phillips 2013; Dodd, Phillips, and Killick 2014; Dodd 2014; Dodd and Petit-Renaud 2015; Ormrod 2015; Killick 2016).

One important topic requiring re-investigation in light of this enhanced access to records is the so-called 'common petition': that is, a petition that did not simply concern the interests of single private parties but claimed to speak in the name of, or was deemed to be of interest to, the generality of the king's subjects. Private petitions have been a focus of interest again since the 1970s as a result of the important work of Harding (1975; 2002: 147–190), Maddicott (1978; 1981; 1984; 2010: 294–297, 371–372), Brand (2004b; 2009) and Dodd (2007; 2009). For the most part, however, relatively little scholarly attention has been paid to the common petition since the seminal work of Myers (1937) and Rayner (1941). More recent research has concentrated on those common petitions which, from the 1340s onwards, were written up on the main parliament roll (Harriss 1975: 356–375; Edwards 1979: 56–65; Harriss 1981: 43–49; Waugh 1991: 202–203; Ormrod 2004: 39–40; Dodd 2007: 140). Both before and after 1340, however, a significant number of petitions that claimed 'common' status and/or were designated as such by the crown were not enrolled, and survive only because royal clerks chose to include them among the bundles of private petitions compiled for each assembly or with other miscellaneous memoranda in the records of the council. As a result of the ways in which these bundles and files were re-organized and published between the eighteenth and twentieth centuries, it became progressively more difficult to identify the discrete body of unenrolled common petitions. The 2003–2007 indexing project revealed the existence of a significant number of common petitions within the wider series of Ancient Petitions. Preliminary lists compiled at that time became the basis for further identifications and transcriptions completed under two awards from the Andrew W. Mellon Foundation led by the University of Toronto and St Louis University. The present volume provides the fruits of that work, creating a critical edition of a series of unenrolled common petitions from the late thirteenth to the early fifteenth century. These documents, hitherto mostly unpublished, constitute some of the earliest records of the English parliament, and yield crucial evidence for the nature and scope of parliamentary business, the development of parliamentary process, and the emergence of what would later be called the House of Commons.

The exact nature of a 'common petition' has been a subject of prolonged debate. The central issue is a terminological one, namely, the ambiguity of the term 'common', and more specifically, whether it refers to the parliamentary commons, the knights and burgesses elected from the thirteenth century as representatives of the towns and boroughs in parliament. Early studies tended to distance themselves from too ready an identification between common petitions and the commons, stressing that the common petition was simply a request made nominally in the name of, and representing the interests of, the broader political community; this stood in contrast to the 'private petition', which aimed at the redress of grievances affecting specific individuals or groups (Haskins 1937; Haskins 1938; Rayner 1941; Morris 1943; Edwards 1979: 44–65). More recent scholarship has reassessed this issue, arguing that, from the mid 1310s onwards, the parliamentary commons largely took over from the barons the right to speak in the name of the 'community of the realm' and thus emerged, by the late 1320s, as the primary authors of the petitions designated as 'common' in the business of parliament (Harriss 1975: 118–121; Prestwich 1983; Ormrod 1990a; Dodd 2007: 128–141; Maddicott 2010: 331–375). Throughout this period of transition, however, we lack detailed information as to who determined the 'common' nature of petitions – an uncertainty made all the greater by a considerable variety of terms employed by the authors to describe the social and political collective in whose name the petitions were made.

Given this ambiguity, the criteria for inclusion within this volume require some further discussion. What are the defining characteristics of a common petition? Most simply, it can be defined in relation to the private petition. The medieval private petition was a request made to the king or his council in parliament, submitted on behalf of a named individual, corporation, or other defined social group. Such requests often dealt with difficult cases which could not be easily resolved through the common law; private petitions therefore provide important evidence of the importance of royal discretion in the dispensing of medieval justice (Dodd 2007: 1–15). There are three key areas in which the private petition differed from the common petition. First, in a private petition, the identity of the petitioner (whether individual or group) was specified; common petitions, by contrast, were usually addressed on behalf of the 'community of the realm', 'commonalty', 'commons' or similar formulations, the implications of which are discussed in Section 2 below. Secondly, private petitions dealt with matters relating only to the petitioner(s), whereas common petitions raised issues of concern to the wider political community. In her seminal study of the common petition, Rayner argued strongly that the defining characteristic of the common petition was its subject-matter rather than its origin; it referred to requests 'concerned with a common or public interest' (Rayner 1941: 204, 570). The third way in which private and common petitions differed concerns the manner in which they were received and answered. Private petitions were received by chancery clerks appointed to sort and pass them on to special committees of auditors or triers made up of members of the nobility, prelacy, and judiciary; only if they required the application of the king's grace were these petitions then passed up for the personal attention of the monarch. Common petitions, by contrast, were submitted directly to the king and council and the responses to them were normally read out in full parliament at the end of the given assembly. There has been some debate as to when this final distinction became conventional practice. While it has been suggested as plausible that some common petitions (especially composite documents comprising what are called in this edition 'multiple petitions') were diverted for the immediate attention of the king and council under Edward I and Edward II, it is only from the beginning of the reign of Edward III that clear evidence becomes available for the existence of distinct processes for the hearing of private and common petitions (*RPHI*, p. xiii; Clarke 1936: 232–233; Rayner 1941: 198–199, 562; Ormrod 1995: 34; Dodd 2007: 132–133).

In response to these continuing ambiguities and uncertainties, Dodd has suggested a three-stage model for the early development of the common petition (2007: 128–155). The first phase was dominated by the grievances of the 'community of the realm', which under Edward I usually meant the barons and prelates in parliament. With the accession of Edward II, community petitions became more directly influenced by the knights and burgesses, whose greater attendance in parliament during this period reflected their development as a political force. However, at this stage, common petitions were still treated in much the same manner as private petitions. During the second phase, from the early years of Edward II's reign until the early 1340s, the parliamentary commons began to exercise political power independently of the barons, and compiled their own schedules of grievances which were received directly by the king and council. The third phase in the development of the common petition came with the inclusion of these schedules of grievances, and the answers provided to them, on the formal record of the parliament roll, which became regular practice from 1343. The common petition continued to develop and adapt during this third phase, particularly from the 1370s when the commons began to adopt or 'avow' those private petitions that they considered to have a sufficiently broad application for presentation as common petitions. Thus, by the late fourteenth century, common petitions included a much more diverse range of requests, reflecting the concerns not only of the general populace, but also of specific regional, social, and sectional groups. This development reflects the growing perception of the commons as a political authority in its own right, as evidenced by the appearance in the late 1370s of private petitions which were addressed to the commons themselves.

For much of the first half of the fourteenth century, then, and to some extent thereafter, the distinction between private and common petitions submitted in parliament was ambiguous. Down to the time of Edward II, the administrative machinery for the presentation of common petitions was not yet fully formed, meaning that common and private petitions were often submitted along the same channels. In the later fourteenth century, the commons sometimes adopted complaints submitted as private petitions which they believed to be concerned with the public interest, and reformulated them as common petitions. Despite this ambiguity regarding their compilation, common petitions may be broadly defined in two ways: they dealt with matters in the collective interest, and, at least from the 1320s onwards, they were sent directly to the king and council rather than to the officials appointed to deal with private petitions.

2. The scope and contents of the edition

For most of the period covered by this volume, *c*.1290–*c*.1420, the text of common petitions, and knowledge of their submission and contents, tends only to survive where there is an extant roll of proceedings of the relevant parliament. The erratic survival of the parliament rolls before 1330, and occasional lacunae thereafter, leaves us largely ignorant of whether common petitions were submitted and heard in the relevant parliaments. The matter is compounded by the fact that, until the 1340s, the clerks of parliament did not necessarily consider the common petitions as a coherent body of material that belonged, as a matter of course, on the roll of parliament.[1] The starting point for the present study is the neglected fact that a certain number of original petitions made (explicitly or implicitly) in the name of the commons survive across the fourteenth and early fifteenth century that either relate to parliaments for which there is no extant roll of proceedings or, for various reasons, were not taken up and written into the official record of the relevant session. Where these can be dated with some certainty to parliaments whose rolls have not survived, they provide the missing evidence both for the submission of common petitions in the relevant assemblies and of the substance of that business and the crown's response to it. Where a petition can be precisely dated to a parliament whose roll is preserved, the original common petition may provide evidence either of the first drafting stage for a petition that appears in modified and developed form on the roll, or that the matter was considered but not selected to be taken forward to the council and enrolled.

---

[1] As with private petitions, a clerk would mark a common petition with the note *Irrotulatur* ('Enrolled', often abbreviated to *Irr*) to indicate that it was included on the parliament roll (Dodd 2007: 326). Only four petitions within this volume bear this note (nos 5, 6, 54 and 72), signalling the fact that the majority of the petitions published here were either rejected or never heard.

Down to the 1330s, it seems that common petitions were submitted piecemeal, some as multiple petitions on single documents but most as single items. From the 1340s, the growing association between parliamentary grants of taxation and redress of grievance encouraged the development of the single 'schedule' of common petitions, submitted in association with the formal document recording the concession of a subsidy in order (implicitly or explicitly) to bring pressure on the crown to acknowledge its thanks for the generosity of the assembly by remedying the concerns of the commons (Harriss 1975: 356–375). In the 1370s, however, a general increase in the scale of the commons' business, and the new practice of avowing private petitions as part of the commons' agenda, mean that the schedules of common petitions and responses appended to or (more usually) copied in a fair hand onto the parliament roll tend to represent a less than comprehensive record of the full amount of business submitted in the name of the commons. In particular, the present collection reveals a significant number of petitions made in the name of the commons in the early years of Richard II's reign which, for various reasons, were not included, or were taken up only in modified form, in the official record of parliament.

From the 1420s, and specifically from 1423, the relationship between original petitions and enrolled common petitions changed again. Now, the clerk of parliament routinely preserved a separate bundle or file of the petitions submitted *by* the commons (both those made in their own name and those that had been submitted *to* the commons and were adopted by them) (Myers 1937: 591–592; Dodd 2007: 187–196). The character of the body of unenrolled material and the relationship between it and the parliament rolls therefore shifted significantly from the beginning of the reign of Henry VI, and the change in practice provides the essential justification for the *terminus ad quem* of the present study. The fact that it is much more straightforward to date unenrolled common petitions after 1423 means that a higher proportion of them have already been published in *RP* and noted in the introductions, footnotes, and appendices to parliament rolls in *PROME*. Taken as a whole, the surviving material for the period *c.*1290–*c.*1420 provides both a substantive addition to the records of parliament and the basis for a significant advance in our understanding of the commons' role in fourteenth-century politics.

The first criterion for inclusion in the current edition is therefore that the petition in question is addressed explicitly (or, from internal evidence, implicitly) in the name of 'the community', 'the commonalty', 'the commons', 'the people', 'the knights, citizens and burgesses', and other related formulations. This is a complex issue, since the language of community, both within parliament and in the wider realm, changed quite considerably across the thirteenth and fourteenth centuries and translations we choose for the various words employed in Latin and Anglo-Norman French can be both problematic and loaded. Magna Carta was forced on a reluctant King John in 1215 by barons claiming to act in the wider interests of the realm, and this set a pattern for the thirteenth century in which the barons largely claimed the right to voice the concerns of the king's subjects. In opposing Henry III in 1258, the barons viewed themselves as *le commun de Engletere* and required twelve of their own to be elected *pur tut le commun de la tere* (*Baronial Movement*, pp.100, 104). In the Declaration of Boulogne issued by a group of barons in 1308, one of the justifying factors was that the authors were acting *de commun assent* (Phillips 1972: 318). In these examples, *commun[e]* (both as noun and as adjective) denotes a collective that historians often call the 'community', but which does not necessarily imply, or implicate, the generality of the king's subjects. It is true that other elements could occasionally be included, as in 1265 when a settlement with Henry III was agreed by *les hauz homes et le commune de la tere* (Maddicott 2010: 259), and in 1297 when the Remonstrances against Edward I were articulated in the name of the *ercevekes, eveskes, countes, barons e tote la comunalte de la terre* (*Crisis of 1297–1298*, p. 115). At least until the early years of Edward II, however, the general consensus is that 'community of the realm' was a term denoting the collective action of the baronage, not specifically of the group that would later be known as the commons (Clarke 1936: 154–172; Prestwich 1983; Prestwich 1990a: 129–145; Maddicott 2010: 324–325). And while it is true that words such as *communitas* and *commune* were sometimes used in the later thirteenth and early fourteenth century to signal the knights, and sometimes also the burgesses, of parliament, we cannot necessarily assume that they denote the concerted actions or views of the entire group of elected representatives in a given parliamentary assembly (Watts 2015: 214–215). Until the time of Edward III, the knights and burgesses were summoned only irregularly to parliament, were treated as separate groups or 'estates' in the working life of the assembly, were sometimes dismissed before parliament was concluded, and were usually excluded from the discussions of major public business held there by the king, council and magnates (Sayles 1975: 94–126). The various forms used in the earlier petitions in this volume show an imperfect and mutable language, with petitions coming from 'the people' (nos 1 and 31), 'the poor people of the realm of England' (no. 3), 'the common people of the realm of England' (no. 22), 'the lieges of the commonalty of England' (no. 19), 'the good people' (nos 20 and 21), and various other associated formulae. With the language of community mainly appropriated by the baronage, other petitioners seeking to represent the wider 'common' voice were thus forced to experiment with various other forms of self-identification.

During the reign of Edward II and the early years of Edward III, however, there was a significant shift and stabilization of terminology. In particular, the defeat and disgrace of Edward II's political opponents at the Battle of Boroughbridge in 1322 created a new dynamic in parliament, where the lords were reduced to a rump and the representative element began more consistently to assert its right to speak for the kingdom at large (Harriss 1975: 98–99; Prestwich 1983; Buck 1983b: 142–147; Ormrod 1990a). During the 1330s the terms 'community' and 'commonalty' were gradually replaced by 'commons' (*la commune*) to describe those who made common petitions in the collective interests of the people (Harriss 1981: 38; Brown 1989: 209–211). Although it is still anachronistic to talk at this stage of 'houses' of lords and commons, there was clearly a sense from this point that the representatives in parliament, for all the diversity of their constituencies, their status, and their interests, formed a collective 'commons' that could speak in the common interest. As the work of Watts (2007; 2015) and Rollinson (2010: 91–100, 143–148, 240–247) has shown, the term 'commons' has a complicated history and later came to be applied not just to the knights and burgesses but to an entire social order. However, in the context of parliament and parliamentary petitions, especially the common petition, 'commons' had a reasonably precise meaning by 1340. To reflect this gradual shift over the first half of the fourteenth century from 'community of the realm' to 'commons', the English summaries of common petitions provided in this volume translate the term *commune* as 'commonalty' when the petition concerned dates from before 1340, but employ 'commons' for those dating thereafter.

There are many other variations upon the theme of community in the address clauses of the petitions published here, and some further explanation is needed as to the criteria for selection. We include petitions made jointly by the lords and commons, but exclude those made in the name of the lords alone where the subject matter clearly applies only to the peers in parliament. Except in cases where there is clear evidence that the matter was taken up specifically by the commons and/or that the commons were included as named petitioners alongside others, we exclude petitions made in the name of other political collectives that had close association with parliament: for example, those from the higher and/or lower clergy of the realm, from the so-called estate of merchants, from the mayor, aldermen, and commonalty of London, and (towards the end of the relevant period) from the Company of the Staple of Calais, all of which groups undoubtedly helped, in their own right, to drive the wider agenda of parliament over the fourteenth and early fifteenth century. Also excluded are those petitions in the name of specific local communities and/or interest groups that were adopted as common petitions and enrolled on the parliament rolls from the 1370s onwards. These requests often reflect the concerns of the groups in question, rather than those of the general populace, and are therefore less illuminating as regards the development of the fourteenth-century parliamentary commons as a collective political entity. Finally, there survive a fairly significant number of original petitions that do not name the petitioner(s). Discretion has been applied to remove those petitions in this category that are very obviously particular to an individual or a corporation, and to preserve only those that appear, prima facie, to address a matter of general importance to the realm at large. In a number of cases, those which pass this first selection can be excluded on the basis of contextual evidence revealing that they were neither written nor adopted by the commons and/or were not submitted in parliament. Those that remain, in this collection, have been closely scrutinized in terms of form, content, and context to establish their credibility as common petitions.

The second set of criteria for selection in this volume concerns the relationship between the original petitions and the parliament rolls. Where an original survives that was subsequently included in identical or near-identical form on a parliament roll (including the separate rolls of petitions made in certain parliaments during the late 1320s and early 1330s), it is excluded here on the basis that it is available in a modern edition in *PROME*.[2] Wherever the original is different from the enrolled version, however, it is edited here: this category includes originals where the enrolment provides only a Latin summary rather than a verbatim transcription (as was frequent practice under Edward I and Edward II) as well as those cases where the enrolled version deviates sufficiently from the original to provide interest and understanding of the process by which the clerks of parliament determined the final text of the common petitions written on the parliament roll. Finally, this collection includes unenrolled common petitions that were transcribed at various points in the seventeenth and eighteenth centuries and were included in the 'Petitiones in Parliamento' sections of *RP*, but which are excluded from *PROME*

---

[2] The same point applies in the three cases where lists of common petitions and the responses to them were enrolled on the dorse of the close roll: in the instances from 1309 (no. 110) and 1325 (no. 116), the existence of originals and/or the absence of full modern editions/translations means they are included here; in the cases of a short series of common petitions from the parliament of January–March 1327 (see Appendix), there is no original, and a full translation of the enrolment is available in *CCR* (itself accessible online).

because they were not enrolled on the parliament rolls. Common petitions that only now survive as earlier transcripts in these sections of *RP* are excluded as a matter of policy on the grounds that there is now no original documentary authority for a new edition.

The present collection cannot claim to be fully comprehensive. The search for common petitions has focused solely on material in TNA, and specifically in the two most obvious of its record series, Ancient Petitions (SC 8) and Chancery: Parliament and Council Proceedings (C 49). There are presumably strays in other series, though a systematic search of Exchequer: Parliament and Council Proceedings (E 175) and spot-checks of other series via TNA's online search facility have not, thus far, brought further eligible cases to light. That there are other relevant materials beyond the holdings of TNA is demonstrated by the existence in a number of non-governmental records of transcripts of schedules of common petitions from parliaments whose rolls have not survived. In these cases, however, the relevant texts are available in modern editions and/or full translations. For the period covered by this volume, the known instances of this phenomenon are: the multiple-clause 'bill' submitted by the 'people of the commonalty of the land' at the Lincoln parliament of January–February/March 1301, surviving in the archives of Canterbury Cathedral (edition in *Parl. Writs*, I, 104–105; full translation in *EHD*, III, 510–512); the common petitions datable to the parliament of March–May 1340 found in the cartulary of Winchester Cathedral (edition in Harriss 1975: 518–520; summary in *PROME*, IV, 275; see also Harriss 1963); the common petitions in the anonymous Westminster chronicle relating to the Cambridge Parliament of September–October 1388 (edition and translation in *Westminster Chronicle*, pp. 356–368; translation in *PROME*, VII, 124–125), and the famous Lollard-inspired bill for the disendowment of the church associated with the parliament of January–May 1410, which is extant in both English and Latin versions in a number of manuscripts (edition in *English Wycliffite Writings*, pp. 135–137, translated in *PROME*, VIII, 509; see also *St Albans Chronicle*, II, 584–589). The net effect is that the present edition, read in conjunction with *PROME* and these supplementary sources, provides full access to all currently known common petitions, unenrolled and enrolled, of the period *c*.1290–*c*.1420. To facilitate understanding of the survival of common petitions over the first half of that period, during which the relationship between unenrolled and enrolled common petitions is so notably complicated, the Appendix provides a chronological survey of all known material for the years 1290–1340.

The common petitions published here are, like the much larger collection of private petitions gathered in The National Archives series SC 8, undated; a dating clause was unnecessary since, from the point of view of the royal administration, the part that needed recording was not the request itself but the action taken as a result of the response. Prior to modern sorting, most petitions would have been datable from their administrative context, either because they were preserved in the original bundles kept for single meetings of parliament, or because they were filed with a dated writ to one of the government offices ordering the appropriate action to be taken. In the nineteenth century, the original files of private petitions compiled in parliament were broken up to create a new, artificial series known as 'Parliamentary Petitions', though not before the creation of a significant number of extant transcriptions by the Record Commission which, in some instances, can help establish the original archival context, and therefore date, of the relevant documents. In the late nineteenth century, this series was itself subsumed into a much larger collection of petitions of other types, creating the current series of Ancient Petitions. In addition, a number of documents were removed from the Parliamentary Petitions and placed elsewhere: for example, in Chancery: Council and Parliament Proceedings (C 49), Chancery: Warrants for the Great Seal Series I (C 81) and Chancery: Miscellanea (C 47). The task of re-establishing the context of, and thus assigning dates to, the individual documents in Ancient Petitions was begun in the 1920s by R.L. Atkinson, and continued during the cataloguing project led by Ormrod and Dodd in 2003–2007 (Dodd 2001; 2009). This was accomplished via cross-referencing, where possible, to existing printed sources such as the published calendars of the patent, close, and fine rolls, of inquisitions *post mortem* and inquisitions miscellaneous (which record actions taken as a result of the request), or by internal evidence such as references to known persons or events; in some cases, quite refined dates can be given to petitions simply on the basis of the specific language used (Sneddon 2009: 193–205). Where no other evidence was available, these earlier attempted archival rationalizations simply assigned petitions an impressionistic date or date range based on the hand. Common petitions for which no immediate cognate is found on the extant parliament rolls are particularly problematic in terms of dating as a result of the often generalized nature of the requests. The editors of this volume have made attempts to contribute to the existing evidence regarding the date of the petitions, and in a number of cases have provided new positive or likely dates for petitions previously misinterpreted or subject only to very impressionistic dating; the basis for these attributions is set out below, in Section 4.

The petitions have been arranged in chapters under different themes, and within these chapters, as far as possible, in chronological order. The themes illustrate the scope of the subject matter of common petitions during this period and the changing political role of the commons over the course of the fourteenth century. Some of the common petitions dating from the 1320s and 1330s, for example, are characterized by a severe anti-baronial stance; they accuse the aristocracy of using their power to oppress the poor and manipulate the legal system in their favour (Ormrod 1990a: 19–24). Many common petitions reflect the role of the commons in providing assent to the king's terms for grants of taxation (Brown 1989: 224–230). Common petitions also provide a very important index of the commons' ability and inclination to expand their horizons beyond the corruption of government and the shortcomings of the law to include matters of growing public interest such as the political economy; in the later fourteenth century, after the Black Death, there is some evidence that they began to support social policies that were increasingly divisive and intended to shore up the interest of the proprietary elite (Ormrod 2010). By the late fourteenth century and on into the fifteenth, the moral force of applying 'common' status to petitions was also somewhat weakened by the increasing inclusion of petitions from individuals and corporations amongst the common petitions presented to the crown (Dodd 2007: 143–196). On the whole, however, the collection of documents presented here provides powerful reinforcement of the view that the fourteenth-century English parliament, and more specifically the parliamentary commons, was a particularly dynamic forum capable of debating the public affairs of the kingdom and bringing significant pressure to bear upon the crown for the remedy of unsound laws and practices and the general promotion of good governance (Ormrod 1995: 30–37; Harriss 2005: 66–74; Maddicott 2010: 352–366, 431–453; Ormrod 2010).

3. Form, hand, and language of the common petition

In both language and form, the common petitions in this volume are not markedly different from the wider body of private petitions surviving in the Ancient Petitions and (until the 1330s) enrolled on the parliament rolls. By the early fourteenth century, the private petition submitted in parliament had assumed a standard form comprising five different elements (Dodd 2007: 281–282). These may be summarized as follows: the address; the name of the petitioner; the grievance; the request for remedy, and a rhetorical appeal that the request might be granted *pur Dieu et en oevre de charite*. However, over the course of the fourteenth century, a number of changes may be observed in the way that these elements of petitionary diplomatic were formulated. In the early fourteenth century petitions tended to be addressed to the king alone, or the king and council, whereas from the 1370s onwards there were an increasing number of petitions addressed to the king and lords (Dodd 2007: 281–282); it is also in the late fourteenth century that the first petitions directly addressed to the parliamentary commons appear. The language of the requests became increasingly elaborate and formal in tone, and as a consequence they increased substantially in length (Dodd 2007: 287–290; Dodd 2014). With some exceptions (such as those where there is no clause explicitly naming the petitioner), the common petitions in this volume conform to this pattern of petitionary diplomatic, and reflect the developments that took place in the way private petitions were formulated. The majority of the requests are addressed to the king or the king and council, but approximately one sixth of them, dating from the late fourteenth century, make specific reference to parliament in their address.

Private petitions employed a number of rhetorical devices in framing their complaints, such as emphasizing the plight of the petitioner, the strength of their oppressors, and the benefits to the king and wider community if the request were to be granted (Dodd 2007: 295–302). These devices all feature in common petitions, but a change in emphasis is perceptible over the course of the fourteenth century. Of particular interest here is the discourse of 'common profit', signifying the mutual interest of the crown and realm. Ormrod has recently argued that the adoption of this phrase in common petitions in the late fourteenth century 'reflected a change in the function and status of the commons, as they moved from the role of humble supplicants for the king's grace to legitimate arbiters of what was, and was not, for the common good' (Ormrod 2015: 221).

For the most part, common petitions are single paragraphs of text, with no distinguishing features in their presentation. However, some depart from this form in that they contain a list of complaints or requests set out in separate paragraphs (sometimes prefaced by a header), usually including a full address only in the first clause, each subsequent request beginning with the words *Item* or *Derechief*. The corpus of common petitions contains a disproportionately high number of multiple-clause requests; approximately one sixth of the documents in this volume fall into this category. By contrast, this type of petition is comparatively rare amongst the private petitions; documents of this type predominantly date from the first half of the fourteenth century, and were more likely to emanate from collective entities such as towns, religious houses or mercantile institutions. It has been suggested that the early schedules of common petitions compiled in the 1320s were influenced in terms of their style and form by the multiple-clause private petitions of the late thirteenth and early fourteenth century, and that both types of document may have arisen for reasons of administrative expediency (Dodd, Phillips, and Killick 2014: 177–178, 183).

Just over half the common petitions published here record a response, which usually appears on the dorse (hence the term 'endorsement'), but occasionally on the face. (In the case of multiple petitions, the relationship between the petitions and the responses is more complex and varied, and is discussed in the notes to individual documents.) In many cases, the responses indicate the context of the petition's presentation rather than any decision taken as a result of the request. As stated above, one of the distinguishing features of a common petition, at least from the early part of the reign of Edward III, was that it was heard in the presence of the king and/or his council. Approximately one fifth of the petitions in this volume give a clear indication that they were received along these administrative channels, as they have been marked *coram rege* or *coram magno consilio*. A minority of the responses make specific reference to parliament, indicating that this was the context of their presentation. As discussed above, in some cases original common petitions may have represented 'first drafts' of matters eventually drawn up on the parliament roll; for this reason, the lack of a response should not necessarily be taken as an indication that the petition in question was altogether unsuccessful.

The petitions in this volume are all in Anglo-Norman French, although there are two that contain short sections in Latin.[3] In this respect they reflect contemporary practice in private petitioning. French predominated in petitions until the mid fifteenth century; Latin was used in only a minority of cases, and English petitions did not appear in any significant number until the 1430s (Ormrod 2009b; Dodd 2011b: 122–123; Dodd 2011b). The responses of the crown to the common petitions are written in both Latin and French (although some of those in Latin are formulaic phrases such as *coram rege*). Latin became less prevalent in the crown's responses after the 1320s, though it did not disappear entirely.[4]

In the majority of cases, we do not know who was responsible for drafting petitions. It is generally accepted that most petitioners would have employed professional scriveners, but a minority may have possessed the skills and knowledge to draw up their own requests.

---

[3] Nos 113 (1322) and 88 (*c*.1380). In the former case, the switch from French to Latin occurs mid-sentence and appears to have no apparent cause, whereas the latter petition includes a quotation of part of a Latin charter.

[4] Of the 127 petitions in this volume, 52 contain no response, 45 contain responses in French, 24 contain responses in Latin (including 5 that have only formulaic phrases such as *coram rege*), 5 contain responses in both French and Latin, and 1 has a response that is illegible. Of the petitions with Latin responses, fourteen date from before 1330, and none are later than 1362.

A full palaeographical survey of petitions has yet to be undertaken, but, based on a preliminary study, Lister M. Matheson argues that, while private petitions might have been drafted by the petitioners themselves or by scriveners employed for the purpose, common petitions were more likely to have been drawn up by government clerks (Matheson 1986: 649).[5] Originating as they did within a parliamentary context, it is possible that some common petitions were drawn up by one of the clerks of parliament who were appointed from the chancery; if this were the case, they should display a similar hand to that of the chancery clerks, a form of anglicana sometimes referred to as 'court' or 'charter' hand (Johnson and Jenkinson 1915: xv–xxi; Hector 1966: 55–65; Parkes 1969: xiv–xvi; Chaplais 1971: 50–53). A number of petitions within this volume display a hand resembling that of the chancery clerks; this is supported by the fact that in several cases, the hand of the petition and its response are very similar.[6] The documents in this category predominantly date from the first half of the fourteenth century; from the 1350s onwards, petitions become more cursive in appearance and begin to exhibit features common to the new 'secretary' script which was adopted in the offices of the privy seal and signet in the 1370s (Chaplais 1971: 52). We can therefore surmise that most of the documents in this collection dating from the second half of the fourteenth century were drafted by professional scriveners and clerks from government offices other than the chancery; in some cases, the MPs themselves may have been responsible for drafting the petitions (Bevan 2013: 228–229). This would have been increasingly the case from the late fourteenth century onwards, when an increasing number of common petitions originated outside parliament as a result of the growing tendency of the commons to avow private petitions which they considered to be in the public interest.[7] This evidence contributes to our understanding of the administrative context in which these documents were created. Ormrod outlines the role of the clerks of parliament in compiling the common petitions which appeared on the parliament roll, which involved 'at least three distinct phases of writing and negotiating, the first phase being the writing up of single grievances in the form of *ad hoc* memoranda, the second being the collection and recording of those items in the "roll" of common petitions (a task apparently undertaken by the "under-clerk",

---

[5] The hand of one of the petitions in this volume (no. 18) bears a strong resemblance to that of the privy seal clerk Thomas Hoccleve. Hoccleve has previously been identified as the scribe of several private petitions: Killick 2011: 87–89.

[6] See, for example, nos 6 (1320), 20 (1327–1330), 24 (mid 14th c.), 31 (early 14th c.) and 116 (1325).

[7] For a later example of a common petition drafted outside Westminster, see Killick 2016.

a chancery official assigned to the commons for the purpose), and the third being the set of decisions taken by the clerk of parliament as to which sections of the commons' list would actually be written up and preserved on the enrolled record of the assembly' (Ormrod, 2004: 46). It is important to emphasize here that the majority of the petitions in this volume were not enrolled; this and the palaeographical evidence suggest that they may represent 'first drafts' of matters which were subsequently rejected or redrafted and presented in another form.

4. Editorial principles

Abbreviations have been expanded silently. Where multiple alternatives exist in orthography, the shortest possible version has been selected (for example, *seign'* is rendered *seignur* rather than *seigneur*). In the case of French and Latin place names, where multiple alternatives exist, the abbreviation has been left unexpanded (for example, *Salop'*; *Linc'*). Missing text and conjectural readings are contained within square brackets, with an explanatory footnote. Interlinear text is displayed within \ /. Punctuation has been added with reference to the five stages of petitionary diplomatic described above. Apostrophes have been added to mark elisions (for example, *d'Engleterre*). The practice of the original documents in capitalizing the word *Roi* has been retained, but in all other cases modern conventions have been observed. In all cases, *i* has been used in preference to *j*, and *u* or *v* used according to pronunciation (see Hunnisett 1977: 29). Any text which falls outside the main body of the petition has been categorized under the heading 'Response'; this includes administrative notes such as *Coram rege* and *Irrotulatur*, in addition to the Crown's substantive answer to the given petition. Unless stated, it is to be assumed that the response appears on the dorse of the document.

An English summary has been provided before the text of each document. This aims to outline the key information contained within the petition: the complainant, the nature of their grievance, and their request for redress. Unless particularly relevant to the substance of the petition, formulaic expressions have been omitted. Where possible, we have adhered as closely as possible to the original text of the petition; however, due to the syntactical differences between Anglo-Norman French and modern English, in many cases it has been necessary to paraphrase for the sake of clarity. While an effort has been made to make the summary as comprehensible as possible to the modern reader, we have preserved technical legal terminology and words or phrases which carry a specific historic meaning.

INTRODUCTION 17

As discussed above, the manner in which the supplicants are described within a common petition is of central importance to our understanding of these documents; for this reason, particular care has been taken in translating these appellations. By preserving as far as possible the language of the original document, we attempt to demonstrate the variations in the way the 'common-ness' of the issue addressed was articulated in the self-conscious identity of the petitioners. For the reasons outlined in Section 2 above, *commune* has been translated as 'commonalty' in petitions dating from before 1340, and as 'commons' thereafter.

The editors have in a number of cases been able to refine the dates ascribed to the petitions in this volume by previous scholars. The dates may be categorized according to three levels of specificity as follows:

a. The petition can be assigned to a specific year on the basis of internal or contextual evidence: for example, through reference to known events or individuals, or due to the existence of supporting documentation such as a dated writ to one of the government offices ordering action to be taken as a result of the request; or because it can be linked to a particular parliament through the existence of a nineteenth-century transcript from the original files of Parliamentary Petitions.
b. On the basis of similar evidence, the petition can either be dated within a specific range, or to within a short period of time either side of a specific year (for example: 'c.1332').
c. The petition can be assigned to a broad date range on the basis of its content, form, hand, and language. In such cases, it will be designated either 'early', 'mid', or 'late fourteenth century', the periods approximately corresponding to the reigns of Edward II, Edward III and Richard II.

5. Referencing

All unpublished primary sources cited here are in Kew, The National Archives (TNA), and are referred to by their call number.

Printed primary sources are cited by short title: a key is provided in the relevant section of the Bibliography. In referencing the parliament rolls and previously published petitions, we give the page numbers for all known earlier editions, principally those in: *Rotuli Parliamentorum*, 6 vols (London, 1787); *Documents Illustrative of English History in the Thirteenth and Fourteenth Centuries*, ed. H. Cole (London, 1844); *Memoranda de Parliamento 1305*, ed. F.W. Maitland, Rolls Series, 98 (London, 1893); *Rotuli Parliamentorum hactenus inediti*, ed. H.G. Richardson and G.O.

Sayles, Camden Society, 3rd series, 51 (1935); and *The Parliament Rolls of Medieval England*, ed. P. Brand, S. Phillips, W.M. Ormrod, G.H. Martin, C. Given-Wilson, A. Curry, and R. Horrox, 16 vols (Woodbridge, 2005). The = sign denotes the fact that the same text is edited in each of the cited publications. The last of these editions, *PROME*, is available in an electronic version (CD ROM: Leicester, 2004); both it and the print version provide the pagination details for the earlier editions, but the electronic version has no pagination of its own. The references provided here therefore allow the reader straightforwardly to track the relevant references in both the electronic and the print versions of *PROME*.

Secondary sources are cited by the author–date system, with full details provided in the Bibliography.

I
MINISTERS AND OFFICIALS

1. Extortion by sheriffs (SC 8/316/E216)
1302

Summary

The people: complaint about the great damage and destruction done to them by sheriffs, who oppress people by appointing men to indict those against whom they bear ill will, or whose property they covet, and then extort money by having them imprisoned and put up for mainprise. In particular, the sheriff of Shropshire has made in excess of £200 from the deliverance of prisoners in this way. Request that the king ordain a remedy against such false indictments.

Response: It is attested before the council by the barons of the exchequer that the sheriff is elected by the whole county, and if they feel themselves injured they should come to the exchequer and justice will be done to them.

Text

A nostre seygnur le Roy e a son conseil se est mustre pur son poeple; par la ou les viscountes funt grauntz damage e destruction \al poeple/ dunt rien ne profite a nostre seignur le Roy, mes son poeple iest rient, par la ou les viscountes e leur clerks a leur grauntz turns par gent qe le viscounte ad procure en chescun hundred qi sunt attitlez a ly de enditer gentz vers qui il ad envie ou mal volunte, ou coveite leur terres ou leur chateus, dunt il prent de lele gentz qi sunt enditez pur suet de prisun, ou pur mettre les par meinprise de les vins dys liveres, de les autres x marcz, cent soutz, plus e meyns, de tieus qi sunt tenuz quant il venent a la deliveraunce les plus lele gentz de tut le pais, e tieux sunt enditez quant le viscounte ad resceu argent de eux qi iammes devaunt iustices ne venaunt, dunt le viscounte de Salop' fist aunt an deus centz e \trente/ treis e les detynt en prisun, dunt Sire William Inge et Roger de Suthcote furent a la deliveraunce, dunt nul de ceux fust penduz, for deus cheityfs qi avoient demore deus ans en la prison, par quey la visconte gayna a cele sule deliveraunce plus de deus cent liveres, dunt graunt hunte est a lele gent estre en prisone e estre reint ia le plus tard saunz desert, dunt graunt aumoyne serroit a nostre seignur le Roy e graunt profyt a son poeple si il vousist ordener certeyne remedie sur teux baillyfs e faus enditurs, qi empoverissent e honissent sa tere e il ne ad nul profyt.

> *Response*: Testificatum est coram consilio per barones de scaccario quod vicecomes est electus per totum comitatum, et si iniurietur eis veniant ad scaccarium et fiet eis iusticia.

Note

This petition was previously printed in Haskins 1937 (p. 316, where the word 'sule' is omitted). It is part of an original file returned to the exchequer from the parliament of July–August 1302. Although in the name of 'the people', the specific complaint against the sheriff of Shropshire (actually the joint sheriff of Shropshire and Staffordshire, in this case Richard de Harley) supports Haskins's suggestion that the complaint derives from the political community of Shropshire. In the *Articuli Super Cartas* of 1300 (*SR*, I, 139), Edward I had granted shires the right to elect their own sheriffs, referred to in the response to this petition. The election in the shrievalty of Shropshire and Staffordshire is the only known use of this right; as this petition demonstrates, the results were disastrous, leading to a power struggle between two local factions (*VCH Shropshire*, III, 17–18; Gorski 2003: 34). The right of election was abandoned in the Ordinances of 1311, although the choice and conduct of sheriffs remained a contentious issue throughout the 1310s and 1320s (see nos 4 and 5).

2. Jurisdiction of forest officials (C 49/5/18)
1307–1327

Summary

The commonalty of the land: complaint that the official of the justice of the forest south of the Trent comes into the country where there are forests and holds inquests in areas in which he does not have jurisdiction, not having regard for those woods that were disafforested by the king's father (in a grant confirmed by the present king), to the harm of the people. Furthermore, the stewards of the forest and their ministers charge people with disputations in places where previously none were charged, which is a great burden to the people. Request for a remedy.

Response: Let it be pursued in chancery, and a remedy be ordained.

Text

A nostre seignur le Roi et a son conseil mustre la comunalte de sa terre; qe cum le lutenaunt sa iustice de la forest de sa Trente viegnie en pays ou forestes sount et preignie ses enquestes par un garaunt, le quel ne veut qil eyt conisaunce par vertue de soun garaunt forqe la demeyne boys nostre seignur le Roy, mesme celui lutenaunt prent ses enquestez et comaunde attachements auxi larges en toutz les lius del dit forest, nent eyaunt regard a la boys qeux furent desaforesteez par le graunt nostre seignur le Roy soun bon piere et par nostre seignur le Roy qe ore est conferme, a diverses grevaunces du people; e les seneschals de la foreste et lour ministres chargent gentz despeutisouns en les lius la ou unke nul ne fuit charge ne demaunde en nul tenps de la foreste ecestes durettes grevaunces, en grant charge du people. De quele chose il prient a nostre seignur le Roy e a soun conseil remedie si lui plest.

Response: Sequatur in cancellaria et ibi sibi fiat remedium.

Note

Complaints about the extent of the royal forests were particularly frequent in the century or so after the Charter of the Forest was first granted in 1217 (Bazeley 1921). The forest became a point of contention in the crisis of 1297–1298, with accusations that Richard I, John, and Henry III had afforested new areas since the reign of Henry II. In 1300 Edward I had been compelled to concede new perambulations of the forests as the price of a tax of a fifteenth, as a consequence of which large amounts of land were taken out of forest jurisdiction (Prestwich 1972: 266–267; Young 1979: 136–140; Prestwich 1988: 518–527). Edward resented this disafforestation, and in the Ordinance of the Forest of 1306 he nullified all perambulations made since 1297 (*SR*, I, 147–149).

The present petition dates from the reign of Edward II or, conceivably, the first parliament of Edward III. In 1316, Edward II ordered new perambulations of the forests in return for subsidies, but his consent was reluctantly given and the surveys were never completed (Young 1979: 144–145). In 1323, the king ordered the keepers of the forest north and south of the Trent to reafforest all lands which had been forest in 1217 (*CCR, 1318–1323*, p. 634; *CCR, 1323–1327*, p. 22). This reafforestation and the actions of the keepers or justices of the forest (or their deputies) prompted complaint in the first parliament of Edward III's reign. There is a damaged petition concerning perambulations and forest officials on the parliament roll for January–March 1327 (*RP*, II, 7 = *PROME*, IV, 7), along with complaints about William Cleydon, former lieutenant of Aymer de Valence and Hugh Despenser as justices of the forest, and an unnamed lieutenant of Henry Scrope, current justice south of the Trent (*RP*, II, 10 = *PROME*, IV, 19–20). The two officers were variously styled 'keeper' or 'justice' at different times, but by the 1320s it is likely – as the present petition implies in the complaint against their lieutenants – that much of their actual work was done by deputies (Neilson 1940: 405).

In the January–March 1327 assembly, Edward III's new regime granted a statute ordering that the Charter of the Forest be 'observed and kept in every article', and that the perambulations of Edward I's reign were to mark the forest boundaries (*SR*, I, 255). It is not impossible that this petition was one of the complaints on the subject of forest jurisdiction and officials presented to the first parliament of 1327, as the culmination of grievances against Edward II's forest policy. While the reference to the 'grant of the king's father' being 'confirmed by the present king' might suggest a date before the deposition of Edward II, the uncertainties over the change of regime in the winter of 1326–1327 meant that some petitions processed in the January–March parliament were in fact addressed to Edward II (Sneddon 2009).

3. Extortion by royal ministers (SC 8/334/E1149)
c.1307–*c*.1327

Summary

Poor people of the realm of England: complaint that no remedy is available against outrageous injustices committed by ministers of the king against the poor, except by writs of chancery and exchequer, which are not upheld without bribes that poor men cannot afford. Request that a punishment might be swiftly ordained, as without this the ministers will not cease to commit wrongs.

> *Response*: The complainants should sue before the king's justices assigned in each county to hear complaints against his ministers, and let justice be done before them.

Text

A nostre seignur le Roy et a son counsell monstrount ses poveres gentz de son roialme d'Engletere; qe com des tortz et outrageous grevaunces fetz par les ministres par colour de lour offitz al poveraille n'est remedie ordine ne purveu, sinoun par les brefs le Roy qe issent hors de la chauncellerie e del escheker, de cesser de la duresce par eus fete al dite poveraille, les queus brefs il ne voillent allouer forsqe a lour volunte, sil ne seit par grant doun fet a eus, quel charge un pover homme ne put endure pur ceo q'il n'ad de quay, ne pur sa povert ne put pluis avaunt sure remedie, e issint demoerent lour tortz e lour gravances e lour desobeissaunce despuniz, e dounent ensample par tiel desobeissaunce as autres qe ne sount pas ministres nostre seignur le Roy d'estre meyns obbeissauntz a les comaundemenz nostre seignur le Roy et a la pes. Par quai ils prient pur Deu et par charite qe tele penaunce \redde/ seit a tels ministres \ordeynez/ livere quant ils serrount de ceo ateyntz, qe sait de profit du poverail kare pur ledger penaunce ne sesserent ils de mal faire.

Response: Sequantur conquerentes coram iusticiis Regis quos ad querelas \de/ ministris suis per singulis comitatibus audire assignantur, et coram eis fiat iusticia.

Note

Although this petition presents a fairly general complaint against the abuses of royal officials, the hand would suggest a date in the early fourteenth century. It is not impossible that it could come from the final years of Edward I, but the contents make it more likely to be a product of the reign of Edward II; the *terminus ad quem* could be in the reign of Edward III, but the fact that the response is written in Latin also tends to suggest a date no later than the 1320s (after which French tended to prevail). The petition alludes to the problem of seeking remedy against royal officials when the latter were themselves instrumental or influential in the serving of the writs of chancery and exchequer that were meant to begin process in the courts; the implication is that a more immediate form of remedy, as provided by bill procedure, ought to be more widely available (*SCCKB*, IV, lii–liii). The response alludes to the provision of just such a remedy before one of the special commissions of oyer and terminer appointed periodically under Edward II (and his successor) to deal with law and order in the shires, which sometimes included the authority to investigate abuse of office by sheriffs and other local ministers of the crown (Gorski 2003: 118; and see nos 4 and 109). The very general nature of the petition makes it impossible to link it decisively to any one of these initiatives.

4. Rights and replacement of sheriffs (SC 8/136/6751)
1311–1331

Summary

The prelates, earls, and barons and all the commonalty of the realm: request that the ordinances on the rights of sheriffs and other ministers be upheld, and that if any sheriff or other minister is accused of going against these ordinances, he be removed and another suitable person appointed.

> *Response*: Let the treasurer and barons of the exchequer order that, if any sheriff goes against the ordinances and statutes of the king, he is to be dismissed and another appointed in his place.

Text

A nostre seygnur le Roi et soen consail prient les prelatz, countes et barons et tute la cominalte de soen roialme; qe les ordinaunces en droit des viscountes e ces altres ministres seient tenutz et gardetz, e qe si nul viscount ou altre ministre soit mys countre les dites ordinaunces, sont remue e altre covenable mys solom les dites ordinaunces.

> *Response*: Mandetur per breve thesaurario et baronibus de scaccario quod ipsi contra ordinaciones et statuta regni de cetero nullum vicecomitem admittant, et si qui contra ordinaciones admissi fuerint quod illos sine dilacione ammoveant et alios iuxta formam statuti admittant.

Note

A note on the guard dates this petition to 1319, although without explanation or obvious justification. It appears to date from the period between the Ordinances of 1311 and the establishment of Edward III's personal rule, although petitions or clauses of multiple petitions seeking action against inappropriate or miscreant sheriffs, as well as attempts to regulate the type of men appointed, can be found throughout the fourteenth century (see nos 5, 7, 11, 109, 114, 117, 118, and 121). In 1300, the *Articuli Super Cartas* had introduced a brief and unsuccessful period where the government experimented with electing sheriffs (see no. 1), which had been ended by the Ordinances in 1311. The new provisions dictated that sheriffs should be appointed by the chancellor, treasurer, and members of the council (or, in the absence of the chancellor, by the treasurer and barons of the exchequer or by the justices of the bench), and that those appointed should be 'fit and sufficient' and hold enough land (*SR*, I, 160). The Statute of Lincoln in 1316 (*RP*, I, 343 = *PROME*, III, 187–188; *SR*, I, 174–175) affirmed the procedure outlined in the Ordinances and came to be viewed as the key legislation on the powers and conduct of sheriffs into Edward III's reign (this is especially evident in responses to several clauses dealing with sheriffs in no. 115). The absence of any mention of this statute raises the possibility that the present petition could date between 1311 and 1316.

It is still possible, however, that the petition dates from some time after the Statute of Lincoln. In 1318 it was ordered that all sheriffs be suspended from office and subject to inquiries into possible misconduct (*RPHI*, pp. 6–7 = *PROME*, III, 257); Edward III repeated the process in 1331 (Morris 1947: 39). The Statute of Lincoln was confirmed by the Statute of York in 1322 (*SR*, I, 189) and by a further statute in 1328 (*SR*, I, 258). The present petition, with its characteristic emphasis on the rights of the sheriff and other officials, could conceivably be a reaction against the drastic measure of wholesale dismissals and a plea for moderation in the general treatment of the official class.

5. Conduct and status of sheriffs (C 49/4/20)
*c.*1318–*c.*1322

Summary

The commonalty of England: complaint that sheriffs and under-sheriffs in the counties take fees, robes, and pensions in contravention of the Statute of Lincoln, which states that sheriffs should not be in the service of great lords in order that they might be loyal to the king and the people and give full attention to their office. Request for a remedy.

> *Response*: A writ should be sent to the treasurer and barons regarding the Statute of Lincoln, and those wishing to do so should make their complaint.
> Enrolled.
> Before the great council.

Text

A nostre seignour le Roi et a soun consail monstre la comunalte d'Engleterre; qe come les viscountes et surviscountes en leur countez pernunt feetz, robes ou pensiouns, ceo cestasavour, ascuns pernunt sessaunte robes et quatre vynt feez et pensiouns en meyme le counte, et ascuns dieux centz, et les surviscountes en pernent meyme les feez, robes, pensions a plus pres come eux poient en pursiwauntz lour meistres, dount la povre poeple ne poient aver nule manere de reisoun ne de dreit encountre nul de ceux ove qi les avauntditz viscountes et surviscountes sount demorretz, et neynt eiaunt regard al estatut de Nichole, qe veet qe nul ne seit senechal ne baillif ne du fee de graunt seignur qe enprendreit le office mes q'il seit tiel q'il pusse de tut atendre al office pur lealment le Roi et le poeple. Dount la dite comunalte prie al dit nostre seignur le Roi qe de ceste duresce lour seit fait remedie.

> *Response*: Seit fait bref as thresorer et barons sur le statut de Nicole, et qe il le facent tenir a la sute de ceus qe se vodront pleindre.
> Irrotolatur.
> Coram magno consilio.

Note

Corruption and malpractice amongst sheriffs was a common concern in the fourteenth century (Gorki 2003: 102–125; and see no. 4). In the reign of Edward II, the links between sheriffs and great lords became of particular significance in the series of conflicts between king and barons, with a struggle for power at the local level amongst retainers of the various factional leaders. The Statute of Lincoln of 1316 (*PROME*, III, 187–188; *SR*, I, 174–175) became the central legislation dealing with sheriffs during the troubled years that followed its enactment (see nos 4 and 115). The reference to that statute means that this petition must date after 1316. There is a very similar though less detailed complaint about sheriffs and under-sheriffs that forms one of four clauses in a petition presented to the parliament of February–March 1324 (no. 114). It seems plausible that the present petition dates from one of the parliaments held between 1318 and 1322, though a later date could also be a possibility. The extant roll of the first parliament after the Statute of Lincoln was enacted, held at York in October–December 1318, records a petition from 'the baronage with the commonalty of the people' asking for the replacement of all except the three northernmost sheriffs on the grounds of misconduct and for an inquiry into the conduct of local officials, a request which the king granted (*PROME*, III, 257). And at the parliament at York in May 1322, the king included the provisions of the Statute of Lincoln in the measures to be re-enacted (Davies 1918: 526). The continuing re-enactment of similar legislation during the remainder of Edward II's reign and the early part of Edward III's indicate that the conduct and status of sheriffs continued to be perceived as a problem (Morris 1947). The present petition was previously published by Davies (1918: 582), and is re-edited here with minor differences.

6. Release of prisoners by the marshal of the king's bench (SC 8/3/129)
1320

Summary

[No petitioner specified]: according to the law of the land, the king should hold in prison any man indicted or charged with felony. However, the marshal of the king's bench is allowing those indicted of homicide or other felonies, who are not repleviable and are delivered to him by the justices to be held in prison, to go free by bail, mainprise or surety, without being returned to the justices. This causes great harm, as the indicted persons sometimes kill, assault, or threaten those who have indicted or accused them. Request for remedy, in order to maintain the peace and punish wrongdoers.

> *Response*: Previously in parliament at York, Henry le Scrope and his colleagues, justices of pleas before the king, were instructed to have such prisoners held, and guards contravening this to be punished. The previous order is to be repeated, or the complainant should have a writ of chancery if he so wishes.
> Enrolled.

Text

A nostre seignur le Roi et a son consail; soit monstre qe tut soit il issint, qe solom la ley de la terre la quele le Roi et touz ses subgitz sunt tenuz a garder auscune gent qe sunt enditeez ou retteez de felounie, et auscuns soyent replevisables et auscuns ne mie, ne pur quant le mareschal du baunk nostre seignur le Roy, auscune gent qe sunt enditeez de mort de homme et d'aultres felounies, por les queles eux ne sunt mie replevisables solom la ley de la terre et lui sunt liverees par les iustices de tenir en prisoun, les lest aler la ou eux voelent par bail, meynpriseion ou plevine sanz remaundement des iustices, dont grant mals avienent en mult de manieres, kar la ley de la terre est enfrainte, et ceux qe deyvent issint estre garde en prisoun et vount issint a large a lur volunte auscune foiz tuent, auscune foiz batent et auscune foiz hautement manacent ceux qe les unt issint endite ou rette de teles felounies, a grant damage et effray de eux, par quei la paes est meyns bon garde et les meffaisours meyns puni qeux ne deussent estre. Dont bon serroit de mettre sur ceo covenable remedie, por la terre meyntenir, la paes garder et les meffaisours punir.

> *Response*: Alias in parliamento apud Eboracum convocato iniunctum fuit Henrico le Scrop et sociis suis iusticiariis ad placita coram rege etcetera quod prisones huiusmodi custodiri facerent et custodes contravenientes punirent. Ideo recitetur prius mandatum et alias iniungatur eidem vel si querens voluerit habeat super hoc breve de cancellaria.
> Irrotulatur.

Note

A Latin summary of this petition, along with the response, is found (twice) on the roll for the parliament held at Westminster in October 1320 (*RP*, I, 372, 374 = *PROME*, III, 410, 412–413), where it is recorded as a 'petition of the commonalty of England' (*communitatis Anglie*). Two parliaments had been held at York, in May 1319 and January 1320, between the appointment of Henry Scrope as chief justice of king's bench (in 1317) and the October 1320 assembly. No record of the instruction noted in this petition exists in the record for 1319, and there is no surviving parliament roll for January 1320. It is likely that, as no additional date is specified, it was the more recent York parliament which is referred to in the response. An additional protest from 'the entire community of the realm', about the large numbers of felonies and disturbances of the peace, is found on the roll of the 1320 assembly (*RP*, I, 371 = *PROME*, III, 381).

The complaint in the present petition was a perennial issue in the fourteenth century. The office of marshal of the king's bench was typically performed by deputies, who sometimes appointed deputies of their own (*SCCKB*, VI, xliv). The lack of a permanent place of detention for persons indicted before the semi-itinerant court of king's bench meant that bail was often determined by the keeper of the local gaol in which the prisoner was detained, making the system capricious and open to corruption (Pugh 1968: 208). The order resulting from the present petition seems to have been ineffective, since a statute of 1331 demonstrates that felons were continuing to be released on bail, and imposed heavier penalties against breaches (*SR*, I, 267). Problems continued: an investigation in 1342 discovered that ninety-one indicted men who should have been held in the marshalsea were actually at large (*SCCKB*, VI, xlv). Statutes of the later fourteenth and fifteenth centuries prohibited bail for certain offences punishable by imprisonment, but not until the power of bail was given to justices of the peace in the fifteenth century was a more practical solution to the question of bail found (Pugh 1968: 206–210; and see also nos 54 and 126).

7. Election of forest officials (SC 8/154/7666)
*c.*1327–*c.*1350

Summary

[No petitioner specified]: complaint that the stewards, lieutenants, foresters, agistors, and other ministers of the king in the forests of England conspire with the sheriffs of the counties to be chosen as verderers and regarders in the forests. As a result, the great trespasses and destruction often done by them to the vert and venison are concealed and unpunished, to the detriment of the king. Request that the king's council ordain that no such minister of the king is elected henceforth to the office of verderer or regarder, but that such men might be ousted and others elected who are sufficient for the task.

Response: [none].

Text

Pur ceo qe seneschaux, lieutenantz, foresters, agystours et autres mynistres nostre seignur le Roi denz ses forestes d'Engletere soi fount par comyn \faitz/ entre eux et les viscountes des countes estre eslieutz verdiers et regardeours dentz les ditz forestes, par qei qe les grantz trespas et destrucciouns sovent par eux mesmes faites de vert et de venysoun denz lour baillysmes serrount concelez et despunyez de ceo q'ils ne se voilliount mesmes enditer des ditz trespas, a grant damage nostre dit seignur le Roi et grant destrucciouns de vert et de sa venisoun. Pleise au bone conseile nostre dit seignur de ordeyner qe nulle tieux senescheaux, lieutenantz, forester de fee ne aultre minister \le Roi/ denz ses ditz forestes ne soient eslieuz desorme es en office de verdier ne de regardeour, mes qe tieux soient oustez et aultres eslieutz sufficeauntez, pur grant salvacioun de vert et de venysoun nostre dit seignur le Roi.

Pur meschief des forestes nostre seignur le Roi en Engletere.

Note

Verderers and regarders were minor officials under forest law, although their roles were essential in addressing forest offences. Verderers were elected in the county court following a royal order to the sheriff after the death or disqualification of an incumbent; they convened the local forest courts to view attachments for vert and venison, and were required to keep the rolls of these attachments and present them at the eyre. Although they had some authority to punish offenders against the vert, their powers were very limited when it came to offences against the venison. Regarders, as the name suggests, were responsible for the regard (a general inspection of the forest to answer specific questions about encroachments and other technical matters), and were appointed by the sheriff in response to a royal command. There were usually twelve such officers at any one time. Under the Charter of the Forest they were appointed every three years, although this rarely happened (Young 1979: 84–87). The sheriff thus had considerable power over the appointment of these officials. Evidence from the thirteenth-century eyre rolls in the Midlands indicates that many of those indicted for poaching were of gentry status or above (Birrell 1982), suggesting that the conspiracy among those of the office-holding class to which this petition refers was a real problem.

This petition is not easy to date. The forests were an issue in the parliament of January–March 1327 (see no. 2), and in June of that year the sheriffs of Yorkshire, Nottinghamshire, Cumberland, and Wiltshire were ordered to renew the oaths of sufficiently qualified verderers in the forests of their counties and hold elections to replace those who were not suitable (*CCR, 1327–1330*, p. 128). It is therefore possible that this petition is linked to the complaints about forest jurisdiction and officials that greeted the accession of Edward III, though a date before 1327 is still possible. Regards declined from the 1340s, and after 1360 effectively vanished south of the Trent, with a formal end coming in 1387 (Young 1979: 157). The recognition that regarders still played a recognized place in forest law would therefore tend to place the petition before the mid fourteenth century.

8. Powers for junior justices (SC 8/79/3921)
Mid fourteenth century

Summary

The commons of the land: the justices of the common bench and the chief justice of the king's bench are able to receive cognizance by writs of *dedimus potestatem* out of the chancery for fines levied in the common bench. Request that junior judges in king's bench might be able to do the same, so that they might lose no power through change of office.

Response: Nothing can be done.

Text

A nostre seignur le Roi et a son conseil prie la comune de la terre; qe come les iustices du comune baunk et le chief iustice du baunk le Roi resceyvent conisances en pais par briefs de dedimus potestatem hors de la chauncellarie pur fines lever en comune baunk, q'il pleise as ditz nostre seignur le Roi et son conseil pur son profit et ese de son poeple grauntier et ordeiner qe les iustices qi sount secundaries en bank le Roi puissent resceyvere tiels conisaunces come les iustices secundaries de comune baunk, par le dit brief ou a meyns les iustices secundaries en le baunk [le Roi, qi ount]¹ estez devant iustices du comune baunk, et puis mys en le baunk le Roi, issint qe par lour remuement del une place taunqe [a l'autre nul poair] lour soit tollet.

Response: Nichil potest fieri.

Note

This petition was previously printed in *SCCKB*, V, p. cxviii, where it was dated to the reign of Edward III. Writs of *dedimus potestatem* empowered named persons to receive the appointment of attorneys for suits to be heard in the court of common pleas or in chancery, to administer oaths of fealty to heirs and various office-holders, and to receive recognizances of documents. Acting by commission in such cases was rapidly recognized to be convenient and desirable, resulting in the increasing use of such writs and their extension to cover the oaths of higher officials such as sheriffs and escheators (C 254, *passim*). It is impossible to date this petition with any accuracy, since no additional context is supplied and there are no corresponding entries on the parliament rolls or in other relevant sources; the hand would suggest

¹ Illegible: text supplied from Sayles's edition.

a date in the mid fourteenth century, at a time when the use of such writs was growing.

9. Stewards holding courts in person (SC 8/80/3953)
Mid fourteenth century

Summary

The commonalty: request that the king order that the stewards 'of the same land' hold their courts in person unless others are put in their place for a reasonable cause, for the profit of the king and the relief of the commonalty.

> *Response*: In the presence of the king and the great council.
> It seems to the king and his council that this should be done, and it is ordered that the ministers do it.

Text

Auxi les comunaltes avaundites prient pur Deux a nostre seygnur le Roy; qe ly pleysse comander qe les seneschaux de meysme la terre tyengnent lour courtz en propre persone, saunz autres mettre en lour leu sy ceo ne soyt par resonable cause, car les dytes communaltes sunt charges auxi grauntment ou plus de leu tenauns des seneschaux qe ne sont des seneschaux meysmes. Par queu les dytes comunaltes prient pur Deux a nostre seygnur le Roy et a son consayl qe lour pleyse cele chose prendre a quex, pur le graunt profyt nostre seygnur le Roy et en aleggaunz de lour graun grevauns.

> *Response*: [Coram rege][2] et magno consilio.
> Il semble au Roi et a son counsail q'il fait afaire, et pur ceo soit mande as ministris qe cest facent.

Note

As the opening 'also' (*auxi*) indicates, this document has become detached from a multiple request, and in the absence of the contextual documentation it is very difficult to establish a precise meaning of 'the same land' (*meysme la terre*) whose stewards were to be ordered to hold court in person. Given that the hand appears to date from the middle of the fourteenth century, one possibility is that the petition refers to the landed estate that was built up by the king's chamber under Edward

---

[2] Text missing: supplied from context.

II in the 1320s and was revived by Edward III between 1333 and 1355 (Tout 1920–1933, II, 314–360; IV, 227–311). Twice in the early 1350s, the principal officer of the chamber estate, the receiver, was ordered to be available at times of parliament to assist in the adjudicating of private petitions that touched upon his area of jurisdiction (Richardson and Sayles 1981, ch. XXII, pp. 34–35). This association, however, remains a matter of speculation, and the document must remain open to a variety of interpretations.

10. Competence of clerks of recognizances of statute merchant (SC 8/80/3958) Mid fourteenth century

Summary

The commonalty: request that only clerks who concern themselves with the points of trade are able to occupy the office of clerks of [recognizances of] statute merchant, and that they write and enrol the bonds by their own hands. Great damage is done to the people when the king grants this office to merchants and gentry who do not know how to carry out their offices, and appoint others in their place.

Response: [none].

Text

A nostre seignur le Roi et a son counseil prie la communalte; qe clercs qi se mellent point de marchaundie puissent occuper les offices des clers de l'estatut marchaund et nul autre, et les obligacions escrivre \et enroller/ de lour maine demeisne auxi come l'estatut voet, car graunt damage est fait au poeple en ceo cas par marchants et vallez qi occupent cels offices du graunt le Roi et poy de tenps y demorent, issint q'il ne sevent lour office dreiturelment \faire/, par ceo qe chescun desire et procure denboter autre.

Note

Statute merchant was a legal process allowing recovery against defaulting debtors (see no. 64). This petition is difficult to date because no action was taken and there is nothing on the extant parliament rolls to suggest similar debates; the dating is therefore based solely on the hand. Throughout the fourteenth century the office of clerk of recognizances of statute merchant was used by the crown as a means of rewarding king's clerks and members of the royal household, who held such posts as sinecures (e.g. *CPR, 1327–1330*, pp. 65, 252; *CPR, 1330–1334*, pp. 52, 103, 212); the absence of any response to this petition, and of any known action to reform the office, suggests that the crown regarded such appointments as a matter of royal grace, in much the same way that it treated certain posts in the customs administration (see no. 80), and resisted any attempt to limit its control and discretion in such matters.

11. Powers for justices of oyer and terminer (SC 8/80/3960) Mid fourteenth century

Summary

The commonalty of the realm: although the king has assigned justices in various counties to hear and determine trespasses and excesses done to the people by sheriffs and other ministers, abuses continue because the appointed justices do not have jurisdiction over extortions or grievances made after the date of their commission. Request that the king order by writs that the justices provide justice for the king and the people for offences committed both before and after the date of their commission, in accordance with the articles contained therein.

Response: The commissions should continue for excesses committed after the date of the commission. If necessary new justices should be added to the commission, and they should have power to hear pleas of rescues made to them in contempt of the king.

Text

A nostre seignur le Roi et a son conseil monstre la communalte du roialme; qe come nostre dit seignur le Roi eit assigne ses iustices en divers counteez a oyer et terminer divers trespasses et excesses faitz au poeple par viscontes et autres ministres, auxi come plus pleinement est contenu en les commissions de ceo faites as iustices avantditz, et les viscontes et autres ministres qi sont ore de novele font auxi grevous extorsions et grevances au poeple come unqes fu fait devaunt, por ceo qe eux entendent qe les ditz iustices n'ont mie poer a conoistre de tieles maneres des extorsions ou grevances faites apres la date de lour commission. Si prie la dite communalte q'il plese a nostre seignur le Roi commander par son bref qe les ditz iustices facent droit au Roi et au poeple \de trespas et excesses/ solom les articles contenuz en lor commission, auxi apres la date come devant.

Response: Continuentur commissiones de excessionibus factis post data comissionum, et innoventur si neccesse sit et addatur in commissionibus de novo faciendis quod iusticiarii habeant potestatem cognoscendi et audiendi querelas faciendas de rescussibus factis eis in contemptum Regis.

Note

The petition is filed next to another one relating to extraordinary judicial commissions (see no. 62) and has previously been dated, by association, to the early 1340s, when there was a particularly important series of investigations into official misconduct in the shires (Jones 1973; Fryde 1975; Harriss 1975: 270–312). However, the hand and the use of Latin in the endorsement may suggest a rather earlier date. Special commissions including powers to pursue allegations of corruption committed by sheriffs and other local officials, usually linked to the more general powers of investigation nicknamed 'trailbaston', were especially regular in the 1310s and 1320s, and continued over the following two decades (Gorski 2003: 118; and see nos 3 and 109). While parliament tended to support such initiatives down to the 1330s, it became opposed after the experience of the very intrusive commissions of 1340 (Verduyn 1993); the fact that the present petition seeks to reinforce the powers of the extraordinary justices again therefore suggests a *terminus ad quem* in the 1330s. 'Rescue' was the unlawful recovery of persons or property arrested pending legal process.

12. Enforcement of the Statute of Purveyors
(SC 8/79/3946)
1363–1377

Summary

The commons: complaint that, although it was enacted recently by statute that no bailiff, either of an earl or of a franchise, was to collect sheaves or other victuals from the poor people of the commons, bailiffs and ministers continue secretly to make such collections, in contravention of this ordinance and to the destruction of the commons. Request that the king forbid such collections in future, with those found guilty to be convicted and seriously punished.

Response: A writ is to be sent to the sheriff to proclaim that no bailiff nor underbailiff nor other warrener is to make such collections unless reasonably due, and if it is found that they do they are to be punished by the justices of the peace and heavily amerced for each suit which they wish to sue for the king or for themselves, before the justices or by writ before the justices of one of the benches.

Text

A nostre seignur le Roi et son conseil prie la comune; qe come nadgaires estoit ordeigne par estatut qe nulls bailifs ne des countes ne des fraunchises \ne sibien autre/ ferreient nulle coillet des garbes ne d'autres vitailles des povres gentz de la comune par vertue de lours offices, encountre quele ordeignance tieux bailifs \et ministres/ priv[ee]ment[3] firent tiels cuillietz de grace, et puis le fount de iour en autre come de chose due de certein [. . .][4] de comune usage, en grant destruition de la dite comune. Qe lour pleise ordeigner qe nulle tielle coillet desormes soit fait par nulle manere, de colour de la comune avantdite, et celui qi purra ent estre atteint soit grefment puny.

Response: Soit bref fait a viscont de faire proclamacion qe nul baillif ne souzbaillif, garener n'autre ne face desore tiel manere de coilliet s'il ne soit resonablement duwe, et si trove soit qe nul de eux le face desore soit puny par les iustices de la pees et grefment amercie a chescuny sute qe vodra sure pur le Roi ou pur luy meismes, devant meismes les iustices ou par bref devant les iustices des un baunk ou l'autre.

Note

Purveyance and victualling was a particular cause of tension between the king and his subjects in the late thirteenth and fourteenth centuries, especially in the 1290s and during the 1330s and 1340s, when the wars of Edward I and Edward III made the greatest demand on supplies (Prince 1940: 365–376; Hewitt 1966: 50–74; Fryde 1969; Prestwich 1972: 114–136; Jones 1975; Maddicott 1975). Parliament proved particularly sensitive over the issue in the 1330s, with several statutes concerned with this subject being passed in the course of that decade (*SR*, I, 262–263, 265–266, 276–277). The first of these, in 1330, recited the provision of the *Articuli super Cartas* of 1300 that purveyance

---

[3] Conjectural: hole in parchment.
[4] One word missing due to hole in parchment.

could only be taken for the king's household (*SR*, I, 137). However, it was not until a statue of 1362, confirmed by Richard II in 1392, that the right of purveyance was formally removed from great lords and restricted to the king and queen (*SR*, I, 373; II, 30). Purveyors became 'buyers of victuals' and were compelled to pay in advance on the open market, as a result of which complaints about royal purveyance lessened considerably (Barnie 1974: 40; Given-Wilson 1983).

The absolute prohibition on purveyance by bailiffs and earls mentioned in this petition indicates that it refers to the 1362 statute, making the parliament of 1363 the earliest from which the petition can date; since it claims that the statute was passed 'recently', the petition can be assumed to have been made before the death of Edward III. The response to this petition, with its command to issue a writ to the sheriff (in the singular), might suggest that a particular county or community was behind this petition, but it is more likely that it should be understood as commanding a general writ to all the sheriffs. Given the emphatic reference to the justices of the peace in the response, the petition may have been submitted after the government firmly established the peace commissions with powers to determine offences in 1368 (Ormrod 2011: 478). Common petitions expressing general concerns about purveyance certainly continued after 1362. The common petitions for the parliament of January–February 1365 began with the standard demand to uphold Magna Carta, the Forest Charter and all other statutes, before specifically asking that the 1362 statute on purveyance be observed (*RP*, II, 285 = *PROME*, V, 181–182). There is a further request found in the common petitions for the parliament of February–March 1371 that the statute be upheld (*RP*, II, 305 = *PROME*, V, 239). It is probable that some lords and bailiffs were still flouting the new legislation in the hope that it would soon be overturned, and that both private petitioners and the commons sought to ensure that the king was resolute in enforcing the statute of 1362 which they had encouraged and which had essentially resolved the issue of purveyance and victualling in a manner favourable to them.

13: Contraventions of the Statute of Purveyors (C 49/8/5) 1363–1377

Summary

The commons: request that no buyer or purveyor take cattle, grain, malt, or other foodstuffs as purveyances for the king's household other than under the form of the statute enacted in 1362, and that they make payments in cash. Recently, the said buyers have taken cattle and other foodstuffs in various parts of England without making payment according to the statute, to the great damage and impoverishment of the commons. Request for remedy.

Response: This is replied to elsewhere.

Text

A nostre seignur le Roi et son conseil prie la comune; qe com en l'estatut nostre seignur le Roi fait l'an trentisme sisme t[...] les purveaunces affaire pur l'ostiel nostre seignur le Roi soit contenuz qe nulle achatour ne purveour prendroit bestaille, bledz, brees [...] vitaille ne cariage affaire pur le dite hostiel forsqe soulement par le fourme del dit estatut, et de ce prest paiem[ent] en poigne; ore de novelle ont les ditz achatours pris en diverses parties d'Engletere bestaille et autres vitailles par [...] faire la paiement solonc le dit estatut, a grant damage et enpoveryssement du dite comune. Dont il prie [remedie pur Dieu et en] oevre du charite.

Response: Il est respondu aillours.

Note

The right-hand side of this document is missing and some of the content and sense has been reconstructed from context. The reference to Edward III's thirty-sixth regnal year, 1362, points clearly to the Statute of Purveyors passed in that year (*SR*, I, 373). This means that the first parliament from which this petition can date is that of 1363, with the terminating date being the end of the reign in 1377. The subject is closely related to no. 12, and the context discussed there applies equally to this one. The request here adheres more closely to the wording of the statute, which limited purveyance to the king and queen and required cash payment for goods. Both petitions serve as a reminder that the sensitive issue of purveyance was not completely resolved by the legislation of 1362.

14. Locations for holding hundred courts (SC 8/40/1953)
c.1376

Summary

The commons of the realm: since ancient times hundred courts have been held in a certain place for the ease of the people, but now the ministers of the hundreds hold them sometimes in one place and at other times in another, in order to amerce the suitors out of greed, to the great oppression of the people. Request for amendment; and, if this is opposed, that the said hundreds might be seized into the hands of the king.

Response: [none].

Text

A nostre seignur le Roi et a son sage conseil prie la comune de son roialme; qe come hundredz de ancien temps fuerent tenuz en un certein lieu come en [...] del hundredes pur ease de pople, et ore les ministres de ceux qi ount les hundredes a [...] tenent les ditz hundredes alafoitz en un place et alafeitz en autre, pur coveitise d'amercier les suteres et autres qi deivent tenir, en grant oppression de people. Pleise ordeiner amendement, et si encontre, facent soient les hundredes seisis en la main le Roi.

Note

This document is faded and stained in several places, making some words illegible. A lengthier, more detailed version of the complaint outlined in this petition is found on the roll for the Good Parliament of 1376 (*RP*, II, 357 = *PROME*, V, 377). The enrolled petition objects that proclamations were not being made at the sheriff's tourns (judicial visitations) to warn people of when the courts of hundreds and wapentakes were to be held by the bailiffs; rather, these courts were being held in secret places and dates, allowing the bailiffs to amerce the people for non-attendance. Although the present petition refers only explicitly to hundreds and not to wapentakes, and omits any mention of the tourns, it is likely that it is related to the one on the parliament roll, and may have been extended and worked up as part of the onslaught against government and its officials by the Good Parliament. The hand would support a date in the later part of Edward III's reign.

Complaints against officials in the hundreds can be found throughout the later Middle Ages, though the specific nature of the grievance here is rather unusual. The enrolled version has a response that the relevant statutes should be upheld and observed. According to the 1225 Magna Carta, reissued by Edward I in 1297, sheriffs were meant to hold their tourns twice each year, after Easter and Michaelmas, a provision affirmed by a statute of 1357 (*SR*, I, 118, 352). The system of hundred bailiffs was quite complex, with some answerable to private lords, others to the sheriff, and still others directly to the crown (Cam 1950: 174). Holding the hundred courts, which could meet as often as every three weeks, was a considerable part of the bailiff's duties, and one which resulted in numerous complaints (Cam 1950: 180). There was potential for corruption in the manner highlighted in this petition, although there is little evidence elsewhere to indicate that it was perceived as a widespread problem.

15. Leasing of franchises at farm (SC 8/104/5194) c.1376

Summary

The poor commons: request that the king order bailiffs of franchises in fee or for life-terms not to lease their offices at excessive farms, greater than in times past, so that the commons are not oppressed and ruined.

Response: [none].

Text

A nostre seignur le Roi suppliont ces pours communes; de ordeyner qe ces qi sont baillifs de fraunchise en fee ou par terme de vie ne lessont lour baillifs a outraiouses fermes mes come en auncien temps furent lesses, issint qe les comunes avauntditz ne soient reyntz ne destrutz par les fermers avauntdites.

Note

The system of appointment and accountability for bailiffs of hundreds and franchises was somewhat complex, but bailiffs typically held their office for a fee (Cam 1950: 174–181). The need to recover that fee and obtain a profit from the office resulted in the leasing of the office – or a part of it – in farm, a practice forbidden by various statutes of Edward III's reign (*SR*, I, 259–260, 277, 284). This petition appears to be related to one on the parliament roll for the Good Parliament of April–July 1376, in which the commons object to the damage caused by the leasing of hundreds and bailiwicks at farm, requesting that the practice be forbidden in accordance with previous statutes (*RP*, II, 333 = *PROME*, V, 322). The response to that complaint, that the relevant statutes should be upheld, acknowledges the problem without providing much of a remedy. The present petition is milder in tone than the one on the parliament roll, in that it calls for an end to leasing at excessive farms rather than a complete prohibition on the practice. Since it refers only to franchises, and not to hundreds, it may have come from one particular group and been developed into a broader, more resolute complaint by the commons as a whole. The Good Parliament levelled a wide range of charges against the government, courtiers, and officials (Holmes 1975: 100–158), producing the greatest number of enrolled common petitions to have survived for a single parliament up to this date. Several of these dealt with local issues that had been taken up by the commons (*PROME*, V, 385–87; Ormrod 2004: 52–53), and it is therefore plausible that, in the broader onslaught against royal government, the commons adopted this particular cause and gave it a wider context.

16. Chirographers' fees (SC 8/102/5055)
1377

Summary

The commons: in the Statute of Westminster II it was ordained that chirographers who engross fines should not charge more than 4s for their fee, but chirographers now hold parties to ransom through exorbitant fees, or otherwise wrongfully delay the parties. Request that chirographers and clerks engrossing fines take only their fee, and that punishment be determined in cases where they take a higher fee or delay parties not wishing to pay more.

Response: This bill is answered among the common petitions.

Text

A tresnoble et tresgracious seignur le Roy monstrent plusours de sa comune; qe come avant ceus heures en l'estatut de Westminster secounde estoit ordeyne qe cyrograffers qi engrosent fines ne prendeyent mez qatre souldz taunsoulement pur lour fee, la les ditz cyrograffers ore preyngnount raunssoun de les partiez outre lour fee outrageousement a lour voluntee demeyne, ou autrement ils tarient les parties torcenousement encountre ley et resoun. Par quoi priount la dite comune en eovre de charite ordeyner remedye, qe les ditz cyrograffers et clerks engrosent fines saunz rien prendre outre lour fee, qar ceo suffitz pur lour travaille, et en cas qe eux preyngnent plus qe lour fee de qatre souldz ou si ils tarient les partiez par cause q'ils ne voillent doner pluis qe la dite fee, qe certayn penaunce soit ordeyne sour eux, pluis grendre qe n'est contenuz en le dit estatut, issint qe le people desorenavant ne soient raunsounez ne issint torcenousement tariez encountre droit et resoun.

Response: Ceste bille est respondu entre les comune peticions.

Note

Chirographers were officials responsible for producing chirographs, documents written in duplicate (or triplicate) on a single piece of parchment, then cut through, to allow all parties to agreement to possess copies which could be compared for authenticity. As the petition states, the Statute of Westminster II of 1285 had fixed the fee of a chirographer at 4s (*SR*, I, 93). This complaint appears to have been submitted in the first parliament of Richard II's reign (October–November 1377), where a common petition of the same matter was answered to the effect that the statute should be enforced (*RP*, III, 20 = *PROME*, VI, 44). The matter had already been raised in the last two parliaments of Edward III (see no. 123), and the present petition was clearly part of the same continuing campaign. That the issue was brought to three successive parliaments indicates that this was seen as a significant issue by at least some of the commons, but the terse response to all three petitions suggests that the government did not see it as a major problem.

17. Castles attached to the office of sheriff (SC 8/21/1029) *c*.1385–*c*.1399

Summary

The commons in parliament: complaint that, although certain castles were always attached to the offices of sheriffs, in order that they might perform their offices and keep prisons there, the king has recently granted them to various people for life. Request that the castles be restored to the offices of the sheriffs.

Response: The king wills it.

Text

A nostre seignur le Roy supplient ses liges comunes en ceste present parlement; come diverses chasteux en diverses parties d'Engleterre furent et ont estee de tout temps appurtenantz et aionts as offices des viscontes, pur faire lour offices et avoir lour gaole illoeqes pur gardir lour prisons, tanqe ore tarde, qe nostre dit seignur le Roy ad grantee la garde des plusours des ditz chasteux as diverses gentz a terme de vie par procurement, paront les ditz viscontes n'ont nulle lieu en certein de faire lour offices, ne de gardir les prisons, a lour grant desease et damage du pays. Qe please a nostre dit seignur le Roy grantir qe les ditz chasteux purront estre reiointz as offices des viscontes avantditz, en eovere de charite et pur profit de vostre roialme.

Response: Le Roi le voet.

Note

This petition is printed in full in *RP*, III, 275 (summary in *PROME*, VII, 169), where it is dated to the parliament of January–March 1390. However, it is found among the collection of unenrolled petitions rather than on the parliament rolls, and the dating of these collections is not always reliable. A statute of 1336 had forbidden the king to give to others the gaols attached to sheriff's offices, an injunction stated more clearly in 1340 (*SR*, I, 277, 284). In spite of this, the crown continued to appoint royal nominees to important gaolerships throughout the fourteenth century, with several appointments made under Richard II (Pugh 1968: 150–151). From 1385, a steady stream of grants of castles, gaols, and other offices can be found on the patent rolls. After declaring his majority in 1389, Richard began to distribute patronage generously, including life interests in castles, to his supporters (Saul 1997: 235–248). The growing number of grants from the mid 1380s led to a complaint from the commons in the parliament of October–November 1386 about the alienation of 'hundreds, castles, liberties and other commodities pertaining to many counties' and the consequent cost to the sheriffs (*RP*, III, 222 = *PROME*, VII, 50), and it is possible that the present petition is a preliminary or alternative version of this entry on the parliament roll. However, it is more probable that it is both a reaction to the cumulative effect of sheriffs' castles being alienated across the fourteenth century and a specific response to the king's actions from 1389. This petition would therefore date from one of the parliaments in Richard II's majority, although it is impossible to state with certainty which one. If it dates from the early 1390s, it seems to have had little effect, since Richard continued to make such grants to his supporters. It is notable that there seems to be no trace of any consequent action in government records, despite the positive response provided.

18. Payment of an annuity to Robert de Markeley
(SC 8/102/5069)
1402

Summary

The commons in parliament: in the first year of his reign the king granted by letters patent to Robert de Markeley, one of his sergeants-at-arms, 12d per day and £10 per year from the issues of the city of London, and a suit of clothes out of the great wardrobe for term of life. The commons assembled at Westminster in the third year of the king's reign ask that this grant be confirmed, in consideration of Robert's service, and that he should also receive certain wages and special fees granted by letters patent of Richard II, notwithstanding statutes or ordinances made to the contrary.

Response: The king of his special grace in full parliament, at the request and prayer of the commons, consents to this petition according to what is contained therein.

Text

A nostre tresredoute and tresgracious seignur le Roy: Supplient voz humbles et foialx liges les comuns de ce present parlement; qe come vous tresredoute seignur, par voz letres patentes faites le [xxvi iour de March l'an de vostre] regne premier eussiez grantez a Robert Markelee, un de voz sergeantz d'armes, dousze deniers le iour et dys livres par an, de avoir [...] issues de vostre citee de Londres par les mains des viscontes d'icell citee, pur le temps esteantz as termes de Pasqe et de Seint Michel [...] aussi et prendroit une robe de la suite d'autres voz sergeantz d'armes chescun an pur terme de sa vie en la grand garderobe par les [mains du gardein d'icell ...] temps esteant, sicome en voz dites lettres patentes est contenuz pluis au plain. Plaise a vostre excellente roiale mageste consideracion avoir a la [...] service du dit Robert, et qe le susdit vostre grant estoit a luy fait de vostre grace especiale, et a l'instance des comuns de vostre parlement [deinz] Westminstre l'an de [vostre regne] tierz, par restitucion face en vostre Chanc[elerie] certeins lettres patentes du Roy Richard vostre darein predecessor, qi dieux assoille, par le quelles a l'instance [...] de son roialme en un son parlement il granta a l'avantdit Robert certains gages et fies especifiez en voz dites lettres patentes, et sur de de vostre [habundante grace a l'in]stance de voz ditz comuns granter et declarer en ce present parlement qe le dit Robert eit et enioie vostre dit grant solonc l'effect et purport de voz lettres patentes [...] estatut ou ordennance fait ou affaire au contraire nient contre esteant, et qe de vostre pluis habundante grace vous plaise granter au dit Robert ce qe luy [est aver] les gages, fie et robe susditz, pur Dieu et en oevre de charitee.

> *Response*: Le Roy de sa grace especiale en plein parlement a les request et prier des communes ad ottroiez ceste peticioun solonc ceo q'est contenuz en ycelle.

Note

The right-hand side of this document is stained and partially illegible; some parts of the text have been recovered by ultra-violet light and some other parts from context. The reference in this petition to the request being made by the commons in the parliament of the third year of Henry IV would suggest that it dates from the assembly of September–November 1402. This actually took place at the very beginning of Henry's fourth regnal year, but had been summoned during the third, so the confusion is understandable (*PROME*, VIII, 154). Robert de Markeley (as his name tends to be rendered in modern forms) had been one of Richard II's sergeant-at-arms since at least 1387 (*CPR, 1385–1389*, p. 391; Given-Wilson 1986: 54–55). The annuity granted him in 1392 and confirmed in 1395 was originally payable at the exchequer (*CPR, 1391–1396*, p. 663), but was transferred to the fee farm of the city of London when it was confirmed by Henry IV in March 1400 (*CPR, 1399–1401*, p. 275). The very large number of royal annuitants that had accumulated by 1399 created a significant financial burden for the early Lancastrian regime, and Henry IV's first parliament called for restraint in the granting of such fees (*PROME*, VIII, 48–49). The enrolled common petitions for the assembly of September–November 1402 include a request that the king should honour his obligations to the long-standing annuitants, with the suggestion that those given more recent promises of payments would have to take second place (*PROME*, VIII, 21). It was in this political context that Markeley was able to persuade the commons to take up own his case for payment. The king's promises of good faith in this and the enrolled petition had little effect, however, and in 1404 there was a general crisis over the payment of annuities that forced Henry IV to put a temporary stoppage on all payments (Given-Wilson 2016: 283–284). For the possible identification of the scribe of this petition, see the Introduction, p. 15 n. 5.

II
CHURCH AND RELIGION

19. Ecclesiastical jurisdiction over secular matters
(SC 8/79/3944)
*c.*1300–*c.*1325

Summary

The lieges of the commonalty of England: complaint about offences committed by ordinaries of the Church, who daily take before them pleas of contract, covenants, debts, and other pleas, greatly damaging and oppressing the people, to the disinheritance of the king and against the dignity of the crown. Any poor man without prohibition who is placed in contempt under their jurisdiction will be made to pay penance or excommunicated, and thus unable to respond in court. Request for a remedy.

Response: If any ordinary of the Church impleads any man in court Christian of things pertaining to the crown, they should have a prohibition and attachment as the law demands.

Text

A nostre seignur le Roi e a soun consail priount ses liges gentz de la commune d'Engleterre; pur Dieu ordeiner faire remedie des grauntz grevaunces qe faitz lour sount de iour en iour par les ordinaires de Seint Eglise, qi eaux fount trere devaunt eaux apleder de contractz, covenauntz, dettes et des aultres plees reals, a graunt damage et oppression al poeple et al desheritisoun nostre seignur le Roi et encountre la dignite de sa coroune, par la raison qe nul povere ne aultre nose porter prohibicion q'est ordeyne en le cas, et si nul le face il sera somouns de office a respoundre de contempt fait a lour iurisdiction, issint q'il sera chacee par penaunce ou de faire fui, qe sera plus grevouse qe raunsoun au Roi duble, ou aultrement il les fount estomenger maliciousement, e puis par tiel estomengement mis encountre eaux il sount forbarrez q'il ne deyvent estre respoundre en nule court en providre, et en contempt de la coroune. Par quei plese a nostre seignur le Roi et au dits consail ordeyner remedie pur les chastier et refreindre de lour grauntz malices avauntdites.

Response: Si nul ordinair de Seint Eglise emplede nul homme en court Cristiene de chose qe appertient a la coroune, eit prohibicion et sur ce attachement come la lei demand.

Note

The question of the jurisdiction of the ecclesiastical courts had been a perennial issue since Henry II issued the Constitutions of Clarendon in 1164. As far as the royal courts were concerned, the ecclesiastical courts had a clearly defined remit, and the development of the writ of prohibition ensured that courts Christian were prevented from encroaching into the jurisdiction of the secular courts, especially in cases concerning contracts and land issues (Adams 1936; Flahiff 1944 and 1945; Helmholz 1975; Helmholz 1981). Complaints about jurisdiction and writs of prohibition are recurring subjects amongst the clerical *gravamina* in the thirteenth and fourteenth centuries (Jones 1966), even though the struggle had effectively been won by the royal courts. The response to the present petition, that the offended parties should obtain a writ of prohibition in the normal manner, tends to suggest that the matter was not viewed as especially significant by the crown.

This petition can be dated to the first part of the fourteenth century, and possibly comes from the final years of Edward I, when the matter is known to have been raised in parliament. The same subject is found in the second part of a Latin summary of a two-part protest from the 'poor men of the land of England' (*pauperum hominum terre Anglie*) on the parliament roll for the assembly of Lent 1305 (*Mem. de Parliamento*, p. 305 = *PROME*, II, 195). It is not impossible that the present document is the original petition lying behind that request. However, although the responses to this petition and to the Latin summary on the parliament roll are very similar, they are not identical. It may be telling that the response to the present petition is in French, which could suggest a date towards the end of the date range, in the 1320s. There was a further petition presented on this subject under Edward II, to the parliament of January–March 1313 (*RP*, I, 293 = *PROME*, III, 63), but this came from the community of Devon rather than the commonalty as a whole, and the king declined to consider the matter.

20. Possession of former Templar lands (SC 8/159/7909) 1327–1330

Summary

The good people: request for the annulment of a statute concerning [lands] lately belonging to the Templars, passed without common assent and by the plotting of Hugh Despenser. Further request that they might resume possession of these lands, and in the meantime have the issues, in such a manner as pleases the king.

Response: The statute should be brought before the council.

Text

A nostre seignur le Roy et a son consail prient ses bones gentz; qe come ils [...] tenoient des eaux pur la defesaunce des ditz Templeres, les queux [...] qe se fist saunz assent de commun par le procurement sire Hugh le Despens[er] [...] ses tut seu ceo qe iustices et gentz de lei disoient expressem[ent] [...] qe cel estatut soit defait, et q'ils puissant reavoir et reentrer les ditz [...] avoir des issues du meen temps, en manere sicome y plest a nostre [seignur le Roy].
Pur le commun [...].

Response: Veniat statutum inde coram consilio.

Note

The right-hand edge of this document is missing, but enough of the text survives for the sense to be clear. Both this petition and no. 21 address the issue of the distribution of the former Templar lands in England, and the two appear to be closely related. Under pressure from Philip IV of France and Pope Clement V, Edward II had reluctantly ordered the arrest of the English Templars in 1308. At the Council of Vienne in 1312, when the Order of the Temple was dissolved, all Templar lands were granted by the pope to the Knights Hospitaller (the Order of St John of Jerusalem). The Templar holdings in England were quite extensive (Perkins 1910), but in England Edward II proved reluctant to enact the papal ruling and many of the Templar estates were granted to others, including several earls (S. Phillips 2010). Not until 1324 was the statute granted which transferred Templar lands to the Hospitallers (*SR*, I, 194–196; and see no. 114). The Despensers seem to have influenced the king in this decision: illegal acquisition of Templar lands was one of the charges against the Despensers in 1321 (*PROME*, III, 429), while the prior of the Order of St John of Jerusalem in England, Thomas Larcher, had to bribe the king and the Despensers to secure the 1324 statute (Hamilton 2010: 224). Following the fall of Edward II, the commons petitioned the parliament of January–March 1327 to revoke the grants to the Despensers, along with the various acts of their regime. Among the petitions is one from the prior of the Order of St John of Jerusalem in England regarding the

Templar lands requesting, somewhat strangely, the return of these to their dispossessed owners (*RP*, II, 12 = *PROME*, IV, 26). There are then no surviving parliament rolls until the one for the assembly which condemned Roger Mortimer in November–December 1330, on which can be found further petitions for Despenser wrongs to be redressed (*PROME*, IV, 122–151 *passim*). In spite of the papal order regarding these lands, their allocation to the Hospitallers was clearly unpopular with those who had benefited or hoped to benefit from the demise of the Templars, and the financial weakness of the Hospitallers – with Larcher an incompetent manager of their affairs – presumably led some to try to take advantage of circumstances (Perkins 1930: 286–287). Although closely related to no. 21, which is datable to *c.*1330, and thus possibly dating from the same year, the present petition could equally have been presented to any parliament in the period 1327–1330. There is no evidence that the matter was ever brought before the council, and from 1329 the king was actively supporting the Hospitallers in obtaining the Templar lands, leading to the appointment of Brother Leonard of Tibertis as prior in 1330 to manage the order's affairs (Perkins 1930: 287–288). The failure of this petition is demonstrated by the fact that by 1338 the Hospitallers had secured control of most former Templar goods (S. Phillips 2010: 235).

21. Acquisition of Templar lands by the Hospitallers (SC 8/79/3938)
*c.*1330

Summary

The good people: the order of the Templars was dissolved by the papacy, and those to whom the escheat falls have taken up their lands. It has since been shown that Hugh Despenser and his son received money from the Hospitallers to use their powers towards the passing of a statute which gave the rights over the Templars' lands to the Hospitallers, despite the fact that they had been advised by the king's justices that this was against the law. Request that this statute might be revoked, that each man ousted by writs issued under the statute without the assent of parliament might be able to return to his lands, and that action be reserved to the king and to all others against the Hospitallers regarding the issues that they have taken in the meantime from the lands and tenements aforesaid.

Response: In the presence of the king.
This should wait until another parliament.

CHURCH AND RELIGION   51

Text

A nostre seignur le Roi et a son conseil prient ses bones gentz; qe come l'ordre des Templiers est et fut defait par l'Apostoille, et puis quele defaute nostre seignur le Roi vostre piere et ses liges hommes, \chescun/ a qi l'escheete apendoit, entrerent sicome ley de terre voleit, la fut ordine trop sutillement et en male manere contre le Roi et ses bones gentz par Sire Hugh le Despenser le piere et le fuiz, pur trop grantz deners outre mesure q'il pristrent des Hospitaliers, apres un parlement fu auxi come eust este en parlement, les ditz Hugh [et] Hugh firent venir les iustices le Roi et \les/ disoient q'il enformassent le Roi s'il poet granter tutes les dites terres et tenementz as Hospitaliers qe estoient as Templiers. Les dites iustices disoient apertement et expressement qe le Roi ne ne devoit ne ne le poiet faire par lei; non pas pur ce les ditz Hugh et Hugh par poair q'il avoient firent a faire un statut, sicome piert par l'estatut qe les Hospitaliers eussent les terres de Templiers, et en le quel estatute poet estre trove qe les iustices ne s'assentirent point, car ils ne peient pur lour serment pur la desheritaunce du Roy et de ses gentz, et disoient qe ce fut contrarie a loi; issi qe cel estatut se fist contre loi et contre raisoun. Par qoi prient ses bones gentz de sa ligeance qe cel eftatut soit deffait et tenu pur nul, issi qe chescun puisse ressortir a soen, desicome par force estoient oftez par briefs qe issirent de tel eftatut nient assentu par parlement, et qe accion soit reserve a nostre seignur le Roi et a toutz autres vers les Hospitaliers des issues qe ils ont pris en le mene temps des terres et tenementz susditz.

Response: Coram rege.
Demoerge tanqe a un autre parlement.

Note

This petition is printed in *RP*, II, 41–42, among a collection of eighty-four petitions taken from transcripts made by Sir Mathew Hale and assigned to the parliament of November–December 1330. Since Hale had access to the files of medieval petitions in their original state, before the archival rearrangement of the nineteenth century, this dating is probably reliable (Dodd 2001: 140; Dodd 2009: 18–19). Although more detailed than no. 20, and addressed more specifically to the matter of Hospitaller possession of Templar lands, the context and basic aims of the present petition are the same, seeking to overturn the grant to the Hospitallers on the grounds that it was achieved by the actions of the Despensers as a result of bribery.

22. Punishing instigators of false quarrels and indictments (SC 8/79/3945)
1334–1335

Summary

The common people of the realm: it was ordained at the parliament recently held at York and decreed by statute that common judgment might be given in all the churches of the realm against maintainers of false quarrels. Since then, there have been more false quarrels than before, since such people do not fear the judgment or punishment of the Church. Further complaint of false speech and false indictments, through which people are daily killed or disinherited and ruined forever. All the commonalty pray that another remedy might be ordained, so that the people are able to live in peace, and the king will not suffer any people in his land who do not fear the law nor wish to be judged by the law.

Response: [none].

Text

A nostre seignur le Roi et a son consail monstrent le comun puple de son realme de Engletere; qe come ordeigne fut a son parlement nagweres a Euirwyk et par estatut illekes fest qe comune centense serrait done en tote eglises de son dit realme sur maintenours de fauce quereles, et sur autre poyns qe sustenent en le dit estatut, en volant et entendant qe fauxine fust destrute et qe tote ces gentz ussent lay et resoun, qe tusiours peux cele dite ordingnance eount plus de fauxe quereles estes enpris et maintenuz qe ne furent avant, par la reson qe il ne doutent le centense de seint eglise ne la paine sur seo ordingne; et auxi bien de faus sermens de faus enditements et d'autre graunt faucines par quex ces lige gentz sunt de iour en autre askuns mors askuns desherites et destrut a tusiours. Par quei tote sa comune prient par cherite qe autre remedie en seo cas soit ordingne, issi qe les le gentz pussent vivere en pees, et qe il ne voile soffrir qe plus de iors soient en sa tere forke le mesmes, cestassavoir gentz qe ne doutent la ley ne par lay voilent estre iustices, ne nul poveres vers eux sute feare qel tort qe il facent.

Note

On the guard, this petition is dated to *c*.1319–*c*.1328 on the basis of the internal reference to a parliament held at York, but this is erroneous. The parliament at York referred to in the petition was actually that of February–March 1334, on the roll of which is a common petition requesting that the king 'ordain concerning false jurors and maintainers of false quarrels' (*RPHI*, p. 234 = *PROME*, IV, 198–199). In response, the king gave the justices power to investigate this matter, but also ordered that letters patent be issued to the bishops ordering that each Sunday, in every parish church, sentence should be pronounced on those guilty of these and other offences. There are no surviving rolls for the next two parliaments, in September 1334 and May–June 1335, and the matter does not feature on the parliament roll for March 1336. As the 1335 assembly was also held at York, it is likely that any reference after this date to a previous York parliament would have included a further and more precise identification of the assembly. It is therefore highly probable that the present petition was presented either at the September 1334 meeting or at that of May–June 1335. The question of conspiracy in trials had been an issue since Edward I's reign (Harding 1983: 98–108), with conspiracy and champerty addressed in a 1330 statute (*SR*, I, 264). It is notable that the commons had no suggested remedy to this problem in the mid 1330s, leaving the king to deal with matters as he saw fit, and that the king's first reaction was to use the clergy as a means to promote the law. Clearly this approach failed, and the problem of false litigation grew as the fourteenth century progressed, with lawyers subjected to particular scrutiny and complaint in this regard in the second half of the century (Musson and Ormrod 1999: 184–188).

The petition is addressed in the name of the 'common people' of the realm, but the request in the final sentence is made by the *commune*, a usage that became more frequent in the 1330s to describe the knights and burgesses of the commons in parliament.

23. Judgments in bigamy cases (SC 8/35/1702)
Mid fourteenth century

Summary

[No petitioner specified]: many felons who are convicted of felonies, and against whom bigamy is alleged, claim benefit of clergy, and although writs in such a case are often directed to bishops in order to have the truth certified, the bishops do not care to return the writs or make certification because of their conscience. The petitioners request a suitable remedy.

Response: [none].

Text

Plese a nostre seignur le Roi et son consaill; qe par la ou plusours felouns sount atteintz de diverses felonies et alleggent clergye, countre queux bigamye ad este allegge, et mesqe diverses briefs en ceo cas soventfoith sont direit as diverses evesqes pur ent certifier la verite, le queux evesqes ne ount pas volu les dit briefs returner ou certifier par cause de lour conscience. Qe plese a nostre dit seignur le Roi et son consaill ordeiner covenable remedie en ceo cas.

Note

The Second Council of Lyons, convened by Pope Gregory X, decreed in 1274 that bigamists were not permitted to claim benefit of clergy. This decision was incorporated into English law two years later by Edward I, in the Statute of Bigamy (*SR*, I, 43), and became known as exception of bigamy. Clerics in minor orders were permitted to marry, but marrying a second time after being widowed made such clerics bigamists. Those judged bigamists in this context were not permitted to claim benefit of clergy. In other words, bigamy was not a crime in itself, but something used to determine the status of clerics (McDougall 2009: 190). As the present petition states, the question of whether or not a man was a bigamist was one for the bishops. If bigamy was determined, a trial could continue; but if the verdict was that the accused was not a bigamist and could thus claim benefit of clergy, he had to be handed over to the ecclesiastical jurisdiction. This practice was confirmed in the parliament of January–March 1327 (*RPHI*, 109 = *PROME*, IV, 38).

The note on the guard of the present petition dates it to *c*.1376 by reference to a common petition about bigamy on the roll for the Good Parliament (*RP*, II, 333 = *PROME*, V, 320). However, both this and a petition from the start of Richard II's reign (*RP*, III, 22 = *PROME*, VI, 48) seek to ignore exception of bigamy and allow men to claim benefit of clergy regardless of the ruling in the bigamy case. Given that the mood of the commons was clearly hostile to the idea of exception of bigamy by the last quarter of the fourteenth century, the present petition seems to date from rather earlier, when the principal issue was that of simply determining bigamy. In the parliament of February–March 1334, a common petition that bigamy should only be tried in the ecclesiastical courts met with a favourable response (*RPHI*, pp. 234–235 = *PROME*, IV, 199). In June 1344, in a petition presented to parliament by the clergy, it was argued that lay justices could not act in cases involving matrimony or bigamy, with the king confirming that such matters should first be referred to the courts Christian (*RP*,

II, 151–152 = *PROME*, IV, 371–372). These cases show that the issues raised in the petition printed here – that cases in secular courts were being delayed by the refusal of the bishops to rule in bigamy cases and determine whether a man could thus claim benefit of clergy – were current in parliament in the 1330s and 1340s, and would suggest that the petition is more likely to date from this period.

24. Legitimization of bastards (SC 8/166/8265)
Mid fourteenth century

Summary

Many people of the realm: various suits are made in the king's courts to legitimize bastards with the agreement of some religious while the statements of other religious are annulled, matters which are normally sent to bishops and other ordinaries to certify. Through these certifications, bastards are suddenly made legitimate, to the disinheritance of those who are not party to such suits and who are not called before the ordinary to argue their case. Request that these certifications should not be a bar to others who were not party to such suits.

Response: He who complains should declare his case in detail if he wishes, and in the meantime the previous law should stand.

Text

A nostre seignur le Roy et a son conseil suppliont plusours gentz du roialme; qe come diverses \sutes/ soient faitez en diversez courtes nostre dit seignur le Roy pur gentz bastardes, moynes, chanoynes, noneynes et altres religiouses par covyne d'altres de lour assent pur les ditz bastardez faire muliereez et a defaire la professioun de tieux religiouses, queles choses sont comunement maundez as evesqes et altres ordenaries de certifier en courte nostre seignur le Roy; de tieles bastardies et professions par queles certifiacions ceaux qi sont bastardz sont sovent foitz faitz mulierees, et ceux qi sont professez par la ley nient professez, en desheritance des altres qi unque ne furent parties a tieles sutes, ne unquore appellez devant le ordenarie de faire ceo qe a lour atient en cest cas. Par quoi pleise qe nul tiel certificacioun sont bare devers altres qi ne furent parties a tieles sutes.

Response: Celluy qi se pleynte declare son cas en especial s'il veulle et en le moien temps estoise la ley devant usee.

Note

Legitimizing bastards was the business of the Church and not of the king's courts. However, property and inheritance law was a matter for secular courts, and it was in relation to inheritance and land ownership that cases of bastardy often arose (Adams 1946; Helmholz 1969). Canon law and English common law were in conflict on the issue of 'special bastardy', where a child was born to parents who subsequently married. In canon law, the child became legitimate through the marriage, but this was not the case in common law, and the difference led to the clash recorded in the 1235 Statute of Merton (*SR*, I, 4): The fact that in such cases an ecclesiastical court might return a verdict of 'legitimate' that would be invalid in common law made the royal courts hesitant about referring bastardy cases in certain circumstances, since the bishop's verdict was considered definitive and the certificate constituted estoppel (Adams 1946: 370–371). This friction between royal and ecclesiastical courts provided an opportunity to use the two systems against one another, as seems to be the substance of the complaint in this petition. It is probable that people were seeking to have inheritance cases referred from secular courts to ecclesiastical ones to obtain certificates of legitimization, which would then allow them to win their cases back in the royal courts, their opponents not having had a chance to object to their legitimization.

The hand of this petition indicates a date in the mid fourteenth century, but it is not possible to assign it to a specific parliament. That the matter was being discussed in this period is demonstrated by a common petition on the parliament roll for January–February 1348, that certifications of legitimacy should not prejudice others who were not party to suits (*RP*, II, 171 = *PROME*, IV, 427–428).

25. Cases at the papal curia (SC 8/134/6683)
*c.*1340–1352

Summary

The people: although no Englishman is obliged to be tried by plea outside the realm, some people, on the basis of false and unsubstantiated accusations, cause cases to be summoned out of England to the papal court at Avignon, to the harm of the people and the great detriment of the crown. Request for a remedy, so that this practice might not become widespread.

CHURCH AND RELIGION 57

Response: For things concerning the crown, there is process in the chancery.
In the presence of the great council.

Text

A nostre seignur le Roy et son counseil monstre son people une comune grevance encontre la corone nostre dit seignur le Roi et encontre roule, dignite et le plee usez; qe la ou nul homme du roiaume d'Engleterre doit estre treit en plee hors du roialme d'Engleterre en nule maniere de plee qe poet estre triez en le dit roiaume, et a la fause et nue suggestion de plusours gentz, supposantz diverses grevances estre faites a eux, les queles poent et deivent estre triez en le dit roiaume, et veuliantz faire blemissementz et preiudices a la dite corone et au dit roialme, et poeple procurerent et procurent de iour en autre plusors del dit roiaume estre somons hors du roialme d'Engleterre countez a Avynoun en le tierz roiaume devant conservatours et lour commissaries et devant autres, encontre tote manere de ley et de reson, et par tiel somons sont faitz diverses proces, et le poeple est trop grevousement grevez, a grant damage de eaux et en blemissement de la dite corone, et pur ce qe chescun homme du roiaume d'Engleterre, clers et lay, par proces de tenps serra en la manere susdite [...]¹ et la dite corone blesmie a chescoun fause suggestion si ce la soit suffert. Prie le dite poeple de ce remedye, et qe tieles ordenances soient de ce faites qe mes tieles grevances ne soient usees.

Response: Les choses appendantz a la coroune sue proces usee en chancerie.
Coram magno consilio.

Note

The 1340s and early 1350s saw the commons generally exercised by the influence of the papacy within England. Clement VI, who became pope in 1342, was widely regarded by the English as a partisan of the enemy French (Wood 1989). Following his accession there was a notable increase in the number of papal provisions made to ecclesiastical livings in England. In response to the clamour of parliament in April–May 1343, the crown issued the Ordinance of Provisors with the declared intention of restricting papal provisions (*RP*, II, 144–145 = *PROME*, IV, 351–352), though the king proved reluctant to uphold this legislation as it threatened Anglo-papal

¹One word here is illegible as the text is faded.

relations (Barrell 1991). Further complaints relating to papal provisions and reservation of English benefices were made in the parliaments of June 1344, September 1346, January–February 1348, and February–March 1351, the last culminating in the first Statute of Provisors (*RP*, II, 153–154, 162–163, 171, 228, 232–233 = PROME, IV, 373–375, 398–401, 427; V, 14–15, 25–27; *SR*, I, 316–318). Related to the concern about papal provisions, and part of the general anti-papal mood of the commons in the 1340s, were complaints about the jurisdiction of the papal courts and the belief that they were being used by the Church to overturn the legal judgments of the royal courts in England. The most famous of these complaints, in the great council of 1353, resulted in the first Statute of Praemunire (*RP*, II, 252 = *PROME*, V, 25–27; *SR*, I, 329). In light of the negative response to the present petition, it is likely that it dates from before the statute of 1353. The rhetoric fits with the general anti-papal mood of the commons in the 1340s, and the petition could therefore be associated with any of the parliaments in the period *c*.1340–1352. Although the Statutes of Provisors and Praemunire effectively conceded the demands of the commons in this period, they were more a symbolic, populist statement than evidence of serious disagreement between the crown and the papacy (Cheyette 1963; Ormrod 2011: 368).

26. Papal income from benefices (SC 8/80/3954) 1369–1377

Summary

The commons of the realm: the pope has often set aside the income of prebends and benefices of churches and cathedrals of the realm for the incumbents of the benefices at their request, but he has recently demanded that this income should be collected and taken out of the realm, to the great harm of the churches and the impoverishment of the realm. Request for a remedy against this new development in the present parliament, to avoid the damage and mischief that will follow.

Response: [none].

Text

A nostre tresredoute et tresgracious seignur nostre seignur le Roi et son tresage conseil en ceste present parlement monstrent les comunes de roialme; qe combien nostre seint piere le pape face sovent foiz sequestrer les fruitz, rentz [et]² oblacions des dignitees, prebendes et autres beneficez es eglises, cathedrales et collegiales deinz la dit roialme, sibien al instance des incumbentz dicelles benifices come al instance des ordinairs et autre pretendantz eux avoir droit as ditz benifices, par cause des plees moves entre eux en la courte de Rome, pur sauver les avantditz fruitz, rentz et oblacions a ceux qi ont droit a eux. Nientmeins le collectour et autres assignes depar nostre dit seint piere par ses lettres bulles demandont ore de novell lez ditz fruitz, rentz et oblacions, et lez facent coillez lever et amesner hors du roialme, al oeps de chambre nostre dit seint piere, contre droit et reson, \en/ perpetuele destruccion des eglises avantdites et en grant enpoverissement de tout le roialme. Plese a nostre dit seignur le Roi et a son dit conseil ordiner due remidie en cest present parlement contre ceste novelte, pur eschuir le grant damage et mischief ensueroit en temps avenir.

Note

Although papal attempts to raise revenue were rarely popular with the commons or the clergy, kings had a more ambivalent attitude as they were often able to profit from the process (Lunt 1934; Lunt 1939; Lunt 1962). Following the outbreak of the Hundred Years War, there were occasional outbreaks of anti-papal sentiment from the commons, which resulted in legislation such as the Statutes of Praemunire and Provisors (see no. 25). One of the commons' concerns was the reservation of ecclesiastical benefices for aliens, which resulted in the first fruits of the benefices concerned being taken overseas. The commons feared that the money thus exported was being used to finance the French war effort. They protested against this practice in the parliaments of September 1346 and February–March 1351, and a number of related issues were incorporated into the Statute of Provisors of 1351 (*RP*, II, 162–163, 232–233 = *PROME*, IV, 398–401; V, 25–27; *SR*, I, 316–318). However, the tenor of the present petition links it more closely to the renewed anti-papal sentiment of the 1370s, between the resumption of hostilities with France in 1369 and the beginning of the Western Schism following the death of Pope Gregory XI in 1378. In February 1373 the papacy attempted to revive the taxation of the clergy in England (*CPL, 1362–1404*, 107). This prompted renewed anxieties about the loss of material resource from the realm. A complaint similar in tone and content to the present petition is found on the parliament roll for November 1373 (*RP*, II,

---

²The upper right-hand corner of the document is torn: text is supplied from context.

320 = *PROME*, V, 285–286), and at the Good Parliament of 1376 there was an onslaught of complaint against the pope and the cardinals, with another common petition presenting a long list of grievances against the pope (*RP*, II, 336, 337–340 = *PROME*, V, 329, 331–337). It is likely, then, that the present petition dates from one of the parliaments held during these last years of the reign of Edward III.

27. Custody of alien priories (SC 8/102/5052)
c.1373–c.1377

Summary

The commons: complaint that, although all the alien priories in England have been taken into the king's hands because of the war, some possessions are farmed to foreign priors, whose many servants act as informants for the French enemy to the detriment of king and realm. Furthermore, many of the possessions farmed to knights, esquires, and other seculars of the realm are wasted and ruined, and some long-established priories are without divine services, contrary to faith and conscience. If a remedy is not quickly ordered then ruin will befall the entire realm. Request to the king and his council to order that all these priories and other possessions of the aliens might be leased into the hands of diocesan bishops, and that they make English monks their deputies, who are able to safely watch over the religious practices and charges of these possessions.

Response: For the profit of the king and kingdom.
This bill is answered among the common petitions.

Text

A nostre seignur le Roy et soun iuste conseil supplient la commune; qe come touz les possessions des prieries aliens dedeyne la royalme d'Engleterre sount en mayns du Roy par cause de la guerre, de qeles possessions plusors sount occupes par prioures aliens a ferme, qe les ount plusors servantz et aultres aliens ovesqes eaux demorranz et venanz de iour en aultre, agardent et gaytont les privetes du royalme et certifiont a nous enmys de France a grant preiudice du Roy et du royalme, et auxi plusors des ditz possessiones bailles a ferme a chevalers et esquiers et as aultres seculers du roialme sount grante gast destruccioun, si bien de boys come de mesons, et ascun des prieries estoyent longement sanz divine service encountre bone foy et conscience, et en cas qe remedie ne soit ent hastiement ordeigne y purront [. . .] destruccioun de tout le roialme. Dount vous pleise qe touz les ditz priories et aultres possessiones des ditz alliens qeconqes soient desore lessez en mayns de diosesans au fyn, qu'ils fasount des moignes Engleys tiels deputes, qu'ils purront governer la religioun, gardre les possessions, ferre les charges de ycele savement, come ils volont respondre a Dieu et a Roy pur les perilles susditez et as fermes ordeignez devant ore.

Response: Regis regni commodo.
Ceste bille si est responduz entre les comunes petitions.

Note

The alien priories in England were regularly seized by the crown during periods of war with France in the fourteenth century, ostensibly because foreign monks were potential spies who exported money from the realm (Morgan 1941; McHardy 1989). The present petition, whose hand is of the later fourteenth century, appears to relate to the seizure ordered at the parliament of June 1369 when, on the declaration of war with France, it was agreed the lands and possessions of all alien religious be taken into the king's hands and then leased back to their priors and proctors (*RP*, II, 302 = *PROME*, V, 227). In 1373 the alien priories lost their automatic right to such leases, and it then became much more common for these to be granted, as acts of royal patronage, to members of the laity, a practice criticized in the present petition (McHardy 1975: 135). Common petitions enrolled on the parliament rolls for November 1373 and April–July 1376 expressed concerns similar to the present petition about the diminution of the divine services offered by the alien priories (*RP*, II, 320, 342–343 = *PROME*, V, 286, 342–344). At the first parliament of Richard II's reign, in October–November 1377, the commons presented a petition requesting that all aliens be expelled from the realm by February 1378, with provision to be made to seize the associated property to the war effort and ensure that divine service continue. The response to that petition, which sets out in some detail the arrangements to be made for the performance of religion in the alien priories, suggests that representations may have been made in the same parliament about the adverse consequences of the general expulsion, though it falls short of the notion that the material resources of the priories should be used to sustain divine worship (*RP*, III, 22–23 = *PROME*, VI, 49–50; Lambert and Ormrod 2015: 16–17). It seems likely, then, that the present petition falls somewhere in the date range roughly bounded by the parliaments of 1373–1377, though it could also be associated with a general concern over the divine services offered in the alien priories that continued through the 1380s and 1390s and formed the basis of experiments made after 1399 with the redistribution of ecclesiastical property for the proper promotion of religion (Thompson 1994).

28. Assessment of clergy property for lay taxes (SC 8/21/1032) Late fourteenth century

Summary

The poor commons of the realm: complaint that since 1292 many lands have been amortized to the Church, and can no longer contribute to the tenths and fifteenths. Recently, the clergy and college members of Oxford have petitioned in parliament for all their purchases of land to be made exempt from such taxes, which would be to the detriment of the temporal lords and commons of the realm. Request that no such petition be granted without common assent.

Response: [none].

Text

[A][3] le Roi nostre tresredoute seignur et a lez seignurs de cest present parlement suppliount touz lez povres comunes de le roialme; qe come plusours gentz de seint eglise, sibien [hommes] de religious, come autres ount purchace et amortize plusours grandes possessions en diverses parties de le roialme puis l'an vintisme le Roi Edward fitz Roi Henry, lez queux possessions ount este assys et de droit soloient estre entre lez gentz laies de le dit roialme, en supportacion sibien de lez [seignurs] temporels come de lez povres comunes suisditz, a la disme et quinzisme quant ascune est a nostre dit seignur le Roi graunte, et ore tarde diverses [gentz de] seint eglise, sibien collegiers, come autres de la ville d'Oxenford queux ount purchace grand partie de la dite ville puis l'an [suisdit], pursuont en ycest present parlement d'avoir tout lour purchace descharge induement dez tiels maneres taxes come desuis est dit, [a grand] destruccion et anientisshement de lez povres burgeys nostre seignur le Roy de sa ville suis dite, et malveys ensaumple et preiudice [de touz] lez seignurs temporels et lez povres comunes de le roialme avantdit. Par quey plese al Roy nostre tresredoute seignur avantdit et a lez seignurs [de cest] parlement ordeigner qe nulle tiele bille issint induement pursue encontre droit et resoun, ne soit esploite ne endose saunz comune [assent] de lez povres comunes de la roialme

---

[3] The left-hand side of the document is faded; missing text has been supplied from the corresponding entry on the parliament roll.

avandit, pur Dieu et en oevre de charitee, considerantz qe lez ditz gentz de seint eglise [pur nulles] tiels purchacez come desuis est dit, ne sont en nulle manere pluis charges a lour disme spirituele, ne a ascune autre taxe [ne subside] q'ils ne fueront devant l'an vintisme le dit Roi Edward fitz le dit Roi Henry.

Note

This petition was previously printed in full in *RP*, III, 275– 276, and calendared in *Oxford Petitions*, p. 150. In both cases, the petition was associated with the parliament of January–March 1390, but this verdict is questionable. There is a petition from the University of Oxford in the same sequence of petitions in *RP*, requesting that since tenants of the university are assessed for the tenth and fifteenth, the masters and scholars should be exempt, but this is similarly difficult to date (*RP*, III, 276, with a summary in *PROME*, VII, 169). It is, however, likely that the petition from the university is the one referred to in this petition, and that the two were probably presented in the same parliament.

The assessment of church lands and wealth of 1291 formed the basis of subsequent clerical taxes until the Reformation, with any lands acquired from 1292 taxed alongside those of the laity (Willard 1907; Willard 1934: 93–102; Weske 1937: 147–148). Any attempt to evade this latter liability would have been unpopular with the parliamentary commons. It is possible, though, that this is an example of an avowed petition, in which the commons agreed to take forward the concerns of interested parties who would have been particularly adversely affected by any such exemption for the members of the University of Oxford.

29. The enforcement of mortmain legislation
(SC 8/79/3949)
Late fourteenth century

Summary

The lords and commons: complaint that, in contravention of the Statute of Mortmain, religious purchase lands and tenements which are enfeoffed to others, who donate the profits from the sale of the lands to the said religious. Request that no land be given or sold to any religious, and nor should they take profit without special licence of the king.

Response: [none].

Text

A nostre seignur le Roi monstrent auxibien les seignures come les comunes; come en ses heures fuist ordeigne en parlement qe terrez ne [...] en mortemayn come piert par l'estatut de religiosis, et ore en fraude del dit estatut les religious purchasent terrez et tenementz et auxint [...] autrideim[4] et fount autres gentz estre enfeoffez de celes terrez et tenementz, et le profitz de celes terrez et tenementz deingnent al oeps del dit [...] les ditz feoffez aliener ceo qe plest a dit religious, pernantz devers eux les deniers pur quey la dite terre est vendu [...] present parlement qe par ceste sotilte ne par nulle autre qe purra estre imagine, qe nullez terrez ne tenementz ne soient donez ne vendu [...] nulle religious purra ascune manere profit prendre par nulle voie sanz especial conge du Roi et des autres seignurages, de qui [...] et si ascun le face encountre qe le Roi et autres seignurages puissant entrer come est ordeigne en le dit estatut et [...] nient amorteez duement qe \ils/ soient tenuz pur nullez.

Note

The right-hand side of this document is missing and it is uncertain how much text has been lost, although the sense is clear. The 1279 Statute of Mortmain (*SR*, I, 51) prohibited the alienation of land to the Church, although a system of special royal licences soon developed (Raban 1982; Brand 2004a). However, more informal arrangements which allowed the Church to continue to acquire land, for example through leasehold, were soon in place (Raban 1974: 6–8). Technically leases were illegal under the statute, although a 1306 case against this was dismissed (*Year Books Edward I*, IV, 148–150). Various systems of indirect acquisition of lands were gradually used by religious houses to circumvent the law, and the attendant bureaucracy and expense of a licence, one of which was to use feoffees (Raban 1974: 12–14). The continued alienation of land to the Church through indirect means prompted occasional complaints in parliament. Abuse of mortmain legislation exercised the commons during the later fourteenth century, with common petitions recorded on the parliament rolls for November 1381–February 1382, November–December 1391 and January–March 1394 (*RP*, III, 117, 291, 319 = *PROME*, VI, 256; VII, 208–209, 269). Royal responses to these complaints were mixed: the 1391 petition resulted in a statute to address the accumulation of lands acquired in illegal or suspect fashion (*SR*, II, 79–80), whereas the king's response in 1394 gave the grievance little consideration. The continued

---

[4] This word is unknown.

appearance of the subject shows that the commons remained unhappy about the failure to enforce mortmain legislation, but it is impossible to provide a more specific date for the present petition than that suggested by this contextual evidence and by the hand, which indicates the late fourteenth century.

30. Limit on sale of monastic benefits (SC 8/79/3929) Early fifteenth century

Summary

[No petitioner specified]: request that no religious might have the power to sell any allowances, corrodies, or pensions, nor make recognisances in any court of sums greater than £40 without the assent of their bishop and patron.

Response: [none].

Text

Plese a nostre seignur le Roi et son bon counseil pur l'amour de Dieu et en oevre de charite et en maintenance de la prosperite de religioun ordeigner en ceste present parlement, qe nul religious de ceste roialme de quele condicion qe soit eit power desormes en avant de vendre null liversons, corrodies ne pensions, [ne][5] nule reconisance faire en nulle court ne nulle grant summe de deniers passant la summe de xl livres, aprester en charge de lour maisoun, sanz l'assent de lour evesqez et de lour patron, et si nul face a contrarie de tiele ordinance qe ce ne soit pas de value.

Note

The sale of allowances, corrodies, and pensions by religious houses was a fairly common practice in the later Middle Ages, although bishops tended to disapprove of a custom which often proved financially damaging (Bell and Sutcliffe 2009: 5–6). Evidence from the diocese of Lincoln indicates that permission was required from the bishop before corrodies could be sold (*Visitations, passim*), since monasteries often found themselves in economic difficulties as a consequence of these sales – although this may not have been a universal requirement. By the end of the fourteenth century, some houses had found their

---

[5] Conjectural (hole in parchment).

commitments in this regard more expensive than they had envisaged, and in certain cases defaulted on them (e.g. Cullum 1991: 6–9). Although the present petition appears, on the basis of the hand, to date from the early fifteenth century, there is no internal evidence which allows for it to be more precisely dated, and there are no corresponding entries on the extant parliament rolls. It is possible that the petition is a reaction to certain abbots attempting to evade their responsibilities for various allowances, corrodies, and pensions, and seeks letters of protection against attempts to default on these obligations, which seems to have been an issue early in the reign of Henry IV. A common petition in the parliament of January–March 1401 sought the repeal of letters of protection against most pleas and legal action (*RP*, III, 469–470 = *PROME*, VIII, 129). There was also an unenrolled petition submitted in the parliament of September–November 1402 that sought to prevent the abbot of Lesnes and other English houses evading their obligations in this regard (SC 8/22/1095 = *RP*, III, 520; summary in *PROME*, VIII, 219). If, as seems probable, the present petition is linked to these complaints, seeking to impose a sustainable level on monastic commitments and ensure proper oversight of their financial affairs, then it is most likely that it dates from the early part of Henry IV's reign. However, the sale of corrodies and other benefits continued in the fifteenth century, including at a value above the £40 suggested in this petition (Bell and Sutcliffe 2009, App. pp. 1–2, 5).

III
LIBERTIES, FRANCHISES, AND RIGHTS

31. Inheritance rights for siblings (SC 8/79/3906)
Early fourteenth century

Summary

The people: complaint that, when a free man dies without having produced an heir but has a brother or sister, the king's ministers sell the land or retain it as an escheat, depriving them of their proper inheritance; request for a remedy.

> *Response*: In the presence of the king and great council.
> The justices are ordered to identify the ministers who do this and stop them, and if there is any reason this cannot be done the king's court is to be certified.

Text

Auxint monstrent vos dites gentz; q'ils sei sentent moult grevees et enpoveres par enchesoun qe quant fraunc homs est mort saunz heir de soun corps engendree, mesque il eit un frere ou un muliereez, vos ministrent vendent cele terre encountre lur leys et lur usages la, ou ils deussent avoir par lur leys lur dreit heritage. Autrement, si enfaunt moerge saunz heir de soun corps il nen portereit mye le heritage apres soun frere, mes vos ministres vendent lur terres a qi qe lui pleyse, ou les detyenent come eschete, et de ces prient ils pur Dieu remedie.

> *Response*: Coram rege et magno consilio.
> Seit mande a la [iustices]¹ se enfourme [queux] ministres ceux sont qi font tieles grevances et les face surser de tieles grevances, et si cause seit pur qei il ne le de mye faire adonqes certefie la court de la cause.

---

¹ Supplied from context, as the text is faded here and in the line below.

68   LIBERTIES, FRANCHISES, AND RIGHTS

Note

The use of *auxint* at the beginning of the address suggests that this document was originally part of a multiple-clause petition, from which it was separated before the answer was written on the dorse. An escheat was land which came into the king's hand as a result of an absence of heirs or because it had been forfeited (Stevenson 1947: 109–110). Medieval inheritance law was complex (Plucknett 1956: 712–724), but the essential position was that collateral branches of the family such as siblings and cousins would normally only inherit if a deceased landowner had no direct descendants. This could naturally result in disputed claims to land. The inquisitions post mortem established if any income or rights were due to the crown, but the land would then have been duly inherited by the heir (if one existed), after due process had established the legitimate heir. Clearly the retention of land as an escheat for any but the permitted reasons was an abuse of office. However, complaints about abuse by royal officials in inheritance cases were not uncommon, and there is no internal evidence which provides a context to this petition, nor is there any direct link to a similar entry on the extant parliament rolls. Such a general complaint could plausibly have come from any point in the later Middle Ages, although the hand of this petition would suggest a date in the early fourteenth century.

32. Increasing farms by fraud (SC 8/79/3920)
Early fourteenth century

Summary

[No petitioner specified]: request that the king and council ordain remedy in cases where certain people of the realm, leasing out their lands at farm, redeem the value or thereabouts and involve themselves in pleas by collusion with other tenants, so that in the recovery higher farms are demanded and the lands extended, to the great disinheritance of the people. Further request that it be ordained in this parliament that those who take such farms might be denied their right of defence.

Response: [none].

Text

Ple\i/s a nostre seignur le Roi et a son conseil ordeiner remedie en cas ou certeinez gens de son reume, lessunt lour terres as ferme, rendent lour value ou ben prede celz, et par colisioun entre teu tenauntz et autre demaundanz se fount estre enplesdez et pays passer par acent de eus, icint qe par le requeverer de plus haut le fe fermes de plus tard demaundes de deveirent esteindre, a graunt deserytaunse de moutz de gens, et qe ordinez seit en se parleament qe en cel cas ceus qi perneunt telz le fermes pussunt estre partye a lour dreit defender.

Note

There is no internal evidence to permit the precise dating of this petition, nor any entries on the parliament rolls that correspond to its demands, even though the text makes clear that it was presented in parliament. The hand would indicate an early fourteenth-century provenance. The convoluted syntax makes it difficult to determine the exact nature of the complaint. The essential issue here appears to be that those leasing out lands at farm were recovering their investment before engaging in legal machinations to increase their income, to the detriment of those leasing the lands. However, protests about collusion and dishonesty in leases and pleas were widespread across the later Middle Ages, and in the absence of further context it is impossible to provide more precise context for the present document.

33. Leasing of waste land (SC 8/257/12802)
1324–1325

Summary

Archbishops, bishops, prelates, earls, barons, and other people of the commonalty of England who are tenants in chief: those who hold their manors of the king, both in the forests and outside them, and whose manors contain wastelands (reed-beds, brush, and other pasture) that contribute little to the issues of their manors, state that they have been in the habit of leasing these lands according to the quality of the soil, by acre, half-acre, and by rood, sometimes for life terms and sometimes in fee, but that the king's ministers have seized the land, because the people who have leased it do not have the king's permission to enter. Request that they might be able to exploit their lands in this way and ease the poor people without hindrance, as it is more to the king's profit than his harm when the manors come into his hand through wardship or in some other manner.

Response: It cannot be done without a new law, something to which the commonalty of the land does not yet wish to assent. Before the king.

Text

A nostre seignur le Roy et a son consail monstrent ercevesqes, evesqes, prelatz, countes et barouns et autre genz de la comunyaulte d'Engletere qe tenent lour manoirs en chief de nostre seignur, \auxibien deinz foreste come dehors/, a queus manoirs illiad gasz appendaunt, ceo est asavoir iaunz, brucre et autre pasture qe poy est de respounse en issues du manoir, dount les seignurages avantditz arentunt lez gasz susdites a pluis pluis et a meyns meyns solomp ceo qe le seoul le demande, et ceo par acre, demy acre et par rode a la foieth en aprovaunt lour manoirs \a la foith a terme de vie et a la foith en fee/, et sur ceo venent le ministres nostre seignur le Roy et fount seiseyr lez gasz issint leseez, pur ceo qe eux ne unt la licence le Roy d'entrer. Par qei les avauntditz ercevesqes, evesqes, prelatz, countis et barouns et autres de la comunyalte prient a nostre seignur le Roy qe eux puissent en tieu manere aprover lour manoirs et le povre pueple eyser saunz estre chalanges, desicome ichet pluis en profit du Roy qe en damage quele hures qe les ditz manoirs devenent en la mayn nostre seignur le Roy par resoun de garde ou en autre manere.

> *Response*: Il ne put estre fait sans novele ley, la quele chose fere la comunalte de la terre ne vult mie uncore assentur.
> Coram rege.

Note

This petition was previously printed in *RP*, I, 416, where it is dated to the regnal year 18 Edward II (July 1324–July 1325). As the *RP* version is taken from a transcript in a manuscript of Sir Mathew Hale, who had access to the medieval files of parliamentary petitions prior to reorganization, the dating is probably reliable (*PROME*, III, 457). The petition can therefore be linked either to the assembly of October–November 1324 or to that of June 1325. It is possibly connected with no. 115, a memorandum of complaints and requests by the people of England presented to the first of these parliaments. The petition is somewhat unusual in separating the petitioners into so many categories, and although they purport to be seeking redress to help the 'poor people', the request ultimately seems to be for the benefit of the tenants in chief named rather than the commonalty as a whole – a tension that is also revealed by the comment in the response that the 'commonalty of the realm' did not wish to assent to changes of the kind proposed.

The dating suggests that this petition may have been prompted by Edward II's policy towards the lands of the so-called Contrariants who had defied him in the civil war of 1321–1322 and bore the brutal consequences thereafter (see also no. 94). Following the king's victory against rebel forces led by the earls of Lancaster and Hereford at the Battle of Boroughbridge in 1322, a significant amount of land was forfeited into royal possession. Initially, Edward was 'eager to reap quick profits while incurring the minimum of costs', and the government leased everything possible (Fryde 1979: 83). In 1324, however, policy changed and all properties worth more than £40 per year were to be stocked with animals and entrusted directly to royal keepers charged with raising their value; those with leases on former Contrariant properties now had a precarious status (Waugh 1975; Fryde 1979: 80–86). Those who had benefited in the short term from leasing Contrariant lands and who had in turn sub-leased the less profitable parts would thus have suffered from the king's desire to maximize revenue and reclaim his lands. Although only tangential, the reference to forests may also have been significant, since the 1320s saw considerable discord about the extent of the royal forests and the misconduct of forest officials (see nos 2 and 7).

34. Accounting at the exchequer (SC 8/167/8336)
1327

Summary

The people of the realm: under Edward II they were required to account for lands in the king's chamber, but they request that they might now make their accounts in the exchequer.

> *Response*: Let it be ordered by writ of chancery that the treasurer and barons of the exchequer should hear all such accounts.

Text

A nostre seignur le Roi et son conseil prient les gentz du roialme, qi deyvent acountes des terres dount sire Edward, piere nostre seignur le Roi Edward q'ore est, avoit ordine d'estre respoundu en sa chaumbre, q'ils puissent acounter a l'escheqier, et qe soit maunde as tresorier et barons du dit escheqier q'ils oyent celes acountes et facent reson.

> *Response*: Mandetur par breve de cancellaria thesaurario et baronibus de scaccario quod ipsi audiant compota omnium et singulorum coram eis computare volencium de terris et tenementis de quibus nuper responsum fuit in camera Regis Edwardi patris Regis nunc, et

faciant ulterius super eisdem compotis quod ad finalem execucionem compotorum fuerit faciendum.

Note

This petition was printed in *RPHI*, p. 284; a Latin version with the same response (from which the word *ipsi* is omitted) also exists in an abstract of a roll of petitions firmly datable to the first parliament of Edward III, in January–March 1327, printed in *RPHI*, p. 150 (= *PROME*, IV, 63). Edward II had made increasing use of the chamber rather than the exchequer as the department in which accounts were to be presented for certain royal manors and lands (Tout 1920–1933, II, 314–360). Edward's relations with the exchequer had often been strained, and a series of reforms had been enacted in the 1320s under the treasurership of Walter Stapeldon (Buck 1983a; Buck 1983b: 163–196). Once the lands of the Contrariants came into the king's hands in May 1322, they had been initially administered by the king's chamber; and although control was officially transferred to the exchequer in July (Fryde 1979: 80, 101), the transfer does not appear to have been completely effected and responsible officials of these and other lands continued to account at the chamber. The response to the present petition suggests a new firmness of purpose on the part of the minority government of Edward III. However, it would take some years for the exchequer to take responsibility for lands administered by the chamber and for the chamber accounts to be transferred to the exchequer, with the process not completed until 1336 (Tout 1920–1933, IV, 230–237). In his analysis of this process, Tout (1920–1933, IV, 231) mentions the present petition but only from a later English copy, and was apparently unaware of the survival of this original.

35. Offences committed within liberties (SC 8/165/8223) c.1330

Summary

The people of the commonalty: the king and his ancestors have granted many towns in the realm the right that residents should not be prosecuted outside the boundaries of their liberties. As a result, these residents beat and kill those coming to the liberties, in the knowledge that they are under their own jurisdiction and may acquit themselves. This is harmful to the crown and people, and they request remedy.

LIBERTIES, FRANCHISES, AND RIGHTS 73

Response: Let those who feel themselves aggrieved sue at common law, and if they cannot be assisted by it, the king will apply another remedy.

Text

A nostre seignur le Roy et son conseil monstrent genz de sa commune; qe come nostre seignur le Roy et sez progeniturs eyent grante as plusours villes deinz son realme qe y ne seyent entaglez de nule part hors de lez bundes de lour fraunchises de nul fayt sayt deinz lour fraunchises, par qi y sount par colour de ceux fraunchises oppressions seur le puple ceo est a savoyre tewent et batent les genz iloqes venantz pur ceo qe y s'aseurent qe il averunt meismes conisaunz de lour fayt demen et aquiterunt eux meismes, issint sount ceux fraunchises grantez en preiudice de la coroune. Por qei la ley ne peut estre servie et en damage deu peuple de quay y priont remedie.

Response: Ceux qe se sentent grevez suent a la comune lei, et sils ne puissent estre eidez par cele, le Roi mettra autre remedie.

Note

This petition was previously printed in *RP*, II, 37, with a complete translation provided by Sayles (1988: 401–402), where it is dated to the parliament of November–December 1330. The *RP* edition derives from a transcript by Sir Mathew Hale rather than the original petition, and is found among a collection of eighty-four petitions dated to the regnal year 4 Edward III (January 1330–January 1331). Modern analysis indicates that Hale was working from an original file of parliamentary petitions, and that the documents in question can be firmly dated to one of the two parliaments of 1330, held in March and in November–December (Dodd 2009; *PROME*, III, 460). It is indeed likely that the present petition dates to the second of these assemblies, at which Edward III formally asserted his majority, brought charges of treason against Roger Mortimer, earl of March, and announced his intention to ensure that the law of the land be upheld and justice done to all (*RP*, II, 52–60 = *PROME*, IV, 103–121). Although common petitions were not enrolled for the relevant assembly, a number of statutes were also issued for the better administration of the courts and legal system (*SR*, I, 261–265).

The particular issue raised in the present petition, concerning the apparent immunity enjoyed by the residents of liberties from the reach of royal justice, was endemic (Cam 1963: 183–204). It came up in the 1320s in connection with the special privileges of the city of London (no. 54), and arose again later in the century in relation to named provincial towns (no. 38). Nor were the problems caused by the existence of separate legal systems in liberties confined to urban jurisdictions: the matter was also a significant cause of friction in larger rural liberties under the control of nobles and churchmen (Holford and Stringer 2010: 1–14). It was difficult for the king to provide any other remedy than the one suggested in this response, that wronged parties seek redress at common law. However, the warning that the king would otherwise seek to assert his own authority may hint at Edward III's particular determination to end the cycle of disorder that had plagued the country during the 1320s.

36. The limits of legal memory in writs (C 49/67/8) Mid fourteenth century

Summary

The commonalty: request that the king decree a time limit for writs of right and other writs in such cases.
   Response: Before the king and great council.
           To be dealt with in our parliament.

Text

A nostre soignur le Roy prie la comune qe lui plese lymiter le temps des brefs de dreit et d'autres brefs en ceo cas.
   Response: Coram Rege et magno consilio.
           Attendre en nostre parlement.

Note

The limitation dates for various writs concerning rights over land and property were changed on several occasions during the thirteenth and fourteenth centuries (Plucknett 1956: 719; Brand 2001). The original limit had been the death of Henry I (1135), although by the time a century had passed it was felt this was too long ago and in 1236 it was changed to the coronation of Henry II (1154). Similar logic, that the passage of more than a century necessitated a new date, resulted in the Statute of Westminster I (1275) setting the limitation dates that continued to be used in the fourteenth century: the coronation of Richard I (1189) for writs of right; the first voyage of Henry III to Gascony (1242) for writs of *novel disseisin*; and the coronation of Henry

III (usually taken as that at Westminster in 1220 rather than the earlier one at Gloucester in 1216) for other types of writ (*SR*, I, 36). Even by the end of Edward I's reign, these dates lay beyond the memory of living men, and by Edward III's time there was obviously a desire to update the law to provide new limits for litigation. However, although there were two precedents for changing the limit, and these indicated that around a century was considered a reasonable time, after 1275 there was a remarkable reluctance by the government to countenance any alteration. The question was raised in parliament in 1322 (see no. 113) but in spite of a determination by the government to make some new statement on limitations (Ormrod 1990a: 27), nothing happened. It may be that the present petition, which can only be impressionistically dated to the middle of the fourteenth century, comes from shortly after the 1322 debate; the response (previously and inaccurately printed by Rayner 1941: 220 n. 1) is not encouraging; it also carries some suggestion that the petition was not originally presented in a formally constituted parliament. The commons returned to the issue of the limitation of writs several times in the period 1369–77 (see no. 41), but there was no further change to the limit of legal memory until 1540.

37. Lands seized by the crown (SC 8/79/3905)
Mid fourteenth century

Summary

Poor religious and other commons of the realm: complaint that, as a result of inquiries made by commissioners and escheators, their lands and tenements have been seized into the king's hands and given to his officers and servants. Request that the king retain the said lands for a certain time defined in parliament, in order that they might sue for their rights, and that in the meantime they should have possession of the lands by sufficient surety found in chancery.

Response: [none].

Text

A nostre seignour le Roy et a son bon counceil priont les povres religiouses et aultres comunes de son roialme; de ceo qe les avantditz religiouses et comunes sont outrageausement greves par enquestes prises par comissioners et eschetours, par cause de qele office trove devant caux terres et tenementz de dites religiouses et comunes sont seiscez en la meyn nostre seignour le Roy, et hors de sa meyn les dites tenementz sont dones et grantes sudeynement a officeres et servantz nostre dit seignour le Roy, par cause de qele graunt les dites religiouses et comunes sont soventfoitz delayes et desherites a toutz iours. Pur qoi pleise a nostre dit seignour le Roy de retener tiels terres et tenementz issint en sa meyn seisitz saunz doun faire par certeyn tenps limyte en le parlement, deynz qele tenps ceaux qe sei sentent greves par tiels enquestes poent suere lour dreit vers nostre seignour le Roy, et aver en le mesne tenps les tenements issint seisitz hors de la meyn nostre dit seignour le Roy par suffisaunt suerte trove al chauncellerie, tanqe terre soit le droit entre nostre dit seignour le Roy et la partie, en overe de charite.

Note

The hand indicates that this petition comes from the mid fourteenth century, but without any additional context it is impossible to provide a precise date. It seems possible, though, that the petition belongs to one of the two periods during the reign of Edward III in which the king and his ministers were subjected to sustained pressure and criticism for the consequences of intrusive royal inquiries in the provinces. The petition may therefore be linked to the special judicial commissions launched in 1340–1343 to investigate corruption and incompetence in local government, which resulted in the temporary confiscation of significant amounts of landed property (Jones 1973; Jones 1974; and see no. 62). Another possibility is that the petition was provoked by a series of inquiries into the crown's feudal rights in the 1360s led by the controversial steward of the king's household, Sir John atte Lee, who was disgraced and dismissed in the parliament of May 1368 (Ormrod 2013b). The relatively unusual identification of the petitioners as 'poor religious and other commons of the realm' makes it possible either that the petition was not submitted in parliament, or that its contents were deemed marginal or inappropriate for inclusion on the schedules of common petitions prepared by the clerks of parliament.

38. The problems of obtaining justice in the great liberties (SC 8/79/3943)
Mid fourteenth century

Summary

The commonalty of the land: request for remedy in that many false acquittances and releases are made in liberties where the king's writ does not run, such as Beverley and Bury St Edmunds, as a result of

LIBERTIES, FRANCHISES, AND RIGHTS 77

which many men are disinherited and ruined and are unable to have security.

Response: Petitions such as this should be put amongst the common petitions in the next parliament.

Text

A nostre seignur le Roi et son consail prie la cominalte de la terre; qe come faux acquitaunces et relesses faitz en foreinz countez, auxibien ou le bref le Roi ne court pas come la ou il court, et en villes des fraunchise come en Beverleye et en le Burgh de Seint Esmond, ent mys avant en la court nostre dit seignur le Roi, en delaiaunce les parties de lour droit, par quoi plusours gentz sount desheritetz anientez de ceo, q'ils ne puissent pluis avant seure. Dount ils prient remedie.

Response: Ponat consimilis peticio inter comunes peticiones in proxi parliamento.

Note

Along with an earlier petition presented on the same subject (see no. 35), this petition addresses an issue endemic in the fourteenth century about the conflicts and delays that arose as a result of the rights claimed by the holders of great liberties to hold their own courts outside the system of justice provided by the crown. The examples given here are the Archbishop of York's liberty of Beverley in Yorkshire, and the great East Anglian liberty controlled by the abbey of Bury St Edmunds; but the petition does not otherwise single these out for criticism in any specific way. The hand of the petition suggests that it was written in the mid fourteenth century. It is tempting to ascribe it to the parliament of January–February 1348, whose records yield two possible contexts. First, the enrolled common petitions from this assembly include no fewer than three petitions on the theme of liberties, demanding the restriction of further creation of the franchises that made up the rights of liberty-holders, the non-alienation of royal liberties, and appeals on judgments given in the courts of the palatinates and other great liberties (*RP*, II, 166, 169, 171 = *PROME*, IV, 417, 422, 428–429). Secondly, in relation to the answer provided to the present petition, there is clear evidence that a fairly significant number of the private petitions submitted in this assembly were not heard while it sat but were deferred for audience at another, called almost immediately after this one ended, and which sat in March–April 1348 (*PROME*, IV, 409); the commons in this second assembly made specific reference to the need for these unanswered petitions to be heard without further delay

(*RP*, II, 201 = *PROME*, IV, 254). The present petition may therefore have been submitted either by an interest group in the name of the commonalty or by the commons as a late addition to their agreed schedule of common petitions; the idea that it might be taken up as a common petition at the next assembly reinforces the argument for a date of 1348, to the extent that a significant number of the common petitions submitted at the second parliament of that year, and the answers to them, referred to the relevant issues as raised at the previous assembly (*RP*, II, 201–203 = *PROME*, IV, 453–459). Neither the specific nor the general issue about liberties appears in the enrolled common petitions from the parliament of March–April 1348, however, and the association of the present document with its immediate predecessor must therefore remain a matter of speculation.

39. False vouchers of warranty (SC 8/335/15823)
Mid fourteenth century

Summary

The commons of the realm of England: complaint that they are often delayed from receiving justice by false vouches of warranty made by people in writs, which are judged to be valid by authority of certain feoffments from which the voucher continues to receive profits, resulting in delay and disinheritance. Request that it be ordained by statute that in all writs in which there is vouching, if the defendant vouches to warranty a certain person and the claimant will swear by peers or otherwise, neither the vouchee nor any of his ancestors should have anything in the claimed land, and that the voucher should continue to take the profits of the lands, and the averment should be received between them if the voucher will wait for it, and if not, then the voucher should put forward another response.

Response: [none].

Text

A chaunceller nostre seignur le Roi monstrent les comuniez de roialme d'Engleterre; qe come ils soient soventfoithe delaiez de lour droit en la courte lour dit seignur le Roi par faux voucher a garant de plusours persones du dit roialme en briefs de forme done et autres briefs semblables, en queux voucher gist par force de certeins feffementz faitz as ditz persones par comyn fraude et collusion pur delaier le demandant de son droit, par la ou celuy qi vouche, nient

LIBERTIES, FRANCHISES, AND RIGHTS 79

contresteantz tiels feffementz, continuelment prent les profitz de les terres e tenementz avanditz, pur queux delaiez les ditz comuniez alefoithe ont este par grante temps delaier, et alefoithe desheritez a touz iours, dont remedie n'ad este ordeine avant sez heures en la courte nostre dit seignur le Roi. Qe pleise a vostre tresgraciouse seignurie, considerant les ditz delaiez et autres periles de desheritement queux purront venir as ditz comunes, par icel enchesoun ordeiner pur comune profit du dit roialme par estatut qe en touz briefs en queux voucher par la ley est done, qe si le tenant vouche a garant un certeine persone, et le demandant voille averer par pairs ou en autre manere come la courte nostre dit seignur le Roi voille agarder, qe celuy qest vouche ne nulle de ces auncestres n'avoit unqes rien en la terre en demande puis le title compris deins soun brief sinoun par collusione et fraude pur delaier le dit demandant de soun droit, et qe celuy qi vouche continuelment prent les profitz de les ditz terres issint en demande, soit l'averement parentre eaux resceu si celuy qi vouche le voille attendre, et si nemye, soit celuy qi vouche bote autre a autre respons, et ceo prient les ditz comuniez en oevre de charite.

Note

This petition was printed, with minor textual variations, in *SCCKB*, III, p. cxxi. Sayles dated it to the time of Edward III; the hand suggests that it is more likely to come from the second half of the reign. Deeds often had a clause in which the grantor promised to warrant the grantee and his heirs, and lords owed warrant to freehold tenants, so that in legal cases these people could be called upon as vouchers to warranty. This acted as a protection to those purchasing land, since warrantors were required to defend the titles of purchasers, and donors (and their heirs) could have no future claim to those titles. Misuse of vouchers for warranty for purposes of fraud or delay was common, and resulted in several attempts to address the problem by statute in the reign of Edward I (Plucknett 1956: 411–412). Unfortunately, there are no entries on the extant parliament rolls of the fourteenth century that offer a more precise context and dating for the debate raised in the present petition.

40. Enrolling of legislation (SC 8/79/3947)
1363–1376

Summary

The commons: request that all the petitions concerning the commons that have been answered and endorsed in the parliaments since the last general pardon made to the commons in 1362 be placed in a statute, together with those that have not yet been made public or executed.

Response: [none].

Text

A nostre seignur le Roi et a son bon conseil supplie sa comune; qe pleise mettre en estatutz et faire publier et proclamer toutes les peticions touchantes la dite comune [...][2] sont responduz et endosez en diverses parlementz avant ceux hures puis la darreine generale pardoun faite a sa dite comune l'an de son regne xxxvi, et les [...] ne furent unqes mys en estatuz publiez ne executz tanqeu cea, pur Dieux et en oevre de charite.

Note

Throughout Edward III's reign, the commons exhibited an explicit preference to have written records of decisions made in their favour during sessions of parliament (Richardson and Sayles 1981, Part II, ch. xxi, pp. 12–13). In the parliament of October–November 1362, Edward III conceded a general pardon to the commons which was recorded on both the parliament and statute rolls (*RP*, II, 272 = *PROME*, V, 149–150; *SR*, I, 376–378; Lacey 2009: 110–112). This concession came to be viewed as something of a precedent, and the commons referred back reasonably regularly to the statute of 1362 as a touchstone of their rights (Ormrod 2011: 481–482). The present petition can be dated to some time between the parliaments of October–November 1363 (the next parliament after the general pardon) and April–July 1376 (the Good Parliament). The latter end of this range is more probable, since the petition seems to suggest that some time has elapsed since the 1362 general pardon; the evident anxiety about the crown's reluctance to enroll other legislation also reflects the generally low statutory outputs of the parliaments of the last years of the reign. There was an unsuccessful effort by the commons in 1372 to define and extend the scope of the 1362 general pardon (*RP*, II, 311 = *PROME*, V, 260–261), but in the assembly of January–March 1377, on the occasion of the completion of Edward III's fiftieth year as king, the crown granted a further, and more expansive, general pardon (*RP*, II, 364–365 = *PROME*,

---

[2] The right-hand side of this document is torn, meaning that in the first two lines the final word is missing.

V, 401–403; Lacey 2009: 115–126). It can therefore be assumed that the present petition dates before this, the last parliament of the reign.

41. The limits of legal memory in writs (SC 8/102/5077) c.1369–c.1377

Summary

The commons of the realm: request that the king ordain a new time for the limitation of writs in this present parliament, on the grounds that the limitation made in the time of Edward I, contained in the Statute of Westminster I, is beyond the time of human memory.

Response: [none].

Text

A nostre seignur le Roi prye la comune de roialme; pur ceo qe le temps de limitacioun dez briefs est molt passe, qe en cest present parlement ordeigne soit novele limitacioun, pur ceo qe la limitacioun faite en temps le Roy Edward fitz le Roi Henry, come est contenuz en l'estatut de Westminstre primer, passe temps de memorie de homme a present.

Note

A note on the guard of this petition dates it to 1378, but without explanation. It is more likely that it dates from the campaign undertaken on this issue in the later part of Edward III's reign. There had been similar efforts to create new limits on the term of legal memory in the 1320s, but these had come to nothing (see nos 36 and 133). There are three instances on the parliament roll between 1369 and 1376 which suggest that the matter raised in the present petition was especially lively towards the end of Edward III's reign. In 1369, a common petition tried to shift the limit of legal memory from the accession of Richard I (1189) to the coronation of Edward I (1274), but met with a blunt refusal (*RP*, II, 300 = *PROME*, V, 224–225). In 1372, in another attempt, the commons were not specific about a new date, instead simply requesting that the limit be shortened; once again, however, the king dismissed the petition (*RP*, II, 312 = *PROME*, V, 264). The third attempt, in a common petition to the Good Parliament of April–July 1376, returned to proposing exact dates to replace 1189 (*RP*, II, 341 = *PROME*, V, 340–341). The 1376 petition specifically states the aim to be the protection of those swearing oaths in inquests, stating that human memory can only remember the last hundred years, which had been taken as the guideline figure in earlier revisions of the date of legal memory (see no. 36). Accordingly, it suggests the coronation of Edward I (1274) as the limit for writs of right and the coronation of Edward III (1327) for other types of writ. The response is more amenable than before, noting that the king would consider changing the law, perhaps reflecting the weak position of the royal administration in 1376. However, there was little statutory legislation in these last parliaments of Edward III and the matter seems simply to have gone into abeyance.

42. Land rights for minors coming of age (SC 8/79/3950)
*c.*1376

Summary

The commons: complaint that fines levied in the king's court on those who have not attained legal age cannot be reversed or annulled, and that through lack of knowledge of the law, bad counsel, or in the case of married women the influence of their husbands, many are thus wrongfully disinherited. Request that those who come of age should have two or three years in which to bring suits before the justices for fines levied during their minority, that they might find proof by averment that the fine should be reversed, and that this right should apply to all under twenty-three years of age.

Response: [none].

Text

A nostre seignur le Roi et a soun conseil monstre la commune; qe come devant ces heurs, fynes q'ent este levez en la court le Roi par hommes ou femmes tanqe come ils furont deins age ne purrent en nulle manere estre reversez ne annullez si la sute ne fuys comense avant ceo qils amendrent a lour pleyn age par la ou femmes covertz par force de lour barouns et autres enfantz deins age nient conissantz la ley estre tiel come desus est dit, et alafoitz par maves conseil ont este destourbez et alloignez q'ils ne purrent faire nulle cuyte tanqe ils fuissent de pleine age, et les femmes par cas tanqe apres la mort lour barons, par ou ils ont en tiel cas sovent este malement disheretez. Par qi pri la comune qe puys enfantz puissent avoir plus large temps come de deux ans ou troiz apres lour plein [age] [...] de comenser tiel seute de annuller et reverser tiel fyn issint leve, tanqe come ils furent deins age issint [...] des iustices ou par autre voie il purra apperir par averment ou par prove estre trove qe la fyn se leva tanqe [...] deins age q'adonqe la fyn soit reverse, nient contrestcant qe la dite seute ne soit comense deyns age et qe [...] a touz iceux qi ne sont pas unqore passe l'age de xxiii ans.

Note

The bottom right-hand corner of this document is missing, but no significant information appears to have been lost as a result. A petition very similar to this is found, albeit with different wording, on the parliament roll for the Good Parliament of April–July 1376 (*RP*, II, 342 = *PROME*, V, 343), and the two would appear to be related. The enrolled version rehearses at greater length the reason why the right to seek remedy should be extended, and differs from the present petition in setting the age limit at twenty-four instead of twenty-three. Given the very complicated relationship between drafts and enrolled version of the common petitions of 1376 (Ormrod 2004: 52–53), however, it seems possible that the present petition represents a preliminary version of that enrolled at the Good Parliament.

Fines were essentially a legal fiction whereby land or property was transferred from one party to another for an agreed sum through a nominal legal process. Invented disputes and the subsequent proceedings allowed a decision to be officially recorded, since fines created a legal record of land ownership, registered on the feet of fines in the court of common pleas. Such legal proceedings provided a title to land which was thus hard to challenge, and could be open to abuse in the way outlined in this petition. Theoretically, minors unaware of their rights could be tricked into surrendering their rights in this manner and then find it difficult, if not impossible, to reclaim their inheritance. Allowing such people time after they reached the age of majority to challenge verdicts reached as a result of bad advice or deceit was a means of preventing the exploitation of under-age heirs. It is hard to say how extensive this problem actually was, since it does not feature otherwise on the parliament rolls of the period. That this complaint was perhaps presented to the Good Parliament might suggest that it was part of the broader collection of grievances against local corruption and injustices which marked this assembly, rather than as a major issue in its own right.

43. Resolving outstanding writs of assize (SC 8/102/5056)
1377

Summary

Lieges of the commons: complaint that many writs of assize of *novel disseisin* and mort d'ancestor purchased in the time of the king's grandfather, some arraigned and others not arraigned, are again in the hands of the sheriffs, to the great damage of the people. Request that the present parliament order that all these writs of assize stand at law, and that commissions be directed to justices notifying them of this, in order that any of the petitioners who have made alienations in the meantime might not be disinherited.

Response: There is a remedy ordained.

Text

A tresnoble et tresgracious seignur le Roi et a soun bon conseille monstrent sy lour plest plusours liges de sa commune; qe come plusours brefs d'assises des novelles disseisine et de mordauncestre fuerunt purchacez en temps son aiel, les queux assises par defaute des iusticez venauntz en paiis sount unquore en mayns de vicountes, ascunes arrayes et ascunes nyent arrayes, en grauntz damages de people. Par quoy plese a tresgracious seignurie en eovre de charite grauntier et ordeyner en ceste present parlement que toutez maneres brefs d'assises en temps soun dit aiel purchasez auxint bien, ceux qeux ne sount pas arrayes come ceux qeux sount arrayes estoysount en lour force, et comissiouns direttes as iusticez faisauntz mensioun de la matere, issint qe ses liges par alienaciouns faitz en le meyne \temps/ ne soyt desherites.

Response: Il y a de remede ordeignee.

Note

An abbreviated form of this petition is found on the parliament roll for the assembly of October–November 1377 (*RP*, III, 20 = *PROME*, VI, 45) and it seems reasonable that this is the base text from which the enrolled version was constructed. Writs of *novel disseisin* and mort d'ancestor had been introduced in the twelfth century to provide a speedy remedy for issues of seisin and inheritance, and prevent protracted legal proceedings (Sutherland 1973; Warren 1973: 337–348). A writ of *novel disseisin* would be purchased by a claimant to land or property, which would cause the sheriff to convene a jury to establish whether the claimant had been unlawfully dispossessed. (The jury had only to determine seisin, not right.) A writ of mort d'ancestor initiated a process to determine the true heir of a deceased landowner. The procedure of *novel disseisin* proved adaptable from the late thirteenth century onwards and effectively rendered mort d'ancestor and other actions obsolete by the end of the fourteenth century (Musson and Ormrod 1999: 122–125). As the intention of these processes was partly (although not exclusively) to provide swift resolution in inheritance disputes, the delay alluded to in the present petition would obviously cause problems for those seeking to alienate or otherwise dispose of lands they believed to be their own. However, there is no evidence on the parliament rolls for this matter having been raised as a concern in the years before 1377.

It is not immediately apparent to what remedy the response refers. It is just possible that a decision made more than sixty years earlier is intended: a petition to the parliament of 1315 had requested that justices might be able to deal with assizes of *novel disseisin* at all times of year, with the response that the justices should attend to them as often as they were able (*RP*, I, 292–293 = *PROME*, III, 62). More likely the sense of the response is simply to confirm existing practice. The government clearly did not perceive the matter raised to be a major problem, and it does not seem to have been brought before parliament again in Richard II's reign. A statute of the parliament of November 1381–February 1382 prevented forcible entries onto land (*SR*, II, 20), a subtle reminder that due process existed for those who believed themselves to have been unfairly dispossessed.

44. Leasing of lands at suit (SC 8/102/5082)
c.1377

Summary

The commons of England: complaint that they are grievously injured regarding lands in hundreds that they hold at suit, and which are leased in parcels to various tenants at will and for terms of years, and in no other way. The bailiffs and farmers of the hundreds distrain the tenants for suit of court before the lessors, even though the lessors have made suit and fine pertaining to the hundred in relation to the relevant lands. Request for a suitable remedy in this present parliament, so that no such suits or fines might be made except by those who have this right.

Response: [none].

Text

A nostre seignur le Roi et son sage conseil monstrent les comunes d'Engleterre; qe come ils soient trop outragement grevez et endamager a cause q'ils tiegnent terres qe deyvent suyte a hundredes, et les lessent par parcelles as diverses tenantz a voluntee et as termes des ans, et en nul autre manere. Les baillifs des hundredes et fermers des hundredes destreignent les ditz tenantz pur suyte faire as ditz hundredes, si avant come leur lessours, par la ou mesmes les lessours ont fait suyte et fyn et qant qe a hundred appent pur les dites terres. Par quoy prient les ditz comunes ent ordeigner covenable remede en ce present parlement, si qe nulles tieles suytes ne fyns soient faitz sinoun par eux qi les deyvent faire de droit.

Note

A note on the guard dates this petition to *c*.1377 with reference to the nineteenth-century Record Commission transcripts. A transcript can be found in TNA PRO 31/7/110, amongst the files of transcripts which preserved the chronological sequence of the medieval files (Dodd 2009: 23). Thus although there seem to be no corresponding entries on the parliament rolls or evidence from other sources that any action was taken as a result, the dating is probably broadly reliable. Those who leased land for a term of years initially had relatively weak protection against the lessor, although the situation changed in the later thirteenth and fourteenth centuries (Plucknett 1956: 570–574). Leases often came with obligations, such as suit of court (in this case, attendance at the hundred court), and the failure to meet such obligations could lead to distraint. This petition appears to suggest a collusion between hundred officials and lessors to extort money from those leasing lands, but general complaints of this nature were common and in the absence of additional information it is impossible to discern a more precise context.

45. Woodland rights (SC 8/102/5092)
c.1377

Summary

The commons of the realm of England: in several counties many lords and many of the commons have woods appurtenant to their manors that adjoin the king's forests. They seek the right to take profits from

LIBERTIES, FRANCHISES, AND RIGHTS   87

these woods and to hunt therein without being impeached or hindered by the wardens of the king's forests, as was lately granted by King Edward the king's grandfather, but is still not enforced.

Response: Within the purlieus they have the right to take profits from their woods, such that no damage or prejudice is done to the king, his tenants, or any others by the enclosure of the copses, and also that they may hunt etc., according to the forest assize.

Text

A nostre seignur le Roi et au consail de parlement monstre la commune du roialme d'Engleterre; qe par la ou en plusours partiez d'Engleterre plusours segnours et aultres de la communalte ount bois aportenauntz a lour manoirs es diverses countez d'Engleterre deintz pourales iouste les forestes nostre dit segnour le Roi, q'il pleise a nostre dit segnour le Roi grauntier a les segnours avaunditz et as aultres eiaunt bois en la manere susdite q'ils puissent prendre profit en lour bois demeyne celles parties, et conge de [...]³ et chacier en lour ditz bois a lour volunte sauntz estre enpechez ou destourbez par les gardeyns de les forestez nostre dit segnour le Roi, come nadgaires estoit graunte par le Roi Edward aiel a nostre seignur le Roi q'ore est, dount rien n'est execut unqore.

Response: En la puralee l'en purra bien prendre profit en lour boys, issint qe nul damage ou preiudice ent se face au Roy ou ses tenantz ou nul autre par la closeure du copys, et aussint ils y purront chacer etc. solonc l'assise du forest.

Note

A note on the guard dates this petition to '?1377', apparently on the basis of internal evidence. The mention of 'King Edward' as the present king's grandfather could be a reference either to the relationship between Edward I and Edward III or to that between Edward III and Richard II; but given the fact that hand of the original is very definitely late fourteenth-century, it seems clear that the petition must date between 1377 and 1399. In that case, the rather general reference to the grant made by 'King Edward' relates quite specifically to the statute made in the first parliament of Edward III's reign, when the crown retreated from the assertive position that it had adopted during the previous two reigns and allowed that the boundaries of

³One word here is illegible due to a tear in the parchment.

the king's forests would be observed as in the time of Edward I; by doing so, it effectively gave up its jurisdictional claims over the 'purlieus', the peripheral areas which had once been forest land but had subsequently been disafforested (*SR*, I, 255; Neilson 1940: 394–397). The 1327 statute was confirmed on a number of occasions under Edward III, though the promise to undertake further perambulations of the royal forests to define the purlieus was never fully implemented (*SR*, I, 257, 261, 265, 275; Young 1979: 146–147). Towards the end of Edward's reign and at the beginning of the next, there was renewed anxiety over the tendency of forest officials to challenge and harass those who held land in the purlieus. In the assembly of January–March 1377, the 'prelates, lords, and commons' petitioned that no man should be punished for hunting within the purlieus (*RP*, II, 368 = *PROME*, V, 409), while three of the enrolled common petitions for the parliament of October–November 1377 addressed hunting, forest bounds, and forest officials (*RP*, III, 18 = *PROME*, VI, 38–39). In all these cases, the response was essentially the same: that the existing law should be upheld. It would seem likely, then, that the present petition dates from the commons' campaign in the first parliament of Richard II; the fact that it was not enrolled may have had something to do either with questions as to the general applicability of grievances that were specified as particular to certain counties or with the fact that its essence was already captured in the three petitions that made it onto to parliament roll.

46. False verdicts in cities and boroughs (SC 8/102/5078)
Late fourteenth century

Summary

[No petitioner specified]: request that the king ordain in the present parliament that attaints might be granted for false verdicts made in cities and boroughs, and that all judgments carried out in the said cities and boroughs should stand.

Response: [none].

Text

Please a Roi ordeigner a ceo parlement qe atteintz soient graunteez de faus veredict fait en citeez et burghs, et en toutez choses executes [. . .] esteantz deins citeez et burghs ne soient arasez.

LIBERTIES, FRANCHISES, AND RIGHTS   89

Note

The right-hand edge of this document is missing; although it is unclear exactly how many words have been lost, the sense is still recoverable. Attaint was a mechanism for reconsidering and reversing verdicts when corruption or dishonesty on the part of jurors was alleged. A new jury would be summoned to review the verdict and also decide whether the original jury had been guilty of perjury. If it was ruled that the first jury had returned a patently false verdict, then penalties included imprisonment and confiscation of lands (Plucknett 1956: 131–132). It has been demonstrated that juries were partial and corruptible in the fourteenth century (Musson 1996: 169–222; Musson 1997; Musson and Ormrod 1999: 186–187), but the complaint is so general that it is impossible to be certain about the date or provenance of this petition. It was self-consciously made and presented in parliament, but there is no trace of it, or immediately corresponding entries, on the surviving parliament rolls. It is therefore dated to the late fourteenth century on the basis of the hand. The explicit reference to cities and boroughs suggests that it could have originated with the citizens and burgesses rather than the commons as a whole, or perhaps even come from a specific town or group of towns, and subsequently been presented for avowal by the commons.

47. Destruction of rabbit warrens (SC 8/146/7255)
Late fourteenth century

Summary

[No petitioner specified]: complaint that many warrens are being destroyed because, when the rabbits go out at night to feed, rogues and wrongdoers come with snares and other equipment and move them into the wild, on the pretext that they are able to take rabbits outside the boundaries of the warrens without breaking the law. They also enter warrens and do great damage. Request for a remedy.

Response: [none].

Text

Come plusours des conyngeirs et garreins des conelx en Engleterre soient en point d'estre destrutz, en ce qe qant les conelx en issent de noet pur lour pestre viegnent en diverses lieux, des garceons et autres riotours ove rees appellez hayes et autres engynes et se movent noet autre parentre les garreins et la savagyne pur le prendre au retourne, souz colour qe par de hors les boundes de les garrennes ils le poent faire saunz offense de la leye, et sovent qant y sont si pris ensi de noet et en obscurritie ils entrent dedeinz mesmes les garrennes et ils font outrageouse destruition, encolourantz q'il le font par de hors. Pleise a nostre seignur le Roi et as seignours de roialme en salvacioun des ditz garrennes ordeigner en ceo present parlement de remedie covenable en ce cas.

Note

In the later Middle Ages, warrens were defined as lands outside the royal forest whose holders enjoyed exclusive hunting privileges over 'beasts of warren', which usually meant rabbits (Young 1979: 97). Rabbit warrens were established on the English mainland from the middle of the thirteenth century, but until the end of the fourteenth, rabbits remained relatively scarce and expensive (Veale 1957). Poaching rabbits could therefore be a lucrative business, and there are numerous commissions recorded on the patent rolls to investigate such offences. However, the issue is not found on any extant parliament roll, and it is therefore difficult to establish a precise context for the present petition. The hand would suggest a date in the late fourteenth century. It is therefore possible – though not conclusive – that it was associated with the sharp decline in the market price of rabbits that set in from 1390 and a resulting concern about those whose livelihoods were dependent on maintaining the exclusivity of warrens (Bailey 1988: 12–15; Veale 2003: 58–59).

48. Answers to be provided to private petitions (SC 8/21/1020)
Late fourteenth century

Summary

The lords and commons of the realm of England: request that it might be ordained in the present parliament that all the private bills delivered to parliament that cannot be endorsed or answered before its departure for lack of time might be endorsed and answered immediately afterwards by certain lords appointed for this, and should be as valid and of the same effect as other bills of parliament; and that this should be done in all other parliaments in times to come.

Response: [none].

Text

A nostre seignur le Roi et son sage conseil supplient touz les seignurs et comunes de son roialme d'Engleterre; q'il soit ordeigne en cest present parlement qe toutes les billes especiales [qeux] sont ou seront donez en cest parlement, qe ne purront estre endossez ou responduz devant le departir du parlement pur brieftee du temps, soient endose et [responduz] bien tout en apres par certeins seignurs a ce assignez, et yce fait soit tenuz si forcible et si valable et de mesme l'effeit come autres billes du parlement et [come ey] faite en pleyn parlement, et ensi soit fait en touz autres parlementz en temps a venir.

Note

The right-hand side of this document is stained and slightly damaged, making one or two words illegible at the end of each line; these have been supplied from the corresponding entry in *RP*, III, 256, where the document appears among a group of unenrolled petitions dated by their editors to 1387–1388. Accepting such dating and assigning it to the Merciless Parliament of 1388, older generations of historians viewed this petition as a precedent for the establishment of the so-called parliamentary committee set up by Richard II at Shrewsbury in 1398 (Stubbs 1896: 523; Steel 1941: 246). However, the dating of unenrolled petitions for Richard II's reign published in *RP* is often inaccurate, and the issue raised here is one that was repeatedly addressed by parliament over the fourteenth century. In a number of assemblies during the 1330s, the commons expressed frustration over the failure to deal with private petitions during a parliamentary session (Richardson and Sayles 1981, ch. xxi, p. 73; and see no. 120), and the same issue arose again, for example, in the parliament of April–May 1379 (*RP*, III, 61 = *PROME*, VI, 123). During the 1340s the common began to press for special committees to deal with outstanding petitions (Dodd 2000: 82); and in the parliament of February–March 1371, a committee along the lines of that requested in the present petition was appointed to stay after parliament had finished in order to deal with outstanding business (*RP*, II, 304 = *PROME*, V, 237). On the final day of the very short second session of the 1397–1398 parliament, which met at Shrewsbury for four days in January 1398, the parliament rolls similarly record a request from the commons for the king to appoint a committee of lords to deal with unanswered petitions (*RP*, III, 368 = *PROME*, VII, 389; *SR*, II, 107). The result was the establishment of a parliamentary committee which ended up having a much broader remit, including a major role in the dispute between the dukes of Hereford and Norfolk (Edwards 1925; Saul 1997: 395–402). Without further contextual evidence, then, the present petition can only be dated by the hand, which is of the late fourteenth century.

49: Ejection from free tenements (SC 8/153/7621)
Late fourteenth or early fifteenth century

Summary

The commons of England: complaint that many people of the realm are ousted from their free tenements and deliberately kept out by force. Request that all those ousted might be restored, and that no man of any condition might prevent their return, on pain of forfeiting his goods and chattels to the king and perpetual imprisonment.

Response: [none].

Text

A nostre tresredoute seignur nostre seignur le Roi et as seignours du parlement monstrent ses communes d'Engleterre; [...] come devant plusours gentz de mesme le roialme sont oustez de lours frank [tenements] [...] roialme et unqore sont voluntrivement detenuz hors par fortmain [...] d'ordeigner qe touz ceux queux sont oustez de lour fraunkes tenements [...] et occupeours et qe nul homme de quele condicioun q'il soit, soit [...] biens et chateux au Roy et corps a perpetuele prison, et qe [...] roialme en tiel cas est avenuz al instaunz de ceux qeux [...] primer estate et si les ditz entrons par le maner [...].

Note

The right-hand side of this document is missing and some words have been lost. Tenants who held by freehold had certain obligations, such as attending seigneurial courts and sometimes being subject to relief and wardship, but were entitled to the protection of the royal courts (Bolton 1980: 20–21). Lords retained some rights over free tenements, especially when there was a question over the succession or the heir was a minor, but they could not evict those in legitimate possession. The present petition is so general that it could plausibly belong to almost any point in the later Middle Ages, and it is only the hand that provides a rough dating to the late fourteenth or early fifteenth century. A statute made in the parliament of October–November 1377 laid down penalties for those disseising others of land (*SR*, II, 3–4). There is an enrolled common petition on the roll of the parliament that met at Gloucester in October–November 1378, complaining about those who dispossessed people and then enfeoffed others; the response to this was a reassertion of the previous year's statute (*RP*, III, 42 = *PROME*, VI, 90). The matter was raised again in the parliament of September–November 1402 (*RP*, III, 497 = *PROME*, VIII, 184), indicating that this was considered a problem throughout the reigns of Richard II and Henry IV.

50. Exemption of purchases from queen's gold (SC 8/102/5086) 1382–1394

Summary

The commons of England: request that the present parliament order the cessation of the practice of taking queen's gold from the buyers of wardships and marriages sold by the treasurer, since the practice is leading to the great impoverishment of the purchasers.

Response: [none].

Text

A nostre tresredoute seignur le Roi et nobles seignurs de cest present parlement supplye la comunealte d'Engleterre; qe come les [ministres] [...] la Roigne [...] l'or la Roigne des gardes et mariages venduz par le tresorer nostre dit seignur le Roi [...] avant come des fines et [...] les tresorer et [...] proces de lever le dit or de ceux q'ont achetez les ditz gardes et mariages de le dit tresorer, en grant poverissement de les ditz achatours, qe lour pleise issint ordiner en cest parlement qe le dit or ne soit demande ne levez de les achatours de biens, gardes et mariages issint par le dit tresorer venduz.

Note

The right-hand side of this document is stained, which accounts for the missing text in the transcription. Queen's gold was a prerogative levy received by the queen consort whenever anyone entered into a voluntary obligation or fine with the king, amounting to a tenth of the value of the total sum. The procedure was outlined at some length in the 1170s in the *Dialogue of the Exchequer* (*Dialogus*, pp. 182–187). By the fourteenth century, there was a degree of uncertainty about the extent of these rights, and both Edward II and Edward III attempted to have the exchequer clarify the definition of queen's gold (Johnstone

1940: 263–265; Liddy 2005: 67–71). Judging from the hand, the present petition dates from the late fourteenth century and is therefore most likely to come from the period during which Richard II was married to Anne of Bohemia, and specifically from early in that period when there was some suspicion about the king's extravagant grants to the Bohemian courtiers who arrived in Anne's train (Saul 1997: 92–94). A common petition on the parliament roll for October–November 1383 states that it had previously been ordained in parliament that queen's gold should not be levied on wardships and marriages granted by the king. This was the very issue raised by the present petition; but there is no direct evidence of such a decision on any extant parliament roll before 1383, and the royal response was dismissive, stating that the practice should continue as it had in the time of Queen Philippa and previous queens of England (*RP*, III, 164 = *PROME*, VI, 356). The present petition is remarkably blunt in its phrasing, and the idea that parliament, rather than the king, could order an end to a prerogative levy suggests this might be an early draft of a petition (even, perhaps, that of 1383) put together by people not familiar with the nuances of the language of parliament. Richard II's second wife, Isabella of France, was only six when they married in 1396 and the controversy over queen's gold does not seem to have been raised during the last three years of the reign.

51. Upholding grants of the Merciless Parliament (SC 8/110/5498) 1399–1401

Summary

[No petitioners specified]: in the parliament of 1388, it was ordained that those who held in tail, in reversion or remainder, and women holding by right of inheritance or jointure, as well as gifts and grants made before the new statute made in that parliament, should be exempted from the force of that statute. Request that those now in possessions of such holdings should have their rights confirmed, and if challenged on the basis of any subsequent gift made by Richard II, should have their suit according to the common law.

Response: [none].

Text

Plese a nostre tresexcellent tresredoute et tregracious seigneur le Roi et as tressages seigneurs de ceste present parlement; considerer qe come en le parlement deinz a Westminstre l'an unszime Richard nadgairs Roi d'Engleterre ordeigne fuit et estable qe les issues en la taille ceux en revercioun ou remeindre ou femmes de lour heritage ou ioncture ove lour barouns diceux qe furount aiuggez en le dit parlement des dountz grantz ou feffementz faitz devant temps limite en l'estatut du dit parlement ne serroient barrez ne forclosez de lour droit. Et granter et ordeigner en ceste present parlement qe ceux qi sont ore en possessioun des terres et tenementz qeux furount des ditz persones aiuggez come issues ou la taille ou en lour revercioun ou en remeindre ou femmes en lour heritage ou ioncture ove lour barouns qe ne lyst a nully qecomqe persones par force d'ascun donne ou grant fait des ditz terres [et][4] tenementz par le dit Richard nadgairs Roi, ou autre donne ou grant fait depuisne temps entrer sur les ditz issues ceux en remeindre ou revercioun femmes de lour heritage ou ioncture, en si [ascun persone ad][5] droit ou accioun as ditz terres ou tenementz q'ils eient lour accioun et sute solonc la comune ley, issint qe les ditz issues en la taille ou en remeindre ou revercioun et les femmes en lour heritage ou ioncture eient respounce come ley et resoun demaundent et ceo por Dieux et en oevere de charite.

Note

Following the condemnation of many of Richard II's supporters in the Merciless Parliament of February–June 1388, the estates and goods of those found guilty were forfeited to the crown. A qualifying clause, generally honoured by Richard II, stated that issues held in tail, those in reversion or remainder, and those held by women by right of inheritance or jointure, as well as gifts and grants of the affected estates made before the new legislation, should be excluded from forfeiture (*RP*, III, 246 = *PROME*, VII, 69–70; *SR*, II, 50–52; Ross 1956). During the second session of the parliament of September 1397, meeting at Shrewsbury in January 1398, the proceedings of the Merciless Parliament were annulled in their entirety and the dispossessed were restored (*RP*, III, 357–359 = *PROME*, VII, 363–367). At his first parliament in October–November 1399, however, Henry IV overthrew the 1398 legislation and restored that of 1388 (*RP*, III, 425–426 = *PROME*, VIII, 30–32). A common petition enrolled on the parliament roll for the same assembly requested that the sales of lands made since 1388 should be confirmed, and the king consented to this, establishing the point in a new statute (*RP*, III, 445 = *PROME*, VIII, 75–76; *SR*, II, 114). The enrolled common petition also mentioned

[4]Conjectural (hole in parchment).
[5]Conjectural (hole in parchment).

entails, jointures, and other titles, but apparently only as an incidental issue, and the crown restricted its response to the question of sales. The present petition, by contrast, prioritizes the cases of those who, because of the nature of their tenure, had been exempt from the 1388 legislation itself and, as a result of the 1398 annulment, had experienced challenges to their rights. An enrolled common petition from the parliament of January–March 1401 raised the specific case of those having protection under the 1388 legislation for lands held in tail (*RP*, III, 475 = *PROME*, VIII, 142–143). It seems likely, then, that the present petition was part of a more general campaign in the first two parliaments of Henry IV to protect the interests of those whose rights had been disrupted, or might be considered vulnerable, as a result of fluctuating royal policy towards the implementation of the forfeitures of 1388.

IV
CRIME, DEBT, AND THE LAW

52. Failure of defendants to answer summonses before inquests and assizes (SC 8/80/3952) Early fourteenth century

Summary

The common people: complaint that those summoned to appear before justices at inquests and assizes do not come for fear of death and other mischief perpetrated by those who do not fear the law, and suitors are thus delayed in recovering by default of suit and greatly impoverished. Request that the king will not suffer this to continue.

Response: [none].

Text

A nostre seignur le Roi et a son cunsail monstrent son comun peuple; qe come ordingne qe gentz soient somons en enq[uests][1] et en assises devant iustices, qe mesmes seux issint somons ne isint desoremes pur \doute/ de mort et de autre mescheif [de] askune gentz qe ne doutent la lay, lur fasent de iour en autre en la plase ou il sunt somons venir, ne la verite [...] issint qe il pardent lur issues, par quei il sunt grantment enpoveris, et la partie issint delaie de son recoverie, [qe] par defaute sa sute covent lesser. Par quei tote la commune prient a nostre dit seignur qe il ne voile mes soffrir [ne] estre fest \cel damage/, de sicome il sunt par son comandement otre lur volunte feat venir a lur custages demayngne.

Note

An earlier attempt at dating this petition, during sorting at the National Archives, associated it with a reference to a petition from the 'community of the realm' submitted at the parliament held at Carlisle

---

[1] The right-hand side of the document is faded, resulting in the loss of the final word of each line: this has been supplied from the context where possible.

in January–April 1307, a reference which is found in an instruction sent to the justices of trailbaston in Devon at the end of the assembly (*CCR, 1302–1307*, p. 531, discussed in *PROME*, I, 130). The link is, in fact, erroneous, and since the matter referred to here is of a very general nature and referred to a problem endemic throughout the later Middle Ages, a positive dating is impossible. The hand is of the early fourteenth century.

53. Repayment of debts from the estates of deceased lords of manors (C 49/8/22)
Early fourteenth century

Summary

The commonalty of the land: complaint and request for remedy, for the common profit of the land, in that many great lords and others suffer damage for lack of a remedy in cases where keepers and bailiffs of manors or receivers of money depart without rendering account of what they have received from the executors. A writ of account is not issuable in such cases, and creditors are unable to take proceedings against the executors, for which many suffer great damage.

Response: A law is not yet ordained in such cases.
Before the great council.

Text

A nostre seignur le Rey et a son consail prie la communaulte de sa terre; qe remedie et ley pur commun profit de sa terre seit ordene en cas ou plusours grantz seignurs et aultres de sa terre grant damage en unt par defaute de remedie, cest asavoir par la ou gardeins ou baillifs de maners ou rescevours de deniers isunt si avant q'il eient nul aconte renduwe de ceo q'il averont resceuw devient lur executours, et [. . .][2] ne veolent pur le testatour aconte rendre, pur ceo qe bref de aconte n'est pas uncore ordene en le cas; et si hom porte [la dette] devers eux exsecutours et hom mette taille tut seit ele ensel du seal, le testatour n'est pas accepte en court pur fait [susdit] de lier les executours a la dette, par qui plusours sunt en grant damage, par quei covenable serreit qe remedie fut en tel [cas].

Response: Non est adhuc lex ordinata in hoc casu.
Coram magno consilio.

---

[2]The right-hand side of the parchment is stained; conjectural text is supplied, where possible, from context.

Note

The issue of how to recover debts owed by those who held in feudal tenure developed out of a series of changes in law and practice during the late thirteenth and early fourteenth centuries, whereby debts owed by the deceased holder of the manor became the responsibility not of his heir but of his executors, who only had the chattels and liquid financial assets of the deceased with which to settle debts (Bean 1968: 32–34). The petition therefore represents a problem endemic in the fourteenth century, and is not easily associated with any particular period or parliament. A clue to its date is provided by the fact that the response is given in Latin; from the mid 1320s, these official notes were much more usually written in French. It is therefore possible to conjecture a date in the 1310s or early 1320s, when the common petitions began, hesitatingly, to deploy the language of 'common profit' in support of changes to the law (Ormrod 2015: 233–242).

54. Privileges of bail in London (SC 8/123/6119) 1321–1327

Summary

[No petitioner specified]: complaint that lawbreakers from London are emboldened to commit murder, as they secure bail and then claim that the liberties of the city put them outside the common law, so that nobody dares to prosecute suits against them, to the great damage of the crown and the peace. Request that the king order that no one be bailed for murder in London.

Response: The issue has been superseded by the eyre.
Enrolled.
Before the great council.

Text

Por ceo qe plusours meffesours de la Cite de Loundres sount molt enbaudiz a tuer les gentz, par la reson q'il puissent estre repleviz tantqe en eyre, et ceo clayment par lour fraunchise q'est hors de comun ley, par quey l'om ne osent la sute faire pur les meffesours qe sount au large, a emblemissement del estat de la coroune nostre seignur le Roy et enfeblissement de la pes. Pleise a nostre seignur le Roy ordener qe desormes nul ne soyt mainpris pur mort de homme en la dite cite.

Response: Le point est anynty en eyre.
Irrotulatur.
Coram magno consilio.

Note

The petition alludes to the rights claimed in the city of London whereby freemen accused of any felony had right of bail until the coming of the king's justices to hear the case. During the eyre of London in 1321, the justices determined that the city should lose this right because John Gisors, when mayor, had knowingly admitted to the freedom of the city a man indicted of felony (*Eyre of London*, I, 67–72), and thereafter the right was permanently lost: this is the position referred to in the royal response to the present petition. The petition must therefore date either to the first parliament to be held after the eyre of London, in July–August 1321, or soon thereafter. On the accession of Edward III in 1327, the Londoners negotiated the restoration and extension of a number of their rights, but failed to receive permission to continue with the custom of bailing indicted felons (*Eyre of London*, I, xix–xxi; Williams 1963: 298–299; Barron 2004: 32–33). For rights of bail, see also nos 6 and 126.

55. The punishment of trespasses (SC 8/261/13018) 1327–1328

Summary

The good people of the commonalty of England: they present transcripts of a petition from the last parliament held at Lincoln concerning trespasses made in the time of the king's father and of a writ to take action thereon, on which nothing has been done. The petition has also been sued before the treasurer, justices, and barons of the exchequer at York since Michaelmas, and no response has been given, to the great damage of the people. They therefore request that the king ordain a suitable remedy at the council now being held at Pontefract, for the improvement of the law and the common profit of the people.

The transcript of the first petition:

> The knights of the counties, citizens, and burgesses complain that many writs of trespass made in the time of the king's father against wrongdoers who have no possessions are suspended, as the justices are reluctant to pass judgement of exigend or imprisonment, but only issue writs of fieri facias or elegit, which

are of no use against those who have no chattels, land, or tenements. Because of this many trespasses remain unpunished, which is an encouragement to wrongdoers and against God and justice. They request that the king ordain that the same process and judgment might be used in all cases pending from the time of the king's father.

The knights, citizens and burgesses request that in the case of those holding estates in other lands by writ of elegit, whose nominees are ousted by writ of *novel disseisin*, that the nominees might be able to recover the estates and hold them for the same term as first set down in the writ of elegit.

Response: [none].

Text

A nostre seignur le Roi et a soun counsail monstrent ses bones gentz de la communalte d'Engleterre cest transescrit d'une peticioun qe vynt du darrein parlement autrefoiz par bref nostre dit seignur le Roi d'assemblez iustices et barons et autres du counsail d'ordener remedie des trespaatz facez en temps le Roi le piere sur trespassours, qe rien n'ount sils des trespaatz soient atteyntz. La quele peticion ad este suye devant les ditz tresorer, iustices et barons del eschekier a Euerwyk puys la Seint Michel en cea, et nulle respounce n'est ouncore sur ceo done, a graund damage du poeple. Par qoi prient les bones gentz de la dite communalte q'il plese a nostre dit seignur le Roi en cest tretyz de Pountffreynt sur ceo ordener remedie covenable, en amendement de la ley et pur commun profit de soun poeple.

C'est le transescrit de la dite peticioun:

> A nostre seignur le Roi et a son counsail prient les chivalers des counteez, citeins des citeez, burgeis des burgs de toute la terre d'Engleterre; qe come plusours brefs de trespaatz faitz en temps le Roi le piere soient pendauntz auxi bien devaunt le Roi mesmes come en le commun bank et en l'eschekier vers plusours maufesours qi rien n'ount par qoi estre iustiseez si noun par lur corps nient plus d'amener a respouns des trespaas avantditz, qe au paiement des damages vers eus par tiel trespaas aiuggez, les iustices et iugges des places avauntditz pur les avauntditz maufesours mener a responce ne voillent l'exigende agarder, ne as damages vers eus recoveretz p[ar] iuggement ne voillent enprisonement aiugger, mes tantsoulement le fieri facias en le brief de elegit, qe de rien ne vaillent ne valer ne poount si noun vers ceus qi ount chattel, terre ou tenementz, par qoi les trespaas faitz par ceus qi rien n'ount demoerent despuny, contre Deu et droiture, a grand esbaudisement des maufesours et deffesaunce de ceus qi le mal ount receu. Par qoi prient les avantditz chivalers, citeins et burgois pur eus et pur toute la commune de roialme q'il plese au nostre dit seignur le

Roi par avisement de son counsail ordener et establir en ceste tretiz de Nicole qe mesme le proces et iuggement soit usee et donee as touz brefs qe sount pendantz en les avauntditz places del temps avantdit, come si le dit Roi le piere ne soi eust pas demys de sa coroune.

Item prient les avantditz chivalers, citeins et burgois pur eus et pur toute la commune de la terre; qe comme il soit ordenee par estatut qe si ceus qi ount estat en autruy terres et tenementz par brief de elegit soient hosteez et destourbeez par bref de novele disseisine, q'il plese a nostre dit seignur le Roi par avisement de soun counsail ordener et establir qe les assigneez celuy qe tiel estat ad par le dit bref, en tiels terres et tenementz eyt mesmes le recoverir sil soit deboute, et issint assignee des assigne chescun pur soun temps durant le terme limitee en l'estente primes faite a la seuyte celuy qe primes seuy le bref de elegit surdit.

Note

This document, and the accompanying transcript of the writ dated 24 September 1327 which survives as SC 8/261/13017, were previously published by Sayles (*SCCKB*, V, pp. cxxxii–cxxxiii); the petition is reprinted here with minor amendments. The parliament of Lincoln of September 1327 was called to deal with imminent danger from Scotland, and was dismissed after eight days because of the news of the death of the deposed Edward II at Berkeley Castle (*PROME*, IV, 82–83). The writ of 24 September (the day after the parliament ended), ordering action on a petition entered 'by the knights of the counties, citizens, burgesses, and commonalty of our realm' (*per milites comitatuum, cives, burgenses et communitatem regni nostri*) therefore provides rare and valuable evidence that other common business of the realm was conducted during this short assembly, whose record is otherwise lost. The transcript of that writ was made to accompany a further transcript of the Lincoln petition itself, wrapped up in the new, supplementary petition as printed here, addressed from the 'good people of the commonalty of England' and submitted (as internal and contextual evidence shows) at a council held at Pontefract during the king's sojourn there in late November 1327 (Ormrod 2011: 611).

The episode is notable in a number of respects. It demonstrates the ability of the political community to seek action on matters decided in parliament but not publicly proclaimed. During the Michaelmas term 1327, some plaintiffs had brought pressure on the exchequer, then residing at York, to observe the decision of the Lincoln parliament; having failed to get satisfaction, they sought out (presumably with the co-operation of the clerks of the royal chancery) a copy of the writ by which the original decision had been communicated to the treasurer. In that transcript was also the vital text they needed to reiterate the Lincoln petition at the Pontefract assembly, and thus bring pressure to bear by pointing out very clearly the failure of the crown to act on its own initiatives. The confidence of those who submitted the Pontefract petition is further highlighted by their reference to 'the common profit of the people', which they may have picked up from the idea that reform would be 'for the good of our people' (*pro bono populi nostri*) as expressed in the writ of 24 September (Ormrod 2015: 230). Finally, the existence of a petition claiming to have been submitted in a council of uncertain composition (the precise word used to describe the assembly is *tretyz*) demonstrates that the crown was under some pressure to admit petitions made in the name of the commonalty not only in fully constituted parliaments but also in other assemblies.

56. The problems of distraining defendants (SC 8/134/6679) Mid fourteenth century

Summary

The poor people of the realm of England: complaint that, if they need to bring writs against the great in which the latter should be required to respond by distraints and issues, the great prefer to lose their issues and suffer the distraint, or have such favour from the king's ministers that the poor people agree to give up their suit. Request for remedy, so that such long process might be avoided.

Response: There is a statute made and ordained on these matters; they should sue as they wish.

Text

A nostre seignur le Roi et a son conseil mustrent les povers gentz du roialme d'Engleterre; qe se eux [...][3] suer envers nul grant de la terre brefs en queux le dits gentz deivent venire en respouns par destrete et issues, les ditz gentz voillant plustost perdre lour issues et suffrir la destrete qe devenir en respouns de la [...] de la demaunde soit grant, ou il averront taunt de favour des ministres nostre seignur le Roi qe les ditz povers coveint pardoner de lour accion, en a despendre nule [...] remedie, qe tiel long processe put estre estourse.

[3]The text is faded and illegible in places.

Response: Il y ad estatut fait et ordine en mesmes les choses; suent s'ils voillent.

Note

This petition refers to the process whereby defendants refusing to answer in court could be subjected to distraint or distress, whereby property, goods, or chattels could be taken by the sheriff and the issues or profits therefrom withheld until they responded to their summonses (Musson and Powell 2009: xx). Distress, as the petition points out, could be a very lengthy process (Blatcher 1936). The main emphasis here is on the way in which the powerful could afford to ignore such measures and, through collusion with court officials, sheriffs and others, wear down lesser defendants so that they gave up their cases. The legislation referred to in the royal response was apparently the Statute of Westminster I (1275), which provided the basis for the process of distraint (*SR*, I, 37–38). The hand of the petition suggests a date in the middle of the fourteenth century, but it is difficult to provide a closer context given the absence of other petitions and statutes on the precise matter raised here. Given the emphasis on the abuse of the law by the powerful and the resulting victimisation of the poor, however, it may be argued that it is most likely to date from the period between the 1320s and the 1340s, when this was a major theme in other common petitions (Ormrod 1990b: 98, 111–112; and see nos 3, 57, 113, and 114).

57. The abuse of the law by the rich (SC 8/80/3956)
Mid fourteenth century

Summary

The common people of the realm of England: complaint that many poor men do not dare to pursue their rights according to the law, for fear of death and other mischief done to them by rich men, who are like kings in their own lands, and who harm them with threats and false indictments. Request that the king properly maintain the rights of the poor, so that they are able to pursue their rights according to due legal process without fear of being ruined by false indictments.

Response: [none].

Text

A nostre seignur le Roi et a son cunsail monstrent le comun peuple de son realme de Engletere; qe come remedie est ordingne a tote gentz, auxi bien au poveres come a riches, de tort a eux fest, qe mesmes seux poveres qele manere tort qe a eux soit fest ne osent lur drait porsure par voie de lay pur doute de mort et de autre meschef qe il lur avendra par ceux riches, qe le ount gre\ve/, car en quel lu qe il pledera ou suera ou a iour d'aniointer en autrement, les riches amesnerent cele cumpaigne, qe pur doute de lour manas et de lur rebukement covent le poveres qi a la volunte de cely qe le ad tant greve en quele manere \qe/ seo soit, et si il se gard hors du pais et hors du chemin son enemy issi qe il ne veule a sa volunte estre tantost le sera enditer de felonie la, ou unkes suspessioun de mal ne sunt en ly trove, et issint par pouwer qe plusours riche gentz sunt auxi come reys en lur paiis demaygne, par tote la tere sunt mesne gentz desherites, ocsis, mahaygnes et autrement manniesces. Par quei il prient tus a lur dit lige seignur qe lur drit governir et en drait maintenir qe ly plese ordiner de ceste plainte remedie, tiele qe riche gentz pussint vocer et qe soit fermement garde et tenus issi, qe ses povere gentz pussent et osent lour drait en fourme de [lei][4] porsure, et issint qe les le gentz ne soient issint destrus par faus enditement sans cause de suspessiun.

Note

The requirement that the law ought to be enforced alike for rich and poor was a commonplace of the political rhetoric of the crown in parliament during the fourteenth century (*RP*, II, 60, 136; III, 32, 228, 257 = *PROME*, IV, 120, 332; VI, 69–70; VII, 63, 131), and was taken up by the commons in petitions and grants of taxes at least during the second half of the century (*RP*, II, 266, 334; III, 14, 101, 285, 301 = *PROME*, V, 126, 324; VI, 31; VII, 196, 220, 228). It was included in the oaths of royal justices and other officers of the crown from at least the thirteenth century, and was reiterated in this context on the parliament rolls during the later fourteenth century (Baldwin 1913: 345–354; *RP*, III, 85 = *PROME*, VI, 176). It is difficult to date the present petition with any precision, but the hand suggests that it was written in the mid fourteenth century. Insofar as it represents a tradition of complaint about the irresponsible behaviour of the magnates, it chimes more closely with anxieties expressed during the 1330s and 1340s than those of the two decades thereafter, when explicit parliamentary criticisms

---

[4] Illegible: text supplied from context.

of the great lords fell away quite markedly (Ormrod 1990b: 97–99, 111–113). The present petition is notably discursive and outspoken on the subject, which may be one of the reasons why it was not apparently answered and enrolled.

58. Holding of inquests on judgments of outlawry
(SC 8/46/2287)
Mid fourteenth century

Summary

The commons of England: men are indicted for felony in foreign counties and outlawed after their death, so that their goods and chattels are seized into the king's hands. The heirs, claiming that their ancestors died before an indictment or outlawry was pronounced, seek inquests in the king's bench; but the justices refuse to grant a *nisi prius* to hold the inquest without express order from the king, causing long and damaging delays. Request that inquests in such cases might be held by *nisi prius* before justices of either bench or before justices of assize.

Response: In the presence of the king.

Text

A nostre seignur le Roi et a son counseil prie la comune d'Engleterre; qe par la ou divers gentz soint endites pur felonie en foreines contees et utlaies apres lour mort, pur qoi les terres et chateux de mesmes ses utlaies soint soises en meine nostre seignur le Roi, sur qoi les heires de mesmes ses soint mis a reverser tiels utlagaries, et se mettent en enquest de baunk nostre seignur le Roi qe lour auncestres murrust devaunt enditement ou utlagarie pronounce en lui, et les iustices de la dit place ne voillent graunter sur ceo nisi prius de prendir enqest en pais saunz especial maundment de nostre seignur le Roi, por qoi le gentz du paies pardount grauntment, et les parties qi suent sount delaies cynk auns ou sys, issint q'il sount grauntment empoveris. Q'il plese a nostre seignur le Roi graunt qe les enquestes en tiel case puissent estre pris par nisi prius desorenavaunt, devaunt les iustices de l'un place ou de l'autir, ou devaunt iustices des assises.

Response: Coram Rege.

Note

The writ and process known as *nisi prius*, formalized in 1285, allowed cases originating in the central courts to be heard in the relevant locality before the justices of assize (Musson and Ormrod 1999: 15–16). During sorting and cataloguing at the National Archives in the early twentieth century, the present petition became associated with an important statute of 1331 that defined the process and circumstances for the granting of pardons of outlawry (*SR*, I, 268). Because of its reference to *nisi prius*, however, it has more recently been linked with the growing interest expressed by the parliamentary commons from the 1340s in the powers of the justices of assize, and has been tentatively dated to the later 1350s (Verduyn 1991: 129–130). The actual issue raised in the petition is very specific, and concerns an attempt to allow inquests on judgments of outlawry where the defendant had been dead at the time of trial to be held under *nisi prius* process in the counties where the original judgment had been made. There are no other particular clues as to the dating of the petition, but the hand also suggests that it was written in the second quarter of the fourteenth century or shortly thereafter.

59. Provision of attaint in cases of false accusation (SC 8/79/3930) Mid fourteenth century

Summary

Many great people of the land and others: complaint that certain people who covet lands, by false conspiracy between them and their allies, bring writs of trespass against their tenants, and speak falsehoods against them, and amerce damages so great that the defendants are not able to pay without selling their lands and tenements, and are disinherited or forced to make a settlement according to the demands of the plaintiffs. This is because in such cases no attaint has been granted according to the law previously observed, and thus many are emboldened to make false accusations. Many of the commonalty of the land request that an attaint upon inquisitions in writs of trespass be granted, or some other suitable remedy be ordained.

Response: It is agreed that they should have an attaint.

Text

A nostre seignur le Roi et a son consail prient plusours gentz de la terre et autres; qe par aide et mayntenaunce des acuns gentz coveitauntz les terres de divers gentz de la terre, qe lour dite coveitise a lour volunte ne pount acomplir, se purchacent par brief de trespas, auxi bien devant iustices assignez d'oir et determiner, come devant les iustices de altres places de la terre vers les tenauntz des dites terres, et par mauveise conspiracie entre eux et plusours gentz du pais lour faus allieez mettaunt sur a les ditz terre tenauntz divers trespas, des queux s'il se mettount en pais les enquestes sount prises a la volunte des ditz gentz par les ditz conspiratours lour allieez, e fausement dient contre les defendauntz, et taxent damages si outraiousement qe les defendauntz ne pount les damages rendre sauntz vendre lour terres ou tenementz, et eux mesmes desheriter ou de fere gree al ordenaunce et a volunte des ditz pleintifs; et pur ceo q'il n'ad en tiel cas nul atteynte grante avant ces oures solonc la lei avaunt usee, plusours gentz qe ne ount regard de conscience ne se doutent de fere faus surment, en confusioun et anyntissement d'autres q'il voillent maliciousement grever. Par quei plusours de la commune de la terre prient qe atteynte sur enquestes en brief de trespass soit grante, ou altre remedie covenable en cel cas seit ordeine.

Response: Il est acorde q'il eient atteint.

Note

The petition was published in the eighteenth century as being of parliamentary provenance but of uncertain date in the reign of Edward III (*RP*, II, 407); the hand suggests that it is from the mid fourteenth century. The address by 'many of the great people of the land and others' requires some explanation. If it were expressed more explicitly as from the lords, or the peers and prelates, then this document would be excluded from the present collection. However, the final sentence shifts the focus to 'many of the commonalty of land', and since the general sense is that a remedy is sought for the benefit of the tenants of the petitioners – people of lesser means – the content and character conform to other petitions of the period made, more straightforwardly, in the name of the commonalty.

The writ of attaint was a provision in law to protect against the consequences of malicious verdicts being given by biased juries. In 1327 and 1331, statutes provided guarantees that the writ of attaint would be available in trespass actions brought both by writ and by bill (*SR*, I, 253, 267). Kaeuper (1979: 757 n. 97) suggests that the present petition prompted the first of these statutes, but it seems more likely that the petition actually alludes to these two measures and complains that they are not properly observed. In the parliament of January–February 1348, the commons campaigned for the extension of the availability of writs of attaint to cover debts cases and crown prosecutions (*RP*, II, 167–168 = *PROME*, IV, 419), and in the assembly of April–May 1354 they successfully secured the dropping of the previous specification that writs of attaint would only be allowed in trespass cases where the damages were assessed above £2 (*RP*, II, 261 = *PROME*, V, 110; *SR*, I, 346). Finally, in the parliament of January–February 1361 (for which no parliament roll survives), a statute was passed extending the writ of attaint to pleas of land and personal actions and (relevant to the concerns in the present petition) allowed that the writ be issued free of charge to poor people (*SR*, I, 366). All of this was part of a larger process, provoked by pressure from parliament, to address the problems of perjury brought on by the extensive use of juries in the judicial system (Musson 2001: 86–87). In this context, it seems most likely that the present petition dates from some time in the 1340s or 1350s.

60. Executors evading debt process (SC 8/79/3941) Mid fourteenth century

Summary

The commonalty: writs of debt are often sued against executors, even to the extent of grand distress; then, by collusion among them, one defaults and the others appear and so save their issues; and thus the process becomes infinite and the plaintiff is left without recovery, for which they pray remedy.

Response: The commons have left parliament.

Text

A nostre seignur le Roi et a son conseil prie la comunalte; qe par la ou bref de dette sovent foith est sue devers executours, tauntqe a la grant destresse; adonqes par coveigne entre eaux un fra defautor et les autres appariront de sauver lur issues, et issint la proces infynit et le pleintif saunz recoverir, de quei ils priount remedie.

Response: La comune est ale du parlement.

Note

This petition is very similar in content and substance to the longer request on this matter at no. 61. The issue raised is part of a more general debate about the responsibilities of executors of wills in the parliaments of the fourteenth century. Executors emerged in the late thirteenth and early fourteenth centuries as having responsibility not only for effecting the testamentary bequests of the deceased person, but also settling their debts (Bean 1968: 131). Here, the specific complaint is about the consequence of the withdrawal of one (or more) of the joint executors of a will such that legal action – in which they shared collective responsibility – could not proceed against them in cases of debt (Goffin 1901: 50). The petition is difficult to date precisely, but the hand suggests that it was written in the mid fourteenth century.

An additional point of interest is raised by the response, 'The commons have left parliament'. There were a number of assemblies under Edward II and Edward III where all or most of the commons appear to have been dismissed (or simply departed of their own accord) before the parliament was officially called to an end, and it is possible that this is the circumstance alluded to in the royal response here (*PROME*, IV, 237, 385–386; V, 6–7, 130, 139; and see no. 81). An alternative interpretation is that the petition was a late submission and that the clerks of parliament disallowed it on the grounds that the common petitions for the relevant assembly had already been submitted and answers been given to them.

61. Executors delaying debt proceedings in court (SC 8/260/12956) Mid fourteenth century

Summary

The commonalty of England: people leave money to others who die before the day for repayment, so they sue the executors; but when the executors are brought forward for grand distress, where there are three executors, two appear but the third defaults. Thus they delay proceedings in court, never coming to answer, and the creditors can never have repayment.

Response: [illegible].[5]

---

[5] This document is very faded, and only partly legible under ultraviolet light.

Text

A nostre seignur le Roi et a son consail monstre la comunaute d'Engletere; qe come eux aprestent lour deners a dyverses gentz a paiez a certeynz iours par lour lettres obligationes, avaunt les iours encoruz les dettours demurent, et ceux a qi la dette est due suent devers les executours pur recoverer lour dettes, et les ditz executours, kant il sont menez a la grante drestresce et il y a tres executours nomes, les deux vendront et la terce sera defaute, et sy fourchent il de iour en iour en court, issint qe iames ne vendront a responz, dount il sont auxi come recoverir de lour dette. Dont il prient qe de ceste duresce soit fait remedie.

Note

This petition is very similar in content and substance to a shorter petition on the same matter, no. 60, where the historical background is discussed. The present document is also difficult to date with any precision. The fact that it addresses the topic in rather more precise terms than the other and uses the technical word *fourch* to describe the delaying of process in the courts may suggest a more expert treatment, but this does not necessarily mean that it dates from after the other. The fact that no response is provided indicates that this issue was not taken up by the royal council (perhaps because of the considerable legal complexities that it raised), and the question of how to deal with defaulting executors remained an endemic problem.

62. Giving of judgments in the county on felonies committed there (SC 8/80/3961) 1341–1348

Summary

People of the commonalty of the realm: many men are indicted for felonies and robberies before justices of trailbaston or justices of the peace, and writs are issued to the justices to bring the records and processes of the indictments to the king's bench for delivery; request that delivery might be made in the county, where the well-respected men of the county are able to be present as a deterrent to wrong-doers.

Response: It pleases the king that the delivery be made in the county, for the ease of his people.

Text

A nostre sei[gnur][6] le Roi et son conseal monstrent les bones gentz de la comunalte de son roialme; qe come plusurs gentz sount endites de diverses felonies \et/ roberies fait en son dite roialme devant ses iustices del traylbastoun et iustices de la pees, et ount entenditz qe brefs sount issues atenz les avantditz iusticez de faire venir touz les recordes et processes des avauntditz enditementz devant le Roi affaire la deliverance de eux illoeqes. Par quey priount les ditz bones gentz a nostre dit seignur le Roi si luy plest qe la deliverance des avantditz endites puisse estre fait en pays la ou l'enditement se firent pur esement du pays, et qe les bones gentz du pays et les muth vanes puissent estre a la dite deliverance en eyde a destruire les malveis.

> *Response:* Il plest a Roi qe la deliverance se face en pais pur esse de son poeple.

Note

The petition refers to a significant point of concern articulated by the commons throughout the 1340s about the work of the extraordinary commissions of trailbaston periodically appointed between 1341 and 1344, and the desirability (articulated increasingly strongly as the decade progressed) for the delegation of powers to people resident in the counties to try cases of felony that were brought before these and other tribunals (Putnam 1929: 33–43; Harriss 1975: 404–406). It is notable that the petition refers to both the trailbastons and the justices of the peace: the latter, who had been in place continuously since 1338 with powers to determine, were not superseded by the trailbastons of 1341–1344, but worked alongside them (Verduyn 1991: 77–93). The commons at the parliament of April–May 1341 had already requested the appointment of 'men of law and others of the region' to deal with cases of criminality and corruption in the localities, but at the time their principal aim was to reduce the oppressiveness of the recently appointed trailbastons (*RP*, II, 128 = *PROME*, IV, 312). In the parliaments of April–May 1343 and June 1344, by contrast, the commons concentrated on achieving modifications within the existing processes (see no. 11). In the latter assembly, the crown responded by withdrawing the commissions of trailbaston and sending pending business on felonies and other offences into the king's bench or before 'other suitable justices assigned by the king' (*RP*, II, 149 = *PROME*, IV, 366; *SR*, I, 300–301). Following the suggestion of the commons (*RP*, II, 148 = *PROME*, IV, 364), the king also appointed a new set of

---

[6] Illegible due to hole in parchment: additional text is supplied from context.

peace commissions for the counties of England, but without powers to determine felonies or trespasses; cases brought before the keepers of the peace would then be referred to ad hoc tribunals with similar staffing to the peace commissions (*CPR, 1343–1346*, pp. 393–397). The peace commissions and the trial commissions were staffed, alike, by the local men recommended by the commons; but over the following five years, only eleven counties were served with trial commissions (Verduyn 1991: 91).

Given the positive response provided to it, the petition presented here seems most likely, therefore, to have been an alternative to the common petition on the matter enrolled on the parliament roll for 1344. Faced with the twin legacy of the trailbastons and the justices of the peace, it seemingly expresses an anxiety over how the new system being worked out at the time of the 1344 parliament would really operate. There are also enrolled common petitions from the parliaments of September 1346 and January–February 1348 recommending the appointment of local men to hear and determine felonies and trespasses in the shires, but these are more insistent about the focusing of such activity on the peace commissions themselves, and in 1348 demanded a guarantee of the withdrawal of trailbastons for the period of the triennial tax granted in the same assembly (*RP*, II, 161, 173 = *PROME*, IV, 396, 434).

63. Exception of villeinage (C 49/67/4)
1348

Summary

[No petitioner specified]: complaint that villeins often implead their lords by writs or bills in foreign counties, where they were not born, in order to gain their freedom from men of that county who have no knowledge of their birth or blood, and in disinheritance of their lords. Request that the king and council ordain that, in cases where a lord claims exception of villeinage on the basis that the villein was born in his manor and seised of him and of his ancestors, the exception, if it is opposed, might be tried by men of the county in which the villein was born, who have true knowledge of his birth and blood, as otherwise great mischief will follow.

> *Response:* It is agreed before the council in parliament that exception of villeinage against the plaintiffs should be accepted, and if the said plaintiffs claim to be of free estate, the matter should be adjourned before the king's bench or

the common bench at the discretion of the defendant, and a writ granted in chancery to the justices to make the adjournment.

Text

Pur ceo qe soventfois auxint qe les neifs empledont lour seignurs par brefs ou billes en foreyn contee par la ou ils ne nasquirent pas, [pur les enfranchier par gentz] de mesme le countee qi ne purront en nule manere avoir cognissance de lour nestre ne de lour sank, en desheritance des seignurs q'ount [neifs quele heure q'ils soient] par eux ensi empledez, et plusours [gentz] de ley sont en divers oppinion le quel excepcion de villenage, si ele soit alegge contre les [neifs serra triee par gentz de] contee en quel les neifs [nasquirent] ou par gentz de forein countee en quel les neifs empledont lour seignours. Pleise a nostre [seignur le Roy et son conseil ordeigner] q'en cas q'ascun seignur alegge avant qecunqes iustices par voie de excepcion contre son nief q'il ne doit [estre respondu, par cause q'il est son neif de son] manoir, de tiel lieu en tiel counte et nasquit deinz meime le manoir, et il seisi de lui et de ses [auncestres come de ses neifs del dit manoir, qe la] dite excepcion si ele soit desdite soit triee par gentz du countee en quel le neif nasquit, [q'ont verraie cognissance de son nestre et de son sank, qar] altrement ensueroit graunt meschief si la excepcion soit triee par gentz de forein countee, qe par tant les neifs serront [enfranchiz par gentz qe ne purront en nule] manere avoir cognissance de lour nestre ne de lour sank, en desheritison des plusours seignurs q'ount neifs quele heure q'ils [soient ensi empledez contre droit et] bone foi, et estre ceo les seignurs serront convictz, de quant qe lour neifs les surmettons par briefs ou billes q'ils pursuent contre lour [seignurs sanz avoir autre] respons a ceo, qe est trop graunt meschief en ley, et qe pleise ordeigner sur ceo tiel remedie qe purra eschure les meschiefs [avantditz].

Response: Il est assentu par le conseil en parlement qe l'excepcion de neifie devers les pleintifs, si ele soit par le defendant devant les iustices purpose qe meismes les pleintifs sont ses neifs et neez en autre contee, soit resceu et allowe, et si les ditz pleintifs respoignent q'ils sont franks et de frank estat, et soi offrent de ce averir qe adonqes sanz aler plus avant en la dite busoigne, aiournent les iustices les dites parties devant le Roy ou en commun bank a l'eleccion le defendant, et soit brief graunte en chancellerie pur le defendant a les ditz iustices avant lour sessions de faire le dit aiournement, et auxint de faire venir le record et proces de la busoigne en l'un des dits places solonc la eleccion del defendant avantdit, si les dits parties averont pledez come desuis est dit et soit l'enqueste prise par gentz del visne du contee ou les ditz pleintifs nasquirent.

Note

This document was printed (from an earlier transcription made by Hale) in *RP*, II, 180; it is re-edited here, correcting some errors in the *RP* edition but also relying on that reading to reconstruct the right-hand side of the original, which is now missing. This seems to form a pair with another extant petition made in the name of the 'all the prelates, lords and peers of the realm, and others having villeins in obedience' (*touz les prelatz, seignurs et peres de roialme et autres qi ount vileyns des obeisans*) (SC 8/342/16148). The present petition does not specify in whose name it was made, but if the two were indeed presented in the same parliament, it could be construed that the one printed here was the commons' version of a concern also being expressed in the lords (Aberth 1996: 102 and n. 28; *PROME*, IV, 406, 436).

At the parliament of January–February 1348, Thomas de Lisle, bishop of Ely presented a series of private petitions concerning his long-standing dispute with Richard Spink of Norwich; Lisle claimed that Spink had been born a villein on the bishop's manor of Doddington in Cambridgeshire, and thus claimed the process of exception of villeinage in order to immunise himself from litigation (Aberth 1996: 100–10). One of Lisle's petitions (SC 8/162/8059, printed in *RP*, II, 192) follows the same line of argument as the present petition, and the endorsements to the two are, in fact, identical. The effect of this judgment by the council was to give defendants who wished to claim exception of villeinage the right to establish the course of further proceedings, as well as insisting that the inquiry on the villein status of the plaintiff take place in the county where the defendant alleged that he had been born. Spink's response to these determinations, submitted by petition in the same assembly, argued that it was impossible to have fair justice under such a scheme, and that the king and council had a responsibility to uphold the principle of *favor libertatis*, which assumed that, in cases of doubt, all men should be considered free (SC 8/342/16148, printed in *RP*, II, 192–193). The endorsement to the latter petition confounded these arguments and effectively gave Lisle *carte blanche* to proceed against Spink on exception of villeinage.

While the judgment might be seen as welcomed by all those in parliament who had an interest in enforcing seigneurial rights over unfree tenants and exploiting loopholes in the law to disable opponents in the courts, the Lisle–Spink case also seems to have raised some anxiety. It is interesting that the only reference to it on the parliament roll for this assembly comes in a common petition expressing concern about the decision to have villeinage tested in the county where it was claimed to apply, since this would inevitably privilege the powerful over the weak; the petition even went so far as to claim that the decision was contrary to the laws and customs of the realm (*RP*, II, 173 = *PROME*, IV, 433).

64. The lands of debtors to be restored on the settlement of their debts (SC 8/177/8824)
1348

Summary

The commons: various men, both from misfortune of war and from other need, have been bound in statute merchant to various creditors, and suffer great damage from favourable extents, imprisonment and livery of their lands to their creditors, and have not been granted re-evaluation or attaint, despite their willingness to make satisfaction. Request that, if debtors, their heirs or executors, or those to whom the reversion of their lands pertains are prepared to make satisfaction, and creditors, their executors or agents refuse to receive their debt and expenses, then the debtors should be able to re-enter their lands and have permanent possession of them.

> *Response:* At the last parliament it was ordained that, in such cases, writs were to be sent to the justices before whom such processes were pending to warn the holders of the lands to be at a certain day before them to receive the moneys, dues, mises, and reasonable costs, and to deliver the lands to those who ought to have them. Those who complain should have such writs.

Text

A nostre seignur le Roi prie la comune; qe come divers gentz, auxibien pur meschief de guerre come pur autre necessite, soi ount liez en estatut marchant en diverses soummes d'argent as diverses creansours, dont execucion est faite de iour en altre par favorable extente, a grande damage de ceux qi sont obligez, auxibien par enprisonement de lours corps come par favorable livere de lour terres, par queux estatutz reex[ten]t[7] ne attaynte pur les dettours n'ad pas este grante, a damage et disheriteson de ceux qi ount este liez, la ou les dettours, lours heirs, lours executours ou ceux a qi la reversion des dites terres apartient ont est prist affaire gree de la dette, ensemblement ad les mises et custages dues par renable acompt. Qe y plese a sa tresexcellente seignurie de ce ordeiner par son bon conseil qe a quele hure qe les dettours, lours heirs ou lours executours ou ceux a qi la reversion des dites terres issint liverez par estatut apartient soient pristz a paier ou faire gree de la dette nient leve, od les mises et custages par renable acompt, et si les creansours, lours executours ou lours assignez ne voillent ou refusent lour dette od mises et custages en la fourme susdite resceivre, qe les ditz dettours, lours heirs, lours executours ou ceux as qeux la reversion [des dites][8] terres apartient, en les dites terres puissent entrer et retenir quitz a eux et lours heirs as touz iours.

> *Response:* Purce qe au derrein parlement feust ordeine qe en tiele cas brief feust mande as iustices devant queux tiel proces pendant de faire garnir le terre tenantz d'estre a certein iour devant eux de recevre les deners, dues, mises et custages resonables, et a deliverer la terre a celui qi la deust [...] de reson [...]ent ceux qi pleindre [...] au tiel brief desore en case semblable.

Note

The procedure known as statute merchant derived from the Statute of Acton Burnell of 1283, amended by the Statute of Merchants of 1285, which provided an effective way of allowing creditors to take proceedings in the king's courts against defaulting debtors (*SR*, I, 53–54, 98–100; McNall 2002). The efficiency of the system clearly raised issues for those who were slow in repaying loans and who, as the petition alleges, then found it extremely difficult to recover their confiscated property. An unenrolled common petition, printed in *RP*, II, 210 and summarized in *PROME*, IV, 442 (but no longer extant), which probably dates from the first of the two parliaments held in 1348 (January–February and March–April), addresses the same substantive issue, and has a long response providing the aggrieved parties with writs of *scire facias* requiring the creditors to be in the appropriate court and receive the repayment of the debt. It is most likely that the petition printed here dates from the second assembly of the same year and was submitted to bring further pressure on the crown for the

---

[7] Conjectural (tear in parchment).
[8] Conjectural (illegible).

enforcement of the new ordinance. It therefore stands as an example of the carry-over of business between successive parliaments and the ability of the commons to recall and react to business undertaken in earlier assemblies.

65. The rights of lords of enfeoffed estates
(SC 8/102/5093)
1377

Summary

The commons of the land: many men give and enfeoff certain persons with lands and tenements on certain conditions, some to acquit their debts and to give alms for their soul; after the conditions are fulfilled, they further entail their lands to people as they please, by reason of which those enfeoffed often retain the lands without observing the conditions or charges, against the will of the feoffer. They request that the king grant to those to whom the lands are thus entailed that, on default of the conditions, they might be able to enter and perform the charges and conditions according to the will of the granter.

Response: [none].

Text

A nostre seignur le Roy et son conseil priont la comune de sa terre; qe come plusours gentz donnent et enfeffent certaignes persones en qi ils s'affient de lour terres et tenementz sur certaignes condiciouns, ascunes pur acquiter lour dettes et pur doner et faire autres diverses almoignes pur lour almes, et apres les dites condiciouns parfournez taillent outre lour terres avantditz as certaignes persones solom ceo qe lour plest, et par cause qe sovent foitz tiels enfeffez retiegnent les terres devers eaux saunz rien faire de les condiciouns ou charges, encountre la volunte lour feffour. Qe please a nostre seignur le Roy grauntier a ceaux as queux les terres sont issint tailles qe pur defaute de les condiciouns nient parfournez q'ils puissent entrer et parfourner les charges et les condiciouns solonc la volunte de donour.

Note

The petition raises the specific issue of what happened when, on the fulfilment of the terms of an enfeoffment to use (that is, a trust), the feoffees neglected or refused to return the lands to the original grantor and instead leased them out on their own terms, thus depriving the original owner of any effective control over the terms under which they were held. The problem had become apparent during the reign of Edward III, both on the royal estates and on those of some of the greatest landholders of the realm; but it was also a much wider issue for lesser landholders as a result of the general proliferation of uses in the fourteenth century (Holmes 1957: 51–57; McFarlane 1973: 217 220; Saul 1986: 23–24; Ormrod 2011: 492–495).

When parliament began to legislate on enfeoffments, in the last session of Edward III's reign in January–March 1377, it was mainly preoccupied with the rights of other parties, specifically of creditors (*RP*, II, 369 = *PROME*, V, 412; *SR*, I, 398). In the first parliament of Richard II, in October–November 1377, however, a statute was passed whose emphasis was much more on preventing collusions that led to the obstruction of the original title; this legislation was to be confirmed and clarified on two further occasions in the fifteenth century (*SR*, II, 3–4, 134, 279; Bean 1968: 125–126; Fratcher 1969: 45 n. 37). There is no petition on the parliament roll for October–November 1377 that relates directly to this legislation, but (in spite of the absence of a response written on the original petition), the substance of the present petition provides strong grounds for assuming that it, or something very like it, prompted the council to action on this occasion. If so, the petition stands as another example of the exceptionally complicated relationship exposed by the records of this assembly between original drafts of common petitions, the schedules of common petitions submitted to the council, and the enrolled versions of the petitions on the parliament roll (see also nos 43, 66, 67, 86, and 124).

66. Debtors imprisoned in the Fleet (SC 8/18/884)
1377

Summary

The poor commons of the land: many men imprisoned in the Fleet on pleas of debt are allowed by the warden to leave the prison to buy and sell, and to spend nights away, so that their creditors can have no recovery against them. They request that the warden be ordered henceforth not to allow any prisoner to leave without satisfying his creditors, except on the king's writ, on pain of forfeiture of his office into the king's hand.

Response: This bill is answered among the common petitions.

Text

A nostre seigneur le Roy et a son counseil suppleient ses povres comunes de la terre; qe come plusours gentz a la sute des partiez sount aiugges a la prison de Flete par plee de dette en la comune bank nostre seigneur le Roy et aillours pur avoir lour recovrir et grant ils sount aiugges a la prison de Flete, le gardeyn de mesme la prison suffre plusours alier a large et faire lour marchandises pour vendre et achatre et gesont les noetz hors de prison a lour volunte, et par tielle colour et sufferance homme ne poet avoir nulle recovrir devers eux, a grant tort, deceyte et anientisshement des plusours gentz. Parquei please a vostre tresgracious seigneurie en oevre de charite \ordeyner due remedie, et outre ces/ commander et charger le gardeyn de Flete et ordeyner qe desornes ne suffre nul prisoner alier hors du prison saunz gree faire a les parties demandantz que ount par iuggement recovriz lour dettes, \s'il ne soit par bref nostre seigneur le Roy/, sur forfete du perdre soun office et seiser la garde du dit prison en la mayn nostre seigneur le Roy, en avantage du Roy et profit de son povre comune.

Response: Ceste bille est respondu entre les comunes petitions.

Note

The untidiness of the document, including the interlineations and occasional grammatical hesitations, and the reference in the response to the common petitions, suggest that it may be a first draft of the more developed petition on debtors in the Fleet prison found enrolled among the schedule of common petitions on the parliament roll for October–November 1377 (*RP*, II, 25 = *PROME*, VI, 55). The response to the petition given on the parliament roll, and the resulting statute (*SR*, II, 4) deal more specifically with the problem raised by the precedence given to debts owed to the crown, and there are grounds for considering that the clerk of parliament actually made a mistake in choosing which of the two petitions to place on the parliament roll (see no. 67).

67. Debtors to the king imprisoned in the Fleet
(SC 8/101/5050)
1377

Summary

The humble commons: complaint that some men who stand accused of debts and damages contrive, by fraud and evil machinations, to become debtors in the king's exchequer, because they have greater suit in the Fleet than in any other prison, causing their creditors to despair of recovery of their debts. Request that debtors should remain in the harshest prison until they can make adequate recompense, and that the warden should stand surety for all debts and damages.

> *Response:* This petition is answered elsewhere among the common petitions.

Text

A nostre tredoute seignur lige le Roi supplient ses humbles comunes; qe come ascuns gentz ont recoveriz dettes ou damages en les courtz nostre seigneur le Roi, et les defendantz ont este agarde a prisoun a y demurer tantqe des dettes ou damages gree serreit fait, la ont les defendantz par fraude et male compassement sei conuz estre dettourx en l'escheker a nostre seigneur le Roi a cause d'aver greindre suete en le prisoun de Flete q'en autre prisoun, par ont les gentz q'ont recoveri pur despoir de lour dettes ont pardonee les greindrez partie pur estre seur del remenant, en grant arerissement des creaunceours et enbaudissement de fauxes creditours et malefesours. Qe plese a sa real seignur le grantier qe si ascun condepnee a sute de partie et agardee a prisoun en manere susdit et en l'escheker ou en comune banc puis soit condempne en ascun summe et commis a Flete q'al maundement des iustices devant qeux le recorde est, le corps soit maunde a demurer en prisone plusdure tantqe il eit fait gree si bien a nostre seignur le Roi, come a chescon autre partie devers qeux il soit condempne, et outre ceo qe le gardein de prison les garde bien sanz les lesser aler hors et sil face q'il respoigne de tote le dette et damages, et soit aussint agarde a prisoun a y demurer tantqe il eit fait gree et outre q'il parde la garde de prisone en apres a touz iours.

> *Response:* Ceste bille si est respondu aillours en les comunes peticions.

Note

A closely related petition, no. 66 (which has more or less the same endorsement), was enrolled in a developed form on the parliament roll for October–November 1377 (*RP*, II, 25 = *PROME*, VI, 55). The answer to that petition, however, relates much more closely to the content of the present document, which raises the specific issue of the problems arising when individuals imprisoned in the Fleet for private debts invented debts owed to the crown at the exchequer such as to have those take precedence over the original debts. Since the wardens of the Fleet were so lax about allowing persons to leave the prison, it could actually be to the advantage of the defendant to invent a debt in the exchequer as a protection against larger debts owed elsewhere. There had been a real case of this abuse in 1375, when the London tailor, Henry Gerard, had conspired with an auditor of the exchequer, William Dounbrigge, to deprive Gerard's other creditors of their dues; and it is possible that the present petition was prompted by that case and/or others like it (Richardson 1922: 42–43; Pugh 1968: 243–244; Dunn 2007: 210–211). Furthermore, the response provided to the enrolled common petition, and the resulting statute (*SR*, II, 4) actually dealt specifically with the issues raised in this petition, rather than the one that was put on the parliament roll. Taken together, then, the two extant originals of petitions on debtors in the Fleet prison submitted in 1377 provide evidence of the complex process by which common petitions were drafted, taken up by the commons, written up for consideration by the king and council, and finally enrolled, with the responses, on the parliament rolls – and of the occasional difficulties of comprehension that can be caused by the apparent enrolment of the wrong petition.

68. The restoration of John of Northampton
(SC 8/102/5072)
1390–1391

Summary

The knights and commons in parliament: request, in consideration of the great injury and affliction suffered by John Northampton, that he be restored to his lands, tenements and goods.

> *Response:* The king wishes to be advised by his council, and to make suitable favour to the petitioner.

Text

A lour tresexcellent et tresredoute seignur le Roy:

Supplient les chivalers et comunes de cest present parlement; qe pleise a vostre treshaute maieste d'avoir consideracion a le grantz meschief et disease les queux Johan Norhamptoun ad soeffrez et deut de votre benigne grace grantier qe le dit Johan poet estre restitue a ses terres et tenementz, et aussi a [ses]⁹ biens, pur Dieu et en oevre de charite.

---
⁹Hole in parchment: text supplied from context.

Response: Le Roy soi voet aviser par son conseille, et faire al suppliant covenable graces.

Note

As mayor of London in 1381–1383, John of Northampton (otherwise known as John Comberton) had aimed to assert the city's control over the victualling trade (see no. 91). This had sparked a bitter dispute with his successor as mayor, Nicholas Brembre, that led to Northampton's arrest and trial for sedition before the king and council at Reading in August 1384 (Nightingale 1995: 270–291). The king quickly remitted the sentence from death to imprisonment (*CPR, 1381–1385*, p. 464), and in June 1386, under the influence of John of Gaunt, allowed Northampton to go free on condition that he never re-enter London (*CPR, 1385–1389*, pp. 158–159). This, however, did not remove the conviction itself, so that Northampton's real estate and chattels remained forfeited.

In the Merciless Parliament of February–June 1388, Brembre himself was tried and put to death (*RP*, III, 229–235 = *PROME*, VII, 83–98; *Westminster Chronicle*, pp. 282–285). It is possible that pressure for Northampton's restoration was brought within the same assembly, but was blocked by the mayor of London, Nicholas Exton, one of Northampton's enemies in the city; certainly, a general pardon issued to the city later in the same parliament explicitly excluded Northampton from its provisions (*RP*, III, 248 = *PROME*, VII, 74; *CCR, 1385–1389*, p. 603; Dodd 2011a: 404–405). The end of Exton's term of office in 1388 finally left the way open for the possibility of a formal pardon to Northampton. In July 1390, at the request of lords residing with the king, John was granted his forfeited goods (*CPR, 1388–1392*, p. 297). Then, in the parliament of November–December 1390, at the request of the commons, the king annulled all the charges brought in 1384 (*RP*, III, 282–283 = *PROME*, VII, 186; *CPR, 1388–1392*, p. 335). Since the latter grant did not mention restoration of lands and/or chattels, however, it seems to have led to continuing uncertainty over which elements of Northampton's property were eligible for return. The present petition implies that John had already been exonerated by the crown, and may therefore be seen either as a supplementary request submitted towards the end of the 1390 parliament or, more likely, as the text from which the clerk of parliament drew up the more extensive and formal common petition on the matter recorded on the parliament roll for November–December 1391; it was on this basis that the crown confirmed the pardon and specified that Northampton should be restored to all his possessions (*RP*, III, 291–292 = *PROME VII*, 209–210).

69. Trial of cases of homicide (SC 8/118/5875)
Late fourteenth century

Summary

[No petitioners specified]: request that the king's justices may go and sit in judgment on all those who are or will be indicted for killing in self-defence within this year and thereafter.

Response: [none].

Text

Plese a nostre seignur le Roy et a son counseil graunter et ordeyner qe teux ceux qeux sount ou qe serroit enditez de mort donne eux defendant, qe les iustices nostre seignur le Roy puissent aler et seer sur lour deliveraunce auxibien dedeinz l'an come apres.

Note

This short document does not name the petitioners, but its form is otherwise compatible with that of a common petition. The hand suggests a date in the later fourteenth century. Between the 1350s and the 1370s it was usually the practice that judgments of homicide and other felonies were either referred up to the king's bench or given by royal judges going down into the shires on circuit as justices of assize and gaol delivery (Powell 1987). From 1380, however, the justices of the peace operating at county level were permitted to determine felonies without the necessary presence of all the assize justices, though at certain times (as in the period 1382–1389) they were required to conduct such trials in association with parallel commissions staffed by magnates and judges from the central courts (Post 1976; Musson and Ormrod 1999: 51, 109–110). In light of the fact that the present petition does not mention the peace commissions and imagines the work to be undertaken purely by judges who 'go' (from the central courts to the localities), it is perhaps more likely to come from before 1380 than after that date, but a more precise context cannot be established.

70. The abolition of the giving of badges by the king and lords (SC 8/100/4985)
1401

Summary

The king's loyal lieges: under his ancestors, the people were well and peacefully governed without division caused by the wearing of badges and other liveries; but lately, the king and other lords of the realm have distributed badges among the commons, which has caused disunity and disturbed the common law of the land. Request that these badges be annulled and withdrawn, in recognition of the great damage that will come to the loyal subjects of the realm.

Response: [none].

Text

A treshaut, tresexcellent et tresdroiturelle seignur le Roy et a soun parlement: Monstrount et suppliount vos loialx lieges; come en temps de vos tresnobles progenitours, iadys Roies d'Engletere, tout le poeple de vostre dit roialme loialment bien et pesiblement ount estee rulez et governez come un comyn entier desouth lour Roy et seigneur liege, saunz desseverance entre eux faitz par conusance du signes ou autres liveres forspris livere de vesture, a graunt unite du poeple enforcement et bone garde de la ley de la terre et comyn droit du roialme, tanqe tarde qe le Roi et autres seignurs du roialme ount donez diverses signes entre la dite comyn a graunt desseveraunce de eux, et sur colour de lour ditz signez de iour en autre maigntenauntz tresmalveys quereles oppressauntz voz loialx lieges et desturbantz la droit et comyn ley de vostre terre, sibien pur doute de l'aliaunce de eux q'enportent les signes suisditz come pur indignacioun des seignurs qeux les donent, parount si bone pees, tranquilite et unite du people, owel droit ne la ley de la terre appesent ne sount meintenuz ne gardes come en temps de vos tresnobles progenitours, a graunt meschief et damage as loialx lieges de vostre roialme si ne soit par temps amendes et redressez. Que please a vostre tresdroiturelle, tresioust et tresloial discrecioun considerer qe tout la poeple de vostre roialme sount vos lieges et entier comyn, a vous come a lour Roy et seignur liege, a vos leyes obeisauntz, et coment q'ils comyn droit et la ley de vostre terre sount oppressez et desseverez par lours veisyns portauntz et usauntz les signes suisditz, ordeigner et estabuler qe les signes avauntditz du ceo enavaunt soient adnulles et retretez, en sustenance de lours loialx aliegeauntz, voz droiturelles leyes et costomez, q'ount est tenuz et usez saunz desseveraunce entre vostre liege poeple et comyn en temps de vos tresnobles progenitours, en oevre du charite.

Note

This petition was previously published by Saul (1990: 314–315) and is re-edited here with minor differences of spelling and punctuation. The parliamentary commons had pressed for restrictions on the granting of liveries by great lords since the 1370s, and from at least 1384 expressed themselves opposed to the specific practice of granting badges ('signs') to retainers. However, the legislation issued before 1399 to regulate liveries and badges did not apply to the king, and Richard II is well known to have made very vigorous use of his own personal badge of the white hart in the 1390s to build up an affinity of followers not only in the royal household but also in the localities (Given-Wilson 1986: 236–239; Bean 1989: 22, 204–205; Bellamy 1989: 81–83).

In his first parliament, in October–November 1399, Henry IV issued legislation severely curtailing the general practice of livery and specifically abolishing the distribution of badges by any lord other than the king, who himself agreed to certain restrictions in his own use of these tokens of lordship (*RP*, III, 428 = *PROME*, VIII, 38; *SR*, II, 113–114; *CCR*, *1399–1402*, p. 182). The present petition most likely dates from the next parliament after this, held in January–March 1401 (Saul 1990: 303). A common petition submitted at that assembly and enrolled on the parliament roll requested the reinforcement of the 1399 statute and further restrictions on the king's use of badges, and resulted in supplementary legislation being promulgated at the end of the assembly (*RP*, III, 477–478 = *PROME*, VIII, 148–149; *SR*, II, 129–130). The enrolled petition and subsequent legislation are quite different in tone and substance, however, from the text presented here. In the notably acrimonious parliament of January–March 1404, the king and council were given information that, 'on another occasion', the speaker of the commons, Sir Arnold Savage, had demanded the full abolition of all liveries, including badges distributed by the crown; the way that the report is constructed on the parliament roll means that the reference can only be to the parliament of 1401 (*RP*, III, 523 = *PROME*, VIII, 230; Given-Wilson 1986: 240). In 1404 Savage claimed, and the commons affirmed, that no such request had been made, presumably in order to guard against the king's wrath. But the unusually explicit political rhetoric of the present petition, with its emphasis on the wholeness of the realm and the idea that all the people should be treated equally as the king's lieges, suggests that it may well be a draft prepared for submission as a common petition in 1401 that was then set aside by the commons themselves under advice that the request was altogether too far-reaching to be agreeable to the king (Saul 1990: 303–304).

V
MERCHANTS, TRADE, AND FINANCE

71. The king's butler and the prisage of wine
(SC 8/202/10065)
1303–1309

Summary

[No petitioner specified]: request that no wines brought into the country by foreign merchants should be taken for the king by the butler or his people without the payment of the custom of 2s for wine of good quality; for if the wines are the king's and the custom is paid, he will lose nothing. A writ on this is requested to all collectors of customs.

Response: Let it be done.

Text

S'il plest a nostre seignur le Roi et son conseil; soit ordeine pur le profit de nostre seignur le Roi qe nuls vyns entrantz le realme d'Engletere a nul de havenes par merchantz estranges, par le botiller ne nul des soens soient amienetz sur le Roi, en oustant le dit nostre seignur le Roi de sa custume de ii. s. du touch, kar tut fuissent les vyns du Roi et le ii. s. paiez, le Roi ne pierd rien; et sur ceo soit mande bref a touz les custumers.

Response: Fiat.

Note

The king's butler exercised the ancient right of the prisage of wine, by which a proportion of each cargo brought into the realm could be taken for the king's use and the supplier compensated at the artificially low rate of £1 a tun. The petition must come from the period between the imposition (in 1303) and withdrawal (in 1309) of the so-called new custom on wine imports, paid only by alien merchants (James 1951: 171; Childs 1990: 22–23). This was the first time since the introduction of the permanent customs system in 1275 that wines were subject to duties in the ports. The arrangements of 1303 did not change aliens' liability to prisage, but required that they be paid the full market value of the wine taken (Lloyd 1982: 27). The implication of the petition is therefore that the levying of the customs revenues on wine taken in the prisage would help compensate the royal coffers at a time when the prisage itself would cost more. The informality of the address clause raises questions as to whether this is to be considered a common petition or merely some form of government memorandum. In spite of the response, there is no known evidence that the crown took action on the proposal.

72. The royal prise of wool (SC 8/77/3808)
1307

Summary

The good people of the land: in 1297 the king ordered all those who had wools to take them to certain places at Easter to find merchants to buy them, on pain of forfeiture; but the wools were taken for the king's use and only tallies were given for them, with no payment, and those who did not bring their wools had them taken without any payment or tallies. They ask that they be pardoned this forfeiture, and that satisfaction be made for these wools as for the others, according to the rolls of the receivers held in the exchequer.

> *Response*: The king pardons the forfeiture and wishes satisfaction to be made, including for those wools not brought and on which no tallies were issued.
> Enrolled.

Text

A nostre seignur le Roi et a son conseil prient les bones gentz de sa terre; qe come nostre seignur le Roi avoit fait crier l'an xxv qe chescun home qui leynes eust, les feist carier as certeins lieus a l'endemayn de Paskes, l'an xxv avaundit, sur forfeture des leynes, e qu'il trovereient[1] marchauntz qui les achatererent. A quel iour le Roi fist prendre a son oeps totes les dites leynes cariees, et enfist faire tailles saunz rien paier. E les leynes qe ne furent nient cariees fist il auxi prendre, auxi come forfaites, et nules tailles n'en feurent faites. Par quei il prient qe cele forfeture seit pardonee, et qe le Roi face gree de celes leynes auxi

---

[1] There is a redundant abbreviation in this word.

come des autres, solonc ceo qe serra trove par roulles des prenurs qe sont a l'escheqer.

Response: Rex perdonat forisfacturum et vult quod satisfiat de lanis sic captis sicut apparere poterit per rotulos captorum qui sunt ad scaccarium, non obstante quod non fuerunt cariate, et quod illi quorum lane ille fuerunt tallias inde non habent.
Irrotulatur.

Note

The prise of wool of 1297 was a compulsory purchase of stocks of this vital product in order to raise money for Edward I's war with France. Credit notes and tallies were given in lieu of cash, and the government was notably slow in honouring its debts to those from whom wool was taken. This had significant impact on the political crisis of 1297–1298 and created long-standing individual grievances for the rest of the reign (Sayles 1952; *Crisis of 1297–1298*, pp. 10–11). It is likely that the petition was presented in the Carlisle parliament of January–April 1307 (for which no official parliament roll survives), since the requested pardon and promise of repayment was issued on 20 June in that year (*CCR, 1302–1307*, pp. 504–505; Lloyd 1977: 95, 325). The text of this document was previously printed, with minor variations of spelling and punctuation, by Haskins (1937: 316–317) and in *Crisis of 1297–1298* (p. 198).

73. The debts of Italian merchant companies
(SC 8/79/3936)
1307

Summary

The good people of the realm: request that the merchants of the other companies of Florence be constrained to make satisfaction for the debts of the Pulci company, as they refuse to come to England to make satisfaction despite letters of protection and conduct; and for remedy against the Ammanati company of Pistoia for their money, the merchants having withdrawn from the realm.

Response: [none].

Text

A nostre seignur le Roi et son consil monstrent les bones gentz de son reaume; des queus les marchandz de la compaignie de Pulchz de Florence \e auxint les marchaundz de Pistoe, Amanachi, emporterent divers summes de deners/, qe come apres le manneis departir des ditz marchandz hors du roiaume d'Engleterre les marchandz de totes les compaignies de Florence demorantz a Londres fuessent areste e leur biens, tant qe homme seut qu'en dreit le potestat et les capitans de la dite cite de Florence, as queus nostre seignur le Roi manda ses lettres especiales par monsieur Gerard de Fresney, qe eus enveassent en Engleterre les ditz marchandz de Pulchz a fere gre a leur creaunceurs eut voussisent fere, e puis apres a la seute \a priere/ des ditz marchandz des autres compaignies de Florence si granta nostre seignur le Roi ses lettres de protection et de conduts as ditz marchandz de Pulchz, teles come eus meismes desirerent de venir en roiaume d'Engleterre pur cele busoigne, les ditz marchandz de Pulchz ne venent pas, ne nul autre pur eus \come il aveint promis/, de fere [gere][2] gre a les bones gentz d'Engleterre. Dont les dites gentz d'Engleterre prient a nostre seignur le Roi qe les marchandz des autres compaignies de Florence demorantz a Londres seient constreinz de fere gre a eus d'Engleterre, desicome ceus \marchandz/ e les autres de Pulchz sont \touz/ de une communaute, qi ne cleim aver nul soverein come Roi ou autre prince qi deut estre requis de dreit fere en tieu cas, fors qe eus meismes qi de ceo ont este requis sicom sus est dit e nul dreit ne ent font.

Ceux de Ama:
Encontre la compaignie de Amanachi de Pistoia; prient les ditz gentz qe remedie leur seit fait de leur argent, de celx marchaunz de la dite compaignie unt emporte hors du realme.

Note

The petition reflects the considerable reverberations resulting in England from the default and collapse around 1300 of a series of Italian banking companies. The Pulci, Ammanati, and others were driven to ruin by their over-commitment not only to the king of England but also to the French and papal governments. The Ammanati company collapsed as a result of Pope Boniface VIII's politically motivated seizure of the goods of the citizens of Pistoia in 1302 (Housley 1982: 238–239). The Pulci withdrew from England

[2] Deleted.

in the winter of 1305–1306 under circumstances regarded within the kingdom as deeply suspect and fraudulent, though they too subsequently went bankrupt in 1309 (Fryde 1951: 346, 350). The petition, originally written solely in reference to the Pulci, was adapted with an interlineation and an additional paragraph to include the Ammanati as well. It must date from between the request issued to the authorities of Florence on 14 February 1307 and delivered by Gerard de Fresney to have the Pulci and Remertini return to London and the safe-conducts issued to representatives of those companies on 6 June 1307 requiring them to present themselves in London by August and satisfy their creditors (*CPR, 1301–1307*, pp. 415, 529). The petition therefore dates firmly to the Carlisle parliament of January–April 1307; many of the petitions presented at this assembly (including one, not surviving, ascribed by the chancery to the 'community of the realm') were not actioned until May and June (*PROME*, I, 129–130). There is no record that proceedings were instigated against the Ammanati. The text was previously printed by Haskins (1937: 315–316).

74. The enforcement of penalties for forestalling (SC 8/73/3615) 1307–1327

Summary

[No petitioner specified]: although the king has ordained that no forestaller or regrater be permitted to trade in any borough, city, or town, they do so in Sussex and throughout the land, causing victuals to be more expensive, so that poor people are unable to live.

> *Response*: Let writs be made to the sheriffs and bailiffs of the area for each person who wishes to sue, instructing that they are not to allow such forestalling.

Text

A nostre seygnur la Roy et a son conseyl seyt demustre; que la ou il est porveu e commande par nostre seygnur le Roy que nul forstallor ne regrater ne seyt en burk ne en cite ne en vile marchaunde, par l'esques forstal e regraterie seyt fest, dount le pais seyt enchiri, taunt de forstallors e regraters sunt en le conte de Sussex e parmi la terre, dount les marches de tote manyre de vitaille sunt enchiris, par que povere gentz ne pount vivere. Dount il prient remedie por Deu.

Response: Soient brefs faitz pur chescun qi vodra sure au viscontes et as bailiffs du pais, q'ils ne soeffrent point tiel forstallerie[3] estre use ne fait.

Note

This petition, whose hand indicates that it dates from the early fourteenth century, does not specify in whose name it was made; the reference to the county of Sussex may suggest that, as in some other cases, it was put together by the parliamentary representatives for the relevant area but written up deliberately to represent a problem general to the realm at large (see, for example, nos 1, 13, 45, and 89).

Forestalling was the practice of buying up goods for sale before they reached the open market in order to push up their price and create larger profit margins for the sellers. The date for the present petition may be fixed within the reign of Edward II, for it was at the beginning of this period, in 1307, that the new king required, for the first time, that ordinances forbidding the practice of forestalling be enforced throughout the land, in conjunction with the well-developed legislation on weights and measures (Britnell 1987). A more precise context could be the decision taken in the parliament of January–March 1315 to address the recent inflation in the price of foodstuffs by fixing compulsory maximum prices for meat, a measure that seems to have prompted a spate of forestalling on a whole variety of foodstuffs imported to the realm (*RP*, I, 295 = *PROME*, III, 67–68; *CCR, 1313–1318*, p. 227; Davis 2012: 224–225; see also no. 79). The fact that the response to the petition is written in French may, alternatively, be taken as evidence that it comes from the 1320s, when the crown shifted away from Latin and towards French as the default language for the endorsements made on both private and common petitions. Whatever the precise date, the response suggests that the king and council were not persuaded at the relevant moment that the petition required any particularly pro-active position to be taken up. While the governments of Edward II and Edward III took firm action on common petitions of the 1310s and 1320s, alleging that forestalling was pushing up the price of commodities in the locations for the meetings of parliament (see no. 79), the answer to the present petition simply allows that those who felt themselves the victims of such practices could have their local officials reminded of the need for vigilance. The response is, however, of some significance in first choosing the term 'regrater' and then altering it to 'forestaller'. There was a technical difference between the two, still quite closely observed in the early fourteenth

---

[3] The word *regraters* has been crossed out and this word substituted.

century, since forestallers were considered to buy in wholesale whereas regraters purchased from retailers. More generally, and especially as the fourteenth century progressed, regraters were considered to fall under the increasingly generic definition of forestalling (Davis 2012: 7–8).

75. The alnage of cloth (C 49/5/23)
c.1307–c.1327

Summary

The commonalty of the people of the realm: it was ordained in Magna Carta that any saleable cloth should be of the width of 2 yards, for which the king has assigned alnagers in various places of the land to collect and inspect saleable cloth in order to check that it is the right size and length and then seal it to show that it has been inspected. However, having trusted the authenticity of this seal, men have bought cloth which is found to be deficient in width or length, to the great damage of the people; and they request a remedy.

Response: Let the treasurer and barons of the exchequer be ordered to examine the rolls and memoranda of the exchequer of the time of the king's progenitors, and the king's alnagers be summoned and appointed to act according to the above request, as was formerly the custom.
In the presence of the king.
For the commonalty of the realm.

Text

A nostre seignur le Rois et soun counseil monstre la comunalte de gentz de son realme; qe come il seit contenuz en la graunt chartre des franchises qe chescun drap vendable soit de la leoure de ii. alnes densz les listes, a quoi sount assignes certeins gardeins depar nostre dit seignur de ve\e/r q'ils soient de tiele assise, et auxint qe come nostre seignur le Roy ad ses alneours en divers lus de sa terre les draps vendables alner et veer q'ils soient de droit assise de longure et puys de les enseeler de seels de loures officez en sengne q'ils soient de droit assise prove, et hors communalment come homme achate les dits draps en affiauns q'ils soient asseiez duement pur taunt come ils sount issi trove enselez, si troeve home meismes les draps en molt feillaunces de leoure et trop de lourz longure, qar tiels draps qeux dussent contener de longure xxx. alnes content mie en la longure forsqe xxviii. et tels draps qeux duissent contenir la longure de xxvi.

alnes ne contenent forsqe xxii. et ascuns forsqe xxi., a graunt damage del people. Dount ils priont qe de ceo remedy seit ordine.

Response: Mandetur thesaurario et baronibus de scaccario quod scrutari fient rotulos et memoranda de scaccario de temporibus progenitorum Regis \infrascripta tangencia/, et vocatis ulnatoribus Regis ordinari faciant quod super contentis in peticione ex iure, fiat prout temporibus progenitorum Regis fieri consuevit.
Coram domino Rege.
Pro communitate regni.

Note

The assize of cloth of 1196, enshrined in clause 35 of Magna Carta (1215), set down provision for a standard width of cloth (*Select Charters*, p. 297); later legislation also defined lengths for various grades of cloth (Bridbury 1982: 106–107). By the later thirteenth century the enforcement of the assize was entrusted to an official who gradually became known as the alnager, and who normally operated through a series of deputies. Until 1353 the alnagers had the power to license sales of cloth that conformed to the assize by applying seals to approved goods, and to confiscate those that failed the prescribed measurements. The present petition probably dates from the reign of Edward II, during which time the English government several times addressed the administration of the alnage (Bridbury 1982: 108). It must date from before 1328, since in that year the compulsory width of 2 yards was modified in the Statute of Northampton (*SR*, I, 260). The hand, and the use of Latin in the response to this petition, also suggest a date in the early fourteenth century. For the changes to the alnage system after 1353, see no. 83.

76. The price of ale (SC 8/80/3957)
1317–1327

Summary

The commonalty of the land: the king and his council ordained in the ninth year of his reign that no ale was to be sold in country towns at higher price than in enfranchised boroughs; this was to the profit of the people, but has now been neglected. They pray that it might be renewed and maintained, for the great salvation of the people.

Response: [none].

Text

A nostre seignur le Roi et a son conseil mustrent la communalte de sa terre; qe la ou ordeine fut par lui et par son conseil l'an de son regne nevisme qe nule serveise serreit vendu en sa terre en ville de upelande, le al[...]⁴ mout plus haut qe a denir en ville de burgh a treis mailis, la quele ordinaunce fit grant profist a son poeple et [...] de plusours genz, et ore est mis en obli. Dount la communaltee prie q'il pusse estre renoveli et comande d'estre tenu, pur grant sauvacioun de son poeple.

Note

The ordinance referred to in the petition was issued in January 1317. It aimed to address the problem of high grain prices resulting from the famine of 1315–1316 by setting upper limits on the price of ale, and (reflecting a similar distinction made in the assize of ale) differentiated between those charged in cities, towns, and urban areas on the one hand and those in rural settlements on the other (*CCR, 1313–1318*, p. 449; Seabourne 2003: 83 and n. 96). The ordinance was in fact issued during the regnal year 10 Edward II (July 1316–July 1317), but the idea that it was made in 9 Edward II may arise from its association with an earlier initiative in the city of London, taken in May 1316, and the more general link with the harvest of 1315 (*CLBL, E*, pp. 71–73; Jordan 1996: 171–172). The petition, which must have been made between 1317 and the end of Edward II's reign, attests to the intensity of the economic problems arising from continued harvest failures between 1315 and 1322 and the inadequacy of official measures to counteract them; although significant efforts were made from 1324 to establish standard weights and measures for ale and other commodities, there is no evidence that the crown responded to this petition by re-establishing compulsory prices either for ale or for grain (Jordan 1996: 171–177; Musson and Ormrod 1999: 90–92).

77. German merchants exporting grain to the enemy (SC 8/79/3948)
1319

Summary

The commonalty of the realm: complaint that merchants of Germany are requesting permission to carry corn out of the realm, claiming that they will take it to Norway and bring back fish and other victuals,

---

⁴The document is slightly stained on the right-hand side.

whereas in fact they sell it to enemies of Flanders and of Berwick and Aberdeen, resulting in an increase in the price. Request that the thirteen cogs belonging to German merchants now at Lynn and charged with corn, malt, and flour should not be given permission to leave, as this would be to the great damage of the realm, and the king would benefit from the collection of so great an amount of victuals.

> *Response*: Concerning the boats loaded, it is agreed by the king and council that they should be released, this time by good security. Concerning the export of victuals by aliens, a prohibition has been expressly made and the king wishes it to remain.

Text

A nostre seignur le Roi et a soun counseil monstrent la comonnalte de son roialme; qe come les marchauntz d'Alemagne suwount d'avoir deliveraunce des bledz de carier hors del roialme, enpromessaunt d'amener les en Norweye et de remener pessoun et autres vitaillies, la il les amenent en Flaundres et a Berwyk et a Aberden, et illoqes vendount lour bledz a les enemys, et puys vount en Norweye et achatent le pessoun et autres mers, et en tele manere unt il les avauntages de touz les terres, et encherissent les bledz en le pays iesqes au double, et issynt unt il amene hors de Lenne puys la Chaundeleure plus de lx. mile quarters, a grant damage de tut le poeple et a grant confort de tut des enemys. Et ore sunt a Lenne xiii. grosse nefs, qe hom apele cogges, charges des bledz et de bres et de flour a la mountaunce de viii. mile quarters, pur queux il suwount ore d'avoir la deliveraunce come de sus est dyt, qe serroit grant damage a granter et encountre l'estat del roialme, kar grant profyt purroyent tant des vitaillies si prestement coilliez faire a nostre seignur le Roi ore en sa guerre.

> *Response*: Quo ad naves artatas ante descensionem concordatum est per \Regem et/ consilium quod deliberatur hac orte per bonam securitatem. Quo ad educationem victualis per alienis suam faciendum inhibitio facta est expresse quam Rex vult quod in suo robore permaneat.

Note

This and the next item reflect the beleaguered nature of English diplomacy in the late 1310s and the growing popular and official suspicion of foreigners that would lead to significant attacks on German merchants during the civil war of 1321–1322 (Fryde 1979: 69–70). This petition dates from after the loss of Berwick from English control with its capture by the Scots in April 1318, and the most likely context is the parliament held at York in May 1319. An embargo on the export of grain and other victuals had been imposed in January 1318 (*CCR, 1313–1318*, p. 588). In April 1319 the crown reminded the authorities of Lynn that this was still in force (*CCR, 1318–1323*, p. 132). Parliament opened on 6 May and continued to 25 May; its extant roll of proceedings includes reference to another petition of the 'community of the realm' (*RPHI*, p. 54 = *PROME*, III, 356). The first element of the response to the petition appears to provide the authority for the orders issued on 12 May that certain alien ships at Lynn should be released so long as they did not trade with the enemy Scots (*CCR, 1318–1323*, p. 135).

78. The manufacture and sale of caps (SC 8/109/5435)
1319

Summary

The commonalty of the realm of England: complaint that, in the king's parliament held at York at Michaelmas 1318, the cappers of Fleet Street in London suggested that no capper make, and no merchant sell, hats made of wool mixed with flock, as a result of which the price of a hat has increased from 6d to 10d. The merchants of Germany and other lands make hats of the cheaper quality, from which the king receives his due custom. The petitioners request that the mayor and sheriffs of London and other officers inquire as to whether the ordinance is to the general profit or that of the cappers, and what loss is sustained to the king's income from the customs as a result.

Response: William Bereford, Hervey Staunton and Gilbert Toutheby are to be assigned to an inquiry into the subject of this petition, and their findings are to be certified in the chancery.

Text

A nostre seignour le Roi et a son conseil mustre la communalte du roialme d'Engleterre; qe com nagaires les overoures des chapeus en Flete Strete de la cite de Loundres, par suggestion faite au dit nostre seignour le Roi et a son conseil en son parlement tenu a Euerwyk en le terme de Seint Michel l'an de son regne duszyme, ont fait purchaz a defendre qe nul overour des chapeus ne feist ne autres marchauntz faire ferroient chapeus de leyne medle de flockes, ne qe nul marchant, denzein ne alien, tiele marchandie mettreit a vente, sur greve forfeture en lour dit purchatz contenue en a acherraunt lour chapeus de meisne, par ceo q'il vend\i/rent avant lour purchaz fait a 6 d., ore vendent \il a/ 10 d., a lour profiz de meisne e \a/ gref damage de son poeple avauntdit, desicom les marchauntz de Alemaine e des autres terres soleyent mener chapeus faitz de leine et de flockes medles bons et covenables, pur le pris en payaunt au dit nostre seignour le Roi sa due custume, qe amounte grande summe par an. Prie la dite communalte au dit nostre seignour le Roi e a son conseil q'il lui plese mander par son bref au meier et as viscontes de Loundres et aillors en son roialme ou mestier serra si lour purchaz avant dit soit pur lour profit de meisne ou pur \le profit/ de commun poeple de son roialme avant dit, et si trove soit par bone enqueste ne pas de lour affinite qe lour purchaz avantdit soit fait pur lour profit de meisne, en ostaunt nostre seignour le Roi de sa custume avaunt dite, et a damage de son poeple soit anenti et de fait.

> *Response*: Ad inquirendum \[tam per][5] mercatores quam per alios per quos etcetera/ super contentis in ista peticione assignentur W. de Beresford H. de Stauntoun] et G. de Toutheby vel duo eorum, et quod facta inquisicione certificent inde Regem indilate in cancellaria sua etcetera.

Note

The original ordinance, referred to in the petition, was issued at the end of the York parliament of October–December 1318, and dated 6 December 1318 (*CPR 1317–1321*, p. 252). It required that woollen caps be made only of wool, without flock added, and that contravention of the new regulation would result in confiscation of the relevant goods or a money penalty. Several private parties brought petitions against named London cappers at the beginning of the York parliament of May 1319 which were drawn together in a summary of charges declaring the offences to be 'contrary to the estate of the common people' (*contre lestatu de commun poeple*), and the justices Bereford, Staunton and Toutheby were assigned to inquire into the matter on 20 May (SC 8/91/4501; SC 8/140/6981; SC 8/142/7086; C 49/5/21; *CPR, 1317–1321*, p. 369). The petition printed here seems to have been prompted by these proceedings and to have been submitted at the end of the parliament, for subsequently, on 5 July 1319, the crown appointed the same three justices as standing commissioners to regulate the cap trade in London (*CPR, 1317–1321*, p. 374).

---

[5]Conjectural. The mounting of the petition obscures these words.

MERCHANTS, TRADE, AND FINANCE 141

79. The price of foodstuffs during the parliament at York
(SC 8/203/10148)
1322

Summary

The good people and common people in parliament: complaint that since the coming of the king to York the price of meat, fish, and other foods has risen considerably. It is said that regraters in the cities of London and York have been forestalling all manner of meat and fish, with the result that they have trebled in value. They request that the king ordain remedy.

Response: Stephen Segrave, John Pecche, Walter Friskney, and Robert Mablethorpe are to be assigned to enquire without delay of the forestallers and of other things contained in the petition, and of the causes, and to ordain a suitable remedy and punish those who are found culpable.

Text

Fait a monstrer a nostre seignur le Roi et a son counseil pur lui et les bones gentz et le comun poeple qi sont venuz a son parlement; qe tutes maners des viaundes, des chares et des pesshons sont si grevousement encheries puis la venue nostre dit seignur le Roi en ville, q'il ne unz poer de gaires de mer si sour ceo aukune mitigac[ion][6] rien seit faite par le dit nostre seignur le Roi et son conseil. Kar dit est qe les regraters de Loundres qi sont y venuz vont dehors la ville en divers lieus en pais et forstallent tutes maners des viaundes, et par covyn entre eux et les regraters de la cite de Euerwyk les unt si encheri a la treble value de ceo qe chescoune chose valoit a la dite venue nostre seignur le Roi, cest a savoir la ou un karkoys de boef ne valut adonqes qe dis sous, hommes ne peut orez meyns avoir qe deux mars ou vint souz; un cass[7] de motoun qe ne valut adonqes qe deux souz sys deners, si il le vendont ore \a/ quatris souz; un saumon quel homme poeit avoir adonqes pur vynt deners ou deux souz, il le sount ore a cynk souz, et issint tutes autres choses des vitailles vendables il les sont ore a la treble value. Par quei pleise a nostre seignur le Roi pur comon bien de lui et de son poeple avauntdit sur ceste grevaunces comander remedie estre fait.

Response: Assignentur Stephanus de Segrave, Johannes Pecche, Walterus de Friskennie et Robertus de Malberthorp ad

[6]Tear in parchment.
[7]Possibly an abbreviated form of *carcois*.

inquirendum indilate super forstallariis et aliis contentis in peticione, et super causis eorundem, et ad ordinandum remedium super hoc competens, et ad puniendum illos quos invenerint culpabiles.

Note

Regraters were small-scale victuallers who purchased in bulk from retailers in order to sell, often in open air, at enhanced prices. Their practices came, informally, under the more general actions taken against forestalling in the fourteenth century (see no. 74). The positive and negative results of increasing demand for food and services in host cities during visits of the royal household and sessions of parliament and the courts were a matter of frequent comment in the early fourteenth century. This petition can be firmly dated to the York parliament of May 1322 since the commission ordered in the response was appointed on 11 May 1322 (*CPR, 1321–1324*, p. 151). The royal household, along with the king's bench, common pleas, and exchequer, had all been located at York since April 1322, and had also resided there in various combinations from late 1318 to early 1320 (Ormrod 2000: 83). In 1327 the crown again took action during a parliament at York to prevent forestalling and the resulting escalation of prices for foodstuffs in the city (*CPR, 1327–1330*, p. 132; *VCH City of York*, p. 99). Conversely, the people of London and Westminster bemoaned the loss to their own retail trade when parliament and the courts moved to York in the 1320s and 1330s (*CIM*, II, 381; Rosser 1989: 120–121).

80. The tronage of wool (SC 8/168/8399)
1327–*c*.1350

Summary

[No petitioner specified]: the king has granted to various people the tronage of wool in various ports of England for the term of their life, together with the keeping of the tron. This used to be in the keeping of the king's customs officers, who had to render account for all the issues, but they can now only account for what the keepers of the tron report to them, to the king's damage. They request a remedy, so that the customs officers are able to monitor any error in the tronage.

Response: It seems to the council, if it pleases the king, that it would be best if the manner of collection of tax on wool, skins, and hides used in the time of Edward I be kept and maintained, and other offices touching the said matters should be kept in the same state, notwithstanding commissions made to the contrary, which should be repealed if it pleases the king.

Text

A nostre seignur le Roi et a son counseil soit monstre; qe come nostre dit seignur eit done a diverses persones le tronage des leynes en diverses portz d'Engleterre a terme de vie, et ont la trone en lour gard, qe ascun temps soleit estre en la gard des custumers le Roi, qi sont [. . .][8] a nostre dit seignur et deyvent rendre acompt de tote l'issue de la dite trone a lour peril, et ne poent avoir conissaunce del pesage, forqe prendre entrer devers eux ce qe les ditz tronagours lour voillent dire et liverer a lour volunte, saunz estre repris des custumers, a grant damage du Roi. Dont bon serroit qe ascun remedie soit ordene pur nostre dit seignur, issint qe les puissent peser quant ils verront defaut en le tronagour.

Response: Il semble au conseil, s'il plest au Roi, qe bon est qe l'estat et la manere quant a coiller des leines, pealx et quirs qeux estoient en temps l'ael le Roi serroit gardez et meinteinez, et qe les issues des tronur et contr[. . .][9] lour et autres offices tochantz les dites choses seient en meisme l'estat, nient contrestant commissiouns faitz au contrer, queles seient repellez s'il plest au Roi.

Note

The reference to the customs system in the time of the king's grandfather places the petition firmly in the time of Edward III, and the hand suggests a date early in that reign. The separate office of tronager or weigher had not been part of the original customs system set up in 1275, but had already come into use by the end of Edward I's reign (Baker 1961: 7), so the response to this petition suggests that the office was a valid one and ought to be continued. The substantive issue may have been around the practice, which became prevalent under Edward II, of reserving the office of tronager as a sinecure for king's clerks and members of the royal household. In May 1331 the government of Edward III attempted a reform of the customs system, including the dismissal of a number of tronagers (*CPR, 1330–1334*, p. 145; Baker 1961: 23–24). Soon, however, the former

[8] Tear in parchment.
[9] Illegible.

practice prevailed and the office reverted to being an honorific title for members of the royal circle. This common petition may have been provoked by the resulting dispute that took place in parliament in 1331 between two high-profile rivals for the office of tronager of Southampton, Roger Byfleet and Roger Lysewy (Baker 1961: 70–71).

81. The state of the king's highways (SC 8/161/8021)
Mid fourteenth century

Summary

The commonalty: request that justices be assigned throughout the land to survey the defects of the bridges and roads of Watling Street and other high roads so that the defects are identified and repaired, as many people have died because of the aforesaid defects.

Response: The commons have departed from parliament.

Text

A nostre seignur le Roi et a son conseil prie la comunalte qe certeyns iustices soient ordinetz et assignez par tut la terre assurvoir les defautes des ponts et passages de Watlyngestrete et des autres hautes estretz, issint qe les dites defautes soient redresser et reparailler et pur le temps avenir continuez, car plusurs gentz sount pery pur la defautes susditz.

Response: La comune est depar du parlement.

Note

Given the importance attached by the medieval crown and society to the maintenance of roads, it is striking how little this matter features in the parliament rolls of the fourteenth century. This petition, which offers rare evidence of such a concern being articulated in parliament, cannot be dated positively to any particular parliament; the hand suggests that it was written in the middle of the fourteenth century. It may, however, be connected with a commission to inquire into the state of the king's highway of Watling Street issued on 20 October 1339 (*CPR, 1338–1340*, p. 362). The parliament of October 1339 (from which Edward III was absent) ended under unusual circumstances, with no organized submission of common or private petitions and with the commons being dismissed early (by 28 October), before business was finally concluded in early November (*PROME*, IV, 237–238). If the 1339 commission did arise directly or indirectly from this petition, then it could have been deliberately backdated to coincide with the period in which parliament was in full session.

82. The measure of a bushel (SC 8/280/13956)
Mid fourteenth century

Summary

The commons of the land: the king has granted that the measure of a bushel should be the same throughout the realm, but some men go to parts of England and measure their malt greater than the king's standard by half a foot of a man, and pile up each measurement in the bushel so that the buyers cannot tell how much is in it, to the great damage and impoverishment of the people. Request for a remedy, for the love of God.

Response: The statute should be upheld in this case, and anyone who complains will be heard by writ at the common law.

Text

Au counseil nostre seignur le Roi monstre la commune de sa terre; qe come en la graunt [...][10] done qe une mesure de bussel soit et doit estre par tut le roialme, par quele mesure [...] la veignent ascunes gentz en ascunes parties d'Engleterre et fount mesurer lour breys q'ils [...] large en leesse qe l'estandard le Roi par demy pee de homme et fount coumbler chescun [...] sur le bussel, issint qe par la laeure des bussels et le coumbler avantditz les achatours [...] un quarter eynz, a graunt damage et empovrisement du poeple et [. . .] des vendurs [...] en cest cas soit ordeigne pur l'amour de Dieu.

Response: Soit l'estatut en ceo cas ordeyne tenuz, et ceo qe se voillent pleyndre soient oiz par brief a la comune leye.

Note

The hand of the petition suggests a date in the middle of the fourteenth century. Magna Carta had ordained that weights and measures should be standard throughout the realm, and common petitions making general requests for the enforcement of the king's standard were submitted in 1322 and 1324 (see nos 113 and 115; Ormrod 1990a: 6–7). Further common petitions resulted in statutory legislation in

[10] The right-hand edge of the parchment is missing, and the text has worn away in parts.

1340 and 1352 and, on each occasion, campaigns of enforcement in the localities (*RP*, II, 240 = *PROME*, V, 46–47; *SR*, I, 285; Putnam 1950: 72–73; Ormrod 1984: 204–210). The present petition and the response may refer specifically to the 1352 legislation, which detailed that the bushel, half bushel, and peck should be in accordance with the king's standard, and made the additional requirement that measures of corn should be struck and not heaped. Further evidence for a preoccupation about the bushel weight is provided by a common petition of 1354, which requested that a definitive measure for the bushel be made in bronze and kept at the Tower of London (*RP*, II, 260 = *PROME*, V, 108). The fact that the present petition is answered favourably raises questions as to why it is not found enrolled in any of the extant parliament rolls of the period; it is possible that it comes from one of the parliaments held between 1357 and 1360, the official records of which have been lost (*PROME*, V, 130–132).

83. The alnage of cloth (SC 8/135/6708)
1353–1373

Summary

The poor people of the commons: request that the king declare in more detail the statute of 1353 regarding the sale of cloth, which ordained that all manner of cloth of regulation size that was put up for sale before the alnager had sealed it and taken the subsidy should be forfeit to the king. They complain that, on the pretext of this statute, the alnagers seize cloth before it has been worked, fulled and cut to the correct length and width, and before the subsidy can be paid, to the harm of them and the king.

Response: [none].

Text

A nostre seignur le Roi et al counsail de parlement mounstrent les povres de la commune; qe com ordeyne soit par estatut l'an xxvii nostre seignur le Roi q'ore est, qe touz manere draps \d'assise/ qe soient mys a vent devant qe soient sealles par le auneur et la subsidie ent paie, fussent forfaites al Roi, par colour de quel estatut lez auneours levent la subsidie dez draps nyent fulles et mettant lour seal, ou autrement lez seisont com forfaites auxi com ils furent fulles et pleynement oeveres la ou lez ditz draps ne poient porter lour certeyn longurs ne layure devant qeux soient fulles ne le seal endurer encountre l'overaigne. Qe plese a nostre dit seigneur le Roi et al counsail a declarer le dit estatut ensi q'il soit entendu dez draps pleynement oeveres ensi qe lez ditz povres pussent lour draps \vendre/ devant ceo q'ils soient fulles sans estre endamagez par lez dit auneours, et le plus tost qe riens deperra a nostre dit seigneur le Roi, por ceo qe la subsidie pout estre leve lez ditz draps en qi mayns q'ils devyndrent apres q'ils soient fulles et pleynement oeveres et portont lour certeyn longure et layure.

Note

The statute of 1353 referred to in the petition relaxed the previous requirement (discussed at no. 75) that cloth which failed to conform to the assize of 1196 had to be confiscated, and instead allowed that such goods could be sold on condition that they were still assessed by the alnager and that an appropriate fine was paid (*RP*, II, 252 = *PROME*, V, 83–84; *SR*, I, 330–331; Bridbury 1982: 47–48). These arrangements were withdrawn in 1373 (*RP*, II, 318 = *PROME*, V, 280, 288; *SR*, I, 395; Harriss 1975: 458–459). The present petition indicates that the alnagers were attempting to circumvent the 1353 legislation by claiming that cloth sales were taking place before they had applied their quality controls, and that they ought therefore to have the right to confiscate such unlicensed sales. The petition perhaps represents initial problems in the application of the 1353 statute, and was therefore most likely presented in one of the parliaments of the mid 1350s.

84. Selling firewood after a great storm (SC 8/79/3916) *c.*1362

Summary

The commons: whereas a great part of the woods of England were felled by a great tempest, tenants who hold such land for a fixed term, for life or in reversion are unable to sell firewood as they are prevented by writs of trespass and waste, to their great disinheritance and damage. For this reason they request that the king grant them the right to sell the firewood felled within their terms and make a profit.

Response: This is answered elsewhere.

Text

A nostre seignur le Roi et a son conseil prie tout la comune; qecom grant partie de touz les boys d'Engletere soit abatuz par grant tempeste du vent, et termers qi ycelex tiegnent a terme des annz ou a terme de vie ne seoffrent eux en \queux/ la revercioun \est/ le busche issint abatuz deinz lour termes vendre ne lour profit faire, a lour graunt disheritisoun et damage. Par quei plaise a nostre dit seignur et a son conseil de granter q'eux a queux le revercioun apent des termes susdit q'ils peussent le busche issint abatuz deinz lour termes susditz vendre et dycele lour profit faire, depuis q'ils sont forclosez des briefs de trespas et de wast.

Response: Responsum est alibi.

Note

The reference is almost certainly to the great storm known as St Maurus' Wind, in January 1362 (Britton 1937: 144–145), and the petition therefore probably belongs to the parliament of October 1362 or shortly thereafter. The hand supports such a dating. However, the response (given, unusually for this date, in Latin) is oblique, and there is nothing on the extant parliament rolls of the 1360s (or other periods) to indicate that the matter was advanced further.

85. The debts of Queen Philippa (SC 8/104/5166) 1376–1377

Summary

The poor commons: request for payment of the household debts of the late Queen Philippa, and for payment of her servants. The late queen instructed her husband the king to set aside sureties for this purpose from her jewels and goods, to the value of 100,000 marks, and the king pledged to honour these debts; however, these have fallen into the hands of Alice Perrers, and as a result the debts have not been repaid, nor the queen's servants rewarded. They request an ordinance for the payment of these debts, as an act of charity and for the love and honour of the people.

Response: [none].

Text

A nostre seignur le Roi et son noble conseil monstrent aschuns de voz povres communes; qe come aschuns diverses debtes lours sont dues pur vitailes prises de eaux pur despenses del hostiel la noble dame la Reine Philippe qi Dieu assoille, queux debtes le noble Roi son seignur et mari lui promist paier as ditz voz commune et lui acquitez et eaux, et en surete a faire le paiement lui plegges sa foie, a cause de quels le surete et ferme esperance de sa promesse, mesme la bone dame dit de sa bouche, mon seignur vous troveres asses de les acquiter et reguerdoner ses povres servantz, et ceo qeux moneies ie metre en vostre disposicion, qi coust apres son trespassement receust ses iouaux et biens a la value de c. mil marz, dont a ceo q'est dit greindre somme qe toutz ses debtes amontount et qeux suffierent pur reguerdoner ses ditz servantz pur lour longe service et travaile sont devenuz as mains et possession Alice de Perers, par quele cause s'il soit par voie d'achate ou autre manere il est bone q'il soit, et riens unquore acquites ne paiez des ditz debtes, ne ses ditz servantz reguerdonee. Sur quoi voz ditz communes et ses ditz servantz vous supplient q'il vous plese par voie de charte [...]" des abues les ditz bons Roi et Reine, et en eide de ditz povres communes et servantz ordener ceo qe bone conscience et foie demandent touchant les ditz bons, queux la dite Alice ad, \aschun ordenance soit fait/ reguerdoner ses ditz servantz et acquiter les dites debtes, en descharge des ditz ulmes et ensi ferres almoigne gaineres ame et honour du poeple.

Note

The petition dates after the death of Queen Philippa in 1369 and apparently before the death of Edward III in 1377. There was no known public criticism of Edward's mistress, Alice Perrers, before the Good Parliament of April–July 1376, and it is most likely that this petition belongs to that assembly (in which Perrers was disgraced and exiled from court) or to the so-called Bad Parliament of January–March 1377 (by which time she had returned to Edward's side). Perrers was subjected to a second disgrace in the first parliament of Richard II, in October–November 1377; among the goods seized from her on that occasion were large quantities of jewels and pearls, some of which may have come from the deceased queen's collection (Ormrod 2008b). Edward III's household had assumed financial responsibility for that of the queen in 1360 in order to try to address chronic problems around Philippa's debts, and following the latter's death in 1369 the exchequer had made numerous payments to her creditors (Given-Wilson 1978a); however, the petition provides evidence that many had still not received satisfaction by the time of Edward III's death. The petition claims that the sums owed amounted to 100,000 marks (£66,667); given other inflated numbers used in the political crisis of 1376, it may simply be taken to indicate a proverbially large

" Illegible.

sum. In calling attention to the enormity of the queen's debts and insisting on Philippa's personal instruction to her husband to honour her debts, the petition reflects both the emerging mythology of a spendthrift queen and the very strong public affection expressed for Philippa in the years after her death (Ormrod 2011: 127–128, 470–471).

86. Accounts for forfeitures of Scottish money
(SC 8/184/9168)
1377

Summary

The poor commons: complaint that a recent ordinance requires them to account in the exchequer for forfeitures of Scottish money, which is to their great oppression and harm. Each year officials are forced to spend in the region of 2 marks or £2 each on going to the exchequer, but account for nothing. As this ordinance is of no profit to the king, they request that it be revoked, and that a writ be sent to the treasurer and barons of the exchequer ordering them to cease to demand such accounts.

Response: Let the ordinance of 1373 be viewed, and let a writ be issued to the exchequer to discharge them accordingly.

Text

A nostre tresredoute seignur le Roi et les autres seignurs de parlement supplient plusours de voz povres communes; qe come par colour d'une ordinance de la forfaiture a moneie d'Escoce ils sont [...][12] au destreinz d'accompter de mesme la forfaiture, et quant ils veignent al Escheker ils n'ent respoignent rien au Roi, \ne ne poent a cause de l'ordinance de mesme la monoie [...] ordeine q'il courge a meindre pris,/ mes font accomptes de nichil [...] chescun an ils despendent en vaine ascuns xl. soldz et ascuns ii. marcz, et tieles sommes en trop grantz molestes et oppressions de le poeple. [Supplient][13] a voz sages discrecions en ese de vostre poeple eiantz regardz, qe nulle profit sourde de la dite forfaiture, ordeigner qe la dite ordinance soit [devoit][14] ouste, et qe brief soit mande au tresorer et barons de

---

[12] The right-hand side of the parchment is stained, meaning that one or two words are illegible at the end of the first three lines and in the interlinear insertion.
[13] Illegible: supplied from context.
[14] Illegible: supplied from context.

l'escheker q'ils cessent desore a demander acomptes de nulli de la forfaiture avantdite.

Response: Soit l'ordinance ent faite en parlement l'an xlviime le Roi Edward aiel icer veue, et solonc la forme dycelle brief fait a l'Escheqier de lour descharger.

Note

The English parliamentary ordinance of 1373 on Scottish money was the first ever attempt to break the traditional equivalence of the English and Scottish pounds and to create an exchange rate between the two currencies (*RP*, II, 318 = *PROME*, V, 281; *SR*, I, 395; Grant 1984: 80–81; Gemmill and Mayhew 1995: 117). The ordinance itself said nothing about the forfeiture of Scottish money, but it appears from a common petition in the Good Parliament of April–July 1376 that the exchequer had begun thereafter to require that local officials make special account for Scottish coin taken within their jurisdiction (*RP*, II, 336 = *PROME*, V, 328). The reference to the ordinance as having been issued under the king's grandfather clearly dates the present petition to the reign of Richard II. Another similar request was enrolled on the roll for the Gloucester parliament of October–December 1378; this time the crown ordered that the exchequer make inquiry into the accounts required for forfeitures of Scottish money and that those which did not bring profit to the king should be annulled (*RP*, III, 43 = *PROME*, VI, 92). The response to the present petition parallels the latter remedy, but is less emphatic. This petition may therefore have been presented in the first parliament of Richard II, in October–November 1377, though it remains unclear why it was not included on the parliament roll for this assembly. Such a dating reinforces historical arguments about the strong continuity both of commons' membership and of political agendas across the last parliaments of Edward III and the first of Richard II (Lewis 1933: 379–385).

87. The debts of Edward III (SC 8/123/6117)
1378–*c*.1380

Summary

The poor lieges of the city of London and other poor commons of the realm: complaint that many of their number are ruined for default of payment of the late king's debts. It was promised at the parliament of Michaelmas 1377 that the creditors would be paid from the goods of the late king, but not all debts have been paid. Thus they request payment, in light of the great harm done to those creditors and as an example to others.

Response: [none].

Text

A nostre tresredoute seignur le Roi et as nobles seignurs de roialme presentz en ce parlement:
Supplient humblement ses poveres lieges de ses cite de Loundres et autre poveres comunes de son roialme, a graunt noumbre creditours au Roi Edward qi Dieux assoille, aiel nostre seignur le Roi q'ore est; qe come plusours de eux aient de long temps est et ore sont a graunt mescheif et poverete et plusours anientiz et destruitz pur defaute de paiement des deniers a eux duez par le dit Roi l'aiel, et a parlement tenuz a Westminstre a la quinzeine de Seint Michel l'an de q'ore est primere fuist parle et sovent depuis ad este promys qe gree serroit fait as ditz creditours des biens q'estoient au dit Roi l'aiel et les queux pur eux paier ses dettes deviendrent as mains de nostre seignur le Roi q'ore est, et sur ceo ascuns certeins persones de Loundres qi se disoient pursuer pur eux mesmes, et pur toutz les autres creditours lour veisynes et ensesoient au conseille continuel clamour et suyte de iour en iour sont paiez et appesez. Il vous pleise par consideracion de iustice et de equite ordeigner qe gree soit fait a tout le remenant des ditz creditours, especialement come entre eux soient plusours moult grauntment plus anientiz et a meschief pur defaute des deniers a eux duez par le dit Roi l'aiel, qi n'estoient les persones a queux gree est fait come dit est, et qe pur les ditz creditours nient paiez il vous pleise tresnobles seignurs ore avaunt vostre departier du parlement ordeigner et assigner de qoi et coment ils serront paiez, pur la pite de Dieu et en descharge des almes, si bien du Roi l'aiel come de ceux qi ount les ditz biens en poair de faire le dit discharge. Ensi qe vostre bon deliverance et bien faire en celle partie puisse et doie estre bon exemple as ditz poveres et autres pur le temps avenir, d'aprestier plus a busoigne, et ensi come il y ad de qoi et les ditz poveres ount suffrez et suffrent de iour en autre graunt destorbance, damage et anientisement, tancome ils ount este en pursuantz ceste busoigne sibien d'autres lour affaires come del longe delaye de lour paiement.

Note

The parliament referred to in the petition was that of October–November 1377; the first assembly at which this petition can have been submitted thereafter was that of October–November 1378. Petitions on the same issue were received in the parliaments of April–May 1379 and November–December 1380 (*RP*, III, 64, 96 = *PROME*, VI, 129, 204), and this petition is likely to have been submitted around the same time. For comment on Edward III's debts, see no. 92.

88. The rights of English merchants trading in Germany
(SC 8/110/5474)
*c.*1380

Summary

The merchants and commons of the realm: in the present parliament they have presented bills to the king detailing the injuries and mistreatment that they have suffered at the hands of the merchants of the company of the Hanse; they ask that the company answer these, since they seek to have confirmation of a charter of liberties and franchises. The charter contains a clause (cited in Latin) that if English merchants in Germany are not as well treated and able to trade freely as German merchants in England, then the king will annul the charter. Their bills prove that English merchants in Germany are not being as well treated as German merchants in England; request that the king and lords annul the charter, or that the merchants of the Hanse answer for the wrongs they have done and make amends for them, on good security.

Response: [none].

Text

A nostre tresexcellent, trespuissaunt et tresredoute seignur nostre seignur le Roi et a ces honurables seignurs dicest present parlement: Supplient humblement voz humbles lieges les marchauntz et communes de vostre roialme; qe come ils ount presente a vostre hautesse en ceste presente parlement certeins billes des certeins iniuries, tortz, robberiez et autres mesprisiouns faitz a voz ditz lieges par ceux de la compaignie del Hans d'Almaigne, des qeux iniuries, tortz, robberies et mesprisiouns susditz voz ditz lieges ount supplies a vostre dit hautesse qe les ditz persones de la dite compaignie respoig[nen]t,[15] en taunt q'ils pursuent pur avoir une confirmacion d'une chartre des certeins libertes et fraunchises ensealles en vostre chauncerie, quele chartre tresredoute seignur comprent en soi

---

[15] There is a small hole in the parchment here: the text is supplied from context.

mesme icestes paroles, cestassaver qe ceux de la compaignie de Hans d'Almaigne averount les libertees et fraunchises susditz: 'Sub condicione quod mercatores Anglici in partibus ipsorum mercatorum Alemannorum cum illuc venerint cum mercandisis suis adeo amicabiliter et honeste ibidem tractentur, et consimilis condicionis existant et libere mercandizare possint sicut dicti mercatores Alemanni hic in regno Anglie tractantur et existunt et pretextu libertatum in dicta carta contentarum suas libere exercent mercandizas. Et si contrarium dictis mercatoribus Anglie in dictis partibus Alemannie aliqualiter fuerit dominus rex vult et intendit de avisamento consilii sui dictam cartam in omnibus suis articulis libertatibus privilegiis et quitanciis penitus et pro perpetuo revocare et adnullare.' Les queles matiers comprises en les billes de voz ditz lieges provent en soi mesmes la contrarie fait come overtement est declare par les ditz billes, q'il plese a vostre dit hautesse adnuller les libertes et fraunchises avantditz ou autrement qe les ditz persones del companie avauntdit respoignent et amendent par suffisant seurte les iniuries, tortz, robberies et mesprisiouns avantditz, pur Dieu et en oevere de charite.

Note

This petition was previously published (under its former reference) in *Hansische Urkundenbuch*, IV, no. 674, where it was associated with the parliament of January–March 1380. In 1377, the government of Richard II had confirmed various privileges granted to the merchants of the Hanse by Edward I, Edward II, and Edward III (*Hansische Urkundenbuch*, IV, 603), but these were withdrawn a few months later and for several years the extreme pressure brought to bear by the mercantile interests in England meant that there was a stand-off between the English crown and the Hanse (Lloyd 1991: 56–61). At the Gloucester parliament of 1378, the Hanse merchants presented a petition requesting the restoration of their privileges; the crown indicated that it was positive about the prospect but insisted that the rights of English merchants be upheld both in the Hanse towns and in Prussia, Denmark, and Norway (SC 8/18/899 printed in *RP*, III, 52, with the endorsement printed in *Hansische Urkundenbuch*, IV, no. 647). The rationale for dating the present petition to 1380 appears to derive from the reference to a clause that the English should be able to trade as freely in Germany as the Germans did in England, which was subsequently agreed in a settlement with the Hanse in September 1380 (*Hansische Urkundenbuch*, IV, no. 696); although this concession was valuable to the English, it actually provided a more restricted range of guarantees than those demanded by the crown in 1378. It should be noted, however, that the tensions did not end at this point, and that there were significant acts of violence and piracy committed by both sides over the following years, culminating in an open conflict between English and Prussian fleets in the estuary of the Zwin in May 1385, which provoked demands for restitution from English merchants in the parliament of October–December 1385 (*CPR 1385–1389*, p. 61; *PROME*, VII, 29). It is possible, then, that the present petition dates from this later assembly or another around the same time.

The petition is notable for being addressed by 'the merchants and commons of the realm': during the early 1380s there are quite a number of petitions made in parliament, some surviving in originals and some avowed as common petitions and enrolled on the parliament rolls, that were addressed in the name of the 'merchants of the realm' or the 'merchants of England'. These, which focused especially (and not surprisingly) on economic matters, reflected a longer tradition of royal consultations during sessions of parliament and of the council with members of the English mercantile elite summoned in their own right or as representatives of the wider mercantile community (Liddy 2001; Dodd 2002). In the present case, however, the elision of the merchants with the commons represents the growing sense that the citizens and burgesses elected to parliament were themselves rapidly emerging as the primary and authoritative mouthpiece for the commercial interest (Ormrod 2009c: 220–225).

89. Waterways in the east of England (SC 8/101/5045)
*c.*1380

Summary

The commons of the realm: many counties profit by the carriage of wool, corn, wines, victuals, and many other goods via waterways; but these often flood, causing disturbance to ports for lack of a strait through which the water can issue. This is to the great damage of the people of Wiggenhall and Ilsington in Norfolk, and to the counties of Cambridgeshire, Huntingdonshire, Northamptonshire, Bedfordshire, Buckinghamshire, Leicestershire, Warwickshire, Derbyshire, and Suffolk. Request that the king inquire into this matter.

Response: [none].

Text

A nostre seignur le Roi en soun parlement monstrent les comunes de soun realme; coment ils a lour tresgrande ease et profist par diverses ewes decura[nt][...]¹⁶ de diverses countees de dit realme puissent carier leynes, bleds, vineres, vitailles et qeleconqe chose qeux leur plerra as portz [...] de illoeques faire leur profist, et auxi coment diverses ewes donees sibien ryvers, come creteniz de ewes qi vignont par pluvie [...] issue parmy les ditz portz, quelle issue s'il soit desturbe ove en nulle partie estreite plusours des valeiez en diverses parties de [...] defaute de issue des ditz ewes serroit surundez, et les cariages des biens susditz retreez, a tresgrande arerisement et destrucion [...] susditz. Porquei suppliont a nostre dit seignur qe lui plese comander soun consail qe si ascun parsune destreiter ascun port du real[me][...] sibien tielles issues susditz a mier come carriages, en ease et profist des ditz comunes as ditz portz serront dest[...] especial les gentz de Wygenhale et Ilsyngton el countee de Norffolk ount faitz en destruition de port de Le[nne][...] damage des counteez de Canteburgg, Huntyngdon, Northampton, Bedeford, Bukingham, Leicestre, Warrick, Derby et Suffolk [...] garant seit desore graunte saunz ceo qi soit bien et apertement entquiz en diverses countees pluis proscheinz quelle [...] serra sibien as ditz counteez come as ditz portz si ascun tiel estreitement soit faite et miz en execucion et [...] gentz de Wygenhal et Ilsyngton susditz sur ceo est grauntee soit sursiz tanqe il soit entquiz en le manere susdite.

Note

Regular flooding, especially from sea inundation, and the associated damage to property and livelihoods, are well attested in the low-lying areas of eastern England throughout the fourteenth century (Bailey 1991). At the parliament of April–May 1379 the people of Wiggenhall, Ilsington, and other villages in the 'marsh of Norfolk' requested an inquiry into the state of the waterways in their area (SC 8/149/7447). A commission had been set up on 28 May, headed by the earl of Suffolk (*CPR, 1377–1381*, p. 363). The precise outcome of the inquiry is not known, but it appears to provide the context for a further petition from the same group of villages, presumably submitted at the parliament of January–March 1380, suggesting that the people of Lynn were proposing (in a counter-petition, seemingly not extant) a narrowing of the waterway, and that this would have a harmful effect (SC 8/146/7272). The present petition, addressed to 'our lord the king in his parliament', suggests that the representatives of the counties that benefited from the waterways opening into the Wash supported the Norfolk villagers and sought to have the matter included among the

---

¹⁶Approximately 3cm of parchment is missing from the right-hand side of the document, meaning that one or two words are missing from the end of each line.

common petitions of this parliament (or one shortly thereafter). The lack of response, and the fact that no trace of the issue can be found on the parliament rolls of this period, may indicate that the clerks of parliament did not see the case for a local issue to become a matter of common interest to the realm at large, though it is to be noted that a range of other concerns for the keeping of the rivers in the fenlands around the Wash did appear in enrolled common petitions of the late fourteenth century (*RP*, III, 95, 272 = *PROME*, VI, 202-3; VII, 164).

90. The gauge of wines (SC 8/109/5413)
c.1381

Summary

[No petitioners specified]: request that the points of the gauge of wines in the previous statute be more plainly declared, especially concerning the measurement of wines and all manner of other liquids brought into the kingdom. This will enable the deputies of the king to carry out their task more efficiently, which will be to the common profit of the king, the lords, and the commons.

Response: [none].

Text

A tresage counseil nostre seignur le Roy; par ce qe les poyntes de la gauge ne sont overtment declarrez en l'estatut ent fait, qe vous plese ordeigner ore a cest parlement qe la dite gauge d'Engleterre puisse estre enlargez par aioustment a ycell, en especial les nouns de touz maners des licours, queux de reasoun deivent estre gaugez come vyns vermail et blankes, sibien douces come asprez, de queconque roialme ou paiis q'avienent d'estre amesnez deinz cest terre, ovesque meell, oyle et tout maner autre licour viegnent en la roialme en queconque vesseill qe poet estre gauge, issint qe l'execucion de la dite gauge puisse estre pluis pleynement parfaite par les deputes le Roy, qele n'ad este einz ces heures, dont ne poet failler, qe grant comune profit sourdra en temps avenir, sibien au Roi come as touz autres seignurs et comunes de la terre.

Note

The gauge of wines was a system by which quantities of wines imported into England were tested in order to prove that they conformed to the standard volumes in which they would then be sold on to wholesalers and retailers. In the parliament of November–December 1380 the commons requested that the crown elaborate its existing legislation on the types of wine and other liquid commodities subject to the gauge, and a statute resulted (*RP*, III, 79 = *PROME*, VI, 206–207; *SR*, II, 16). Given that it does not name the petitioners and that it is addressed to the council, the petition printed here cannot be definitively associated with parliament, though its assertion of common profit to the lords and commons of the land may suggest such a context (Ormrod 2015). It is most likely therefore to date from the next parliament after 1380, that of November 1381–February 1382, or shortly thereafter.

91. The fishmongers and victuallers of London
(C 49/9/20)
1383

Summary

The commons: request that the king, with the agreement of the lords spiritual and temporal in the present parliament, grant that the mayor and aldermen of the City of London should oversee the assize of all manner of victuals within the liberty of the city, not being in any way restricted by the Statute of Fishmongers made in the last parliament. They ask that they might be able to inspect any victuals, including fish, to ensure that they are of sufficient quality, are sold at a reasonable price, and not in secret but in the appointed places, and that victuallers who are found to be dishonest should be punished as the case requires, without any interference from the statute.

Response: Let it be sent to the lords.
The said statute should be enforced in all other articles.

Text

Prient les comunes; qe please au nostre tressoveraigne seignur le Roy, par le consentment des seignurs espirituelx et temporelx en icest present parlement assemblez et auctorite de mesme le parlement, graunter et ordeiner qe les mair et audermans de la citee de Loundres pur le temps esteantz, qi par raison de leur offices et auxi par force des diverses libertees et fraunchises a mair et citeins de mesme la citee par les tresnobles progenitours du nostre dit soveraigne seignur grauntez et par luy mesmes confermez et en diverses parlementz ratifiez et establiez, deivent garder l'assise de toutz maners vitailles deins la liberte du dite citee, ne soient ascunement par force ou colour de l'estatut des pessoners fait en le darrein parlement restreintz de user lour iurisdictioun touchant la reule et governance de qiconqes vitailles et vitaillers, sibien pesson et pessoners come autres, eins q'ils puissent faire avoir et envoir leur surviewe, serche et assaie de qiconqes vitailles, q'ils soient saives bones et couvenables et venduz au due temps et resonable pris, et nonpas en mussettz mais places overtz a ceo limiters; et les vitaillers q'ils trouverent defectifs a l'encountre de punier et chastier solonc qe le caas requiert et raison demande, saunz estre vexez, molestez ou enquietz par nully soubz colour dicelle parolle, destourbance ou ascunes autres generales paroles contenuz en le darrein estatut avantdit.

> *Response*: Soit baille as seignurs.
> Pur ben toutfoith qe le dit estatut estoyse en sa force en toutz autres articles.

Note

This petition has its background in the bitter disputes between rival factions in the city of London during the early 1380s (Nightingale 1995: 263–291). In the parliament of October 1382, the city officials petitioned for legislation that would severely limit the autonomy of the fishmongers and other victualling trades and thus subject them to the authority of the controversial mayor, John of Northampton (*RP*, III, 141–143 = *PROME*, VI, 301–303). The resulting legislation was enshrined as the so-called Statute of Fishmongers (*SR*, II, 34). At the same time the fishmongers, led by Northampton's rival, Nicholas Exton, successfully sought the protection of the crown against the vengeful instincts of the mayor and his party (*RP*, III, 143 = *PROME*, VI, 304–305). The petition printed here must have been presented at the parliament of February–March 1383, but did not find its way onto the parliament roll, which refers to the ongoing dispute between Northampton and Exton only in a general common petition for the restoration of the franchises of the city of London (*RP*, III, 147 = *PROME*, VI, 316). The present petition, clearly inspired by Northampton, aimed to ensure that the Statute of Fishmongers did not inadvertently restrict the city's control over the victuallers by asserting his right to deal with all issues not clearly covered there 'as the case requires and as reason demands'. The endorsement, although resorting to the legislation of 1382, hints that the lords were otherwise inclined to allow Northampton discretion on doubtful points. The fact that the petition was not enrolled may suggest, however, that the council was reluctant to accept to such a position, possibly because of the inevitable disputes that might then arise over the scope and authority of the statute. The matter was resolved at the parliament of

October–November 1383 by the government's agreement at once to annul the Statute of Fishmongers and to confirm the comprehensive authority of the mayor of London over the victualing trades (*RP*, III, 160, 161 = *PROME*, VI, 345–346, 349–350). This led the victuallers into a direct confrontation with Northampton that resulted in the latter's disgrace, trial, and imprisonment in 1384, for which see no. 68.

92. The debts of Edward III (SC 8/101/5031)
1388

Summary

The poor commons of various cities and boroughs: they have lent great sums of silver for the maintenance of the wars of Edward III, and although the treasurer is aware of these loans, several of them remain unpaid, to their very great impoverishment. They request that the king command the council in the present parliament to arrange repayment of these loans, by assignment or in another manner, in order that the petitioners' condition might be improved, and that they might be able to lend further sums in the future should the necessity arise.

Response: They should make their requests to the executors and administrators of the goods of the said king.

Text

A nostre seignur le Roi et a soun conseil suppliount ces poiveres comunes de diverses citees et burghes; qe come ils apresterunt en meintenance des guerres nostre seignur le Roi, aele nostre seignur le Roi q'or est, grandes sommes d'argente; dount le tresorer nostre dit seignur qi ore est ad tresbon conisaunce de quelles aprestes, plusours de eux ne sount unqore repaiez, a leurs tresgrandes enpoverissementz. Qe plese a leur dit seignur eier compassion as enpoverissementz des ditz comunes, par encheson du desport de leurs ditz aprestes et as grandes \charges/ q'ils ount suffertz en autre manere, de comander son sage consail en ceste present parlement q'ils ordeinent ascun remedie, qe les ditz comunes puissent estre paiez de leurs sommes issint apresteez, par assignement oue en autre manere, en relevement de leurs estatz et q'ils puissent estre de la grendre volunte et poair de leurs biens aprester si tiel si grande necessite surviegne.

Response: Facent lours pursuites as executours ou administres des biens le dit Roi.

Note

Prior to re-sorting in the nineteenth century, this petition was part of an original file of documents relating to the parliament of February–June 1388 (printed in *RP*, III, 255). Both this petition and no. 87 probably allude to the £40,000 of loans that Edward III's government took from the magnates, bishops, ecclesiastical institutions, and urban corporations in 1370 in order to support the recently revived war with France. Because the credit system changed after 1371, with reliance on a small group of brokers centred on key individuals in the royal household, the lenders of 1370 found themselves repeatedly unable to gain satisfaction at the exchequer, and many were still without payment when Edward III died in 1377 (Ormrod 2011: 526–527, 542–544). Common petitions on this matter in the parliaments of April–May 1379 and November–December 1380 had been answered with promises that the new king, Richard II, would deal with the matter as soon as he could; and in 1380 it was reported that most of the debts had now been paid (*RP*, III, 64, 96 = *PROME*, VI, 129, 204). The response to the present petition suggests that, by 1388, the scale of the remaining debt was felt sufficiently contained to be assigned not on the exchequer but on the personal estate of the late king, which was also subject to a protracted settlement under Richard II (Given-Wilson 1978b). However, Edward III's debts were still being cleared in the exchequer in the 1390s (Ormrod 2011: 527).

93. The re-establishment of the customs service at Ipswich (SC 8/118/5865)
1406

Summary

The commons and merchants of England: request that the staple and shipping of wool, hides, and wool-skins from the port of Ipswich might be maintained; if it please the king, that he might ordain and grant in this present parliament for the ease of the merchants that the wool customs and subsidies and the staple and tronage of wool might be the same in the port of Ipswich from this day forth as it was formerly, any letters patent made to the contrary notwithstanding.

> *Response*: The king, with the advice and assent of the lords spiritual and temporal in parliament, has approved this petition, to be in effect until the next parliament.

162   MERCHANTS, TRADE, AND FINANCE

Text

A tresexcellent et tresgracious seignur le Roy:
Suppliont les communes et marchantz d'Engleterre; coment l'estaple et l'eskyppesoun soleit estre des leins, quirs et peaux lanutz save et seure a le port de Eyppewych, que pleise ordeigner et granter en ceste present parlement pur lennes de voz custumes et subsides et pur ease et salvacioun des marchantz et de lour leins, quirs et peaux lanutz qe l'estaple et l'eskippesoun des leins, quirs et peaux lanutz, ove le tronage des leins, soit en mesme le port de Eyppewych de ceo iour enavant come soleit estre avant ces heures, ascunes lettres patentes ent faitz a contraire non obsteantz.

Response: Le Roy, del advys et assent des seignurs espirituelx et temporalx en parlement, ad ottroiez ceste peticioun, adurer tanqe a proschein parlement.

Note

The town of Ipswich campaigned actively in the reign of Henry IV for its right to be a head-port for the royal customs system, and in the process came into competition with the towns of Lynn and Great Yarmouth (Amor 2011: 55–56). In January 1404 Great Yarmouth was granted the right to act as the sole head-port for the counties of Norfolk and Suffolk (*CPR, 1401–1405*, p. 369). At the parliament of October–November 1404, however, the crown consented to a petition of 'the commons and merchants of England', enrolled among the common petitions, and allowed that both Ipswich and Great Yarmouth be open simultaneously until the next parliament (*RP*, III, 555 = *PROME*, VIII, 309; *CPR, 1401–1405*, p. 475). The present petition dates from the next parliament, held in March–December 1406. It is clearly modelled on that of 1404, claiming again to be from the 'commons and merchants of England'. It was not, however, enrolled, but preserved in a file of petitions from this parliament which also included a request from the town of Lynn that it, too, be re-established as a head-port for the customs in wool (SC 8/121/6017). (Both petitions are printed from the originals in *RP*, III, 560 and summarized in *PROME*, VIII, 414.) The crown responded in June 1406 by closing Great Yarmouth and allowing Ipswich and Lynn to export wool until the next parliament (*CPR, 1405–1408*, pp. 188, 209). The petition, like that of 1404, represents the ability of the urban interest to influence proceedings in parliament and have the requests of individual towns articulated as though they were those of the kingdom at large; in the present case, however, the burgesses of Ipswich and their representatives failed to have the petition recorded on the official roll of the 1406 parliament. For another common petition invoking the merchants of the realm, see no. 88.

VI
WAR, RESISTANCE, AND REVOLT

94. Fines by adherents of the Contrariant lords after civil war (SC 8/80/3955)
1322

Summary

The knights of the shires and all the commonalty of the land: request that the king appoint justices to take fines from all those former adherents to the king's rebels and enemies who wish to come forward voluntarily and make fine for their trespass according to their wealth and the quantity of their lands. By this means the king will have profit and the commonalty of his land will be put at ease.

Response: It is the council's opinion that, if it pleases the king, this should be done.
In the presence of the king.

Text

A nostre seignur le Roy priount les chivalers des countez et tote la commune de sa terre; qe luy plese de sa grace assigner auskuys iustices de prendre fyn de touz ceux qe furount aerdaunz a ces rebelles et enemys qe vodrount venir de gree et conustre l'aerdaunce et faire fyn au Roi pur lur trespass is lur power et la quantite de lur terres, et par tieu manere porra le Roi hastivement avoir graunt profist et sa commune de sa terre estre esee.

Response: Avis est au conseil si il plest au Roi qe ceo serreit afaire.
Coram Rege.

Note

At the Battle of Boroughbridge in March 1322, Edward II defeated his cousin, Thomas of Lancaster and the other so-called Contrariants who had rebelled against the king in protest at the growing influence at court of Hugh Despenser the elder and the younger. Lancaster and his principal allies were put to death and their lands were confiscated to the crown ([J.R.]S. Phillips 2010: 394–409; and see no. 33). The parliament that was convened at York in May 1322, in the aftermath of the battle and judicial executions, was the occasion for the present request, aimed at protecting the lives and possessions of Lancaster's lesser adherents and thus limiting the violence of the royal reaction. Notwithstanding the request that fines be assessed according to capacity to pay, those who secured such releases after July 1322 had to offer a very high price (Fryde 1979: 69–77), and in Edward III's first parliament is was decided, as a matter of general discretion, to release from liability those who still owed contributions towards the fines of 1322 (*CCR, 1327–1330*, p. 98; *CMR, 1326–1327*, p. 50 n. 2; Ormrod 2008a: 83). The present petition is notable as an early expression of the idea that the raising of income from the exercise of the royal prerogative would be to the 'ease of the people' by unburdening the 'commonalty of the land' from other fiscal exactions (Ormrod 2015: 236). A previous edition of the petition was published by Davies (1918: 597), and it is translated by Sayles (1988: 365).

95. The ministers of Thomas of Lancaster
(SC 8/144/7193)
1322

Summary

The poor people of the land: complaint about the wrongs and oppressions inflicted upon them by the stewards, bailiffs, and other ministers of Thomas, formerly earl of Lancaster, who levied prises from the people, brought the king's tenants under the jurisdiction of the earl by their power, and took services and customs due to the king. Request that these ministers might not be restored or given office until they are tried by jury.

Response: The king will be advised on the contents of the petition.

Text

A nostre seignur le Roy e a soun counseil prient le povers gents de sa terre; si li plest q'il voille avoir regard de lur estat endreit des counseillers, seneschals, baillifs e autres ministres qe furent ove Sire Thomas, iadis counte de Lancastre, qe menerunt le poeple en graunt angusse par prises e en autre manere torcenousement, e tresterent les tenaunts nostre seignur le Roy denz la fraunchise le count par poer, e leverent de eus servise e custumes avaunt dues al Roy, e moldes autres tortes firent, ausi bien a nostre seignur le Roy com al pople, qe ben serra trove quel houre q'il plest a nostre seignur le Roy a tel ordeyner ses iustices. Dount il prient a nostre seignur le Roy pur son profist demeyen e pur relevacioun de son pople \qe/ teles maners des seneschals e baillifs ne seient recounseillez de court ne mys en offiz, taunke lour estat soit trie par pays, kar taunke il sount si ben de court, e ount tel ados, il entendent nostre seignur le Roy de eus mesmes saunz recoverer.

Response: Rex habebit avisamentum super contentis in peticione.

Note

The petition dates from shortly after the fall and execution of Thomas, earl of Lancaster, in March 1322. It was published in the eighteenth century when it was still preserved in a file of parliamentary petitions dating from the regnal years 15 and 16 Edward II (July 1321–July 1323) (*RP*, I, 394). There are only two parliaments at which it can therefore have been submitted: those held at York in May 1322, and November 1322, for neither of which a parliament roll survives (*PROME*, III, 433–438). The petition employs the confiscation of Lancaster's estates as an opportunity for a general inquiry into alleged oppressions committed by his officials. In that it expresses anxiety about these officials being subject to formal legal process, it is perhaps more likely to date from after the decision in July 1322 to allow those implicated in Lancaster's rebellion to make fine for relief from justice in July 1322 (see no. 94), and may therefore probably be dated to the November parliament. In the aftermath of the civil war of 1321–1322, there were many private petitions claiming compensation against the Lancastrian estate (Ormrod 2008a: 82; Harris 2009; [J.R.]S. Phillips 2010: 415); although the present petition is made in the name of 'the poor people of the land', there is no evidence that it was dealt with in a different manner from those entered by private individuals.

96. The services of the Cinque Ports (SC 8/179/8927) c.1360–c.1385

Summary

The commons of England: in former times, the people of the Cinque Ports had a fleet and exercised power over the sea, so that no nation would dare to attack the realm for fear of their power, for which defence the king's ancestors granted them their franchise and the name of barons of the Cinque Ports, as stated in their charters. They complain that the people of these ports have relinquished their ships and purchased lands and tenements in the country, and thus no longer maintain the defence of the realm for which their franchise was granted; thus they pray remedy.

Response: [none].

Text

A nostre seignur le Roy monstrent la comune d'Engleterre; qe com les gentz des Cink Portz en auncien temps soleyent estre on port de navye et de poair depar la mer, qe nul nacion ne fuist si hardi de grever la roialme pur doute de lour poair avanditz et tele defense fesoient en portz, pur quele bon defense les progeniturs nostre seignur le Roy lour graunta lour fraunchise et lour dona noun des barouns des Cink Portz, en tiele manere pur salvacion de roialme et defense maintener et garder come apiert par les chartres des progeniturs nostre seignur le Roi avanditz a eux grauntez, les queux diont: 'pro salvacione et defensione regni nostri'. Plese a nostre seignur le Roi entendre qe les ditz gentz du portz la fortesse et poair de navye sunt relinquy par purchas de terres et tenementz en pays, issint lour defense et salvacion du roialme pur quele salvacion et defense la franchise lour fuiste graunt, et dount ils priont remedie.

Note

A note on the guard dates this petition to the Good Parliament of 1376. However, although there is a common petition about the Cinque Ports on the parliament roll for that assembly, it is not of the same content as the present one (*RP*, II, 352 = *PROME*, V, 366–367). The rights and privileges of the Cinque Ports had been established throughout the Norman and Angevin periods, and in 1290, in return for service in Wales, Edward I had confirmed these privileges and exempted the barons from various levies and from the jurisdiction of shires and hundreds, in return for providing fifty-seven ships for fifteen days in response to a royal summons (*CChR, 1257–1300*, p. 344). It does not seem that the Cinque Ports ever performed this service in full, and during the fourteenth century their fleet declined; by mid-century, many other ports were providing ships and only Sandwich of the Cinque Ports was able to make any meaningful contribution to English naval efforts (Rodger 1996: 644–646). In spite of this failure to meet their obligations, the Cinque Ports continued to receive their privileges and exemptions.

It seems likely that the present petition dates from the end of the reign of Edward III and the earlier years of Richard II, during which the pressure of naval defence was especially acute, and a recurrent and lively topic of discussion in parliament (Sherborne 1994: 29–53). There is evidence of several complaints about the Cinque Ports being made in parliament in the later part of Edward III's reign and the early years of Richard II's, especially from the two counties – Kent and Sussex – in which the ports lay. In 1363, a commission was appointed in response to a parliamentary petition (no longer extant) from the people of Kent complaining about the barons of the Cinque Ports (*CPR, 1361–1364*, p. 451; *PROME*, V, 171). As well as the 1376 petition (submitted by the people of Sussex and taken up by the commons), there is an enrolled common petition from the parliament of November–December 1380 requesting that the Cinque Ports, together with the palatinate jurisdictions of Cheshire and County Durham, being exempt from ordinary taxation, should nonetheless be charged to aid with defence (*RP*, III, 94 = *PROME*, VI, 199). The present petition accords with the theme found in these cases: that the barons of the Cinque Ports were accumulating lands and liberties instead of contributing the naval power that was the price of their privileges. In the absence of any further contextual evidence, however, it can only be assigned an impressionistic date based on the hand and the wider debate about the state of England's fleet.

97. The problem of fugitive villeins (SC 8/183/9131)
c.1370–c.1400

Summary

The commons of the realm: many villeins escape from their lords and flee to other counties or cities, and by collusion with others obtain false writs of trespass or of contract in those counties against their lords; when their lords claim villeinage, the justices take the inquests in the counties where the villeins are, and where they claim free status, rather than in the counties where they were born. In this way many lords have suffered great disinheritance, and the commons request that the king ordain a suitable remedy.

Response: [none].

Text

A nostre tresredote seignur le Roi prie la commune de son roialme; qe pur ceo qe diverses meschiefs, desheritisons sount avenuz devant ses heures, sibien a seignurs come a plusours autres du roialme, de ceo qe lours neyfs futivis hos de lours seignuries et demurantz en estraunges countees ou grant citees, ount portez brief de trespas ou d'autres contraites devers lours seignurs fayniantz le trespas ou le contraite estre faites en les ditz estraunges countees, par faux covine entre eux et autres de les ditz estraunges countees pur enfrauncher les ditz vileyns, et sur ce grant lours seignurs sont mesnez en respounce, et ount plede qe le dit vileyne ne serra respond, pur [. . .]¹ est lour vileyne de lours maners en le countee ou les ditz vileyns furont neez, et les ditz vileyns ount pledez fraunk et de fraunk estate, les iustices ount usez de prendre l'enquest pur trier la dite vileynage de ditz estraunges countees ou les ditz vileyns issint, par fraude soposent le trespas ou le contrait estre fait et nemy des countees ou les ditz vileynes furont neez, par quel meschief plusours du roialme ount sovent foith desheriteez en grant ensaumple de desheritisoun de touz les seignurs en temps avenir. Qe [ple]² plese a vostre graciouse seignurie ore en ceste present parlement ordiner sur cel meschief covenable remedie.

Note

The problem of runaway serfs was endemic in the fourteenth century and intensified after the Black Death (Hilton 1983). In 1348, at the instigation of parliament, the crown had reformed the process on the writ *exceptio villenagi* in order to make it easier for lords to challenge presumptuous villeins who attempted to take legal proceedings against them in the courts (*RP*, II, 173 = *PROME*, IV, 433, with discussion in *PROME*, IV, 406), and in 1352 parliament successfully secured a promise that, when lords brought writs of neifty claiming rights over fugitive villeins, the accused could not take indefinite refuge by counterclaiming with writs *de liberate probanda* that offered them protection until their status was properly tested by legal process (*RP*, II, 242 = *PROME*, V, 52–53; *SR*, I, 323; Ormrod 1990b: 147). None of this did very much to address the key issue, to which the present petition drew attention, of the difficulties arising when fugitive villeins were residing in counties beyond those where they were born and where their lords needed to claim them in order to assert their seigneurial rights. In the parliaments of November 1373, October–December

¹Tear in parchment (one word missing).
²Crossed out.

1385 and November–December 1391 the commons presented petitions similar in content to the present one, though making more explicit the idea that former villein tenants were often protected by the strong desire of self-governing cities and towns (including London) to uphold the point that serfdom did not run there and that all their inhabitants were free (*RP*, II, 319 = *PROME*, V, 284; *RP*, III, 212 = *PROME*, VII, 23; *RP*, III, 296 = *PROME*, VII, 218–219; Bailey 2014: 299). All of these received evasive answers that suggest some doubt as to whether the common law could provide effectively for the problem. The precise moment at which the present petition was framed remains ambiguous, and it is dated here impressionistically, and on the basis of the hand, to the last quarter of the fourteenth century.

98. Recovery against those taking alleged villeins out of the king's jurisdiction (SC 8/102/5057)
c.1370–*c*.1400

Summary

The commons of the realm: complaint that, throughout the realm, some men have taken others, claiming them to be their villeins, and brought them out of their counties to places where the king's writ does not run, so that the sheriffs are unable to secure *capias* or exigend over them or bring them to answer by distress or in any other manner. They request that the king ordain that *capias* and exigend might be awarded in such cases as in replevin, as was ordained previously by statute, and that this should extend to suits made in the past as well as in times to come.

Response: [none].

Text

A nostre seignour le Roi et a son consail du parlement monstrent la comune de roialme; q'une comune grevance ad este parmy mesme la roialme, avant ces hures de ceo q'ascuns ount pris diverses gentz, seurmettantz les estre lour villeins, et les ount amenes hours des countes ou ils estoient pris et ascun foith aillours, ou brief le Roi ne court pas, issint qe les viscountes ou ils estoient pris n'autres viscountes la brief le Roi court ne poient faire, la deliverance de corps ensi pris par brief de replegiare, sour qi avant ces hures capias et exigend n'ount pas este agardes par la ley sa en arer use, et sovent ceux qe fount tieux prises n'ont terre ne rente n'autres biens, ne lour corps n'ount este troves en mesmes les countes, n'aillours d'estre mene en response par destresse n'en autre manere. Par qi supplie la dite comune qe ordeyne soit qe capias et exigend soit agarde en tiel cas come en replegiare de prise des avers, come est ordeyne avant ces hures par estatut, considerant la meschief estre greyndre de pris de corps de homme si la deliverance ne soit fait de sa franchise prover solonqe la ley de la terre qe des prises des avers ou d'autres biens, et ceste estatut l'estende as prises faites si bien en tepms passe come en temps avener.

Note

The notes on the guard of the original of this petition date it to the late 1370s on the basis of the Record Commission transcription, though there is no other direct evidence to confirm such a dating. The hand is indeed that of the later fourteenth century, and it may be worthy of note that the address to 'the king and council of [the] parliament' is found in private petitions and common petitions enrolled on the parliament rolls that date predominantly from the 1370s to the 1390s (SC 8/18/900; SC 8/22/1053; SC 8/90/4470; SC 8/93/4615; SC 8/94/4666; SC 8/106/5295; SC 8/125/6229; SC 8/129/6426; SC 8/144/7159; SC 8/147/7346; *RP*, II, 347; III, 47 = *PROME*, V, 354; VI, 47). The present petition refers to the provision, under the Statute of Westminster II of 1285, whereby lords who sought to distrain their tenants for services under the process of replevin and found difficulties having the matter settled in lesser courts could have the case removed before the king's justices (*SR*, I, 72). The petition sought to have the same principle applied in actions of *capias* (for the arrest of the defendant) and exigend (the prelude to outlawry).

One reason why the petition was not answered or included among the extant schedules of common petitions on the parliament rolls lies in the apparently tangential comment that those who took away tenants claimed that they were then their own villeins, which would have meant that the defendants in such cases were not immediately subject to the common law. This petition therefore offers an alternative perspective on the issues raised in no. 97, by demonstrating the difficulties faced when lords of free tenants wished to proceed against them in the king's courts but were confounded by others' claims that the persons in question were their villeins. The fact that these two issues existed in tension with each other reflects the general lack of cohesiveness among the proprietary elite as to how to deal with peasant tenants' increasing reluctance, after the Black Death, to fulfil both free and unfree services to those claiming to be their lords (Hatcher and Bailey 2001: 116).

99. Scottish and English prisoners of war
(SC 8/102/5090)
1377

Summary

The commonalty of the realm; request that John Mercer of Edinburgh and many others of Scotland who have been taken and arrested should not be delivered until Thomas de Musgrave and many others, who have been imprisoned in the castle of Dunbar by the earl of Dunbar of Scotland, are delivered.

Response: [none].

Text

A nostre treshonure seignur le Roi et soun counsail priont la comnalte \de soun roialme/; qe come une John Mercer de Edenburgh et plusours autres d'Escoces sont pris et si en meste, q'ils ne soient my deliveres tanqe monseignur Thomas de Musgrave, Thomas de Musgrave le fitz, Thomas de Blencanhop de Helbek, Piers de R[...],[3] William de Stirkland, Roger de Stirwyth et plusours autres soiont delivers, queux sont pris et emprisonez en la chastel de Dunbarre par le count de Dunbarre d'Escocez, le quel ne les voet deliverer en nule manere.

Note

The petition almost certainly belongs to the parliament of October–November 1377. At the beginning of the assembly, instructions were given that John Mercer 'of Scotland' and his unnamed son, currently in the king's custody, be handed over to the earl of Northumberland (in his capacity as a warden of the marches of Scotland) and delivered before the council in the capital (*CCR, 1377–1381*, p. 20). An order allowing Northumberland to claim expenses for this activity was issued 'by the council in parliament' in November (*CCR, 1377–1381*, p. 39). There are issues over whether this is the same John Mercer who, with his son Andrew, was responsible for a series of raids on the east

---

[3] Illegible due to tear in parchment.

coast of England at the end of Edward III's reign and the beginning of Richard II's; the chronicler Thomas Walsingham identified this John as closely connected with the French court (*St Albans Chronicle*, I, 222—227; Campbell 1965: 208 and n. 3). Thomas Musgrave, keeper of Berwick-upon-Tweed, and his grandson (*sic*) Thomas had been taken prisoner near Melrose during a raid into Scotland in the August 1377, and were released on security by the Scottish earl of March after an agreement was reached in January 1378 (Roskell, Clark, and Rawcliffe 1992: III, 810). The present petition therefore represents the anxiety of the polity over the security of the realm in the early months of Richard II's reign and its keen perception of the need to retain valuable prisoners of war for the purposes of negotiation.

100. The ransom of Sir Matthew Gournay (SC 8/103/5114) *c.*1377—*c.*1381

Summary

The commons of the realm of England: Sir Matthew de Gourney fought in the wars of the present king's grandfather in Poitou, and rebuilt as new a castle called *le Herbergement* for the advancement and upkeep of the war and in defence against the king's enemies. He was captured three times in one year, to the great impoverishment of his estate. He then returned to England to obtain counsel and aid from the king, and without warning he and his lieutenant Sir John St Loo were taken and placed in irons in the Tower of London, and kept until they paid the king 3,600 marks sterling. The commons thus beseech the present king to make restitution for the great losses and damages that Sir Matthew has undergone, as an example so that all his subjects might have a greater desire to serve him in his wars in times to come.

Response: [none].

Text

A lour tresredoute seignur le Roi monstrent les comunes de vostre realme d'Engleterre ore a ceste present parlement; qe come un de voz liges Sire Mayheugh de Gourney estoit avant ces heures en les guerres nostre treshonure seignur le Roi vostre ayelle, qi Dieux assoille, es parties de Peyto en quels parties le dit sire Mayheugh fist reparailler et tout de novel edefier un chastel l'en appelle le Herbergement, en encrees et meintenance de voz guerres et en defens de voz enemys, en quel temps le dit sire Mayheugh estoit pris trois foitz en un an en le service nostre dit seignur le Roi vostre ayelle, l'une foitz par tresoun, l'autre foitz enavant devers nostre dit seignur le Roi vostre ayelle par son comandement qant il gist enbataille devant Parys, la tierce foitz enreturnaunt par son comandement pur estre un des reparrons des parties de Peyto ensemblement ove monseignur Guylliem de Feltoun, le quel sire Mayheugh acquita lui mesmes, et tout sa companye qi furent pris ovesqe lui a grant enpoeverissement de son estat, sur qei le dit sire Mayheugh vient en Engleterre a pursure a son dit seignur le Roi le ayelle et a son bon conseill d'avoir ewe eide, remedie et reward de sa grant perde et poevertie q'il avoit suffer, et sodeinement tost apres sa venue en icell parties d'Engleterre le dit sire Mayheugh et ovesqe lui sire Johan Seynloo, q'estoit son lieutenaunt du dit chastel, furent pris et mys en dure prisoun et en feers en le Tour de Londres, et en grant distresse sanz cause et iugement retenuz tanqe le dit sire Mayheugh avoit paie a nostre dit seignur le Roi le ayelle mille mille mille vi. c. marcz d'estirling mitre les despenses le dit sire Mayheugh, de qoi suppliont voz ditz comunes qe vous please de vostre haust et tregraciouse seignurie ordeigner et faire restituissioun des grandz perdes et damages qe vostre dit lige sire Mayheugh ad ewe et suffert par icelles causes, et en descharge del alme nostre dit seignur le Roi vostre ayelle, et en ensample qe touz voz liges eyount le meillour volunte de vous server en voz guerres en temps avenir.

Note

Sir Matthew Gournay (as his name is usually modernized) was a prominent soldier from a minor landed family in Somerset. He had been involved in the war in Brittany and other parts of northern France during the later 1350s and was a conservator of the Anglo-French truce of 1360 (Jones 2004). However, like a number of other English captains operating in northern France, he had refused to abide by the terms of the truce, by continuing to engage in the war of succession in the duchy of Brittany; his arrest and detention in 1361 (along with John St Loo), as well as the fine paid for release, as referred to in this petition, are well attested (*CPR, 1361–1364*, pp. 144, 186). In the Good Parliament of 1376 the commons supported a complaint from Gournay and others about the burden of their service in the wars, and especially the high ransoms that they were forced to pay when taken prisoner (*RP*, II, 343 = *PROME*, V, 344–345). The crown is unlikely to have regarded Gournay's debt on the fine of 3,600 marks as requiring the same consideration it might give to those owing ransoms to foreign captors; but during the following winter, when the king's chief minister William Wykeham was disgraced and put to trial, it was alleged that the fines had been Wykeham's own idea, and were an unwarranted imposition (*Anonimalle Chronicle*, pp. 96–100; Ormrod 2011: 491). Public sympathy for Gournay may therefore have been increasing around the time of Edward III's death, and the present petition represents an attempt by the commons in the early parliaments of Richard II to secure a more lenient policy. It has been argued that the common petition of 1376 that names Gournay was the work of Sir Thomas Fogg, another of those named therein and an MP in the assembly (Ambühl 2013: 207). The present petition is likely to have been the consequence of similar lobbying. Compare the petition made on behalf of Sir Geoffrey Workesley (no. 105).

101. Extortions committed since the Peasants' Revolt (SC 8/98/4885) 1381–*c.*1385

Summary

The poor commoners; lately, in the time of the uprising, wrongdoers committed damages and trespasses against various people. Those who suffered damages have compelled others, by threats to life and limb and by false imprisonment, to make fines and redemptions, some of £40 and some of £20, and others more or less than this, and have taken damages, some of 10 marks, some of 100 marks or £100, and others more or less than this. The parties ruined by these extortions are in no way guilty, and the matter is to the great destruction and perpetual oppression of the commons and against the king's peace. They request that the king and his council ordain in this present parliament a remedy for theses extortions, grievances, and oppressions, and that those who are responsible might be brought before the king and council and duly punished, as a warning to other such extortionists.

Response: [none].

Text

A nostre tresredoute seignur le Roi et soun sage consail ore en ceste presente parlement supplient ses poveres comuners; qe come nadgairs en le temps de rumere diverses meffesours aragez ount faitz diverses damages et trespasez as diversez gentz, et aprez ceo mesmez lez gentz qi ount heus et sustenez lez damagez et grevauncez susdits ount compellez autres diversez gentz par manasce de vie et de membre et par fauce imprisonement de faire a eux fynes et raunceons solomc lour volunte, de mesme ascun a qaraunt livrez, ascun a vynt livrez, ascun a pluis, ascun a meynz, la ou lez ditz gentz issint destruiz et par extorceon anientissez ne furent unqes de rien coupablez; et ascunez preignont pur la damage \de/ dys marcz, cent marcz ou cent lyvres, et issint de graunde a pluis, a graunde destruccion et perpetuele oppression de voz ditz comuners, encontre la peas nostre dit seignur le Roi. Qe plese a nostre tresexcellent seignur le Roi et son sage consail ceo en ceste present parlement de ordeyner a voz ditz comuners dez ditz extorceons grevaunces et oppressions due remedie, restitucion et recoverer, et qe ceux qi ount lez ditz extorceonz et oppressions a voz ditez comuners faitz et lour mayntenours puissent estre devant vous et vostre dit consail si duement punissez, qe autrez tiels extorceoners puissent estre garnez par eux sessez tiels oppressions faire a voz comuners, pur Dieu et en oevre de charite.

Note

The petition reflects the considerable confusion that resulted from the attack on persons and property during the Peasants' Revolt of 1381. In its criticism of those who used the high state of tension resulting from the revolt to extort fines and damages from innocent parties, it reflects the parliamentary commons' concern to ensure that the pursuit of the principal perpetrators of the revolt was tightly focused and did not result in the kinds of irresponsible and vindictive behaviour reported here (Tuck 1984). The petition is otherwise difficult to date but, like others reflecting upon the aftermath of the revolt, seems most likely to have been registered either in the parliament of November 1381–February 1382 or in one of the assemblies of the years immediately following.

102. The criminal status of those put to death during the Peasants' Revolt (SC 8/20/970) 1381–*c*.1385

Summary

The commons of the realm: in the recent uprising of 1381 the leaders — such as Walter Tyler in Kent, Jack Straw in Essex, John Hanchach in Cambridgeshire and Robert Phippe in Huntingdonshire — were not convicted by process of law, but were arrested whilst committing treason and beheaded by the king's ministers in order to prevent their rescue by their followers. The commons request that they be adjudged and declared in this parliament as convicted rebels and felons, just as if this had been done by due process of law, as their heirs are demanding their lands and tenements as if they had died as the king's loyal lieges.

> *Response:* It is agreed in this present parliament that those who were put to death during the insurrection are to be considered as convicted felons.

Text

A tresexcellent et tresredoute prynce nostre seignur le Roy et son tresnoble counsaille en ceste present parlement supplient les comunes de son roialme; qe come en [temps de insurreccion] des comunes en diverses countees d'Engleterre, cestassavoir en les countees d'Essex, Kent, Cantebrigge, Huntyngdoun, l'an de soun regne quarte trayterousement [encountre] lour ligeance soy leverount, come a vostre hautesse et partout la royalme est notoriement conutz, et quex malfesours en les dites countees ascunes de eux lour [furent capitaines], principales, chevynteyns, pur amesner et exiter tous les comunes de royalme a destruer vous lour seignur liege et touz les gentiles de mesme le royalme, come [Wauter] Tylere del countee de Kent, Jakke Strawe en Essex, Johan Hanchach en le counte de Canterbrigge, Robert Phippe en le countee de Huntyngdoun [quex ne furont] par comune cours et processe de ley atteintz, mes fesantz lour dites tresounes prises, par voz ministres pur ceste cause hastiement decollez, pur eschewer rescous des [ditz] chevynteyns par les comunes a eux aerdauntz, as quex meliour resistence adonqe par discrecioun de tieles gentiles ne purreit avoir este fait, pur salvacion de lour [dit seignur liege] et l'estat de son royalme qe les ditz Wauter, Jakke Strawe, Johan Hanchach, Robert Phippe soient aiuggez et declarez en ceste parlement atteintz come rebelles et felounes nostre seignur le Roy encontre lour ligeance, si avaunt come ils ussent estez atteints en lours vies par appel enditement ou altre processe de ley, qar lours heires demandent lours terres et tenementz en manere come ils ussent estez mortz voz loiaux lieges.

> *Response:* Est acorde en cest present parlement qe ceux qeux furent mys a mort en temps de insurreccioun soyent tenuz com felouns convictes.

Note

The petition is printed in full in *RP*, III, 175, where it appears among a series of unenrolled petitions ascribed to the regnal year 7 Richard II (June 1383–June 1384), the date also assigned in the Record Commission transcript. The right-hand side of the original is stained, and the lost text has been recovered using the earlier edition. *PROME*, VII, 29 provides a summary of the petition and assigns it to the parliament of October–December 1385. The reference in the petition to events in the regnal year 4 Richard II (June 1380–June 1381) makes it possible that the petition was submitted as early as the parliament of November 1381–February 1382. It seems most likely, however, to have been the consequence of actions taken in that assembly and that of October–November 1383. In the assembly of 1381–1382, all those who had participated in the Peasants' Revolt of 1381 were permitted to come forward and request pardons, with the exception of 287 named individuals still liable at law for the actions they had undertaken during the uprising (*RP*, III, 103, 111–113 = *PROME*, VI, 222–224, 240–247). In 1382 the commons requested that the pardon be made general and the crown agreed to apply it to all those implicated in the revolt except the 287 men listed in the earlier schedule and a handful of others (*RP*, III, 139 = *PROME*, VI, 295). In the parliament of February–March 1383, the commons aimed to settle continuing uncertainty by asking that no one be excluded from the amnesty except the 287 men named in 1381, and a statute was issued confirming this position in May 1383 (*RP*, III, 147 = *PROME*, VI, 315; *SR*, II, 30–31). The present petition seems to have been made soon after this. The four men named were not among those on the definitive list of excluded persons, and the effect of the 1383 statute was therefore presumably to allow the families of those put to death during the revolt without formal convictions to argue the case that they were included implicitly in the amnesty and thus to recover their property. Of the four named examples given, John Hanchach of Shudy Camps offers the most obvious case where relatives would seek restitution. Hanchach, who was put to death on the orders of Henry Despenser, bishop of Norwich, for his part in the attack on the manors of Thomas Heselden in Cambridgeshire, was a substantial freeholder with some aspiration to gentry status (Hilton 1973: 141, 181, 215; Dobson 1983: 239). It is interesting that the commons were sufficiently sure of the existence of the elusive 'Jack Straw' (whose existence many historians challenge) to be able to name him as one of those whose relatives were also trying to seek recovery of property.

103. Malicious counter-suits in the king's courts following the Peasants' Revolt (SC 8/101/5012) 1381–c.1388

Summary

The liege commons of the realm: complaint that they have suffered great oppressions and mischiefs and loss of goods, lands, and tenements from wrongdoers and their abettors. They have pursued these people in the king's courts; but, by malice and conspiracy, the wrongdoers have indicted them of various felonies and had them imprisoned, and they cannot get released until they produce pledges and sureties that they will pardon the wrongdoers' liability for their earlier actions. The commons request that the lords and council ordain that these pledges and sureties be nullified, that the wrongdoers and their abettors be punished, and that the commons might be able to recover their goods and chattels. They further request that such an ordinance be held lawful from 1 May 1381, the time of the uprising of the commons of England.

Response: [none].

Text

As tresgraciouses seignours et chivalers de touz le counteez d'Englet[er]re[4] en cest present parlement ensemblez supplient treshumblement et requirent les lieges comunes de la roialme; qe come les ditz lieges comunes ont suffrez grandez oppressions et meschiefs, desheritesons et perdes de lour biens, terres et tenementz ove chateux par les meffesours, abbettours et lour maintenours du dit roialme, dount ces heures dont les ditz lieges comunes ont longement pursuiez en les courtz nostre seignur le Roi pur lour ditz terres, tenementz, biens et chateulx recover, sur quel les ditz meffesours ont de lour grande malice et conspiracie faitz torcenousement enditer les ditz lieges comunes de diversez feloniez, a cause de forbarrer et excluder lez ditz lieges comunes de lour droit et pursuite recover en les courtz suisditz, par colour des quels enditementz ont pris les ditz lieges comunes et meignes al prisone, et illoeques ont durement a grandez meschiefs et oppresions, tenuz tanqe les ditz lieges comunes troveront plegges et certeignez seurtes de pardoner et relesser as ditz meffesours toutz lours acciouns par eux faitz as ditz lieges communes. Qe plese

---

[4] The scribe omitted the 'er' abbreviation.

a nostre tresnobles seignuries et tressages conseille d'ordeigner qe tieux obligaciouns, seurtez ou autres escutz ensi grande oppression des ditz lieges comunes soient tenuz par nuls sur certeigne peine, qe les abbettours et les meyntenours des ditz meffesours soient punisez et eient mesme le punissement come les ditz meffesours, et ensi ordeigner qe les ditz lieges comunes puissent lour biens et chateux ensi pardux recoverer, par cause del prisonement avantdit, et qe cest ordeignance teigne lieu auxibien du primer iour de Maii l'an du regne le Roi Richard quart, du temps del insurreccioun des comunes de Engleterre, come en temps avenir.

Note

The petition refers explicitly to the Peasants' Revolt of 1381 in requesting that an ordinance be issued, backdated to the eve of the uprising, addressing the problem raised here: that is, of defendants in cases before the king's courts taking out malicious actions against the plaintiffs in order to compromise or invalidate the latters' causes. The problem has nothing in itself to do with the rising of 1381, although there is some inference that the 'wrongdoers' who abuse the 'liege commons' in this way were of inferior social status. The parliament of November 1381–February 1382 fixed 1 May 1381 as the *terminus a quo* for offences related to the rebellion that were covered under the terms of the general pardon offered by the government of Richard II (*RP*, III, 103 = *PROME*, VI, 223–224; Lacey 2009: 152), and the present petition clearly references this. The mention of 'King Richard' rather than 'the king who now is' might suggest that the petition dates after 1399. However, the debates in parliament on the implications and consequences of the Peasants' Revolt were most intense in the years down to 1388 (Tuck 1984). The argument for an early dating is also borne out, at least to a degree, by the unusual address clause: 'To most gracious lords and the knights of all the counties of England assembled in this present parliament'. Petitions addressed jointly to the lords and commons seem first to have developed during the effective minority of Richard II, and other early cases of address to the knights, rather than to the whole of the commons, have been noted (Myers 1985: 14–15). In the early fifteenth century, by contrast, it was much more usual for petitions to be addressed to the lords *or* to the commons (Dodd 2007: 166–187). The petition thus represents an interesting case of one group claiming to act for the 'liege commons' seeking to have its case taken up by another group within the parliamentary commons, and apparently failing in the process.

104. Rights of freeholders ejected during the Peasants' Revolt (SC 8/102/5088)
1381–c.1388

Summary

The commons of England: in the recent revolt many people of the realm have been ousted from their freeholds, rents, and services, including men of the Church, and even now are detained from their possessions without due cause and by force. They request that the king and lords in parliament ordain that all those who are ousted from their freeholds might be restored to their tenements without any further process sued against the said intruders and occupiers, and that no man of any rank be so bold as to keep such possessions, on pain of forfeiture and imprisonment. They further request that writs might be sent from the Chancery to the sheriffs in each county where such a case has occurred, and that those ousted might have seisin of their properties and be able to pursue their rights by the common law.

Response: [none].

Text

A nostre tresredoute seignur nostre seignur le Roi et as seignours de parlement monstront ses comunes d'Engleterre; qe come en le grant rumour ore tard et puis le comencement de cest present parlement sibien come devant, plusours gentz de mesme le roialme sont oustez de lours frankes tenementz, rentz et services, sibien gentz de seinte eglise come d'autre en plusours lieux parmy le dit roialme, et unqore sont voluntrivement detenuz hors par fortmain en maintenance de lours maufaitz. Qe pleise a nostre dit seignur le Roi et as ditz seignours du parlement d'ordeingner qe touz ceux queux sont oustez de lours frankes tenementz come dit est soient restitutz a lours tenements sanz pluis outre processe assuer vers les ditz intrusours et occupeours, et qe nul homme de quele condicioun q'il soit, soit hardy en avant de deteiner ne maintener tiels possessions sur peine de forfeiture de terres, biens et chateux au Roy et corps a perpetuele prisone, et qe brief hors de la chancellarie nostre dit seignur le Roy soit directe as viscontz de chescun countee du roialme ou tiel cas est avenuz al instaunz de ceux qeux sont oustez pur les metter en possession et seissine peisibille des ditz tenementz come en lour primer estat, et si les ditz entrours par le maner avont droit pursuont par le commune leye.

WAR, RESISTANCE, AND REVOLT   183

Note

The specific mention of *le grant rumour* – 'the Great Rumour' – may suggest that the petition refers to the series of confrontations that took place in the south of England during 1377 between feudal lords (including some important ecclesiastical institutions) and their unfree tenants (Faith 1984). However, the concerns expressed over this episode in the parliament of October–November 1377 were focused on the challenge to lords' rights to command labour services from villeins, rather than on the preoccupations of the present petition, which are about the unlawful seizure of property. It seems more plausible, therefore, that the petition refers to the Peasants' Revolt of 1381, which was itself referred to regularly in the first parliament after the rising as *le grant rumour* (*RP*, III, 98–100, 106 = *PROME*, VI, 214–217, 229). The Record Commission transcription of the petition also assigned it to the regnal year 5 Richard II (June 1381–June 1382), though this may have been informed by its contents as much as by its archival location. The debates on the implications and consequences of the Peasants' Revolt were most intense in the parliaments from 1381 to 1388 (Tuck 1984), and it is likely that this petition, though not incorporated into the enrolled common petitions of this period and not immediately referenced elsewhere, was part of that more general discussion.

105. The ransom of Sir Geoffrey Workesley
(SC 8/103/5109)
*c.*1381

Summary

The commons of the realm of England: concerning the king's humble servant Geoffrey de Workesley, who has served for a long time as squire and knight to the king, his father, and his grandfather, and has been often taken and ransomed in the king's wars, because of which he is in great debt. He obtained advancement through marriage to the daughter of Thomas de Felton, but while he was overseas in the king's service his servant, Thomas Pulle, defiled his wife and encouraged her to obtain a divorce, by which falsity and treason Geoffrey has lost the advantage of his marriage and his inheritance. It is well known that when Geoffrey and Thomas met at Reading at the recent council, a dispute arose between them in which Thomas was wounded, but that he recovered from this wound. Thomas is now dead, and his friends seek to impeach Geoffrey for his death, saying it was caused by this wound. Considering these circumstances, the petitioners request that the king take Geoffrey into his grace and give him a pardon as a work of charity.

Response: [none].

Text

A nostre tresgracious et tresredoute seignur le Roy prient les comunes de vostre roialme d'Engleterre; qe come vostre petit bachiler Geffrai de Workesley eit servi de long temps en estat de esquier et en estat de chivaler a luy noble et puissant seignur et prince vostre pier, de qi le dit Geffrey prist son ordre de chivaler a le bataille d'Espaigne, et aussi a luy noble et puissant Roy vostre aiel, et depuis a vous en voz guerres tout son temps, en quelles ad este sovent foitz pris de guerre et n'ad reguerdoun ne relevement avant ces heures, paront il est mis a grant meschief et est endettez a somme nient portable, et nadgairs le dit Geffrey et la fille et une des heirs de monseignur Thomas de Feltoun feurent mariez ensemble pur avancement du dit Geffrey, le quel Geffrey pluseurs ans apres le mariage continuee pur la grant affiance q'il avoit en une Thomas Pulle son servant a temps q'il passa outre mere en vostre service, assigna le dit Thomas d'estre entendant a sa dit femme pur la sauve et honeste garde de mesme sa femme en sa absence, li quele Thomas Pulle come fauce et traitere a son dit mestre fit vileine a soun meistre et [parmist][5] defoilla sa femme en sa absence, et entre ce procura et excita la dite femme pur faire faucement une devorce entre le dit Geffrey et sa femme, par quel faucete et treson il ad perdue son avancement de son mariage d'une grant heritage, come overtement est connu apres le temps les ditz Geffrey et Thomas encontrerent a Redyng a darreine conseil illoeqes et sur le dit cause paroles sourdrent entre eux si qe le dit Thomas feuste naufreez, de quelle plaie le dit Thomas feust garrez come sembla a plusours gentz, et a la et chivacha overtment et depuis esposa la dit femme, par quelle esposaille chescun homme purret bien coniser la faucine et treson du dit Thomas, mes ore le dit Thomas est mort, et les amys du dit Thomas pur empecher le dit Geffrey diont q'il morist de la plaie susdit, la ou il morust en son propre defaut et nemy de la play. Par quoy pleise a vostre hautesse et noble seignurie considerer les grandes causes suisdites et sur ceo prendre le dit Geffrey a vostre benigne grace et mercy et luy ent faire vostre gracious pardoun oevere de charite.

---

[5] Illegible due to tear in parchment: supplied from Record Commission Transcript, PRO 31/7/107, no. 12.

Note

Sir Geoffrey Workesley (sometimes modernised as Worsley) was a Lancashire knight who served with Edward III in France in the 1350s and the Black Prince in Castile in the 1360s, and made an advantageous marriage with Mary, the heiress of Thomas Felton, a fellow-soldier who completed his career as long-serving seneschal of English Gascony. Geoffrey was taken prisoner by the French at Pontvallain in 1370 and put to ransom (Walker 1990: 75). Much of the rest of his career was spent abroad attempting to build up the financial resources required to settle debts accumulated in the payment of this ransom. His plight was recounted in a common petition on the parliament roll for the Good Parliament of 1376, which named a number of career soldiers who were in difficulty as a result of high ransom demands (*RP*, II, 343 = *PROME*, V, 344–345; Ambühl 2013: 207). When transcribed by the Record Commission, the present petition was thought to date from the regnal year 5 Richard II (June 1381–June 1382). Internal evidence also supports its specific allocation to the parliament of November 1381–February 1382, or soon thereafter; the reference to a great council held recently at Reading most likely relates to the assembly summoned there in August 1381, the same month in which Workesley was retained by John of Gaunt, duke of Lancaster (*Westminster Chronicle*, pp. 18–21; Walker 1990: 75, 283). It has been argued that the 1376 common petition was engineered by one of Workesley's associates and an MP in the relevant assembly, Sir Thomas Fogg (Ambühl 2013: 207), and the present petition may have arisen from similar lobbying in 1381.

Geoffrey Workesley died in early 1385, after which further disputes continued over his and his wife's inheritances (*VCH Lancs*, IV, 376–392; Walker 1990: 162). The dispute during his own lifetime with Thomas Pulle is not attested in other sources, but a petition submitted by Geoffrey's kinsman Robert, later in the 1380s, claims that Mary Felton had entered a nunnery and was then seeking to annul her monastic vows in order to reclaim her lands (SC 8/146/7276).

106. Villeins participating in Bishop Despenser's crusade (SC 8/102/5087) 1383

Summary

The commons in parliament: many villeins recently rose against their lords with the purpose of obtaining their freedom, on which remedy was made in parliament; but many villeins and neifs in various counties are now setting out to cross the sea with the bishop of Norwich to be free of their lords. They request common remedy, such that lords may delay and prevent their villeins from the voyage according to the law of the land without incurring the penalties of the papal bull granted to the bishop.

Response: [none].

Text

A nostre seignur le Roy supplient les comunes en ceste presente parlemente; qe come plusours vileins et neifs nadgairs leverunt en countre lour seignurs a purpos d'estre enfranchis, a quel temps bone remedie yfuist ordeigne en parlement, par quey plusours vileinz et neyfs de la terre en diverses countez soy ordeneints du passer la meer ove l'evesque de Northwych en ceste viage par cause d'estre alarge de lour seignurs. Qe please d'ordeigner commune remedie issint qe lez seignurs ypuissent arester et destourber lour vileins et neyfs du lour passage soloume ceo qe la ley de la terre ad este usee de tut temps, issint qe lez ditz seignurs n'encourgent la sentence par force de la bull grante par la pape al dit evesque.

Note

Late in 1382 it was agreed that Henry Despenser, Bishop of Norwich, would lead an English military expedition against the count of Flanders, Louis of Male; because the governments of Richard II and Louis supported different sides in the papal schism, Despenser was able to persuade Urban VI to give the campaign the status of a crusade. Over the winter of 1382–1383 significant numbers of people in England, from a wide variety of social backgrounds, sought to participate and reap the rewards of salvation (Housley 1996: 90–98; Saul 1997: 102–105). The petition dates from the parliament of February–March 1383, at which the advanced preparations for the campaign were discussed (*RP*, III, 144–146 = *PROME*, VI, 309–313). The opening clauses, referring to the recent Peasants' Revolt and to the formal repeal, in the parliament of November 1381–February 1382, of the manumissions of villeinage that had been temporarily conceded by the young king during that crisis (*RP*, III, 100 = *PROME*, VI, 216), were clearly meant to add force to an argument that villeins be debarred from participating in the crusade. The absence of a response and the non-enrolment of the petition on the parliament roll, however, strongly suggest that the royal council, and especially the ecclesiastical element within it, was not convinced either of the appropriateness of disqualifying the unfree from involvement or, indeed, of its ability to protect lords from liability to the excommunication that was known to befall those impeding the course of this crusade.

107. Fugitive villeins taking refuge in boroughs
(SC 8/22/1070)
1397

Summary

The commons: request for remedy in the situation where villeins belonging to lords, bishops, abbots, priors, and others flee to market towns, which claim that their franchises give them the right to detain such people. As a result, the lords are unable to take them back, to their great damage and disinheritance; and many lords do not dare to constrain their villeins to perform their services for fear that they will flee.

Response: [Let it be sent] to the lords.

Text

A nostre tresdoute seignur le Roy et a lez seignurs de cet present parlement suppliont les comunies; qe pur la ou ore tarde les veleines dez seignurs, evesqes, abbes, priours et autres gentiles de realme fuount de iour en autre as veiles marchauntes, qi claimont deteneir teils veleins par lour frauncheys et les teignont ensy forcibelement, qe lez seignurs a qi lez veleines sount ne powerent eux reavoir, a graunt disheritesoun du ditz seignurs et genteiles, et a graunt damage de iour en autre de ceo ent veint, pur ceo qe les veleines qi sount ore en possessions du ditz seignurs et genteiles veiount qe nuile remedie est fait de ceux qi sount feuez as ditz veiles marchauntes, yssint qe ore plusours veleines contredeiont defaire lour services et custumes a lour seignurs, et lour seignurs n'oisount eux constraindre de faire[6] lour service pur doute de lour fuist avauntditz. Qe pleise du ordeigner remedie pur eschewer le disheritesoun et damage qe purroit ent avenir.

Response: As seignurs.[7]

---

[6]The words 'de faire' are written as a single word in the original, but divided here for clarity of meaning.
[7]Written on the face at the head of the petition.

188

Note

The petition is printed in full in *RP*, III, 448, among a group of unenrolled petitions assigned to the parliament of October–November 1399. In fact, these all belong to the parliament of January–February 1397: see *PROME*, VII, 329, where the present petition is summarized. The address to the king and lords is symptomatic of the process by which common petitions were referred to the lords for approval before going to the king and council for a final decision; the note 'As seignurs' above the body of the petition is a contraction of 'Soit baille as seigneurs', denoting the decision to send the petition on to the lords, which first appeared in the 1390s (Myers 1985: 64; Dodd 2007: 169).

Throughout the fourteenth century, but especially after the Black Death, there were concerns over unfree tenants leaving their manors without permission and taking refuge in enfranchised towns where custom required that all inhabitants be free (Hilton 1983). A common petition in the parliament of November–December 1373 about villeins fleeing to London is a notable case in point (*RP*, II, 319 = *PROME*, V, 284). The issue seems to have escalated after the Peasants' Revolt of 1381. A petition on the matter in the parliament of October–December 1385 resulted in legislation attempting to uphold the residual rights of lords over alleged villeins who used their residence in cities and towns to sue them in the courts (*RP*, III, 212 = *PROME*, VII, 23; *SR*, II, 38), but further petitions on the matter in the parliaments of November–December 1391 and September–November 1402 suggest that little changed (*RP*, III, 296, 499 = *PROME*, VII, 218–219; VIII, 189; Bailey 2014: 299). The present petition is more concerned than others of the period with the actual recovery of the persons and enforcement of services from runaway villeins, and represents something of a last-ditch attempt to enforce serfdom before its general collapse in the fifteenth century.

108. Scottish raids on the northern counties
(SC 8/22/1090)
1402

Summary

The commons of the realm: complaint that the counties of Northumberland, Cumberland, and Newcastle upon Tyne are greatly impoverished by attacks from and expeditions against the Scots, destruction of goods, chattels, towns, and bridges by sudden floods, charges laid on Newcastle upon Tyne to find victuals and ships for the king and to provide a hundred watchmen on the city walls each night, and losses in hosts and expeditions, as a result of which a thousand or more people have fled out of the area. They request that these counties be discharged of all escapes of felons, fines, issues, amercements, tenths and fifteenths, debts, loans, accounts, and arrears of tenths and fifteenths, debts, loans and accounts, whether tried or not determined, and that they might have an allowance for this in the exchequer, so that they might be able to repair their estates and defend their borders in times to come.

Response: The king has granted this petition according to its tenor.

Text

A nostre tresredoute et tresexcellent seignur le Roy: [...]

Supplient voz humblez legez voz comons de vostre roialme ore assemblez, en relevacioun de voz contez de Northumberland, Cumbr' et Novell Chastell [sur Tyne, de touz lour perdes et] meschiefes [ore tarde hewes par] l'Escoce, cestassavoire des graundes chivachez et arsures sur eux par l'Escoce grauntez, chivachez par eux hors de lour contes [envers l'Escoce, destruccions des biens, chateux, villes et pontes par soddeigne creteigne] d'ewe, trover des plusours niefs par Novell Chastell bien vitailles et armes sur la mer, fesantz agaitz sur les murs de Novell Chastell par [cent persones chescun noet, de par plusours autres grauntz perdes] par hostes chivachaucez, sibien ore tarde \par le/ lieutenant [et] par autres grauntez hostez devant, par cause de quex perdes et mischiefs mille [persones et outre sont fuez hors du pais. Qe plezse a vostre roiale maieste] pardoner au voz dictes trois contes, et au chescun persoun des mesmes les contes relessier et dischargier au cest foith touz maneres des [eschapes des felonyes, fynes, issuez et amerciementz, touz maneres des] dismes, quinszymes, dettes, prestes et acomptes, et arrerages des dismes, quinszymes, prestes et d'acomptes, triez ou nient terminez, et d'ent [d'estre allowes en vostre Escheqer, par cause des queux grace et pardons] voz dictes lieges puissant avoire greindre volunte en lour pais de reparer, et lour terres et heritages de gayner, et mueth parter lour chargez, et defendre [lour marchez en temps a venir, pur Dieu et en oevre de charite].

Response: Le Roy ad grantez ceste peticioun selonc le purport d'icell.

Note

The petition was printed in the eighteenth century, when it was still in a file annotated as belonging to the parliament of

September–November 1402 (*RP*, III, 518, summarized in *PROME*, VIII, 218); it is re-edited here, though text now irrecoverable as a result of staining has been supplied from the earlier edition. It is the only petition in the 1402 file to have been made in the name of the commons, the others being from private individuals and corporations; the inference is that, in spite of its 'common' status, it was heard by the triers of private petitions rather than being sent on to the king and council and then being included among the enrolled common petitions for the assembly. There was a long tradition across the fourteenth century of requests made in parliament for reduction of the fiscal burden on the northern counties in recognition of the poverty they experienced through Scottish raids (*Northern Petitions*, pp. 135–136, 154–157; *AP Northumberland*, pp. 210–211, 219–222; Willard 1908; Briggs 2005). Under Richard II there were a number of requests for remissions made on behalf of the people of Northumberland, Cumberland, and Westmorland (in various combinations) that were adopted and enrolled as common petitions (*RP*, III, 80–81, 270–271, 280, 295 = *PROME*, VI, 166; VII, 160–161, 181, 216). Under Henry IV, however, such petitions – even when, as here, explicitly adopted by the commons – tended not to be written up on the parliament roll and simply resulted in the appropriate statements of exemption recorded on the patent rolls (*CPR, 1399–1401*, pp. 444, 449, 453; *CPR, 1401–1405*, pp. 381, 465, 468; *CPR 1405–1408*, p. 380; *CPR, 1408–1413*, p. 192); the present petition resulted in one such action, issued on 20 November 1402 (*CPR, 1401–1405*, pp. 181–182). It was now usual only to enrol petitions that called for extraordinary special measures in relation to the economy, security, and good order of the northern counties (*RP*, III, 639, 662 = *PROME*, VIII, 491, 548–549). The routinized approach to granting fiscal exemptions through letters patent to the county communities of Northumberland, Cumberland, and Westmorland continued under Henry V (Ormrod 2013a: 199).

VII
MULTIPLE PETITIONS

109. Common petition in nineteen parts (SC 8/155/7740)
*c.*1305–*c.*1331

Summary

[No petitioners specified]:
1. The king's estate and the peace of the realm.
2. Purveyance not to be taken by anyone except the king, and paid for within forty days.
3. [Purveyance not to be taken against the will of the provider.]
4. The assize of bread and ale to be properly maintained.
5. [Conspiracy.]
6. For the common profit of the realm, no reprieve should be granted in cases of robbery and murder committed openly in the kingdom against the king's estate and to the damage of his people.
7. The king should forbid threats to life and chattels, and battery, since these often lead to homicide, on which point trailbaston is too lenient.
8. No undue interference in assizes by lords, and that the king make inquiry by good and loyal men; the people cry and pray remedy, for God.
9. [Curfew in cities and boroughs.]
10. [Murders committed in country areas at night; taverns and liquor.]
11. Constables to be attentive to their responsibility for keeping the peace.
12. That the requirements of the Statute of Winchester regarding the night watch be enforced; great damage occurs to land from neglect of this point.

13. That the king should ordain regarding ravishment of women, which is widespread, and on which the people pray remedy.

14. That no sheriff or coroner have office unless . . . he serve the people, and that he not appoint deputies.

15. [Peaceful passage through the realm.]

16. [?Military service.]

17. [Felony and trespass.]

18. [?]

19. [Counterfeit money.]

   Response: [none].

Text

[A nostre seignur] le Reoy:

1. Qe la Roy et son conseil voyllont ordeyner qe l'estat le Roy soyt [. . .] son people [. . .] vivere en pes et par ley de la terre et [pur destruccion de lour][. . .] par prisis.

2. Qe nul ne preyngne prisis en la terre forqe le Roi a sa [. . .] et de ceo estre payez le dens le qarante iours.

3. Item; qe nul ne entre en [. . .] meson soit autre [. . .] de seignur de l'ostel ne reyn de luy ne preynant autre sa volante.

4. Item; qe l'asise de [. . .] et de serveyse seyt autrement garde qe ne est done [. . .] au grant damage.

5. Item; qe les fraternetes et les conspiraiturs [. . .] borowe [. . .] quis par bon instuit et leaux [. . .] sanz nul [. . .] seyent a la volunte le [. . .] ne qe iammes teuz ne seyent en enqueste [. . .] ne en [. . .] serra prise ne nul de lour asante.

6. Item; qe le [. . .] pur son profit et le comun profit de son realm sanz nul desport faire de robbours et meurdresours fait apertement en son realme contre l'estat le Roi et au \affray/ et damage de son people, qe par tiel affrai et damage purra sourdre atre en son realme.

7. Item; qe le Roy defende manas de vie et de meuble et baterie en son [rea]lme, qe par batrie et manas veynt omycide qe tralbaston pase trop leger sanz reson.

8. Item; qe le Roy ordeyne qe nul homme de seygnury ne se melle des [assise] suie se touche sa persone propre ne ne[1] qe nyle ne \en/preynant clamure pur deseriter le tenauntz par leie, et apres l'asise passe si avera le meyntenour la terre a grant damage de people, et qe le Roy face enquere par bons et leaux tiels et fra son profit qe assez il ount tiels si il asassent pleindre, dont le people crie et prie pur Dieu remedie.

9. Item; qe [...] ne seyt overte en cite ne en borou apres courfu.

10. Item; [...] ne seyt morte sur opelond du solayl rescoursaunt tanke [...] et si un uyt trove autre seyt la taverne a la volunte le Roy [...] vyn seyt serveyse ou autre licour qe a tavernis dens la nut sy venent les robberies et les mourdris et autre grant maus en la terre.

11. Item; qe les conestables qe ount la pes agarder, qe il payent charge qe il gardent autrement la.

12. Item; qe il ne fount a qe les veylles se facent solom l'estatut de Wincestre, ou grant damage vient en la terre par defaute de garde.

13. Item; qe le Roy ordene de ravisement de femmys qe hom use partoute la terre communement, a grant defayt du Roi et touz les granz de la terre et damage des almys et de coers a les persoins; dont le poeple prie de ceo remedie.

14. Item; qe nul viscount ne coroner ne seyt sy il ne seyt home [...] [...]aunt en pais pur servir le people, et en nul outre office pees du Roy et coun[sel] bons et leaux, et qe il ne eyt nul lutenaunt.

15. Item; qe [...] et prive pur [...] passer parmy la terre autre si beyn parmy citez et borows cum par [...] et [...] en la terre sauns estre despitousement a resconue en areste mes si il ey fait chose [...] faire ne dust [...] iescune a forme de ley pur l'estat le Roy sawer, et ne nyle a toller le Roy [...] qe beyn le fait qaunt mesmes prent vengaunce cum [...] et autel parmy la terre.

16. Item; qe quel oure qe la Roy [...] ne y voynent a force [...] en [...] seygnur [...] pur servir le [...] du Rey et de realm.

17. Item; [...] avant le parlement si par felonie ou trespas [...] este use pur [...] au Rey et a les grans de la terre et par cas a tous le realme.

---

[1] The second 'ne' is probably a scribal error arising from a line break between the repeated 'ne's.

18. Item; qe nul [...] home ne femme ne [...] outre une nut si meme voille [...] pur luy et [...] faitz qe par tel herb[...] [...].

19. Item; qe le fause moneie seyt desore [...].

Note

This previously unnoticed document is very badly damaged: there is a large hole in the upper left-hand side and two further smaller holes further down, and much of the extant text is too faint to be recovered even under ultra-violet light. The hand is conversant with chancery styles of the first half of the fourteenth century, and the relative brevity of the individual entries tends to suggest a date relatively early in that period. The document is written up as a piece of contiuous text, but is broken up here into its constituent items. Unfortunately, the precise nature and meaning of some of these items is very difficult to discern. The document cannot categorically be claimed as a common petition since there are no petitioners specified, and it is possible that it is akin to some of the conciliar memoranda compiled in the early fourteenth century that captured within them the substance, and sometimes the text, of common petitions (see also no. 113). On the other hand, there is an explicit address to the king at the outset; there is an elusive reference to parliament in item 17; and the document frequently deploys language and rhetoric used in known common petitions of the early fourteenth century, including the bemoaning of damage done to the realm and people, and the formulation 'the people cry remedy' in items 8 and 13 (Ormrod 2015: 229–234). All of this suggests that the document is, indeed, an addition to the list of schedules of common petitions known to survive from the early decades of the fourteenth century.

In terms of date, there is a clear terminus *a quo* in the reference to trailbaston at item 8. The trailbaston commissions (a nickname derived either from the sticks carried by criminals or from the motif of the staff of justice) were set up in 1304–1305 in response to major concerns over public order in the realm (*PROME*, I, 114; Harding 1978; Phelan 2000). The present document does not necessarily comment on the first round of trailbaston proceedings. Further general commissions of oyer and terminer to address problems of corruption and lawlessness – issued, for example, in 1307, 1314, 1323–1324, 1328–1329, and beyond – were also known by the informal terminology of trailbaston (*CPR, 1301–1307*, pp. 542–543; *CPR, 1313–1317*, pp. 128–130; *SCCKB*, IV, li–lxvi; Verduyn 1991: 13–42; Green 2002: 171). It is certainly notable that many of the concerns in this document relate quite directly to the original articles of trailbaston issued in 1305, with their emphasis on undue interference in legal process through maintenance and intimidation, the committing of violent crimes (including those committed at night), and – the subject of a supplementary ordinance in 1305 – the offence of conspiracy (*RP*, I, 178; *RP*, I, 183 = *PROME*, II, 444–445; Musson and Ormrod 1999: 49). But a case could equally be made that a number of the concerns over law and order expressed here show a close affinity with the statutory legislation of the parliament of September–October 1331, for which no common petitions were included on the parliament roll; in particular, the important reinforcement provided in 1331 to the Statute of Winchester of 1285 on the treatment of those who broke curfew and rode by night in a threatening manner reflect issues raised in the present document at items 9, 10, and 12 (*SR*, I, 268; Putnam 1929: 28).

The document draws attention to several other major concerns in public life during the early fourteenth century that may also assist with the question of its date. Item 14, on the office of sheriff, is difficult to interpret owing to the loss of some crucial text, but it may be a request that sheriffs be residents in the counties where they held office: if so, it was part of a long debate on this matter throughout the thirteenth and fourteenth centuries that was regularly re-stated as official policy by the crown under Edward II and Edward III (Saul 1981: 108; and see no. 118). Much more prominently, items 1–3 relate to the problem of purveyance, and particularly stress the abuse of this right of compulsory purchase of foodstuffs by lords and other people of power. The petitions are insistent that the right of prise should belong only to the king and be applied with the consent of the provider, with repayment being made within forty days. Purveyance was a subject of regular concern in parliament under Edward I, Edward II, and Edward III, and several statutes of the period reinforced the *Articuli super Cartas* of 1300 in requiring that prises be taken only for the king's household (see nos 110 and 113). The specific point made here about repayment is not part of that body of legislation, but instead refers to the 1225 version of Magna Carta, as confirmed in 1297 and subsequently, which required that officials (both royal and seignorial) taking corn and other goods should repay the provider within forty days (*Select Charters*, pp. 342, 350). The emphasis is rather different from that which prevailed in the debate over prises at the beginning of Edward II's reign, articulated in the Stamford Articles of 1309 (no. 110) and the Ordinances of 1311, which concentrated on the abuse of this prerogative by the officers of the king (Prestwich 1990b: 4–6; Maddicott 2010: 306–308, 333). It could be that the request for the enforcement of the assize of bread and ale that follows on at item 4 is linked to the initiatives taken at the start of the period of famine in 1316–1317 to regulate the price of grain and ale (see no. 76). But the concerns in the present document may also fit rather more obviously with those found in no. 113 and other contextual documentation from the 1320s, which suggest a growing anxiety over the abuse of prise by the lords of the realm during the political disturbances of the civil war of 1321–1322 and the deposition of Edward II (Ormrod 1990a: 19–20). A case can therefore be constructed for linking the petitions on purveyance made here with the statutes issued by Edward III from the parliaments of November–December 1330 and September–October 1331, which emphasized that the prerogative of purveyance should be exercised only by the households of the king, the queen, and their children (*SR*, I, 262–263, 265–266).

Finally, item 19 of the present document refers to 'false money': that is, the problem of imported silver coins made on the continent to imitate and replace English sterling. This had been a major issue in the 1290s. Although it had largely been addressed by a series of reforms in the royal mints in 1300–1302, the crown expressed persistent concern over the possibility of a new influx of counterfeit coin during the 1310s and 1320s, and the impression thus given may have perpetuated the public fears apparently represented in the petition given here (Mate 1972: 69–74; Mate 1975: 11–14; Allen 2012: 259–261). From 1331 the parliamentary debate about the coinage turned away from counterfeit imports and towards the more fundamental problem of the general shortage of bullion (*RP*, II, 61, 105 = *PROME*, IV, 159, 243–244; *RPHI*, p. 237 = *PROME*, IV, 201; Mate 1975: 13–14); the emphasis of the present document therefore suggests that it dates from before this time.

It is notable that item 13 expresses concern about the enforcement of the existing thirteenth-century legislation on the ravishment of women (a term covering both abduction and rape) (Dunn 2013). While there are general grounds for assuming that ravishment was both under-reported and under-prosecuted in the first half of the fourteenth century (Hanawalt 1979: 104–110), no other general debates on this crime are known in the English parliament prior to 1382 (*RP*, III, 139–140 = *PROME*, VI, 296; *SR*, II, 27; Post 1980). What is especially striking here is the way that the petition expresses concern not only about the rights of the king and the male relatives of the abducted woman, but also about what such crimes did to the 'souls and hearts' of the relevant people – a rare example in political documentation of this period of the affective impact of negligence in the proper enforcement of the law.

While a precise context for this important set of petitions therefore eludes us, its contents suggest that it must have been compiled some time between the instigation of trailbastons in 1305 and the early years of Edward III.

110. Common petition in eleven parts (the Stamford Articles) (SC 8/294/14698 and C 54/127, m. 22) 1309

Summary

The commonalty of the realm requested that the king consider these articles at the parliament held at Westminster in April 1309, in return for their assent to a grant of a twenty-fifth. The king gave his response at the parliament held at Stamford in July of the same year. The articles and responses follow.

The good people of the realm who have come to parliament are much grieved because they are not being governed according to the articles of Magna Carta, and because of wrongs done to them by the king's ministers. They request a remedy on the following:

1. Complaint that those claiming to be the king's ministers take grain, malt, fresh and salted meat, poultry, and fish without paying or giving any other guarantee, to the impoverishment of the people.

    Response: An ordinance concerning such prises was made during the time of Edward I, which should be upheld.

2. The king's ministers take 2s per cask of wine, 2s per cloth imported by foreign merchants, and 3d of each pound of merchandise sold by weight, to the damage of the people, since the price of such commodities has increased by a third.

    Response: The king orders that this petty custom be removed, and the king to be advised on the advantage that should result; saving the ancient duties and the customs previously granted.

3. Complaint that, although the king has commanded that coinage which circulated in the time of his father might hold the same value as previously, the merchants in cities, boroughs, and towns disobey this command, and double the value of currency.

    Response: The king wills that writs be sent to all the counties of England proclaiming that the coinage should circulate at its correct value, on grievous penalty.

4. Complaint that stewards and marshals continue to sue all manner of pleas without proper authority, contrary to legislation made in the time of Edward I. Because of this the people are much grieved and impoverished, and they request a remedy.

Response: The king orders that stewards and marshals are not to sue any manner of pleas except those ordained by his father in the ordinance that was enrolled in chancery.

5. Complaint that stewards and marshals go about the country holding pleas and amercing towns and boroughs, outside their jurisdiction and without warrant, to the damage and impoverishment of the people; request for a remedy.

Response: The king wills that the pleas of the marshalcy are only to be held in areas under their jurisdiction: that is to say, within twelve leagues of the place where the king is resident, according to the aforesaid ordinance.

6. Complaint that the knights and men of cities, boroughs, and towns who come to parliament to deliver petitions concerning the grievances of the people for which no remedies are available under the common law cannot find men to receive these petitions, as were appointed in parliament during the time of the king's father.

Response: The king wills that in his parliaments henceforth men might be assigned to receive petitions, and that the petitions should be delivered by his council, as they were under his father.

7. Complaint that the king's receivers of prisage at fairs and in cities throughout the realm take more than is necessary, and sell the surplus for their own profit, to the great harm of the king and his people; request for a remedy.

Response: The king wills that the ordinance that was made concerning such prisage in the time of the king his father should be kept and upheld, as is contained in the rolls of chancery.

8. Complaint that law suits tried in the king's courts are often delayed by protections and writs of privy seal, to the great damage of the people.

Response: The king wills that protections with exemptions from pleas should henceforth not be granted to anyone, except to those who go out of the realm in the king's service, and that the chancellor is not to issue them in any other case.

With regard to writs under the privy seal, the king wills that the ordinance made under Edward I, and which is held in the chancery, should be kept.

9. Complaint that felons indicted of larcenies, robberies, homicides, and other felonies are too easily able to purchase pardons, so that those who have indicted them do not dare to remain in their country for fear of such felons, and many do not make indictments for this reason.

Response: The king wills that henceforth no pardon for felony should be granted except in those cases where it used of old to be granted: that is to say, if a man kills another by misadventure, in self- defence, or in madness, and this is found by the verdict of the justices.

10. Complaint that, although it is ordained that common pleas in the king's court should be tried in a certain place, the king's ministers try such pleas before the gates of their castles, against the form of the law; request for a remedy.

Response: The king wills that the constables of castles should not distrain people to plead before them in a foreign county, or in any manner than was formerly observed.

11. Complaint that, although various people of the realm hold their tenements in chief of the king, and have held them since time immemorial, the king's escheators come and seize their lands and oust them by inquests, without their having the right of appeal in the king's court; thus the people are much grieved.

Response: The king wills that if the people and their ancestors have held the tenements since time immemorial, as the petition supposes, the escheators should not interfere.

And it is ordained and ordered by our lord the king, with regard to those who wish to plead to the chancellor, that if any man go against any of these said points, the chancellor, by writ of the great seal, should make a remedy as he sees fit. And the king has also charged the said chancellor and his other ministers that each of them correctly observes the aforesaid points.

Text

Les articles souz escritz furent baillez a nostre seygneur le Roy par la communalte de son roialme a son parlement qu'il tynt a Westminster au mois de Pasche l'an de son regne second; au quel parlement le Roi pria d'aver une ayde de sa terre, e les laies gentz granterent au Roi le xxv denier, par tieu condicion, q'il meist conseil e remedie en les articles avantditz. E la Roi a son parlement a Staunford, commenceant le Dimeynge prochein apres la Seint Iak l'an de son regne tierz, ordena respons et remedie a meismes les articles, lesqueux respons et remedie il fist notefier a son poeple a son dit parlement a Staunford, et les queux sont cy dessouz escritz, c'est asaver apres chescun article le remedie qe y est ordene.

Les bones gentz du roialme qi sont cy venuz au parlement prient a nostre seigneur le Roi q'il voille si lui plest aver regard de son povre poeple, qe molt se sente greve, de ceo q'il ne sont pas menez sicome il deussent estre nomeement des pointz de la grant chartre, e prie de ce, si lui plest, remedie. Estre ce, prient a nostre seygneur le Roi, si lui plest, q'il voille oir les choses qe molt ont grevez son poeple, et uncore grevent de novel de iour en autre, par ceux qui se dient estre ses ministres, et mettre y amendement, si lui plest:

1. Adeprimes, des bledz, brees, chars fresches et salees, et toute manere de polaill, peisson de meer et de eawe duce, pris par ceux que se dient estre ministres le Roi, qe rien ne paent, ne autre certeinete par taille ne en autre \manere/ ne font au poeple le Roi; par quoi son people est enpoverez.

    Response: A cest article est respondu, q'il y avoit une ordenaunce fait de tieux prises en temps le Roi Edward, pere nostre seigneur le Roi qui ore est, la quele ordenance hom entend qe soit covenable pur le Roi, et profitable pur son poeple, et voet nostre seigneur le Roi qe cele ordinaunce soit tenue et garde en toutz pointz.

2. L'autre, qe le Roi par ses ministres prent de chescun tonel de vin ii. soldz, de chescun drap qe marchandz aliens font venir en sa terre ii. soldz, et de chescune livre de aver de pois, iii. deners, au damage du poeple, qe par tieux prises achate le poeple au tierz deners plus q'il ne soleit.

    Response: Nostre seigneur le Roi, a la requeste de son poeple grante qe cele petite custume de vyns, de draps et d'aver de pois soit souztrete et oustee a la volunte le Roi, pur saver quel profit e quel avantage accrestera a li et a son poeple par cele souztrete, e puis en aura le Roi consail selonc l'avantage q'il y verra, sauves totes voies a nostre seigneur le Roi les auncienes prises et custumes auncienement dues et approvees.

MULTIPLE PETITIONS 201

3. Le tierz, qe la ou le Roi ad commande que la monoye d'esterlings qe aloit en temps le Roy son pere, a qui Dieus face merci, feust tenuz aussi bone come elle feust en le temps son pere, les vendours es citez, burghs et es autres villes marchandes desobeissaument ne le font pas, mais encontre son mandement vendont au double value et plus cher en moltz \des/ lieus de sa terre, par quoi le poeple est molt enpoveri.

   Response: Le Roi voet qe briefs soient enveez en toutz les contez d'Engleterre, a faire crier qe la monoie courge a sa droit value, sicome elle soleit en temps son pere, et sur ce grevouse peyne, et qe hom n'encherisse les choses pur la monoye, car la Roi la voet maintenir aussi bone come elle soleit estre.

4. Le quart, qe comme le poeple se senti molt greve et travaille en temps le Roi leur seignur son pere, a qui Dieu face mercy, de ce qe seneschaus et mareschaux plederent moltz de maners des pledz qe a eux n'afferoient a pleder; et as pleintes de son poeple, qe par tieux pledz feust grevez et enpovery, fist remedie et establi certeins pointz et articles, des queux et de quoi seneschaus et les mareschaux doivent devant eux aver conissance a pleder; les seneschaus et les mareschaux qe ore sont, ceux pointz ne ceux articles ne fount ne ne gardent, ainz enlargissent leur iurisdiccion e leur poair encontre l'ordenance et l'establissement son pere, qui Dieu face merci. Dont son poeple est molt greve e enpoveri, et de ceo prie remedie.

   Response: Le Roi voet qe seneschaux et mareschaux ne teignent autre manere de pledz, ne en autre forme qe n'estoit ordenez par le Roy son pere, qui Dieus assoile, et q'il ne passent desoremes cele ordenance, q'est enroullee en chauncellerie.

5. Le quint, qe les seneschaux et mareschaux ou il vount par pais, hors de la verge ou leur poair n'est pas, tenent pledz, amercient burghs et villes grevousement sanz garant, et au gref, damage et enpoverissement du poeple; par quoi le poeple prie remedie.

   Response: Le Roi voet qe les pledz de la mareschaucie ne soient tenuz forsqe deinz la verge, c'est asaver deinz les xii. lieues enviroun la ou le corps le Roi serra, et selonc l'ordenance avantdite.

6. Le sisme, qe les chevaliers, gentz de citez e de burghs e d'autres villes qi sont venuz a son parlement par son commandement, pur eux et pur le poeple, e ont peticions a liverer pur tortz et grevances

faites a eux qe ne poent estre redrescees par la commune ley, ne en autre manere santz especial garant, il ne troevent hom qe leur peticions receive, sicome soleit estre au parlement en temps le Roy lour seigneur son pere, qi Dieu face merci; et de ce prient sa grace et remedie.

Response: Le Roi voet qe en ses parlementz desormes gentz soient assignees a receivre peticions, e qe elles soient delivres par son conseil, aussi come estre soleient en temps son pere.

7. Le septisme article, qe la ou le Roi ad ses pernours de prises faire en feires e cytez parmi le roialme, les pernours le Roi pernent plus qe ne busoigne al oeps le Roy, ceux meismes le livrent as autres pur marchander a lour[2] pren demeyne e au profit a qi il le delivrent, et au damage le Roi e de son poeple. Dont le poeple prie remedie.

Response: Le Roi voet qe l'ordenance qe fu faite de teux[3] prises en temps le Roi son pere soit tenue et gardee, la quele est contenue es roules de la chancellerie.

8. Le oytisme, qe par la ou il y ad suite faite selonc[4] forme de lay en les banks nostre seignur[5] le Roi, sovent par protections e par bref dessouz la targe sont lour[6] dreitures delaez, a grant damage du poeple.

Response: Le Roi voet qe protections od les clauses d'acquitance de pledz ne soient grantes[7] desoremes a nulles gentz, forsqe a ceux qi vont hors du roialme en le servise le Roy por[8] grosses busoignes du roialmes, \et[9] le Roy ad charge lor[10] chanceller q'il ne les face en autre manere;/[11] et quant as brefs de la targe, le Roi voet qe l'ordenance soit gardee qe en fust faites[12] en temps le Roi son pere, la quele est en chancellerie.

9. La noevisme, qe par la ou larons sont enditez de larcines, roberies, homicides et autres felonies faites, trop legerement purchacent la

---

[2]C 54/127: 'leur'.
[3]C 54/127: 'tieux'.
[4]C 54/127: 'solonc'.
[5]C 54/127: 'seygnur'.
[6]C 54/127: 'leur'.
[7]C 54/127: 'grantez'.
[8]C 54/127: 'pur'.
[9]C 54/127: 'e'.
[10]C 54/127: 'le'.
[11]This text is not interlineated in C 54/127.
[12]C 54/127: 'faite'.

chartre le Roi de sa pees, par quoi ceux qi les ont enditez ne osent demorer en lour pais pur doute de ceux larons, et plusors[13] se retreent de enditementz faire par cele encheson. Dont le poeple prie remedie.

Response: Le Roi voet qe desoremes ne soit grante pardoun de felonie, forsqe en cas ou auncienement soleit estre grantez, c'est asaver, si hom tue autre par mesaventure, ou soi deffendant ou en deverie, et ce soit trove par record de iustices.

10. Le disme, qe par la ou les communs pledz du bank le Roi des contez doivent estre pledez en certein lieu, la viegnent les ministres le Roi de ses chasteaux, et treent en tieu manere les pledz devant les portes des chasteaux, contre la forme de la ley; et de ce prie remedie.

Response: Le Roi voet qe les conestables des chasteaux ne destreignent gentz a pleder devant eux nul play de forein conte, ne deinz conte autrement qe auncienement soleit estre fait.

11. Le unzisme, qe par la ou diverses gentz du roialme tenent lour tenementz en chef du Roi, et unt tenuz eux et lour auncestres du temps dont memorie n'est, viegnent les escheturs le Roi et seisent lour terres, et les oustent par enquestes q'il font de lour office, sanz appeller en la curt le Roi; dont le poeple se sente molt greve.

Response: Le Roi voet qe des tenementz qe gentz et lour auncestres ont tenuz du temps dont yl n'y ad memoire, sicomme la peticion suppose, les escheturs ne se mellent par encheson del primer entre.

Et ordenez est et comandez par nostre seigneur le Roi qe a ceux qe se voudront pleinder a chauncellier, qe nul hom soit venuz encontre aucun des ditz pointz, le chanceller, par bref du grant seal, en face tele remedie comme il verra qe face a fere par reson. Et le Roi ad aussint charge le dit chanceller et ses autres ministres qe chescun endrait li garde les pointz avantditz.

Note

A full text of the so-called Stamford Articles appears on the close roll for the regnal year 3 Edward II (July 1309–July 1310), where

---

[13] C 54/127: 'plusurs'.

it is recorded on an additional membrane or schedule attached to m. 22 (C 54/127; *CCR, 1307–1313*, p. 225). The text from the close roll was published *in extenso* as an appendix to the late eighteenth-century edition of the parliament rolls (*RP*, I, 443–445) and selections were published (in the original and in translation) in a number of later collections of constitutional documents (*Select Documents*, pp. 6–8; Sayles 1988: 290–291). SC 8/294/14698 is a verbatim version of the close roll entry, but it is incomplete, with only the preamble and items 1, 2, 7, 8, and 9 appearing, and some of the extant text being stained and faded. The configuration of the document strongly suggests that a lower portion has been cut away, and that the original layout contained the preamble and items 1–6 of the Stamford Articles on the face, with items 7–11 on the dorse. The layout of SC 8/294/14698 also implies that the grievances were written up first and the responses added (in the same hand) once the council had determined its views; this, coupled with the interlineation in the text of the response to item 8, suggests that this document represents the rough notes from which the fair copy was written up on the close roll. Given the historical importance of the Stamford Articles and the absence of a modern complete edition, the entire text is reproduced here, using SC 8/294/14698 as the base text for those items that appear in it (with footnotes indicating places where this diverges from the close roll), and the close roll as the base text for the others.

As the preamble to the document makes clear, the petitions that it incorporates were submitted at the parliament held at Westminster in April–May 1309, which was attended by representatives of the shires, cities, and towns. This assembly granted a tax of a twenty-fifth in support of the Scottish war, on condition that the king consent to the eleven articles of reform set out here (*PROME*, III, 11–13). Edward II's responses to the conditions were delayed until the meeting of the next parliament, and the tax itself remained in abeyance. The assembly that met at Stamford in July–August 1309, which also included county and urban representatives, returned to the question of the tax and the conditions attached to it. In return for consent to the restoration from disgrace of his favourite, Piers Gaveston, and as the price of the tax that he needed to put into commission, the king and council provided a series of positive responses to the petitions entered in the earlier Westminster parliament (Maddicott 1970: 103–104; *PROME*, III, 15).

The ways in which these responses were announced and implemented was complex. In June and early July the king had already given a foretaste of the policy to come on item 1 in a series of proclamations for the proper administration of royal purveyance (Phillips 2010a: 158). Item 3, which dealt with concerns over a possible devaluation of the coinage, resulted in a writ dated from Stamford on

5 August requiring proclamation of the king's intention to hold firm to the standard set for the currency under Edward I (*CCR, 1307–1313*, p. 225; Allen 2012: 148–149). A few weeks later, from Kings Langley on 20 August, writs were issued for the proclamation of a statute (subsequently known as the Statute of Stamford), which responded to items 1, 4, 5, and 8 by confirming the relevant clauses of the *Articuli super cartas* of 1300 that regulated royal purveyance, determined the jurisdiction of the steward and marshal of the king's household, and restricted the use of the privy seal in matters relating to the common law (*SR*, I, 154–156, reciting *SR*, I, 137–138, 139). The text of the statute continues with responses to items 10 (on the holding of common pleas in a fixed place; see Clanchy 1985) and 2 (the abolition of the so-called new custom paid by alien merchants since 1303; see Lloyd 1982: 30). Thereafter it simply refers in general terms to other requests made to the king, and provides a statement, based on that added at the end of the text of the Articles, that the chancellor and others had been required to uphold the king's concessions and should ensure that anyone aggrieved on any issues raised in the 'ordinance' could have access to the law via writs issued from the chancery. The king having thus acknowledged the conditions attached to the tax granted in May, commissions for the collection of the twenty-fifth were finally issued on 26 August (*CPR, 1307–1313*, pp. 183–186).

The Stamford Articles have been recognized for some time as one of the earliest full schedules of common petitions that articulate the interests of the parliamentary commons and their constituents (Harriss 1975: 110–111, 120). While item 11, complaining about unjust actions taken against those who held estates in chief of the king, might be supposed to represent an issue closer to the hearts of the barons, the subject-matter of the document as a whole is readily associable with an emerging agenda of the representative element in parliament found in other extant common petitions of the early fourteenth century: for example, item 1 on purveyance (see nos 109, 113, and 120), item 2 on the new custom of 1303 (see no. 111), item 7 on the king's rights of prisage (see no. 71), and item 9 on charters of pardon (see nos 111, 118, and 120). The most powerful reason for associating the Articles with the commons, however, is the content of item 6, on the receiving and answering of private petitions brought to parliament by the representatives of the shires, cities, and towns. Either because of the vexed political relations between Edward II and the magnates and a resulting desire to have parliaments sit for as little time as possible, or because of an abortive attempt to streamline parliamentary business and cut back as a matter of policy on the number of private petitions submitted there, the fact that such petitions were not being processed was clearly a matter of significant concern, and would come up again in the provisions for the governance of the realm made in the Ordinances of 1311 (Dodd 2007: 71–74). The fact that this issue was not referred to in the Statute of Stamford does not necessarily mean that the crown sought deliberately to suppress its own positive response to the item: both the Articles and the Statute of Stamford suggest that the king's answers to the full set of the Articles were announced verbally in parliament, and the question of guaranteeing the right to submit and have responses to private petitions was arguably more a matter of parliamentary procedure set by this kind of memorandum than it was something on which formal legislation might be issued.

The omission of this and other items from the Statute of Stamford also serves to highlight the comparative weakness of parliament's efforts to try to make grants of taxation absolutely conditional on the redress of grievances. Later in the fourteenth century when parliament more regularly attempted to link grants of taxation to common petitions, it proved impossible to uphold the idea that the tax would only be paid if the king provided positive responses to every petition (Harriss 1975: 356–375; Ormrod 1990b: 63–67). The fact that Edward II's government managed to avoid proclaiming a number of the responses it had made to the Stamford Articles and restricted itself to maintaining a reference copy of them on the close roll suggests a regime determined, wherever possible, to hold to its rights. A similar phenomenon may be noted later in the same reign, when, after the York parliament of May 1322, the crown established remedial legislation responding to a range of issues arising as a result of the formal withdrawal of the Ordinances of 1311 and other issues probably raised by recent common petitions. The text of this legislation was written up on the dorse of the close roll by way of providing a record of the action, but there is no evidence that it was ever issued for proclamation in the shires and therefore became part of the law of the land (*RP*, I, 456–457 = *CCR*, *1318–1323*, pp. 557–558; Davies 1918: 490–494; Ormrod 1990a: 3–4).

111. Common petition in four parts (SC 8/156/7796) c.1309–c.1318

Summary

The knights of the counties and the good people of the cities [...]:

1. Request that the king should not grant charters of pardon for murder so readily, as this encourages felons and wrongdoers and is to the detriment of the peace.

Response: [Note commenting on the retrospective nature of charters of pardon.]

2. Concerning the half a mark custom of wool [and a new levy] made without common assent, they request that the [new] charge be withdrawn, and the collectors of customs desist.

   Response: The matter is understood, and the king wishes to pay the associated costs to sellers and buyers.

3. [Sense lost].

   Response: It is also agreed that this be done.

4. [Sense lost].

   Response: It is agreed.

Text

Les chivalers des countes et les bone gentz de cites [...] a nostre seignur le Roy et a son soun counseil comaunder amend[...] [...] southescrites:

1. Enprimes, ces chartres de pardoun de mort de homme et des [...] trop comunement, en abaudizement des felouns et de meffesours a [...] et arerisement de la pees, qe mes ne soient si legerement grauntes [...].

   Response: [...] avise avant qe desore grante tieles chartres et non eent de son temps.

2. Ensement priount qe de la custume de leyne de demy mark [...] pris et [...] charge de novel comaunde a lever saunz commun assent [...] houste et [...] et coilours de la custume de surseer et ceo est paie [...] prest soit [...][...]rer ceo qe il ount paie.

   Response: La chose est deprist, et le Roi ent fait sute de paier de la chose en charge del vendour qe del achatour, et pur ceo s'en voet suffrir le [...].

3. [...] plest [au seignurs][14] a nostre seignur le Roy [...] ses iustices [...] qe ne soient nomez viscountes et seneschals [...].

   Response: Acordez est qe ensi soit.

4. [...] en pais par bone gentz [...].

[14] Crossed out.

208   MULTIPLE PETITIONS

Response: [...] qe serront \enxi/ [...] acorder [...].

Note

This schedule of petitions is severely damaged, with sections of the top right-hand and bottom left-hand torn away, and much of the rest creased and stained. The responses, written into the space left between each item, are in a different hand from that of the petition itself. In spite of the fact that damage renders several sections of it unintelligible, the document is of considerable interest in providing early evidence of the role of the knights of the shires and the urban representatives in petitioning the crown and in asserting the right of common assent to fiscal impositions. It is likely that the first line refers not only to the knights and citizens but to the burgesses as well; the remaining survivals of the heading suggest that the schedule of petitions arose from a specific instruction to the commons that they address the king and council on matters of concern to the commonalty.

The precise date of the petition is very hard to determine. Item 1, on the granting of pardons for homicide, was a lively issue throughout the reigns of Edward I and Edward II and the earliest extant and datable common petition on the matter is the schedule of petitions submitted in the parliament of April–May 1309 (at which representatives of the counties and the urban areas were present) and subsequently put to formal record on the close roll, complete with the king's responses, at the parliament held at Stamford in July–August of that year (no. 110). The Ordinances of 1311 aimed to restrict the abuse of charters of pardon, but the very general provision made there, and the issues surrounding the legality and enforceability of the Ordinances, meant that controversy continued on into the reign of Edward III (Lacey 2009: 76–77).

Item 2, relating to the taxation of trade, is still more challenging to disentangle. The available text suggests that the issue being addressed was not the so-called ancient custom of half a mark (6s 8d) per sack of wool exported from the realm, which was granted by parliament in 1275 and collected permanently thereafter, but rather one of a sequence of further impositions made on overseas trade after 1294. One possibility is that the document alludes to the debate over the withdrawal of the so-called new custom of 1303, which was imposed with the consent of a group of foreign merchants (and applied only, in a direct sense, to them) and which was again criticized at the parliament of April–May 1309 and withdrawn both under the Stamford Articles of 1309 and the Ordinances of 1311 (Lloyd 1982: 26–30; and see no. 110). However, the reference in the royal response to the repayment of 'sellers and buyers' makes it more likely that the imposition referred to by the commons here was a forced loan. The two prises (compulsory purchases, made on credit) of wool made by Edward I in 1297 resulted in long-running complaints, still rumbling on at the time of Edward II's succession, over the repayment of creditors (Lloyd 1977: 87–95). Another, perhaps stronger possibility is the forced loan on overseas trade imposed in 1317. In light of the explicit assertion made here that the elusive new charge had been made 'without common assent', it is significant to note that the official memorandum proposing the 1317 levy explicitly asserts the right of the king to exploit the romano-canonical doctrine of necessity as justification for the forced loan; although Edward II sought some form of consent from a group of merchants summoned to a council at Nottingham in July 1317, no authorization was sought from full parliament for the forced loan (Ormrod 1991). The forced loan was designed to run for a year, to the end of September 1318, at which point it was supposed to be repaid. At the full parliament that convened at York on 20 October and ran to early December, an elaborate list was compiled of the various private petitions submitted, sorted into different categories. One category, 'of debts sought from the king' (*de debitis petitis de rege*), included a petition from 'the merchants of England' (*mercatorum Anglie*) on 'the loan of sacks of wool' (*de dando mutuum de saccis lane*) (*RPHI*, pp. 73–74). Whether the present schedule of petitions can be positively associated with this particular assembly remains a matter for further debate, but the association would provide some evidence to support the view that the statutes issued from the York parliament of 1318 were themselves a response to matters raised in otherwise lost common petitions registered on this occasion (*PROME*, III, 248; *SR*, I, 177–178).

112. Common petition in two parts, on inheritance and inquisitions (SC 8/80/3951)
1319–1325

Summary

The commonalty of the land of England:

1. It was granted in the Statute of Gloucester in 1278, at the request of the commonalty, that if a man alienates in fee lands or tenements inherited from his wife, his son and heir might be able to demand and recover such lands. They request that the pleas which are

pending before the justices of the bench regarding similar cases might receive the king's final judgement.

Response: A similar petition was answered at the Lincoln parliament and similarly at the last parliament at York.

2. Request that, as stated by the Statute of Westminster II, those who plead in the king's court under inquisition are allowed an essoin at the first day following the inquisition, but that judgement not be delayed by a second essoin.

Response: Nothing can be done without changing the law.

Text

A nostre seygnur le Roi e a soen conseil pri la communalte de sa terre de Engiltere:

1. Qe il les voil de sa grace remedi graunter, qe par la ou nostre seygnur le Roi pier nostre segnur le Roi qi ore est en le sime an de son regne a Glowcestre a la request de la communalte de sa terre graunta par estatut, qe si hom alienast en fee teres ou tenementes q'il tint par la lay de Engiltere del heritage sa femme, son fiz e heire, a qi nule heritage decent de part son pier, ne serrait pas forsclos de accioun par le fete son pier a demaundere e recoverere le heritage sa mere par le pier aliene, tut face la chartre le pier mencioun qe ly e ses heires seynt tenuz a la garantie, qe en autel maner voil nostre segnur le Roi ore graunter de sa grace qe le fiz par le fete sa mere tenaunt terres ou tenementes en dower ou en autre maner a terme de vie, ne seit forsclos d'accioun a demaundere e recoverer son dreit par sa mere aliene en fee, a qi nule heritage de par la mere decent tut seit il \son/ plus procheyn heire de saunk, e qe les plees qe sunt pendaunz devant iustiis en baunk tuchaunt meme le cas puissent prender final iugement de la grace nostre segnur le Roi en la fourme de susdit.

Response: Quo ad primam peticionem: ad consimilem peticionem responsum fuit in parliamento Lincolnie, sicut patet per indossamentum peticionis tunc porrecte et similiter ad ultimum parliamentum Eboraci.

2. Ensement, la ou il est contenu en la statut de Westmustre le secunde qe si hom enpleyde en la court le Roi se mette en enquest qe alowe ly seit au primer iour une essoine, si qe as autres iours ensuanz l'enquest ne seit deleye par essoyne, qe en autel maner

voil nostre seygnur le Roi graunter de sa grace qe si parties en sa court pleydent e decendunt en iugement qe au primer iour seit alowe une essoine, si qe as autres iours ensuaunz le iugement par autre essoine ne seit delaye.

Response: Quo ad secundam peticionem: nichil potest fieri sine mutacione legis.

Note

This set of two petitions was previously published by Sayles (*SCCKB*, IV, cxvi) and has been re-edited here with minor amendments. In the original, there is a space left after both items as though to allow the insertion of the individual responses; in fact, the responses are both written on the dorse, but are interspersed in the edition provided here in order to clarify the items to which they refer. The two requests are not naturally linked, although both are loosely concerned with inheritance rights and associated inquisitions. As stated in the petition, one of the provisions of the 1278 Statute of Gloucester was that a son could recover lands which he should have inherited on his mother's side but which his father had alienated (*SR*, I, 46). In 1285, the Statute of Westminster II had permitted a man an essoin (an excuse for not attending court) on the first day only, but stated that the case could not then be delayed any further (*SR*, I, 85).

Questions about inheritance and alienation of land can be found frequently in private petitions of the reigns of the first three Edwards, but this petition must date to the period 1316–1325. The Lincoln case referred to in the response was addressed in the assembly of January–February 1316 through a private petition from John of Bordesden, who claimed that John of Garton had granted him the reversion of lands held for life by Ada of Ritton, but that Ada had instead alienated those lands to her son; the response refers to the provisions of the Statute of Gloucester but does not give a definitive answer, instead stating that the statute must be explained to the magnates adjudicating the case (*RP*, I, 336 = *PROME*, III, 171). This means that this petition must have been presented before the next Lincoln parliament, held in September 1327, which effectively restricts it to the later part of Edward II's reign. There were parliaments at York in October–December 1318, May 1319, January 1320, and May and November 1322. As the 'last parliament at York' is mentioned after the Lincoln parliament, the first assembly this can be is that of 1318, which makes 1319 the earliest possible date for this petition, although there is no corroborating evidence on the surviving parliament rolls (which exist only for 1318 and 1319). Although Sayles suggested a more limited range of 1319–1322, there is no obvious reason why this petition could not alternatively have been presented in any of the parliaments of 1324 or 1325.

113. Common petition in twenty-three parts (C 49/66/29)
1322

Summary

[No petitioner specified]:

1. When a lady who holds lands in dower alienates them in fee, her heir should not be prevented from claiming them after her death, as is set out in the Statute of Gloucester; and likewise for the heir of a tenant who alienates by the courtesy of England.

   Response: It is lawful that henceforth this be done regarding land held in dower or by the courtesy of England.

2. That damages are not awarded in writs of disseisin, as they are in writs of possession of grandfather and great-grandfather.

   Response: [none].

3. When sheriffs or bailiffs return only small sums of money, a lord has no averment against them, contrary to the Statute of Westminster.

   Response: An averment is admissible against both bailiffs and sheriffs when they return very small issues.

4. Sheriffs appointed to gaol delivery do not visit every prison, and take bribes, yet go unpunished.

   Response: The justices assigned to gaol delivery will make enquiries on such concealments and punish the sheriffs, and if any wish to sue regarding this matter, they will be received by the king.

5. In pleas of champerty no man should have the right to bring an action except the king, as they do not have the power to guarantee surety in a process of champerty.

   Response: It would be well to keep this in mind.

6. A steward of a great lord should not make any false presentment at the leet of his lord such that people have no recovery in chancery.

MULTIPLE PETITIONS 213

Response: [none].

7. It would be to the profit of the king and the people if all the justices concerned with the crown sent their documents to the exchequer annually, so that the goods forfeit from those who have been judged guilty can be thus annually levied.

   Response: This will be discussed at the next parliament.

8. Previous discussion and agreement on the limitations applying to writs of right have not had effect.

   Response: Writs of right should be limited by the reign of Henry III, writs of possession at the coronation of Edward I, and writs of *novel disseisin* at the time of the latter's voyage to Gascony.

9. It is stated in Magna Carta that if an heir is under age, his lord might not have the ward of him nor of his land before he has taken his homage.

   Response: [none].

10. Memorandum regarding those who hold escheats in the hands of the king.

    Response: See article 30 of Magna Carta.

11. In writs of trespass and of oyer and terminer, people do not bring damages of trespass of fourfold or more, so that a low-born man cannot have attaint and brings another plea.

    Response: [none].

12. At the last parliament it was agreed that process in the writ of debt be altered, but the writ of pone speeds up the process by only one day; since the Statute of Merchants was altered, the matter needs attention, as those who live in distant parts of the land are not able to come to make recognisances in a court of record.

    Response: [none].

13. That these important matters be recorded in a statute.

    Response: [none].

14. For remedy against false returns of bailiffs of franchises.

    Response: As above.

15. To ordain that the chattels of felons and fugitives, the rights of a year, waste, deodand, shipwreck, and other such profits that are only levied in eyre, might be levied from year to year for the king's

profit, just as other lords have levied them by charter since ancient times.

Response: [none].

16. That all weighing equipment used for buying and selling be fair, as the balances of the realm are false, to the great damage of both the great and common people.

    Response: Let it be executed by writ.

17. To reform all measures of grain, wine, and beer throughout the realm, and that officials be appointed to monitor this in each county or other district.

    Response: Let it be carried out as above.

18. Regarding the wool staple, that it be ordained that cloth be made in England.

    Response: [none].

19. That the wearing of fine furs might be restricted.

    Response: It is recorded elsewhere.

20. To ordain remedy in cases where those who have carried off the goods of great lords die, and the goods fall into the hands of their executors.

    Response: The executors should have action by writ of trespass for goods that the testator carried off half a year before his death, and of other goods of which the testator was impleaded at time of death.

21. Complaint against the oppressions made by some lords of the land, who take grain, animals, hay, oats, meat, and other victuals from the people where they live without their consent and often without paying anything, or paying much less than the true value. Similarly, when such great lords pass through the land they lodge with abbots, priors, and other men of the Church against their will, and if the wardens of these places are not ready to receive them, they break down the doors of their barns, granaries, and cellars and take straw, fodder, wine, meat, and all other victuals without paying anything. This is against the law concerning poor and rich, as if a man of the people goes to one of the houses of the great lords and takes anything without consent, he is accused of theft and robbery. Thus they request that the statute made regarding such cases in the time of the late king might be renewed, and

some explicit words inserted to restrain the great lords from such oppressions.

Response: The statutes made on this are sufficient, but in order that they are carried out inquiries are to be held according to the form of the statute.

22. Complaint that when an ordinary man impleads a great lord, he will be so threatened by the lord that he will hardly dare to sue his plea in the king's court, and if he sues the jurors he will also be threatened; so that ordinary people do not dare to speak the truth, and many trespasses remain unpunished.

    Response: [none].

23. Complaint that sometimes a plaintiff in a case of trespass impleads some of his own party, and brings one of them to answer, and by their deceitful defence and damages extracts a great sum in fraud and then flees. Request that in such cases remedy might be made by attaint, or in some other way.

    Response: As above.

Text

1. De ce qe par la ou dame qe tent en dowar aliene en fee et se oblige a la garr, et son heir est barre le quel q'il eit par dessent ou noun apres la mort la femme, si issint ne soit qe le fitz ou heir ne y ne mette chalange selonc la forme del estatut de Gloucestre avant la mort la mere; et si tenaunt par la curtesye d'Engleterre aliene, son heir n'est par barre s'il ne eyt par dessent a la value.

    Response: Il semble q'il est leu qe desore seit fait de alienatiour faites par ceux qui tienent en dower ou autrement a terme de vie sicome etc. par la curteisie de Angleterre.

2. De ce qe damages ne sunt pas agardes en bref de entres sur la disseisine, auxi com en bref de possessioun de aeel et besael.

3. De ceo qe quant les viscountes retournent quod mandaverunt ballivo libertates alicuius qui michi sic respondeat, et le baillif ne respount forsqe de xii d., home n'ad nul averement contre cel retorn, tut seit il contre le estatut de Westminster.

    Response: Il semble qe l'averement gist vers le baillif come vers viscountes quant ils responount de tres petites issues.

4. De ce qe viscount a la deliverances des gaoles ne vienunt pas avaunt touz lour prisouns, mes retinent pur douns a lour volente ceux q'il volunt, saunz penaunce pur ces aver.

Response: Il semble q'il est bien qe si nul viscounte face nul concelement de prison ou enditement soit le viscounte eit la prison d'un an et soit rende a la volunte le Roi, et qe chescun qui voudra soit resceu a suier pur le Roi en cel cas, et les iustices iadumeins qui serount assignez a la deliverance de la gaiole[15] enquergent sur tieles concelementz et punissent le viscont come desues est dit.

5. De ceo qe en plee de champard nul home ad accioun fors qe le Roy, par qey nul home ad volente assewre en ce proces de champard.

Response: Il semble q'il est bien qe homme enpense.

6. De ce qe q'avant un seneschal d'un graunt seignur vodra nul grever fest presenter a la lete soen seignur ascun faus presentement, et fait avisiers saunz aftererement a sa volunte, de qei il ne ad nul recoverer en la chauncellerie de cel faus presentement.

7. Par ceo qe avant ces houres ad este parle qe ceo seroit profit a nostre seignur le Roi et au poeple pur divers resons qe touz les iustices se mellent de la corone, d'an en an enveiassent lour escrites a l'escheqer, issint qe les chateux foirfaitz et autres profitz nostre seignur de ceux qui ount lour final iuggement puissent estre levez d'an en an, al oeps nostre seigneur le Roi et de ceaux qe les deurent aver par leur fraunchises.

Response: Semble qe ceo serroit a parler au prochein parlement.

8. Item, de ceo qe avant ces houres ad este parle des limitacions des brefs de droit et d'autres, la quele parlaunce n'estantes uns uncore en efect, semble qe ceo seroit a parler pur le profit du Roi et le poeple.

Response: Il semble qe bref de droit soit limite de tute le temps le Roi Henri, brefs de possession etc. du coronement le Roi Edward, bref de novele disseisine de son passage en Gascoigne.

9. Item, de ce q'est contenu en la graunt chartre qe si heir soit dedeinz age, soen seignur n'eyt la garde de ly ne de sa terre avant ceo q'il eyt pris son homage, la quele chose n'est pas tenue

---

[15] The words 'enquergent facent' have been deleted here.

devers nostre seignur ne vers autres qe sont en le cas semble, qe par la sentence qest done sur la dit chartre qe cel point fust amesure.

10. Item, memorandum de illis qui tenent de escaetis in manu regis existentibus.

    Response: xxx capitulo magne carte.

11. Item, de ceo qe en brefs de trespas et d'oier et terminer gentz n'ount une concience de mettre les damages du trespas a quatrebles ou plus, qe droit ne seroit par taunt q'ome ne put une aver atteinte sur damages en trespas, tut le put homme aver en autre plee, pur ceo qe malice se crest de iour en autre, et semble qe seroit bien de mettre remedie.

12. Item, de ceo qe au darein parlement fust acorde qe le proces du bref de dette fust encorcy par diverses causes, et ordeine soit a ceo q'est dit qe il n'y ad autre abreggement forqe en lieu de summons mettre pone, le quel n'est abreggement forqe d'un iour. Semble qe depuis qe statut de marchand est defait, q'ant a commune qe ceo sereit bien qe le proces de bref de dette sereit plus abregge, qar gentz qe demourent en forein pays de la terre ne pount en tenz lour contractz venir de fere reconisances en courte qe port record.

13. Item, de mettre les bons pointz en estatut.

14. Item, de [...][16] remedi contre faus retours des bailiffs de franchises.[17]

    Response: Ut supra.

15. Item, de ordener coment les chateux des felons et futifs, an et wast, deodandes, wrec de mere et autres tieles profitz qi ne se lievent forsqe en eyre, peussent estre levez de an en an al oeps le Roi, sicome autres seigneurages le lievent a lour eops, qe tiels profitz pernent par chartre ou d'antiquite.

16. Item, de mettre totes balaunces en fyn, auxi bien pur vendre come pur achater, q'ar homme dist qe tutes les balances du roialme sunt fauses fors celes qe sunt de feures, a graunt damage des grauntz et a commun poeple.

[16] Illegible.
[17] This item is crossed out.

Response: Soit mis en execution par bref.

17. Item, de redrescer totes les mesurs de blee, vin et de cervise par tut le roialme, et de mettre conservatours sur ceo en chescun countee ou autre garde.

    Response: Soit mis etc. come amount.

18. Item, de l'estaple des leins, et de ordener qe draps soient faitz en Engleterre.

19. Item, del user des riches pellures estrescer.

    Response: Par aillours est remembre.[18]

20. Item, de ordener remedi contre ceux qui emportent les biens des grauntz seignurs et des autres, quant eux gisent en lour moriaunt et tost apres la mort, devant qe les biens viegnent as les mains des executours, et cel cas avient sovent.

    Response: Il semble qe bon seroit qe les executores eient action par bref de trespas des biens le testatour emportez un demi an davant sa mort, et des autres biens dont le testatour morust empledant.

21. Come Roi soit tenu par son serment de meintenir la leye de sa terre, la quele leye doit estre une pur povres et riches, le poeple de ceste terre auxi bien gentz de seinte eglise come autres se sentent mout greve par oppressiones qe ascuns countes, barons et autres grauntz de la terre fount sur eux, cestasavoir par la ou tieux seignurs sount demorantz il fount leur prises de bledz, bestes, feins, aveynes chars et autres vitailles sur le people, enviroun auxi bien en marches come dehors, contre gre de gentz, sovent saunz rien paier, et s'il paient ceo sera mout meins qe la verrai value. Et ensement qaunt tieux grauntz seignurs passent parmi la terre il vount gisir sur abbes, priours et autres gentz de seinte eglise contre lour volente, et si les gardeins des lues ne soient prest de les receivre il fount debriser les oeus des graunges, garners et celers et pernent son litere, provande, vin, chars et tutz autres vitailles sauntz rien paier auxi come en l'article avant, et issi n'est par la ley uve endroit des povres et des riches, qar si un home du poeple venist a une des mesuns des grantz seigneurs et riens preist illoeqes contre le gre le gardein, homme lui surmettroit larcine et roberie, et partaunt selonc la lei porteroit myse de vie et de membre. Dount il semble q'il seroit bon qe l'estatut fait en tieu cas en temps le Roi qi mort est feust recite, et ascuns expresses

---

[18]This is the response to both items 18 and 19.

paroles mys pur refrendre les grauntz de tieux oppressiones fere et conforter le poeple de vivre en quiete, qe le dit estatut seit fermement garde.

Response: Il semble qe les estatutez sur ceo faitz son suffissantz, mes qe il soient mis en execucion enquerrours assignez solonc la fourme de les estatutz.

22. D'autre part, par la ou un home du poeple emplede un graunt seignur, il sera taunt manace par le graunt seignur qe a peyne osera il suer sa querele en le court le Roi, et s'il sue les iurours du pais serount auxint taunt manace q'il ne oserount aprocher la court le Roi pur nul verite dire, par qei plusours trespasses demoerent despuniz, a graunt damage et du Roi et de partie.

23. Item, il avient aucune foiz qe pleintif en trepas emplede auncun de sa covine ovesqes autres, et mette unx de sa covine plus tost a respons, et par lour feinte defens et damage taxez a trop outrageous somme en fraude et a fui, qe nuls des autres apres puissent ceux damages amesurer, qe en ceo cas soit fait remede par attente come desus est dit, ou autre remede trovez.

Response: Ut supra.

Note

The document is not headed and its appearance and form suggest that it is a composite of conciliar memoranda and of summaries and fuller transcriptions of petitions submitted in parliament. The scribe of the main items left spaces between each of them, and the responses are written into these gaps in a different hand. The date remains uncertain, but the fullest analysis suggests that the document is closely associated with a parallel (and in some places verbatim) conciliar agenda produced at the time of the York parliament of May 1322 and that some or all of the issues that it addresses had been raised in that assembly (Ormrod 1990a; the version of the document given there, pp. 27–31, has been revised for this edition). The reference to 'the last parliament' in item 12 is in this respect ambiguous, and could refer either to the assembly of July–August 1321 or to that of May 1322: no additional evidence has been established for a debate on the writ of debt at either of these assemblies.

The petitions reveal the knowledge and competence of their authors in crafting and justifying their arguments. Item 1 refers to the Statute of Gloucester of 1278 (*SR*, I, 47, 48), item 3 to the Statute of Westminster II of 1285 (*SR*, I, 80–81), item 9 to clause 3 of Magna Carta (the

1216 version, as confirmed in 1217, 1225 and thereafter: *Select Charters*, pp. 337, 341, 350), and item 11 to the revisions of the Statute of Merchants made under the Ordinances of 1311, which remained in force after some of the Ordinances were reissued in 1322 (*SR*, I, 165; *RP*, I, 456–457). Item 21, the longest of the entries, refers both to the statute of 1300 (the *Articuli super Cartas*) on the regulation of purveyance (*SR*, I, 137) and to the king's coronation oath to uphold the laws (*Foedera*, II.i, 33); it also deploys the motif of the obligations of the king to represent the interests of all, rich and poor alike, found elsewhere in common petitions of the fourteenth century (see nos 56 and 57). The more general reference to a statute made in the time of the late king in item 21, concerning magnate abuses of purveyance, is probably linked to the *Articuli super Cartas* of 1300 (*SR*, I, 30). The crown followed suit. In the response to clause 8, it proposed that the limits of legal memory should be undated beyond those set by the Statute of Westminster I (1275) (see also no. 36). And in its answer to item 10 (which is not set out as a petition, but as a memorandum, but appears to follow on from item 9), it referred explicitly to the solution provided by 'clause 30' of Magna Carta (meaning, it seems, clause 31 of the 1225 version: *Select Charters*, pp. 338, 343, 350).

The highly disturbed nature of English politics in 1322, following the Battle of Boroughbridge and the execution of the king's cousin Thomas of Lancaster and several of his leading supporters, meant that very few of the issues raised in this agenda were addressed substantively or prompted actual initiatives by the crown. It is not surprising, then, that a number of them were taken up again in the list of common petitions compiled in the parliament of October–November 1324 (no. 115). Indeed, in some cases – for example, the issues over the keeping of prisons (item 4), the penalties of the eyre (item 15), the regulation of weights and measures (item 16), the encouragement of domestic cloth manufacture (item 18), and sumptuary legislation on the wearing of fur (item 19) – the matters were of sufficient import and the common petitions were sufficiently persistent for them to be taken up after the fall of Edward II and became the basis for legislative initiatives in the early years of Edward III (Plucknett 1940: 116–126). The document therefore provides an important record of a range of perennial and systemic issues on which the council, the lords, and the commons could all identify the need for reform. In particular, the anti-baronial stance of some of the issues – including those articulated in clauses that appear to draw on petitions (item 21 on purveyance, and item 23 on abuses of the law) suggest that the elected representatives in parliament, the knights and burgesses, were contributing actively to political debate in the parliaments of this period (Ormrod 1990a).

114. Common petition in four parts (SC 8/108/5398)
1324

Summary

The commonalty of England:

1. The exchequer demands repayment of debts dating from the time of Henry III and earlier, by which the people are greatly impoverished. Some of the debts have been pardoned and others paid, but the receipts have been lost.

2. The poor people of the realm were accustomed in the times of the king's forefathers to petition in the chancery, but now must speak directly to the king or pay in order to obtain a writ. They request remedy, that the poor might have the same access to the law as the rich.

3. Request that the king provide remedy against the sheriffs and under-sheriffs who continue to take fees, robes, and pensions in contravention of the Statute of Lincoln, which requires that no sheriff should be in the service of a great lord, in order that they might better serve the king and commonalty.

4. Concerns about the damage that will result if the lands of the Templars are granted to the Hospitallers, as this will cause the pope to dissolve all the religious houses of England and to depose the archbishops and bishops, which would be a grave impoverishment to the land and detrimental to the dignity of the crown.

Response: Those who feel aggrieved should come to the king and he will do right.
In the presence of the king.

Text

1. A nostre seignur le Roi et a soun consail monstre le commonalte d'Engleterre; qe come il sont grantmentz grevetz par diverse demaundes qe venont par summones hors del eschekere du temps le Roi Henry le voil, et du graunt temps avaunt et apres des autres progenitours le dit nostre seignur le Roi qe ore est les queus dettes les uns furount pardonez et les autres paiez les queus acquitances et tailles sont peris et ars, par quele demaunde le people est moult enpovris. Pleise au dit nostre seignur le Roi qe de ceo voille aver

regarde en eide du povre people relever qe grace et remedie fut fete.

2. Derecheif monstre la dite commonalte du realme au dit nostre seignur le Roi; qe come le povre people du realme solieit en temps de ces progenitours estre bonement delivers en la chauncelerie par lour peticion solomp ceo qe le cas fust, et ore nul ne puet illoqes remedie aver, ne bref si ne soit de meime chose saunz parler au Roi ou doner deners au nostre dit seignur le Roi, et nul pour homme ne puet poynt siwere la court tauntqe il pussint au Roi parler, ne d[ener]s[19] ount pur achatre la ley de la terre devers la court nostre dit seignur le Roi. Par qei le dite commonalte priount au nostre dit seignur le Roi qe pleise a sa seignurye qe de ceste chose remedie fust fete, qe les povre gentz pussint auxi bien ateyndre la lei come les riches, si lui pleise.

3. Derecheif monstre la dite communalte du realme a nostre seignur le Roi; qe come les viscountes et suthviscountes en lour countez pernont feetz, robes et pensions, ceo est asaver les uns pernont plus et les uns meyns, dount le povre people ne poet aver nule manere de reisoun ne de droit encountre ceaux ove qi les avantditz viscountes et suthviscountes sont demerez, e neynt eant regard al estatut de Nichole, qe voet qe nul viscounte soit seneschal du graunt seignur, ne de nuli retenaunce, mes qe tiels yseient qe puissient de tut a cele office atendre, pur lealment le Roi et la communalte server. Dount le povre people prie de ceo remedie.

4. Derecheif priont la dite communalte au dit nostre seignur le Roi q'il voille aver regard des terres et tenementz neasgeres au Templars, qe eux ne seient grantez a Ospitalers, pur divers mescheifs et desheritances qe puissunt eschoire au dit nostre seignur le Roi et a sa coroune, ceo est asavoir qe si les avantditz Ospitalers puissunt par tiel voie ateyndre a les teres et tenementz avantdites, ceo serreit un informacioun a l'apoistaille a defere totes la religious d'Engleterre, et a deposer les ercevesqes, evesqes d'Engleterre et assigner lour lay feetz a un ou a deux de ces parenz, solomp ceo qe lui plerra atener de la court de Rome, et issint devendreit il veisyn au Roi d'Engleterre la, en ceuax qe tenoit ore les dites terres sont ces suges, et cel qe parteynt au spiritualte il dorreit a divers freres chescun iour un deux marks ou vynt southe pur faire le office, solomp ceo qe les eglises fussunt petites ou graundes, et le remenaunt qe parteynt a la spiritualte freit il paier a la court de Rome a sa tresurie, dount cest chose chorreit gravment

---

[19] Illegible due to tear in parchment: supplied from context.

enpoverissement de la terre et emblemyssement et desheritaunce de sa dignite et de sa coroune aperte. Par qei la dite commonalte priont au dit nostre seignur le Roi qe de cel mescheif voille aver avisement par son bon consail qe remedie fust faite.

Response: Celi qe seut grevee veigne et le Roi li fera droit. Coram rege.

Note

This schedule of four common petitions was first noted by Rayner (1941: 552–553) and dated by her to some point between 1316 and 1324. Buck (1983b: 145) and Ormrod (1990a: 6) date it positively to the parliament of February–March 1324 (for which no parliament roll is extant), which promulgated the statute assigning the Templars' lands to the Hospitallers, an impending action referred to in item 4 (*SR*, I, 194–196). Item 1 was published by Buck (1983b: 176), items 2 and 3 by Ormrod (1990a: 6 n. 3, 20 n. 1); item 3 is a slightly shorter copy of an apparently earlier petition on sheriffs (no. 5). The document has been fully re-edited for publication here. The items are written up as a continuous series, without spaces between them; the responses are written on the dorse.

The matters raised in this set of common petitions were of significant political sensitivity in 1324. The question of the levying of the ancient debts of the crown, raised in item 1, arose from a major campaign launched by Edward II's exchequer, which raised regular complaints in the early 1320s (Buck 1983b: 134; Ormrod 1990a: 13). The second item, suggesting the problems arising from an insistence that private petitions be dealt with by the king in person, reflects the growing sensitivity during this reign about the reservation of common law matters to the royal grace and the disposition of royal judgements under writs of the privy seal (Davies 1918: 136–158; Wilkinson 1924; Trueman 1956). Item 3 reflects the general anxiety throughout the early fourteenth century on the abuse of office by sheriffs and, like other petitions of the period (nos 5 and 115), refers explicitly to the efforts to regulate the office and address corruption among sheriffs under the Statute of Lincoln of 1316 (*PROME*, III, 187–188; *SR*, I, 174–175). The final item harks back to the decision of Pope Clement V in 1312 to suppress the Order of the Temple and to assign its property for the support of crusading in the Holy Land. Many of those who had been given custody of the confiscated estates in England at the time of their original seizure by Edward II in 1308 were understandably reluctant in and after 1312 to hand them over to the Knights Hospitaller. At the moment of its inception, then, the 1324 statute seemed to suggest that lay lords in England would be unjustly stripped of assets they had come to assume were theirs. In fact, the statute allowed a right of appeal, so that very little of the Templars' property actually changed hands (Phillips 2009: 4–8; and for the subsequent history of this statute, see nos 20 and 21). With its lengthy criticisms of the curia and treasury of Rome, the final item in this set of common petitions also reflects the more general anti-papal sentiment running among the English political community throughout the fourteenth century.

115. Common petition in seventeen parts (C 49/5/25) 1324

Summary

The people of England:[20]

1. Complaint against unlawful practices by mayors and bailiffs in cities and towns, and request that the customs of towns should be set down in writing and examined by the king's council, so that those that are unlawful should be abolished.

   Response: He who feels himself oppressed should complain.

2. Request that mayors, aldermen, and bailiffs of towns should not be vintners or other merchants, as they abuse their office by forestalling goods and raising the price of many necessities.

   Response: Another remedy is ordained.

3. Complaint of disturbances of the peace in towns, and lack of agreement on when the common bell should be rung; also, that these towns wish to have the proceeds of the murage to build town walls, as these are often misappropriated.

   Response: Regarding the first part, the mayor and aldermen of London are to be summoned on Tuesday next to decide for which emergencies the common bell should be rung. Regarding the second article, certain loyal men are to be assigned by the king in each town which at this time has murage, pavage, and pontage, to hear from those responsible the way in which these are spent.

---

[20] The document is damaged and parts of the text are illegible and irrecoverable.

Memorandum regarding murage etc.[21] If the auditors in charge discover that anything has been concealed or held back, then those responsible are to complete the work under the supervision of the auditors, and then be punished.

4. Request that a fixed weight be agreed throughout the realm for measures of grain and other goods, as is ordained in Magna Carta.

Response: On Tuesday let it be noted from the rolls of chancery what was done in the king's tenth year.

5. Complaint of the waste and destruction committed by the keepers of lands of heirs who are under age at the deaths of their predecessors.

Response: Let the Statute *de Custodiis* be observed.

6. Request that the Statute of Lincoln on sheriffs and bailiffs be upheld.

Response: The king wishes and commands that the statute be observed.

7. Complaint that sheriffs and bailiffs at tourns and views of frankpledge imprison people without cause, against Magna Carta.

Response: The bishops and nobles will consider this matter.

8. Complaint that sheriffs and bailiffs of franchises amerce people and acquit them as they please, to the great oppression of the people and in contravention of Magna Carta.

Response: Let the remedy that is ordained in chancery be maintained.

9. Complaint that the great fairs of England extend beyond the limits of the time appointed and assigned, disturbing many people and damaging trade, as the merchants do not know when they should come or go. The commonalty, both merchants and people, request that no fair might be held outside the time appointed by warrant, and that those who remain longer be punished.

Response: The barons [of the exchequer] are to find a solution on a precedent from the king's tenth regnal year.

10. Complaint that sheriffs and others who keep prisons should not accept ransoms in return for releasing those indicted by plea, as was ordained in a former statute.

---

[21] This item is on a strip of parchment fixed to the document lower down its face. A mark indicates that it is a continuation of the response to item 3.

Response: Let a remedy be observed as is ordained by statute.

11. Complaint that sheriffs' clerks take bribes for the execution of writs.

    Response: Let the Statute of Lincoln be observed.

12. Complaint about sheriffs [meaning lost].

    Response: Let the same statute be observed.
    Our lord the king commands that the said statute might be observed in all points, and that any who complain of wrongs done against them should have a writ in chancery.

13. Complaint about the proliferation by sheriffs of the office of bailiff errant and of putting the office to farm; the bailiffs have too many clerks and catchpoles, riding and on foot, and all of this is to the great oppression of the people and contrary to right, reason, and the ancient custom of the realm.

    Response: Let a remedy be made according to the Statute of Lincoln.

14. Complaint that, although the king recently pardoned his people all debts dating from the time of his ancestors to the twentieth year of his father's reign, his sheriffs in each county again demand these debts by order of the exchequer, to the great oppression and impoverishment of the people.

    Response: It is testified by the treasurer and barons of the exchequer that a writ was sent according to the form of the pardon.

15. Request that the amercements, fees, and chattels of felons and fugitives, and other dues that bishops, earls, barons, and other nobles receive from their men and their tenants by the franchises they hold from the king might be valid in the exchequer, without oppressing the people.

    Response: The king wishes that the allowances made to the lords in such cases by the treasurer and barons of the exchequer be carried out according to due process.

16. Complaint that the chattels of felons and fugitives and the annual profits of their lands, which are owed by right to the king or others, remain in the hands of the sheriffs or the towns until the eyre, which sometimes does not take place for thirty years, by which time the goods are spent by those who have them in their keeping.

    Response: The justices will consider this and inform the king.

MULTIPLE PETITIONS 227

17. That Christians commit usury in various ways, some covert and some open, to the great oppression of the people.

   Response: The bishops will be called to consult with the magnates and justices.

Text

Fet a remembrer qe le peple d'Engleterre se sent souvent oppres e greve en tut autres choses de cestes suthescriptes:

1. De ceo qe meirs e baillifs e ceux qi assigne sunt a garder les citez e les graunz viles en roialme font plusours cors e duresces a gentz [foreins][22] qi venent de denz leur poair, e avowent leur fetz par usages qe sunt de tut contrariez a ley et ensement a resound, et font tieles usages kaunt leur plest. Dount grant seurte serreit au pople qe tuz les usages qe citezeins e burges du roialme cleyment aver de denz leur villes et [citees][23] le pople seyent mis en escrit et liveres al escheker denz certeyn temps, et illoeqes seyent bien examines par sages du counseil le Roi, et si akuns seient trovetz contrariez a resoun seient aneintyz, car coment qe eles seient contraries a la ley e les ne deyvent pas estre contraries a resoun.

   Response: Qui se sentiat gravatum, conqueratur.

2. Item; de ceo qe par tut en graunt viles nule certeyn assise de payn, vin ne cerveise n'est garde ne forstal ouste ne forstaller puny, pur ceo qe les mairs, les audremanns et les baillifs qi deyvent mesmes les villes garder et le pople de denz demeraunz et repeyrauntz a dreit treter et justisce sunt vineters, et unt leur fourns et leur bracines et marchaundunt de totes choses qe a marche venent, et par colour de balye forstallunt les chose vendables; issint qe comune des gentz ne poent avenir, si noun par [...] eux et de ceo [deivent] la outraiouse chierte qe ili ad de tutes choses, et meement des vitailles, dount hom covient estre sustenu. E semble qe grant profit serreit a common pople qe ceux qe deyvent ceux offices a justicer forstallours et meytenir assise de payn et de vin et cervoise ne se entremerssent poynt de marchaunder com comon marchaunz, taunt com [qeux] seient en comon office.

   Response: Alias ordinatum est remedium.

---

[22] Conjectural.
[23] Illegible: supplied from context.

3. Item; de ceo qe les graunz villes sunt malement governez et gardez, de ceo qe en chescune ville s'est piecea contente, et de iour en altre se acrest alliaunce entre foreins ioefnes et autres a fere bateries et meyntenaunces acontre la pes, et a ceo si une medlee se comence entre deus ou treis meyntenaunt unt en costoume de soner common seyn, a quoi tauntz se assemblent qe ceux qe la pees deussent garder ne unt poair de les iustiser, a grant peril de tuz qe sunt repeiraunz et conversaunz en granz villes; et semble qe par la ou comoun seyn se soune la commune deust respondre du fet qe avounent estre [...] si mal en avegnie dount les iustices ne suffisant agre fer[ent], ou au meyns des corps des meffesours. Et estre ceo par la ou comounes de tieles villes purchacent d'aver murage pur les villes enclor, auxi bien a seurte du pais come des villes, et le murage est coly des biens de bone gent du pais et des autres, qe leur biens y enveyent ou menent ceux des villes qi coillent le murage se enrichissunt et nel mettent pas de grant partie, en ceo a qoy le Roi las graunte au damage du pople.

Response: Quo ad primam partem vocentur maior et aldermanni London' die Martis proxime futuri, et sciatur ab eis in quibus casibus communis campana pulsatur etc.
Quo ad secundum articulum, assignentur certi fideles regis in singulis villis que a tempore regis habuerunt muragium, pavagium et pontagium, ad audiendum compotum inde etc. debite modo.
Quo ad muragium etc: et si auditores compoti inveniant aliquid concelatum vel retentum et opus pro quo \huiusmodi muragium etc/ concessum fuit non sit perfectum, tunc id quod concelatum vel retentum fuerit ponatur in reparacione operis per visum auditorum et aliorum quos \ad hoc/ deputaverint, et concelatores et retentores etc puniantur ad vel mitatem etc. Et si opus perfectum fuerit, tunc illud residuum remaneat domino regi et nichilominus culpabiles puniantur supradicto modo.

4. Item; de ceo qe nule certeynte de pois ne de mesure de ble ne de autres choses, qe par pois et mesure sunt vendables at atachables, ne eyt tenu nule part du roialme a forment graunt damage, auxi bien des graunz come de comoun poeple et en peril des almes de ceaux qe en coupe sunt par la sentence done sour la grante charter, en la qele entre altres choses est contenu qe une mesure de vin, de ceruise, de ble et de pois seit par tut le roialme [...]

mes q'il ne furent poynt contenu en la chartre commune, resoun le demaunde qe ensi soit.

Response: Die Martis deferantur rotuli cancellarie de hiis quod anno decimo facta fuerunt.

5. Item; de ceo qe les heirs auxi bien des graunz come des mene gentz, qi en temps de mort de leur auncestres sunt denz [age . . .][24] garde sunt come reyntz et destruiz par le wast et destructioun que home fet de leur heritages en temps de garde ia fait qe la dite [. . .] et fraunchises par la dite sentence affirme soit contenu, qe les gardeyns ne deyvent prendre forsk resonables issues [. . .] saunz destructioun et wast des homages ou des choses, et a ceo duraunt la garde deyvent sustenir les biens qe a leur sunt [. . .] choses en auxi bone garde come eux les averont resceu.

Response: Videatur statuta de custodiis etc.

6. Item; de ceo qe l'estatut de vicscountes et de ballifs qe fut fet au dareyn parlement de Nichole en [. . .] pas este tenuz ne encore n'est, a mount graunt damage du Roi et de [. . .] pople.

Response: Le Roy veut et comande qe le statut soit garde.

7. Item; de ceo qe vicscountes et ballifs en les tourns et vewes de frank plege [. . .] de ces font enprisoner la gent et le pople [. . .] leur volunte [. . .] estre deyvent enquerables [en court de viscounts] [. . .] frank plegge se tenount seient [mis] en certeyn [. . .] contre la graunt chartre demaunde a qe nul homme seit atteint par presentement sauntz respons.

Response: Deliberent prelati ac proceres.

8. Item; de ceo qe vicscountes et ballifs des fraunchises et de hors et autres [. . .] ceux qe sunt amerciez de quit eux a leur volentez, en graunt oppressioun du peple et countre la graunte charte.

Response: Seit garde remedie q'est ordene en chancellerie.

9. Item; de ceo qe les graunz feres d'Engleterre qe sunt graunte et ordene al esement du pople en divers pais auxi bien com a profit des seinurgages a qi les feres sunt demoerent et sunt tenuz outre temps limite et assigne, issint qe la continuaunce hors de resoun de une feire fet destourbaunce a mouz des altres. Dount les pais sount le plius deseseement,[25] terres et seignurages des feyres perdent leur profitz, les marchaunz ne sevent kaunt il deyvent

---

[24] From this point onwards, four or five words are illegible at the end of each line.
[25] *Sic*: the correct form would have been the past participle of the verb *deseser*.

certeynement venir ou departir [...] quoi le meyns y venent et le meyns de marchaundises sunt illoeqes perts et [terres]. Prie la comunalte auxi bien des marchaunz com de poeple qe le temps de feires ancienement ordene et limite seit garde saunz pluis longe continuance, issint qe nule feire seit tenue otre le temps limite et le garaunt de la feire, et qe certeyne peyne seit mis a ceux qe pluis longues y demoerent qe le garaunt de la feire ne demaunde.

Response: Iniunctum est baronibus quod informent [...] anno decimo de premissis facta fuerunt.

10. Item; de ceo qe vicscountes et autres qi ount gardes de gaoles ne soeffrent saunz rauncioun prendre des gentz endites lesse par pleynte, ia seit qe statut soit fet sont en graunt temps passe.

Response: Observentur remedia ordinata per statuta.

11. Item; de ceo qe vicscountes par tut sont a temps des ore fere les execuciouns des brefs par leur clers et leur escrites par procurement les parties [...] as bailifs et hundreders as queux les execuciouns apendent de par noun dreit [...] mye a altre si ne soit en defaute de [vie], et c'est chose est a tresgraunt oppressioun du pople et encontre l'estat de tuz les grauntz et autres du roialme.

Response: Observetur statutum Linc'.

12. Item; de ceo qe vicscountes levent les ballifs de soutz eux [...].

Response: Observetur idem statutum.
Nostre seigneur le Roi comaunde qe le dit statut soit garde en tutz ses pointz, et qe s'il nul se pleigne de chose faite encontre ceo eit bref en chancellerie pur le Roi et pur le meismes, et aussi seit feite bref pur le Roi a celi qi vodra sue pur le Roy.

13. Item; de ceo qeu un counte ne soleit estre qe un ballifs erraunt, ou deus ou plus pur mettre en execucioun les maundemenz le Roi et du vicscounte en defaute des ballifs hundredres deinz fraunchise et de hors si defauteiont, et ceux ballifs errauntz soleient tuz estre trovez des vicscontes ore mettont les vicscountes par tut plusours ballifs errauntz et les balient l'office aferme et eux ont plusours south eux, clers et kachepols a chival et a piee et chescun devaunt un certeyn, et tut en tresgraunt oppressioun du pople et en countre dreit et tote manere de resoun et de auncien usage du roialme.

Response: Fiat remedium quia tanget statutum Linc'.

14. Item; de ceo qe par ou le Roi qe ore est pardona nadgweres a son pople totes maners des dettes com des amercimentz de issues

forfez et par bref ave de tut le temps de ses auncestres al an vintisme du regne son pere, uncore ses vicscountees de chescun counte unt mesmes les choses en demaunde par les somonses del Escheker, a mout graunt oppressioun et enpoverissemenz du pople.

Response: Testificatum est per thesaurarium et barones de scaccario quod per brevem de scaccario missum est per antiquas summonitiones ad illum finem quod corrigantur iuxta forma pardonacionis, et Rex sic precepit fieri cum festinatione et quod ex habundanti fiat inde breve de cancellarii.

15. Item; de ceo qe les amerciementz, fyns, chateux de felons et de futifs, et autres dettes qe prelatz, countes, barouns et autres gentz vut rescever de leur hommes et leur tenauntz par les fraunchises qe eux unt du Roi et de ses auncestres tut iours curent avaunt en somouns del Escheqer, saunz estre alowe a nient graunt oppression du pople.

Response: Quant a proces de alowance fere en tieus cas ceo appertent as tresorer et as barouns; et le Roi veult qe il facent due process, et qe apres alowance fait as seigneurs des fraunchises seient ceus deschargez vers le Roi qe sont assignez a autres par celes allowances, et de ceo seit fait bref de chancellerie.

16. Item; de ceo qe chateux des felouns et de futifs et le profit del an et le wast de leur terres et tenementz qe de dreit appertenent au Roi ou as altres qi aver les deussent par leur fraunchises demoerent en meyns des vicscountes ou des villes tantqeu heire, sauntz estre liverees au Roi ou as seignurs as qi ceux apertenient par leur fraunchises, a graunt damage du Roi et des seignurs avauntditz et des gentz de villes; car coment qe gentz seint dampneez devaunt iustices pur felonie ou larcine ou outlaghes et par taunt leur chateux seient forfeiz, mesmes les chateux demorent en garde de vicscounts ou de villee tauntqeu heire, qe par caas ne sera pas tenu une feze denz trente aunz, a dunqes seront les biens despendus et gastes par ceux qe les aveyent en garde et leur heirs ou autres qi rien de ceo averont enchargeez a estre ne la meite ou pluis ou par cas tut concelee sauntz estre presente en heire, et issint les perde le Roi ou ceux qi par fraunchise aver les deussent.

Response: Les iustices s'avisent et certefient le Roy.

17. Item; de ceo qe Cristiens sont usurers en diverses maneres, aucunes covertes e aucunes overtes, a grant oppression du people; qe remedie soit fate.

Response: Prelati vocatis \magnatibus et/ justiciariis deliberent.

Note

Items 4–8 and 10–16 of this memorandum, along with English summaries of the other contents, were previously published by Ormrod (1990a: 31–33); all of the recoverable text from the damaged original has been transcribed anew and re-edited here so as to present as much as possible of this important document. The date was determined by Rayner, who noted that the response to item 4, concerning weights and measures, can be cross-referenced to an entry on the fine roll for 3 November 1324 that itself specifies actions previously taken in the tenth regnal year of Edward II (July 1316–July 1317) (*CFR, 1319–1327*, p. 314; Rayner 1941: 554–555). On that basis, the document must have been compiled and annotated at the parliament that met at Westminster in October–November 1324. A short official account of this parliament survives, detailing the king's response to advice provided on the current dispute with France (*RPHI*, pp. 94–98; *War of Saint-Sardos*, pp. 95–97; *PROME*, III, 444–446; Bradford 2007: 259–262, with detailed justification for dating; Bradford 2011: 205–206); but no other business of the assembly was put on this record.

The heading to the present document, 'Memorandum ... ' (*Fet a remembrer...*) highlights the fact that this is not necessarily a schedule of common petitions in the developed sense in which we have them from the 1330s onwards, but a working set of notes capturing the substance of the complaints and requests made during a political assembly and the decisions made upon them. The responses, written into the spaces between the items, are in a different hand from the main text, appear as scrawled notes, and are written variously in Latin and French; for lack of space, the response to item 3 had to be continued on a strip of parchment added on further down the document. These features suggest that the text is the actual working document used when the contents were addressed by the king's council. It is all the more remarkable, therefore, that the complaints and requests appear to preserve so much of the form and language of a series of common petitions submitted in the given assembly. The petitioners are referred to as the 'people of England' (*le peple d'Engleterre*) in the heading. It has been remarked in relation to the anti-urban stance of items 1–3 that the parliament of October–November 1324 included representatives of the shires but not of the cities and towns (Ormrod 1990a: 6 n. 4).

On the other hand, item 9, on the dates of fairs, claims to speak in the name of 'the commonalty, both merchants and people' (*la communalte auxi bien des marchauntz com de poeple*). All of this evidence suggests that this document is a complex composite built from a series of written petitions and oral communications brought to the clerks of parliament and judged by them suitable to send forward to the council.

References to statutes and previous government actions in the document make it clear that both the petitions and the responses looked back extensively to precedents for action undertaken in the reign of Edward I and earlier in the reign of Edward II. The answers to items 10–13 all cite the Statute of Lincoln of 1316, which defined the office of sheriff and continued to be regarded as the central legislation on the powers and accountability of these powerful and often controversial ministers into the reign of Edward III (*SR*, I, 283; *RP*, I, 343, 351 = *PROME*, III, 187–188, 204; *RPHI*, pp. 225, 233 = *PROME*, IV, 190, 198; Morris 1947: 42–43; and see nos 5 and 114). The petition at item 15 makes allusion to the statute of 1316 that pardoned all outstanding communal fines imposed by sessions of the eyre before 1291 (*SR*, I, 281–282). The response to item 9 refers to an initiative taken in February 1317, when the chancery had ordered a general inquiry into the charters it had granted to the holders of fairs in order to determine the precise dates and duration under which they were entitled to run (*CCR, 1313–1318*, p. 456). The response to item 5, with its mention of the Statute *de Custodiis*, refers further back in time to clause 16 of the Statute of Marlborough of 1267, which defined the rights of under-age heirs during the time their lands were held in wardship by their lords (*SR*, I, 23–24; Waugh 1988: 66; Brand 2003: 474–475).

In spite of the apparent lack of compositional wholeness, the substantive points raised by this document are in fact rather more coherent and consistent than is the case in some other schedules of common petitions surviving from around this time. The petitions are, in effect, blocked into sub-sections, with three significant themes emerging: urban issues (items 1–3), sheriffs and other shire officials (items 6–8, 10–13) and the profits of royal justice (items 14–16).

There is little evidence, however, that the crown was inclined to take more positive action to deal with the issues raised. Such inertia is explained partly by the diplomatic emergency brought on by the War of Saint-Sardos and partly by the way in which some of these petitions directly confront contentious policies associated with the ascendancy in the king's council of Hugh Despenser the elder and younger. Item 14 reminds the king of the promise made in 1316 to withdraw the threat of levying communal fines on local communities for the chattels of felons and fugitives, and item 16 points up the anomalies that arose when the now very irregular visitations of the eyre put these and other ancient rights of the crown into commission. The decision to revive the judicial instrument of the eyre in 1321 after a long period of inactivity had effectively superseded the guarantee of 1316 and generated suspicion and complaints that the exchequer would once again start to levy penalties relating to the period before 1290; in spite of the assurance provided in the answer to item 15, there is clear evidence from the mid 1320s of the inclusion in the summonses of the sheriffs of estreats imposed in former eyres (Buck 1983a: 210–212; Ormrod 1990a: 23–24; Lacey 2009: 106–107). The matter had already been raised as an issue of significant concern in the common petitions of 1322 (no. 113) and was now, in 1324, addressed in some detail, from the point of view both of the shire communities at large and, more specifically, of the threat thus posed to the holders of franchises. While this issue was, in isolation, of relatively restricted import, it reflected wider concerns both about the grasping nature of the crown's fiscal policy in the mid 1320s and about the manipulation of justice, especially the eyre, for the purposes of royal profit (Crook 1982; Buck 1983b). As with a number of sensitive issues raised in the common petitions of 1322 and 1324, no effective solutions were found until the next reign: in this specific case, the matter finally came to a head in the parliament of March–May 1340, when Edward III was forced to issue a statute pardoning the penalties of the eyre in return for a generous grant of taxation (*SR*, I, 281–282; Fryde 1969: 260–261; Lacey 2009: 107–109). The case therefore stands as an example of the significant difficulties involved in translating common petitions into government policy under Edward II, and of the consequent uncertain connection between schedules of common petitions and the official record of parliament during the 1320s.

116. Common petition in five parts (SC 8/8/392)
1325

Summary

The king's liege people:

1. Their ancestors have given many tallages to the king's ancestors in order to have the Charter of the Forest, but recently the king's ministers south and north of the Trent have come and taken back vills, lands, and woods, destroyed ditches, and disrupted agriculture, to the great damage of the people and against the

charter. They pray remedy, for God and the soul of the king's father.

Response: It pleases the king that the justices of the forest and their ministers be called before the bishop of London, the chancellor, Geoffrey le Scrope and William de Herle, so that those who wish to plead regarding the taking of land or woods might be heard and the justices and their ministers defend themselves. Also the king's sergeants are to be called to search the exchequer for evidence on this matter, that there might be profit to all concerned.

2. Complaint that many people have been imprisoned and their lands and goods seized, without being convicted by process of law, solely on the false accusations of malevolent persons who are adherents of the king's enemies. Request that they be released, and that henceforth no such arrests be made without due process of law.

Response: Those who are taken by such accusations are to come to chancery and have justice, and henceforth the king does not wish anyone to be arrested contrary to the law of his land: if anyone is, he is to sue, and justice will be done.

3. The tenants of various honors which have come into the king's hand through forfeiture of the rebels were previously able to purchase lands and take feoffment without permission from the lords, but now the king's escheators and other ministers seize the lands as though they were held of the king in chief, which is contrary to Magna Carta; request for a remedy.

Response: With regard to taking fines for the purchase of lands held of honors in the king's hand, the king is to have the same status as the previous lords, according to the tenor of Magna Carta, saving his rights in other matters.

4. Complaint that various lands have fallen into the king's hands by forfeiture of rebels that have been seized wrongfully from others by force, and although inquisitions have been returned in chancery about this, no issue of law has been made. Similarly, lands, manors, vills, and franchises in various counties have been seized by the king, although ownership can be proved by charter. Request that the king order issue of law for such lands, when their title can be proved by inquisitions or by charters.

Response: Regarding the first point: they are to show the inquisitions in chancery, along with any charters or fines they have, and if everything is in order justice is to be done.

The same for the second.

5. Complaint that they have delivered petitions into various parliaments, some of which are adjourned before the king and some before the chancellor, but nothing is done; for which they request a remedy.

Response: It pleases the king.

A petition for the whole commonalty of all the realm.

Text

1. A nostre seignur le Roi mustrent ses liges gentz; qe come leur auncestres et eux eyount donetz plusours taillages as auncestres nostre seignur le Roi pur avier la chartre de la foreste, la quele chartre nous avions del nostre seignur le Roi qe ore est conferme, pur le nostre a lui largement donaunt, puis viegnent les ministres de les forestes de sa Trente et dela, et ount repris en forest villes, terres et boys auxi entierement come unqes furent, encountre la forme de la dite chartre a grant damage de son poeple, et fount abatre fosses et desturbent leur gaynage, et pernent de eux grevouses et sovernels redempciouns e grant destruccioun du poeple, de quey eux prient pur Dieu et l'alme son piere remedie.

Response: Il plest au Roi qe les iustices de la foreste d'une part et d'autre et lur ministres seiont appelez devant l'evesqe de Londres, le chanceler, sire Geffrei Lescrope et sire William de Herle, et ceux qi se vodrent pleindre de purprist de terre ou de boys faire encontre reson et droit seient oyis, et les iustices et lur ministres seient aussint oyis en lur defense, et droit seit fait au Roi et as autres, et sur ceo seient appelez les serianz le Roi pur le Roi, et tantost seit mande as tresorer et chamberlein q'il cerchent en l'escheqer [...][26] put estre trove pur le Roi de la foreste, et qe ceo seit profit tute veys.

2. Et auxint sire prient voz liges gentz; qe come plusours gens de vostre roialme, chivalers, dames et autres sunt pris et emprisone, et lour terres, chateux seisitz par ascusement, sire, a vous feit des gentz malvoillauntz d'aherdaunce a vos rebels ou a vos enemys ou d'autremantz solom lour malveise contruveure, la ou eux ne sunt enditetz n'en autre manere atteynz solom la ley de vostre terre.

[26]Two words are illegible here due to a stain on the right-hand side of the parchment.

Pleyse a vostre haute seygnurye qe desore tieux attachemens ne se facent par simple acusement saunz proces de ley, et qe de ceux ensi pris et emprisonetz voillietz comaunder deliverance solom la ley de vostre terre.

Response: Ceux qi sont pris par tiel accusement voignent en chancelrie et averont droit, et desoremes le Roi ne vult pas qe nul seit pris contre la ley de la terre, et si nul seit, sue et droit ly sera fait.

3. Auxi prient voz liges gentz qi tenent de diverses onours devenuz en vostre meyn par forfeiture de voz rebels; qe com en temps avant qe celes terres et onours devyndrent en vostre meyn il poient achater terres et prendre feoffament saunz aver conge de seignurages, et ore voz eschetours et autres ministers, quant terres deinz le ditz onours sunt purchasetz, seissent les terres com s'ils fuissent tenuz de nostre seignur le Roi en chief com de la coroune, qe est encountre la forme de la grant chartre; dount il prient remedie.

Response: Quant a fins prendre pur purchace des terres et tenementz tenuz de honurs esteanz en la mayn le Roi, eit le Roi mesme tiel estat come les seignurs avoient solom le purport de la grant chartre, sauf au Roi ses droitures et ses prorogatives en autres choses.

4. Auxi prient les dites gentz pur tote la commune; qe come diverses terres ore sunt devenutz en la meyn le Roi par forfeture de ces rebels, les quels il purpristerent par force de seignurye et par disseisyn feit a divers gentz; dount plusours enquestes sunt returnez en chancelrie et nul issue de ley est feit, a grant arerissement de people. Ensement de terres, manoirs, villes, fraunchises en divers counteez les quels sunt seisitz en le meyn nostre seignur le Roi, tut eyent ils chartres de ses progenitours ou de lui meismes nul remedie n'est feit, par ount ils prient a sa seignurie qe des tieles terres, manoirs, villes, rentes, baillies de fee et fraunchises ensi seissiez en la meyn le Roi il voillie comaunder issue de ley solom ceo q'ils purrount mustrer par enquestes ou par chartres de ses progenitours, ou de lui meissmes, q'ils eient resoun de tieles terres avoir, et ceo prient ils pur le esement de son poeple.

Response: Quant al primer point, veignent en chancelrie et mustrent lur chartres et fyns s'il eyent et les enquestes, et si totes choses seient trovez [cleres][27] qe besoignent seit fait droit. En mesme la manere au secunde.

---

[27] Illegible due to stain on right-hand side of parchment, and supplied from *RP*, I, 430.

5. Et aussint sire prient voz liges gentz; que par la ou il ount boute avaunt leur peticiouns en divers parlementz de divers grevaunces, ou les unes sount adiournees devaunt le Roy et les autres devaunt le chaunceler, dount nulle issue n'est faite; qu'il plaise a vostre haute seignurie comaunder remedie.

Response: Il plest au Roi.

Billa pro tota communitate totius regni.

Note

This schedule of petitions was written up with space between each item; the responses are written into these gaps, in a different hand from that of the main text. The document can be positively dated to the parliament of November–December 1325 on the basis of a transcription of its contents (including the responses) found on the dorse of the close roll for the regnal year 19 Edward II (July 1325–July 1326). The entry on the close roll is headed 'the following petitions were granted in parliament at Westminster on the octaves of Martinmas in the year 19 Edward [II], by the king with the assent of the prelates, earls, barons, and others then in the said parliament' (*Memorandum quod petitiones subscripte concesse fuerunt in parliamento apud Westmonasterium convocato in octabis Sancti Martini, anno regni Regis Edwardi filii Regis Edwardi decimo nono, per eundem regem de assensu prelatorum, comitum, baronum, et aliorum in dicto parliament tunc existentium in forma que sequitur*) (*RP*, I, 430 = *CCR, 1323–1327*, pp. 539–540). The text given in the 1325 document, edited here for the first time, differs in some details from that provided on the close roll: the latter contains an additional petition concerning the franchises of the city of London, while the final clause of the response to item 1 in the document published here (*et sur ceo seient appelez ... qe ceo seit profit tute veys*) does not appear on the close roll (Rayner 1941: 555–556). In 1325, the bishop of London referred to in the response to item 1 was Stephen Gravesend; the chancellor was Robert Baldock, archdeacon of Middlesex; Geoffrey le Scrope was chief justice of the king's bench; and William de Herle was a justice of common pleas.

The form of the schedule provides some of the clearest evidence that, by the mid 1320s, the commons in parliament were taking on the primary function of expressing the grievances of the realm before the king (Ormrod 1990a). It is addressed in the name of 'the king's liege people'. Item 4 explicitly states that these 'liege people' were speaking for 'all the commonalty'. The reference in item 5 to the delivery of petitions by the liege people also seems to make the point clearly, though the expression here makes it possible that the reference is to private petitions instead of (or as well as) common petitions. Finally, there is the elaborately written Latin annotation at the foot, 'A petition for the whole commonalty of all the realm' (*Billa pro tota communitate totius regni*), whose addition suggests that the clerks of parliament may have been complicit with the commons in pressing their case to represent the commonalty in parliament.

The crown's apparent willingness to address the complaints raised here and to formalize them in the memorandum on the close roll is the more striking given the controversial nature of some of the demands made. Items 2–4 reflect the notorious activities of the crown following the civil war of 1321–1322, when many lands were seized from persons indicted, or merely suspected, of involvement in the cause of Thomas of Lancaster; during the mid 1320s, and especially after the deposition of Edward II in 1327, hundreds of private petitions flowed in complaining of the hardships and injustices resulting from the brutality of the government, and especially of the king's principal henchmen, Hugh Despenser the elder and younger (Harris 2009). There is also abundant evidence to support the complaint in item 5 that petitions submitted in parliament were not being processed and answered in timely fashion. The crown itself had acknowledged as much in 1320 and 1322; and despite its expressions of good intent typified by the blithe response to the present petition, the problem continued to be acknowledged by all sides into the early years of Edward III (Sayles 1988: 353, 361, 408, 412; Dodd 2007: 71–76; see also nos 110 and 120). However, it is also to be stressed that in this instance (as indeed with the earlier Stamford Articles) there is no evidence that the memorandum made on the close roll in 1325 was publicized as an ordinance or statute. The record therefore appears to be a rather token gesture of goodwill to the domestic political community made at a moment of high tension when the king needed consent to controversial policies being developed in connection with the current conflict with France, known as the War of Saint-Sardos (*PROME*, III, 450–451).

117. Common petition in three parts (C 49/8/23)
*c.*1327–*c.*1337

Summary

[No petitioner specified]:

1. Complaint that people arrested and imprisoned for felonies and trespasses made against the peace have remained in prison for long periods without having delivery, because of the costs incurred by their imprisonment or because the justices have not come into

the county to deliver the gaols. Request that the justices of assize be ordered to hold gaol delivery sessions and charge the sheriffs to carry out the delivery as the law demands; that the justices hold sessions in each county where they are assigned at least twice a year; and that any sheriff who does not obey these terms lose his office and be punished.

2. The common people are greatly delayed from having justice in the king's court as a result of the false returns of sheriffs, especially in cases where a great man is party to the suit against a poor man. Request that, in such cases, the justices amerce the sheriff at their discretion, having regard for the damage that he has done to the party through such false returns, where the party has an averment against the sheriff.

3. The commonalty are greatly grieved in cases where they plead or are impleaded in the courts against great men and others of the realm, because they do not dare to take their pleas elsewhere, in accordance with the law, in cases where they are not able to have justice. They request the king that the justices of assize inquire into such matters, and that in such cases the franchise be seized into the hands of the king until the lord has made a settlement for the trespass and damages.

Response: [none].

Text

1. Primerement, por ce qe grantz mals sont avenuz par cause qe ceux qi ont este pris et emprisonez pur felonies et trespas faitz contre la pees a la suite le Roi, si bien par enditementz come par autre manere, ont demorez treslongement en prison sanz deliverance aver, cestassaver, aucuns pur gaigne qe les viscountes et gaolers ont pris por suite de lor prison, aucuns autres par favour pur lour procurer amistee en le meen temps par la ou ils sont coupables, et aucuns pur lour poverte, et aucuns autres par cause qe les iustices n'ont pas fait session sur la deliverance des gaoles ou ne sont pas venuz en pais par long temps. Si plest il au Roi qe les iustices assignez a prendre les assises et a les gaoles deliverer parmy le roialme soient iurez, qe maintenant faites lour sessions sur les assises, ils serront sur la deliverance des gaoles par la ou ils sont assignez, et chargeront les viscountes de faire venir touz cieux prisons devant eux et le pays pur lor deliveraunce, et facent la deliverance tielle come la ley demande sanz autre delay, et q'ils ferront session en chescun countee par la ou ils sont assignez au

mains deux foiz en l'an, et qe chescun viscounte soit iure desore q'il fra les prisons et le pays pur lour deliverance venir avant les ditz iustices a chescune session, et s'il nel face, perde son office et soit mercie a la volunte le Roi.

2. Item, por ce qe le commun poeple est grantement delaie de droit aver en la court le Roi par cause de trop petites issues retornees par faux retornes des viscountes, meement en cas ou aucun grant est partie a la suite d'un povres homme. Si plest il au Roi qe en cas ou trop petites issues sont retornees sur aucun grant ou riches homme bien conu, qe les iustices n'acceptant point tieu retorne, mes amercient le viscounte selonc lour discrecion, eant regard au damage q'il ad fait a la partie parmy tieu faux retorne, ou eit la partie le verrement devers le viscounte sicome estoit ordene devant ces heures s'il soit demande.

3. Item, por ce qe la commune est grantement greve par la ou ils pledent ou sont empledez en les courts des grantz et autres de roialme, par cause q'ils n'osent pur doute des seignurages remuer les pleez hors des dites courts selonc ley en cas ou ils ne poent droit aver es meismes les courts. Si plest il au Roy qe les iustices assignez a les assises prendre en pays a chescune session enquergent de tieu chose, si bien a la suite le Roi come de partie, ou en cas qe tieu durete soit trovee, soit la court ou la franchise seissees en la main le Roi tanqe le seignur eit fait gree au Roi pur le trespas et a la partie des damages.

Note

Although this schedule of petitions has no formal address clause, the matters that it raises, and particularly the claim to be speaking about or for the 'common people' (item 2) and 'commonalty' (item 3), strongly suggest that it was compiled by the commons. The scribe who drew it up left spaces between each item for the responses to be added; the absence of such responses raises questions, however, as to whether it was actually accepted by the clerks of parliament as a common petition to be forwarded to the king's council.

The petition was previously published by Sayles (*SCCKB*, V, p. cxliii), who dated it impressionistically to the reign of Edward III. The issues raised were indeed matters to which parliament consistently referred throughout this period, but the particular focus of anxieties suggests a date early in the reign. Under the Statute of Northampton of 1328, confirmed in 1330, the justices of assize were required to deliver the gaols of the counties within their circuits; the statute of 1330 added the additional specification that the visitations should occur at least three times a year (Musson 1996: 118–121). Complaint continued over the non-observance of this legislation, including a common petition in the parliament of February–March 1334 (*RPHI*, p. 234 = *PROME*, IV, 198–199). It might be assumed that the request in item 1 of the present document that the gaol deliveries take place at least *twice* a year would have to have been made before the statute of 1330. But it is to be noted that opinion on this matter continued to vary, and the lower expectations set by the commons in parliament sometimes reflected their understanding of what could actually be achieved: by the time of the Good Parliament of April–July 1376, in fact, they were simply asking that gaol delivery take place in each county at least *once* a year (*RP*, II, 334 = *PROME*, V, 325). By that stage, however, the visitations of the commissioners of gaol delivery had become less crucial as a result of the emergence, during the 1350s and 1360s, of the justices of the peace, who gradually secured the authority to give judgment at least on trespasses and worked in close conjunction with the overlapping personnel of the assize and gaol delivery commissions (Powell 1987; Musson and Ormrod 1999: 50–53). This suggests that the issues raised in the present document were more keenly felt during the early years of the reign.

Further justification for the dating is provided by the notably hostile stance taken up towards the great men of the realm in items 2 and 3. During the 1320s and 1330s the parliamentary commons often made explicit criticisms of the great lords for their abuses of the legal system, and especially the crime, noted here, of maintenance. Although concerns about maintenance remained a regular feature of the common petitions for the rest of the fourteenth century, the specific comments about the magnates tended to fall away after the 1340s as a result of a growing association of interests, in the wake of the Black Death, between the commons and the lords (Harriss 1975: 509–517; Ormrod 1990b: 97–113). It therefore seems appropriate to date the present document more specifically to the first decade of the reign of Edward III.

118. Common petition in three parts (SC 8/80/3959) c.1329–c.1341

Summary

The commonalty of the land:

1. Request that sheriffs, under-sheriffs, bailiffs, hundreders, and other ministers who have been summoned before the justices for conspiracies, confederacies, and other falsities, and who have purchased charters of pardon and been restored to their offices,

might be ousted from the king's service, notwithstanding the charters.

2. Request that no sheriff, under-escheator or bailiff henceforth be appointed if he does not have sufficient land and tenements in the same county such as to answer to the king and the people, according to the recent statute made at Westminster.

3. Complaint that, whereas many men purchased lands and tenements in the time of King John, Henry III, and Edward I, the escheators now find by inquest that the lands were held of the king in chief and were alienated unlawfully. They request that a remedy is ordained so that impeachments are not made regarding these lands.

Response: For those wishing to sue this petition: concerning the first point they should have a writ to the sheriff that no such person be retained in the office of sheriff.

Text

1. A nostre seignur le Roi et a son counseil prie la comune de la terre; qe viscontes, suthviscontes, baillifs, hundreders et autres ministres queux ont este commiz en la place le Roi devant ses iustices et devant iustices errantz et autres iustices assignes des conspiracies, confederacies et autres fausines, et queux par lour subtilteez ont puis purchacez chartres nostre seignur le Roi de pardon des meismes les choses, et issint sont restituez a lour offices et font greindres malveisteez et extorsions au poeple qi faire ne soleient, soient ousteez de service nostre dit seignur le Roi, nemye contre esteant les dites chartres.

2. Item; come contenu soit en l'estatut drein fait a Westminstre qe nul visconte, sutheschetour, baillif de franchise, wapentak, hundred ne trithing soit desore s'il n'eit terre suffisalment en meisme le countee dont respondre au Roi et au poeple si homme se voudra pleindre, prie la dite comune qe nul haut eschetour ne suthvisconte ne soit desore s'il n'eit terre ou tenementz suffisant come desus est dit.

3. Item; come plusours gentz en temps le Roi Iohan et le Roi Henri et auxi en temps le Roi Edward le ael, avant l'estatut, eussent purchacez divers terres et tenementz a tenir de lour feffeours, et ore les eschetours, voillantz grevez la people, font de iour en autre par colour de lour offices diverses enquestes des tieux terres et tenementz, par les queles ils troevent q'ils feurent tenuz du

244   MULTIPLE PETITIONS

Roi en chief et alienez sanz conge, et issint parvent deviers des gentz par extorsion et autres grevances les font, et ascunefoitz ils seisent [ascuns] les terres en la mein le Roi. Prie la dite comune qe remedie soit sur ceo ordene, issi qe empeschement ne soit fait desore par eschetours pur purchaz des terres et tenementz qe feurent tenuz du Roi en chief et alienez avant l'estatut.

Response: Celui qi vodra sure ceste peticion: quant au primer point eit bref au viscont qe mes nul tiel soit receu en nul office de viscont.

Note

This set of common petitions is written up in a fair hand on the face of the document; the single response is written, in a different hand, on the dorse. The reference to King Edward 'the grandfather' (*le ael*) clearly places the document after the accession of Edward III in 1327; the legislation referred to in item 3 is the Statute *de Donis* of 1285 (*SR*, I, 96). The dating was refined by Rayner (1941: 553), who argued, on the basis of the reference in item 2 to the 'recent statute made at Westminster', that it came from some point between 1332 and 1335. In fact, the issue raised in the relevant item – about the need for sheriffs and other county officials to hold land in the relevant shire so that they could be held accountable and if necessary punished for their actions – was a regular feature of royal legislation in the first decade of Edward III and beyond, with statutes on the matter in 1328, 1330, 1331, 1336, and 1340 (*SR*, I, 160, 174, 258, 264, 266, 277, 283; Morris 1947: 47–49; and see nos 4, 5, 109, 114, 115, 117, and 121). The reference to the investigation of sheriffs and other county officials by a variety of judicial tribunals (item 1) is also sufficiently general to apply to the whole of the first half of Edward III's reign (Verduyn 1993; Musson and Ormrod 1999: 48–50). In default of further positive evidence, the petition is therefore assumed to date at some point shortly after one of the statutes on the qualifications of sheriffs issued between 1328 and 1340.

119. Agenda for reform in ten parts, embedding common petitions (C 49/33/22)
1331

Summary

1. First, for remedy in the situation where executors or others who are impleaded by writs of debt or contract then fourch, so that the plaintiffs are unable to bring the plea to conclusion.

Response: It will be discussed.
   It seems that it would be well to do this.

2. That the ordinaries should not entrust administration of wills to executors who do not have sufficient land or tenements to be justiciable and brought to answer in court to creditors.

   Response: It will be discussed.

3. That sheriffs arrest indicted men and accept fines in exchange for their release, so that the indictments are dismissed without them undergoing gaol delivery. The justices at each gaol delivery should have the power to investigate, judge, and punish those sheriffs and bailiffs of franchises who are found guilty of this practice, and to re-arrest all those indicted so that they are delivered according to the law of the land.

   Response: It will be discussed.

4. For remedy against those people indicted of felony who, not daring to attend the delivery for fear they will be condemned, sue a writ of chancery to make the indictments go before the king, and thus by their suit are delivered and the felony remains unpunished; no further writs of this kind should be issued out of the chancery without good cause, and this cause expressly noted in the writ, and that the case should not be judged elsewhere except before the king.

   Response: It will be discussed.
   The chancellor will advise.

5. Although the king is held by his oath to give justice to all so that the peace might be maintained in his realm, many murders, homicides, robberies, and other various felonies that are committed in the Cinque Ports are not brought to justice, because of which the king loses the escheats, chattels of felons and fugitives, and other various profits. Request that the king ordain that the warden of the Cinque Ports makes an annual tourn throughout the area to inquire, hear, and judge all manner of murders, homicides, and felonies, and see that justice is done, in respect of the king as well as the other party, as there is no other eyre where this matter might be dealt with or judged.

   Response: It will be discussed.
   It will be done by commission made to the warden.

6. People throughout the realm commit acts of outlawry, and then return themselves to the king's prison and make the court understand that they were in prison in Colchester or elsewhere at

the time of the outlawry, procuring men to give accounts to certify this to the sheriff, for which the king and the lords lose the profits and escheats that they should have from the outlawry. Request that such unsubstantiated accounts should not be accepted by the sheriff without averment from the local area.

Response: It will be discussed.
Let it be done.

7. Complaint about false jurors, who take bribes to be on juries so that no one might be attainted by such suits. Request that they might be banished for term of life, because at the moment there is insufficient deterrent against giving false testimony.

Response: A remedy will be discussed.

8. Complaint that defendants in all manner of pleas who plead outside the eyre are able to recover damages, with the exception of writs of right. They ask that a remedy be ordained, as was agreed in parliament, concerning the illegal purchase of attachments and prohibitions.

Response: It will be discussed.

Concerning parliament [...]:[28]

9. Complaint that where a lord has a bastard tenant who has a mortal illness, he is dispossessed of his land. Request that the land should revert to the lord after the tenant's death.

Response: It will be discussed.

10. Complaint that people who are taken and imprisoned for felony or robberies of which they feel themselves guilty procure an approver from Newgate prison to appeal them for a crime committed in a foreign county, so that they are ordered by writ of of the justice to go to Newgate or the place where the appellant is, and there are delivered by favourable inquest. Request that henceforth felony might first be judged by men of the locality where the felony was committed, and that sheriffs might not be able to change the cause of the indictment or conceal it.

Response: It will be discussed.

---

[28] From this note onwards, the text continues on the dorse of the document.

Text

1. Le primer, la ou executours ou autres obligez en commun seyent enpledez par bref de dette ou de covenaunt et fourchent, qe les pleintifs ne pount ateindre a fin du ple, soit ordine remedie.

    Response: Loquendum.
    Il semble qe il serroit bien qe en cas ou l'om oblige.

2. Item,[29] qe nule administracioun seit baille par ordinere as executours qi ne pount estre iustices par lei ne menez en court a respondre as creauncers, par la qe un des executours est tiel k'il nadz terre ne tenement par qei estre iustice, et si ne serra iames home respondu en la court le Roi de sa dette.

    Response: Loquendum.

3. Item,[30] seit ordine remedie de viscuntes qi pernent les gentz enditez et par fin les lessent aler et besillent les enditements, saunz iames les faire venir a la deliveraunce de geole, et tout les cyeus il lesse par plevine, la plevine n'est iames mostre a la deliveraunce de geole. Parount bon serreit qe les iustices a checune deliveraunce de geole eussent poer d'enquere et terminer et punir teuz viscuntes et baillifs de fraunchise qi serrunt trovez copables, et outre faire reprendre touz les enditez taunt qe il seient deliverez solum ley de la terre.

    Response: Loquendum.

4. Item, seit fait remedie de ce qe divers gentz, enditez de felonie, n'osent atendre la deliveraunce pur doute d'estre dampnez, fount sure bref de la chauncelerie de faire venir les ditementz devaunt le Roi, et issi par lur sute demene sunt il delivere et la felonie domert despunie, par qei bon serreit qe mes teu bref ne isse hors de chauncelrie saunz bone cause, et cele cause expressement notee en le bref, et seit la cause [qe ne peust aillurs estre terminee sinoun devaunt le Roi].[31]

    Response: Loquendum.
    Soit avise le chanceller.

5. Item, pur ce qe nostre seignur le Roi est tenu par sun serment a faire droit a touz et qe la pes seit maintenu en son realme, voille ordener qe les murdres, homicides, roberies et autres divers felonies qe sunt faitz en les Cinc Ports dount iames iustice ne dreit

---

[29] This item is crossed out.
[30] This item has been crossed out.
[31] These words are struck through.

n'est fait, par qei nostre seignur le Roi pert les eschetes, chateux des felons et futifs et an et wast et autres divers profitz si droiture en fust fait. Plese a Roi ordener qe le gardein des Cinc Ports checun an face sun tour parmi les Cinc Ports pur enquerre, oyr et terminer touz maneres de murdres, homicides et felonies issint qe dreit seit fait auxibien a la sute le Roi come a sute de partie, kar il ne venent a nule autre eyre ou la chose peut estre manie ne termine.

Response: Loquendum.
Soit fait par commission done al gardein.

6. Item, seit ordine remedie par la ou gentz parmi le realme sunt utlagez et puys se rendent a la prison le Roi et fount entendaunt a la court qe il furent en prison en Colcestre ou aillurs a temps del utlarie, par qei hom maunde a viscunte de certifier la court si il furent en prison a teu temps, les viscuntes pernent des uns loer et returnent fausement qe il furent en prison a teu temps, par qei le Roi et les seignurages perdent les profitz et les eschetes qe lur dussent encrestre par la utlarie. Bon serreit qe mes teu simple respouns de viscute ne seit accepte pur de faire tiele utlarie saunz averrement de pays del vygne, dount il se dient aver este en prison et qe cel averrement seit pris devaunt le Roi.

Response: Loquendum.
Fiat.

7. Item bon serreit de mettre remedie vers faus iurours, qi pernent lower des parties d'estre en iurees si nul seit atteint de tieles prises, q'il seyent exulez a terme de lur vies, pur ce qe faus serment a temps qe ore est n'est pas dute ne iames ne serra taunt com il pount estre assoutz d'autre qe de evesqe.

Response: Loquendum est [remedium].[32]

8. Item, seit ordine remedie qe les defendauntz en touz manere des pleez qi serrunt pledez hors de eyre des iustices, forspris bref de dreit, peussent recoverer damages, de ce q'il sunt a tort travaillez, s'il ne peussent mostrer q'il eyent provable et renable cause de mover en manere de ple [par la][33] [...] qe autrefoiz fust acorde en parlement pur les prelatz \non est verum/[34] quant il furent a tort travaillez par attachement sur la proibicioun.

---

[32] Conjectural.
[33] Conjectural.
[34] Interpolation in another hand.

Response: Loquendum est.

De parliamento [...]:

9. Item, soit ordene remedie pur le seignur qe la ou si [...]³⁵ bastard tient de lui terres et gist en sun mal moriaunt, la vient un sun [...] disseise de sa terre, seit remedie ordine a seignur apres la mort sun tenaunt bastarde, kar autrement demorra la terre a touz iours a celui qi la avera a tort occupe.

Response: Loquendum.

10. Item, soit fait remedie par la ou gentz sunt pris et enprisonez pur felonie ou roberies dount il se sentent copables procurent acun des appellours de Neugate qe les appelent de acun fait, fait en forein cuntee, et par taunt sunt il maundez par bref de iustice de Neugate de venir a leu ou le appellour est, et illeqes sunt delivere par favorables enquestes, auxibien de la felonie faite en forein cunte com del appeale; ben serreit qe desormes la felonie pur la quele il sunt en prisun seit primes terminee par gent del vignee ou la felonie fust faite, en ce k'il seyent maundez al appellour, et qe viscuntes sur quant k'il pount forfaire mes ne chaungent la cause de les enditementz ne nule enditement concelent.

Response: Loquendum.

Note

This document was previously published by Sayles (*SCCKB*, V, cxxxvi–cxxxviii) and has been re-edited here. The items of the main text are written up on the face and dorse, with the responses provided in a different hand and written closely into the gaps between the items. Sayles noted the Latin heading on the dorse, *De parliamento*, as though it were a general response to the whole document, but items 9 and 10 are written below it and have their own responses; it is more likely that the annotation was an attempt at a cross-reference to a parliament other than the one in which this was drawn up. Item 8 refers to the parliament of York of May 1322, which re-issued the relevant clause of the Ordinances of 1311 (*SR*, I, 160; *PROME*, III, 434), and provides a *terminus a quo* for dating this document. Rayner (1941: 557) argued that the document is most likely to be associated with the parliament of September–October 1331. The opening speech given at this assembly declared that one of the parliament's purposes

---

³⁵ The text is faded.

was 'to ordain how the [king's] peace might be better kept'; and the commons were subsequently ordered to consider this question, the chancellor commenting that 'the peace has not been kept as it should since the last parliament' (*RP*, II, 60 = *PROME*, IV, 155–157). There are no common petitions enrolled on the parliament roll for this assembly, but a number of private petitions submitted on the occasion referred to abuses of the law (Verduyn 1993: 859–860), and it seems likely that the document presented here was the result of a consultation between the council and members of the commons during the session of parliament. In spite of the deletion of parts of the text and the rather elusive initial response to many of the items, a significant statute was issued at the end of the 1331 parliament addressing a number of the issues of public order and legal process raised in the memorandum, including the regulation of outlawry (item 6), the treatment of corrupt jurors (item 7) and the use of approvers from Newgate prison (item 10) (*SR*, I, 265–259; Verduyn 1991: 35). Not all of the statute was determined by this agenda, and not all the remedies it provided followed the recommendation of the consultation. But the take-up is sufficient to warrant the view that this document was a significant element in framing the government's judicial programme.

The document cannot be read as an unmediated common petition. Its clauses do not conform to the opening diplomatic of common petitions in this period, but read rather as notes for consideration: the formulations 'let a remedy be ordained' (*soit fait remedie* with variations) and 'it would be good if...' (*bon serreit*, with variations) strongly suggests that it is a conciliar memorandum. However, there is an occasional drift into forms and rhetoric closely associated with petitioning, which suggests that this, rather like no. 115, is a hybrid document incorporating both conciliar memoranda and common petitions.

120. Common petition in nine parts, with separate schedule of responses (SC 8/272/13584 and SC 8/272/13587)
1337

Summary

The commonalty:

1. Request that Magna Carta and the Charter of the Forests might be upheld and maintained in all points, along with statutes

and ordinances made regarding purveyors and suppliers for the household of our lord the king and the queen and their children, in order to avoid damage to the people.

Response: The king wishes that the previous statutes and ordinances should be observed on all points, and if anyone feels aggrieved, let them sue for remedy against the trespassers, whether they are the king's purveyors and ministers or anyone else.

2. Request that the commissions of oyer and terminer begun at Nottingham regarding thieves and disturbers of the peace might be maintained in all points.

Response: Because the commissions were granted at the request of the commons for the destruction of evil-doers, but many have complained that the said commissions are more damaging to the great and good than to such evil-doers, the king will order his justices to employ the commissions in due and proper manner; and if they do not, he will order them to be repealed.

3. Complaint that thieves and felons attempt to enlist in the king's wars in Scotland and thereby gain pardon for their crimes. Request that the king receive no such felons into his grace, or accord them the rewards due to his liege men.

Response: The king does not wish to grant charters of pardon other than those that should be granted in accordance with the oath made at his coronation.

4. Request, regarding those indicted of felonies who flee into neighbouring counties, that the justices be able to send writs to the sheriffs in those counties ordering them to pursue and arrest the fugitives, so that they might be brought to justice.

Response: The king wishes that the course and process used in the eyres and in writs of oyer and terminer be upheld by the justices.

5. Complaint that, whereas it has been ordained by statute that nothing should be taken from its owner without his consent, certain people by means of their commission take wheat, barley, hay, peas, oxen and pigs, money, and armour without paying anything, and levy taxes upon the people of the countryside at their will, at which the people feel themselves much aggrieved. Request that no free man should be liable to such taxation without the common assent of parliament.

Response: The king wishes that no collections should be made other than those ordained by statute, and that the justices now assigned in the counties have power to hear and determine the complaints and do right, at the suit of the king as well as the party.

6. Request that the king provide arms and wages for the soldiers currently being selected by commissions made throughout the land, as the country is much burdened and charged by many taxes and other grievances.

Response: The king does not wish to charge his people in any other manner than under his predecessors.

7. It was ordained that the quota levied under the tenth and fifteenth in 1334 should not exceed that of 1332, but those assigned to raise the taxes have raised them in cities, boroughs, and counties, to the great grievance and impoverishment of the people and against the agreement of the king and the commons. Request that these increases might be overturned.

Response: The king allows that the tax last granted might be paid in accordance with what was granted, and that in times to come such taxes might be levied in such a manner as will be granted.

8. The commonalty of the cities and boroughs request that they might be able to have and use their franchises and free customs in the manner they have been accustomed to since time immemorial, and that the Statute of York, which is for the sole profit of foreign merchants and to the damage of the aforesaid cities and boroughs, might be annulled.

Response: The statute has been made for the common profit, and at the request of the commons, so the king grants that if any feel themselves wronged, they should come to the chancery and present their grievance, and thus justice will be done.

9. Complaint that many petitions have been put forward in parliament that have not yet been fully answered. Request that all petitions put forward in parliament by the commons might be fully answered before parliament adjourns.

Response: All the petitions previously presented by the commons in parliament have been fully answered before adjournment; regarding individual petitions presented at this parliament, the king wishes that the auditors should try and determine them before the adjournment.

This petition was answered on the Thursday in the first week of Lent, the same day that the commons submitted a petition sewn to this one, and left parliament.

Text

Ista peticio liberate fuit viii die parliamenti.

A nostre seignour le Roi prie la commune:

1. Qe la grant chartre et la chartre de la foreste et les autres estatuz et ordeinaunces grauntiez seiont meintenuz et tenuz en tous poynz, et auxi l'estatuz et ordeinaunces fetez sur les purveours et pernours pur les osteaux nostre seignour le Roi et la Roine et lur enfaunz seiont gardez et meintenuz, pur les grevaunces et damages qe le people sent encontre estatuz et proclamacions sur ceo \fetez/.

    Response: I. Quant au primer point, tochant qe la grant chartre et la chartre de la foreste et les estatutz et ordenances seient tenuz, il plest a nostre seignur le Roi qe les dites chartres, estatuz et ordenaunces einz ses heures faitz seient gardez et tenuz en touz points, et en cas qe nul se sent greve de damage a li fait countre la forme des ditz chartres, estatutz et ordenaunces, sue devant eux as queux il attient de mettre remede countre les trespassors, et reson et droit li serront faitz, auximent contre les purveors et ministres nostre seignur le Roi, ma dame la reigne, com countre autres.

2. Item, prie a nostre seignur le Roi la commune; qe come nostre seignour le Roi par son bon consail granta a Notyngham, en aide des bons et en destruant larons notories et communs destourbours de la pees en meigntenaunce de la pees nostre seignur le Roi, commissions a certeignes genz en cheskun countee d'enquere oier et terminer totes maneres felonies et trespas, les queux ont bien commence, et la pees par tant le mieux asseure. Pleise a nostre seignour le Roi qe les commissions soiont meintenuz en tous poyns.

    Response: II. Quant au secund point, tochaunt les commissions de trailbastoun, por ceo qe les dites commissions feurent grante a la request de commune a destruction des malveis, et plusours avant ces houres se sount pleint, et de iour en altre se pleinent, qe les dites commissions tournent en diverses lieux en damage des grantz et des bons plus qe en chastiement des ditz malveis, le Roi commaundera a ses iustices q'ils usent les commissions en due et bone manere, et s'ils les en usent en bon \manere/, selonc l'entencion de nostre seignur le Roi, il s'en soeffra, et si ceo noun, il les comaundera de repeller.

3. Item, pur ceo qe les notories larons et felons enditiez devant les ditz iustices de diverses felonies sei confortent et sei abaudisant de ceo q'ilz sont en esperaunce d'aler en la gerre nostre seignour le Roi devers Escoce ou aillours ou nostre seignour le Roi avera a faire, et par taunt aver chartre de pardoun des totes maneres de felonies. Prie la dite commune q'il pleise a nostre seignour le Roi de receyure nuls tiels larouns notories escumigies a sa grace, ne d'aler nule part en son service, depus q'il poet aver assez des autres bons et vaillauns de ses liges genz, kar par tieux larouns escumigiez ia bone bosoigne ne se fra nule part.

Response: III. Quant au tierce point, tochant chartre de pardon, le Roi n'est pas en volunte de graunter tieles chartres altrement q'il deit affaire, solonc son serment fait a son encouronement, et ne il n'kad fait puis son derrein parlement.

4. Et pur ceo qe tieux enditiez se vount defuians et wakerauns en autres counteez qe de ces en queux il sont enditiez, prie la dite commune qe les iustices devant queux il sont enditiez puissent maunder lur brefs as vicountes en queux counteez il serront trovez, de \les/ pursuire, arestier et prendre, et les amener devant les ditez iustices [il]oeks[36] aprendre ceo qe lei vodra.

Response: IV. Quant au point tochant qe les endites en un counte fuent en altre, nostre seignur le Roi voet qe cours et proces usez \en/ les eyrs et auxint en brefs de oier et terminer se tiegnent devant les ditz iustices.

5. Item, prie la dite commune; qe come par final accord du parlement, et sovent en estatut reduit et pur lei affermee, est ordine qe nul, de quele con[dici]on q'il soit, freit prise en le roialme contre gree de celi a qui les choses sont, countre queux acord, estatut et ordinaunce certeignes genz [par] commission pernent, et par autres deputiez desouz eaux prendre font, auxi

---

[36] A section of the parchment is missing from the left-hand side of SC 8/272/13584.

bien sur la terre marine come en plus haut pais, bleez, [org]es, fenes, peys, bofs et bacouns, argent et armures, sauns paie fete, et asseont et levont des genz du pais certeigne somme d'argent a lur volunte, dount le people se sent outraiousement grevez, et prie qe tieles commissions soient repelez, de sicome nul frank homme ne deit estre assis ne taxe saunz commun assent de parlement.

Response: V. Quant au point tochant qe gentz deputez par commissions a prendre bledz font leur prises auxi bien sur terre marine com ailleors, nostre seignur le Roi voet qe nules prises se facent autrement qe n'est ordeine par les estatuz, et qe les iustices qi ore sont assignez es countes par commissions eient poair d'oier et terminer les pleintes et faire droit, auxi bien a la seute nostre seignur le Roi com de partie.

6. Item, pur ceo qe commissions sont faits par tote la terre de eslire genz armeez de certeignes armures et archers et autres genz au piee, dount le pais avant ses houres ad estee mult grevee de trover lur armures et lur gages, prie la commune qe a quel houre q'il plest a nostre seignour le Roi d'aver les corps a sa volunte, q'il les troesue lur armures et les paie lur gages devant lur aler, de sicom la terre est mult greve et charge par plusours taxs et autres grevaunces.

Response: VI. Quant au point tochant les commissions d'eslire genz armez de certeines armures, nostre seignur le Roi ne voet charger son poeple altrementz n'en altre manere qe ad fait en temps de ses auncestres.

7. Item, prie la commune; qe come l'an utyme fu grantee a nostre seignour le Roi la dyme et la quinzime a la somme dont le Roi fust servi l'an syme, come piert par les roulles retournez en l'escheker l'an syme avantdit, a queux temps ceaux qi furont assignez de lever et receyvre les ditz taxs encrutront de lur teiste demeigne citiez, bourghs et les communaltiez des contieez a greinoure somme qe ne fust devant en l'an syme, a grant grevaunce et enpovrissement du people, countre le grant et l'assent de nostre seignour le Roi et la commune en plein parlement. Pleise a nostre seignour le Roi qe l'encrees soit oustiee, soulonc l'assent et le grant avant dit, pur ceo qe le people est plus enpovri que ne soleit estre.

Response: VII. Quant au point tochant qe l'encres fait es taxes de disme et quinzisme seit hoste, il plest a nostre seignur le Roi qe le tax derrainment grante seit paie solonc com qe il est grantez, et qe en temps avenir tieles taxes seient levez \en manere com/[37] eles serront graunte.

8. Item, prie la communealte des citiees et bourghs; qe com meimes les cities et burghs soient foundez en afforcement du roialme, et auncienement enfranchiz pur certeignes fermes et rentes paier au Roi, qe les citeins et burgeis puissont aver et user lur franchises et lur frаunchs custumes en la manere q'ils les ont eu et use du temps dont memorie ne court, et qe l'estatut n'ad guerres fet a Euerwyk en contraire, a la suite des marchaunz aliens pur lur singuler profit et a damage des avantditz citieez et bourghs, soit repele et tenu pur nul.

Response: VIII. Quant au point tochant qe les citez et burghs puissent user leur fraunchises, por ce qe le dit estatut ent fait estoit fait pur commune profit, et ce a la request de la commune, il plest a nostre seignur le Roi qe si nul se sent greve, viegne en chauncellerie et monstre sa grevaunce, et illoqes reson serra faite.

9. Item, prie la commune; qe com plusours peticions ont este mys avant en parlement le queux ne ont mie estee respounduz pleinement, pleise a nostre seignour le Roi qe totes les peticions mis avant en parlement \par la commune/ soient totes responduz avant le lever du parlement.

Response: IX. Quant au point tochant qe les peticions de commune seient respondues, totes les peticions einz ces heures mises par le commune en parlement ount este respoundues pleinement devant le departir des ditz parlementz, et quant as singuleres peticions ore baillez a yce parlement, nostre seignur le Roi voet qe les auditeurs ore assignez pur les trier les trient et terminent avant leur departir de mesme le parlement.

Le jeudy en la primere simeigne de Quaresme si estoit respons done as gentz de commune a ceste peticion, et meisme le iour avoient ils conge a departir, et si baillerent le dit jeudy une peticion cossu a ceste.

Note

This set of nine petitions from the commonalty, with a parallel series of official responses written on a separate document, has elicited

---

[37] Substituted for 'solonc com qe'.

significant interest among historians. The petitions and responses were published *in extenso* by Richardson and Sayles in 1935 (*RPHI*, pp. 268–270); the two documents are re-edited here with minor amendments. The preamble, the substantive text of the petitions, and the notes at their foot are taken from SC 8/272/13584; the responses are provided in SC 8/272/13547, where they appear with the Roman numerals included in the text here. For ease of interpretation, the responses have been separated out and placed under the relevant petitions in the summary and text.

Richardson and Sayles argued that these petitions and responses belong to the parliament of February 1339 (*RPHI*, pp. 267–268), a dating supported by Rayner (1941: 558–559) and Harriss (1975: 97 n. 1, 248 n. 2), and maintained by Sayles in his later translation of items 5 and 9 (Sayles 1988: 426). Fryde (1969: 259), however, argued that the petitions should be associated with the parliament of March 1337, and further analysis supports this suggestion.

The Lent parliament of 1337 was summoned to meet on 3 March. The writs *de expensis* for the commons were issued on Thursday 20 March (which fell in the second week in Lent) (*CCR, 1337–1339*, pp. 113–114). However, there is evidence that the assembly was drawn to a close before this, by Sunday 16 March (Tout 1920–1933, III, 62 n. 1), in which case the reference in the note at the end of the set of petitions that they were answered, and the commons left, on 'the Thursday in the first week of Lent' (13 March) fits well into a reconstructed chronology. Other substantive reasons can be given for a 1337 dating. First, the commissions of oyer and terminer mentioned in item 2 as having been issued at Nottingham (in October 1336), and noted under their nickname of 'trailbastons' in the royal response, were withdrawn later in 1337 on the outbreak of the French war (Verduyn 1995: 2); they were therefore already completely superseded by the time of the 1339 parliament. Secondly, while many commentators have assumed that the expressions of anxiety in relation to war must have been provoked by the Anglo-French dispute, it is the war with Scotland, which had been going on since 1333 and had already created huge pressures of its own (Maddicott 1975), that provides the explicit or assumed context for complaints about military pardons (item 3), purveyance (items 1 and 5), and the raising and equipping of armies (item 6). Thirdly, and decisively, the statute made at York referred to in item 8 is not, as Richardson and Sayles assumed, the legislation of 1337, but the Statute of York of 1335, which upheld the rights of aliens to trade freely in the realm and proved highly controversial with London and other towns and cities of the realm (*SR*, I, 270–271; Sergeant 1918: 276–277; Ormrod 2011: 117). Finally, and more generally, the king was not present at the parliament of February 1339, being then detained at

Antwerp in preparation for campaigning against the French, so that it is highly unlikely that the royal will articulated in the responses to the petitions could have been sought, expressed, and communicated between the eighth day, when the heading to the petition says it was delivered (and which, assuming that the 1339 assembly started on time, was 11 February) and the adjournment of the parliament just a week later on 19 February (*PROME*, IV, 234).

The complaint at item 9 about unanswered petitions requires some comment. In 1332–1333, several assemblies had been held at which, for procedural and practical reasons, petitions were not accepted or answered. The main concern in these assemblies was over the resulting delays in providing responses to private petitions (*RP*, II, 65, 66, 67 = *PROME*, IV, 168–169, 174, 183). But in the parliament of January 1333 one of the common petitions requested that 'all unanswered bills delivered by the commonalty in various parliaments in the time of our present lord the king' should be answered in this assembly (*RPHI*, p. 224 = *PROME*, IV, 190; Richardson and Sayles 1981, ch. xxi, p. 73). The schedule of petitions presented here shows signs of modification, with an interlineation inserted in item 9 to specify that the petitions under consideration were those submitted 'by the commons'. In fact, the royal response addresses both common petitions (which, it claims, had all been answered) and private petitions, where the reply provides specific evidence that panels of auditors were appointed in the relevant assembly.

No parliament roll survives for either the March 1337 or the February 1339 assembly. Given the similarity of tone and content between the petitions set out above and other sets of common petitions found on parliament rolls of the 1330s and 1340s, and given the generally positive if rather evasive answers provided in the royal responses, it seems likely that the clerks of parliament would have considered including this business on the official record of the assembly. The note at the end of the petitions, that on the final day of the parliament the commons also submitted a petition 'sewn to this one', raises questions as to whether the related document survives among the documents surveyed in this collection, or elsewhere.

121. Common petition in two parts, concerning royal officials (C 49/7/11)
Mid fourteenth century

Summary

The commons:

1. [The damage to the commons and the king as a result of annual tenure of office, possibly by sheriffs and escheators.]
2. [Problems arising when sheriffs and escheators confound the proper administration of royal escheats to serve their personal interests.]

Response: In the presence of the king.

Text

1. A nostre seignur le Roi et a son conseil prie la comune de sa terre; pur profist le Roi [. . .][38][. . .]illies a demorer par un an, et par la reson de lour petit demoer ils seoffrent les choses [. . .] damage de Roi; q'il lui pleise de ce ordiner remedie.

2. Item, pur ce qe plusours [. . .] meismes en [. . .] sovents foitz divers alienacions faites en autres seignuries des terres, qeux sont [. . .] par la reson qe les seignurs des les seignuries purrount estre faites viscountes et eschetours apres eaux nul ne voet faire [. . .] [dem]orer en le dit office issi [. . .] Roi perde sa seignurie en plusours lieux, et est en poynt d'estre desherite, q'il [. . .] qe plusours tenauntz le Roi [des] terres en divers countez et deivont et le heir ne voet mye suyer le diem clausit extremum, forsqe del eschetour [. . .] et les eschetours en autres countez la ou il ne tient poynt en chief [. . .] la reson q'il ne poount mye avoir conusaunce en queu [. . .] du Roi [. . .] sovent foitz la garde des terres qeux sount mys tenuz et ou plusours cas autres profitz, a tres grant damage [. . .] qe lui pleise [. . .].

Response: Coram rege.

Note

This common petition is significantly damaged, and the sense is not fully recoverable from the available text. Item 2 is mainly concerned with the offices of sheriff and, more particularly, escheator; on these grounds, the petition might be thought to date between 1341, when the two offices were reorganized to be held concurrently by the same individual, and 1357, when the escheatries were again separated from the shrievalties (Saul 1981: 135). If these are the offices referred to in item 1, however, then the apparent emphasis on the adverse effects of

---

[38]The majority of text on the right-hand side of the document is illegible due to a stain on the parchment.

annual turnover might point to the period after 1371, when it became standard practice to appoint a new set of sheriffs every year (Gorski 2003: 38–39). It is just possible that this petition represents the basis of the important statute regulating the office of escheator, issued in 1362 (*SR*, I, 374–375): the legislation cited the complaints of the commons as the basis for remedial action, but there are no extant common petitions on the matter enrolled on the parliament roll for this year. Since a definitive reading of the document is impossible, it is dated here impressionistically, on the basis of the hand, to the mid fourteenth century.

122. Common petition in five parts (SC 8/109/5429)
Late fourteenth century

Summary

[No petitioner specified].

1. Request that the king and the lords in parliament ordain remedy for the common profit of the realm that cases of *novel disseisin* might not be delayed through default of the defendant.

2. Request that, if any vill or franchise is exempt from paying expenses to the knights of parliament, it might be made clear who pays and who does not, because sometimes half the county claims exemption; that the expenses might be apportioned by good men in full county court sessions, and when the sums are allocated to the bailiffs and hundreders that these then be assigned by good men within the relevant hundreds, in order that no more is paid than is set out in the king's writs.

3. Complaint that the counties of Suffolk and Norfolk are charged in the exchequer for a sum of £100 called the 'ancient increment' against common right, which the sheriffs do not wish and are unable to bear, and which is to the great detriment and ruin of the common people. Request that the king abolish the sum or make another remedy.

4. Complaint that collectors of fifteenths, tenths, and subsidies granted to the king and commissioners of the same hold various meetings and take excessive sums for supplying indentures and acquittances, to the injury of the people. Request that the king ordain by statute that no more than 3d be collected from each vill, as was the old practice.

MULTIPLE PETITIONS 261

5. Complaint that the stewards of lords and ladies of the realm take excessive fines from various tenants who hold land in chief. Request that such sums and fines might be removed, or the stewards punished.

Response: [none].

Text

1. Plese a nostre seignur le Roi et as seignures du parlement pur comune profit du roialme, qe en assise [de novel][39] disseisine et en chescun [...] plee personel la ou l'enquest est agarder par defaute d'il defendaunt [...] [veigne] en propre person [devaunt le] prise du l'enquest [...] resteu de [monstrer] cez evidencez et auxi de chalanger l'enquest, a cause qe la queles parties sont [...] dis annez iournment, ne ont iurez devers qeux home poet aver soun recoverer.

2. Item, si nulle ville ou fraunchise soit exempt q'il ne paiera as coustages du chivalers du parlement, q'il soit mys en certeyn qeux paieront et qeux noun, qar en divers countez la moyte du countee ne voet rienz paier, et q'il soit aporcionez par bonez gentz en pleyn countee, et qaunt lez sommez sont mys et lyverez as baillifs et hundreders qe celle somme soit mys par bonez gentz de mesme le hundred, issint qe nulle pluis ne soit paie qe n'est compris deynz le briefs de Roy.

3. Item, qe lez countez de Suffolk et Norffolk sont chargez en l'escheker d'un somme de c. livres appelle 'vetus incrementum' encontre comune droit, quel somme lez viscont ne voillent ne poent porter, mesme lez prignent de ceux qeux sont menez al gaole par lez briefs le Roy, quel est graunt arerisement et anientisement du comune poeple, q'il please au Roy d'ouster celle somme ou de feare autre remedie.

4. Item, pur ceo qe coilliours de quinzeines, dymes et subsidies grauntez au Roy et commissioners de yceux fount divers cessions et parnount outrageouses sommez pur endenturez et aquitauncez; dont le poeple se sont greve. Qe please a Roy de ordeigner par estatut qe de entier coilliet, quel q'il soit, ne soit pris d'un ville qe trois deners, come ad este en aunciens temps, et sour ceo ordeigner certeyn peyne.

---

[39] The upper section of the parchment is damaged; where possible, missing text has been supplied from the context.

5. Item, pur ceo qe les feoders dez seignurs et dez dames du realme parnont outrageousez destressez de divers tenantz par aval, tan q'ils fount divers fynz la ou ils purront estre servyz par suffiseaunt destresse de lour tenantz qeux teignont en chief, qe tiels destressez et raunseonz soient oustez sour grief peyne.

Note

This previously overlooked schedule of five petitions does not specify by whom the requests were made, and in particular the fiscal elements (items 2–4) make it possible that the list was drawn up by a lobbying group (possibly led by the knights of the shires for Norfolk and Suffolk) intent on exposing local problems that had more general significance and might therefore be adopted as common petitions; the assertive use of 'common profit' in justification of the demands made is striking at this level of petitionary activity (Ormrod 2015). The address to 'the king and the lords in parliament' suggests that the document cannot date from earlier than the 1370s, when this formulation was first adopted (Baldwin 1913: 389; Dodd 2007: 97). The best clues as to a more precise date, however, are provided by items 2 and 3.

Item 2 refers to the debate, current since the 1350s, over the right to claim exemption from payment of the expenses of the knights of the shires for attendance at parliament (Latham 1933; Cam 1963: 240–2). None of the other extant common petitions on this matter are especially close in form and detail to this, but the fact that the matter was regularly and keenly debated in the late 1370s and 1380s suggests that this petition may form part of that sequence of complaint (*RP*, II, 258, 287, 368; III, 64, 212 = *PROME*, V, 103, 185, 410; VI, 129–130; VII, 22). A further petition in the Cambridge parliament of September–October 1388 led to a statute on the matter (*Westminster Chronicle*, p. 365; *PROME*, VII, 125; *SR*, II, 59; Tuck 1969: 238–239); if the present petition had been made after that date, it seems more likely that it would have referred to this legislation. Item 3 refers to the debate, first opened up in the Good Parliament of April–July 1376, over the so-called ancient increments charged by the exchequer on sheriffs over and above the standard farms of their counties (*RP*, II, 349 = *PROME*, V, 359–360; Morris 1947: 75–78). The case of the shrievalty of Norfolk and Suffolk was first mentioned in the parliament of October–December 1385, and the specific and general issues around this matter were raised repeatedly into the 1390s (*RP*, III, 211, 305, 321–322 = *PROME*, VII, 21–22, 235, 275–276). Relief was supposedly provided by a statute issued in the first parliament of Henry IV (*SR*, II, 114–

115); although grievances continued thereafter, the petitions lodged in parliament on behalf of Norfolk and Suffolk and other affected counties always now referred specifically to the remedy of 1399 (*RP*, III, 592, 614, 635–636; IV, 12 = *PROME*, VIII, 380–381, 431–432, 483–486, 541–543; IX, 24–25). The general inference, then, is that this schedule of petitions dates from somewhere between the mid 1370s and the late 1380s.

Item 4, on the taking of fees by the collectors of lay taxes for the issue of receipts to local collection areas, is also interesting in providing rare evidence on what was considered the appropriate going rate for such documents: elsewhere, the practice tended only to be noted where corrupt officials were accused of extorting larger sums for delivery of acquittances (Willard 1947: 218).

123. Common petition in two parts, on chirographers' fees and the tithe of *silva cedua* (C 49/69/23)
1377

Summary

The poor commons:

1. It was previously ordained by statute that chirographers should not take fees, but they continue to take great sums beyond that which is due, causing people to suffer great delays and losses. A remedy was requested at the last parliament, but nothing was done; thus they request that something might be done to prevent this felony.

2. At the parliament held at Westminster in 1371 the commons requested the king to define the tithe of *silva cedua* and clearly to state at what age the wood might be tithed, which was not adequately declared at the time. They now ask that the king clearly define the said tithe, for God and as a work of charity.

   Response: Concerning chirographers, the existing statute should be observed.

Text

1. A nostre seignur le Roi et a son bon conseil monstre sa pover comune; qe come autrefoitz fuist ordeine par estatut qe le cirograffer ne prendroit souldz pur le cirograffe faire et ore il

prent grandes sommes outre ceux mater, souldz de chescun fyn et plousours autres fees par lui acruez, et nientmeins il carie et delaie le poeple, pur tieux choses de iour en iour et terme en terme s'ils ne lui donent a tant come ils duissent du resoun, par quele cause plousours gentz lessent de pursuier ou lever tieux fines au grandes perde de ses fines et au grande damage du poeple, du quele chose remedie fuist prie au darrein parlement et rien n'est fait. Priont ore remedie et qe certeine peine soit mys sur les feloniez a l'encontre, pur Dieu et en oevre de charite.

2. Item monstre la dite comune, qe par la ou en parlement tenuz a Westminstre l'an nostre seignur le Roi qarant et quint estoit prie au Roi a declarer ceste paroles silva cedua et demettre en certein du quele age le bois serreit disme, quele chose come il sembl[...][40] suffissantement respondu en cel temps. Par qoi ils priont a ore de le declarer et mettre en certein et auxint [...] pur Dieu et en oevre de charite.

Response: Quant a cirographer estoisent l'estatut ent faitz.

Note

These two otherwise unconnected common petitions, written on a single membrane, must have been submitted at the last parliament of Edward III, held in January–March 1377 (*PROME*, V, 427). In the first item, the reference to the statute defining the fees taken by chirographers is to the Statute of Westminster II of 1285 (*SR*, I, 93), and the reference to a petition on the matter made in the last parliament clearly cross-refers to a common petition on the roll of the Good Parliament of April–July 1376 (*RP*, II, 337 = *PROME*, V, 330–331). The second item refers to the petition made on the tithe of *silva cedua* (cut wood) in the parliament of February–March 1371 (*RP*, II, 305 = *PROME*, V, 240) and the statute made in response (*SR*, I, 393); the matter had been a regular issue in parliament for some time, and both in 1373 and now in 1377 it was claimed that the decision of 1371 had not been enforced (*RP*, II, 319 = *PROME*, V, 282; Adams 1937: 20–21).

For the parliament of January–March 1377 we possess the originals of a number of private petitions that were subsequently avowed, or adopted, as common petitions and included in the fair copy of the schedule of common petitions on the parliament roll (*PROME*, V, 391). It is possible that the two petitions in the present document

---

[40] The bottom right-hand corner of the parchment is missing.

were composed by the commons themselves, or by special interest groups hoping to have their campaigns taken up by the commons. The fact that the petition on the chirographer was answered certainly suggest that the document was forwarded with the other common petitions for judgment by the council, and the fact that they were not subsequently included on the parliament roll of this assembly may have been a matter either of conscious decision or of mistake and negligence by the clerk charged to compile the final version of the roll. The frustration of the commons is reflected in the fact that the question of the fees of chirographers was taken up again in the next parliament, of October–November 1377 (no. 16).

124. Common petition in two parts, on pleas outstanding from the previous reign and the offence of maintenance (SC 8/102/5096)
1377

Summary

The lords and commons of the realm of England:

1. Request that the king ordain in the present parliament that all pleas, legal processes, and suits pending during the time of his grandfather should be enforced in court with the same authority as before his death, in order to avoid the disinheritance of the people.

2. Request for a statute that no lord or any other should undertake any manner of legal action or business against them by maintenance, on pain of certain punishment, considering that the commons are not able to have any law or reason, given that the jurors dare not speak the truth for fear of such maintainers.

Response: [none].

Text

1. A nostre seignur le Roi et son tressage conseil suppliont si lui pleise les seignours et comunes de son roialme d'Engleterre; qe pur escheuer desheritance [et autres][41] meschiefs et perils qi

---

[41]The document is slightly damaged: missing text has been supplied from Record Commission Transcripts, PRO 31/7/110, no. 31.

purront avenir a vostre poeple en processes des plees et pursuites qe estoient pendantz en temps vostre aiel en diverses p[laces] qe il [plese] ordeigner en cest present parlement par avis de vostre tressage conseil un general remedie, qe touz maneres des plees et processes et pursuitz pendantz en touz vos courtz quele part q'ils soient soi tiegnent en meisme le course et force q'ils furent le proschein iour de court devant le moriant de vostre dit aiel.

2. Et auxint qe lui pleise, en socour et relevacioun de sa dite pover comune ordeigner par estatut en cest present parlement, qe nul seignour n'autres n'enpreignont sur eux de meinteiner nuly en null manere de querele ne busoigne a cause de gaigne ne autrement, sur certein peine sur ceo ent a ordeigner, eant regard qe vostre povere comune ne poiont avoir nulle leye ne resoun, ne les iurours n'osent dire la verite pur doute de tiels maintenours.

Note

Internal evidence indicates that these two petitions, written on a single piece of parchment, must have been submitted in one of the early parliaments of Richard II; the references to the previous king as the present king's grandfather in item 1, and the likelihood that the request made there came as quickly as possible after the death of the old king, suggest that the most probable parliament in which they were composed was the first one of the new reign, in October–November 1377. Unlike the pair of unenrolled common petitions surviving from the last parliament of Edward III (no. 123), those given here have no response, and it is therefore unclear whether they were ever forwarded to the council for consideration. There were a number of issues regarding the crime of maintenance dealt with at the first parliament of Richard II, but none of the legislation accords directly with the nature of the second item of this set of petitions (Bellamy 1989: 81). There is certainly an important difference between the main series of common petitions for the October–November 1377 parliament, which are described as 'the petitions submitted to parliament by the commons' (*les peticions baillees avant en parlement par les communes*) (*RP*, III, 15 = *PROME*, VI, 32) and the first clause of this unenrolled schedule, which specifies the petitioners as the 'lords and commons'. Note, however, that item 2 claims only to be made for 'the said poor commons'; given its stance against lords engaged in maintenance, it is unlikely to have received the endorsement of the peers. This emphasizes the absence of any obvious link between the two items and the occasional or accidental nature of their juxtaposition.

125. Common petition in two parts, on the jurisdiction of the constable and marshal (C 49/8/19)
c.1384–c.1410

Summary

The commons:

1. Request that no man might be forced to go before the constable and marshal to answer for debts or contracts if they are not the party under contract, but might be in a position to sue under the common law.
2. Request that heirs, executors, and administrators of goods of any person might be completely discharged of such suits before the said constable and marshal, and placed under common law.

Response: In the presence of all the lords of parliament.

Text

1. Item, prie la comune; qe nulle homme soit constreint de venir devant conestable et mareschalle a respondre de dette ou contrait s'ils ne soit mesmes partie a contrait, mes soit mys a suer a la comune ley.
2. Item, [qe][42] heirs, executours et amynestratours des biens de queconqe persones soient outrement descharges de tiels suytes devant les ditz conestable et mareschalle, et mys a la comune ley.

Response: Devant touz les seignurs du parlement.

Note

The 'Item' with which the first of these two linked petitions begins suggests the document as it now exists may originally have been part of a longer set of petitions. The constable and marshal were hereditary offices whose roles were fundamentally military, although the development of their functions and rights from Norman origins is imperfectly understood (Prestwich 1996: 171–175). Their responsibilities gave them joint jurisdiction over certain military matters, in the form of the court of the constable and marshal. From the reign of Richard II, the commons were of the belief that this court

---

[42] Illegible due to tear in parchment: supplied from context.

was exceeding its legitimate powers. The essential complaint – about the usurpation of power by the court of the constable and marshal of matters which should be dealt with under the common law courts – occurs several times on the parliament rolls in the late fourteenth and early fifteenth centuries. The first occasion on which the matter was introduced was in the parliament of November–December 1384, when the commons complained that many issues touching the common law were coming before the constable and marshal, with the king granting the request that matters should be dealt with in their appropriate jurisdiction (*RP*, II, 202 = *PROME*, VI, 425–426; *SR*, II, 37). A second instance is found among the enrolled common petitions for the parliament of January–March 1390 (*RP*, II, 265 = *PROME*, VII, 148), the first half of which is linked to the present petition in its request that the court of the constable and marshal should have no cognizance of any contract made within England which might be tried at common law, unless it only concerned arms. The response in 1390 stated that the remit of the constable was wider than this, and allowed a writ under the privy seal to cease cases begun in the court until the king's council had time to consider them; this decision was entered onto the statute roll (*SR*, II, 61–62). The third occasion when this issue was raised was in the parliament of January–March 1401, in a much lengthier common petition which, after requesting the enforcement of the statute of 1384, also sought that those inheriting lands (by escheat or verdict in the royal courts) from those sentenced in the court of the constable and marshal should be free of those judgments (*RP*, III, 473 = *PROME*, VIII, 137–138). The present petition could relate to any of these occasions, although the contents connect it most closely to the common petition of 1401, which in turn was reiterated in the parliament of January–May 1410 (*RP*, III, 625 = *PROME*, VIII, 462). The grievance of the commons related only to jurisdiction within England; it seems to have been accepted that the constable and marshal had jurisdiction over all matters outside the realm, as decreed in a statute of 1399 (*SR*, II, 116) and confirmed in response to a common petition at the parliament of September–December 1429 (*RP*, IV, 349 = *PROME*, X, 405).

126. Common petition in four parts (SC 8/230/11479) Early fifteenth century

Summary

The commons of England:

1. Request that clause 35 of the Statute of Marlborough be upheld, which states that no one might be able to distrain his free tenants without the king's writ, nor force them to take oaths against their will. Complaint that the stewards of the courts of barons, bailiffs, and hundreders distrain free tenants to come to the courts to be on inquisitions, and if they do not come they amerce them grievously; request that such ministers might be judged in their lordships, and if they distrain free tenants or levy amercements they should forfeit their office and pay damages to those concerned.

2. Request that collectors of taxes be ordered to take only the customary sum for acquittance from their sub-collectors in the vills, because, whereas before they took 2d for an acquittance, now they take 12d or 2s.

3. Request that ordinaries, officials, and deans only take the customary sums for testaments, because, whereas before they took 12d or 2s, now they take 40s or £10 or more.

4. Request that it should be clearly ordained what amount sheriffs should take for sureties of prisoners, as they currently take large sums, which is to the damage of the people.

Response: [none].

Text

1. A nostre seignur le Roy priount ses communes de Engleterre; qe luy plese ordener qe l'estatut fet a Marleburg' soyt muth tenuz queil ne ad este devant ces oures, queil estatut est en tel paroles capitulo tricesimo quinto nul desoremes pusse destreyndre ses francs tenaunz a respoundre de lur fraunk tenement ou de nule chose qe apartuent a fraunk tenement saunz bref le Roy, ne ni face ses franks tenaunz iurer countre lur volente, desicome nul ne deyve ceo fere saunz comaundement le Roy, neynt contre estyant ceste estatut le seneschaus de court de barounes, balyes, hundreders et lur mynistres destreynt fraunks tenauntes de venir a lur courtes et hundredes d'estre en enquestes entre parties pledants devant eux, et si les fraunks tenauntes ne venant d'estre en enquestes devant eux sils \les/ amercient grevoussement de court en court, et les amerciements levont par destresces, a grant damage de tut le commune. Par qei plese a vostre treshaut seignurie de ordeiner a cet parlement qe tus telis barouns, seneschau, balyes et hundreders et lur mynystres soynt iurs desormes par lour seignuries avant qe fascent plus en lour office, que iles ne destreynderent ne telis amercements leverount de nul

frank tenaunt, ne par nul voys les constreyderount de venyr devant eux pur estre en enqueste, sur peyne de foriurer lur office a tus iours si de ceo soyent ateyns a synt de parties ou a synt de la Roy, et sur peyne de fere gre a le partie qe issint \serra/ destreint et greve de se damage a treble et outre de estre en la greve mercy nostre seignur le Roy.

2. Plese auxi a nostre seignur le Roy de ordeyner ceo qe les colyors de taxis nostre seignur le Roy prendront de lez southcoliours de villez pur lour aquitaunces desore a eux, qar avant ses houres ils soleyount prendre forsqe deux deneres pur un aquitaunce, et ore ils prenderount dusze deners ou deux souldz ou plus a lour volunte, a grant oppressioun du poeple et enpoverissement.

3. Plese auxi a nostre seignur le Roy de ordeyner qe lez ordinaries, officiales, coronours et denes prignount du poeuple le Roy forsqe resonablement ne pur prener de testament forsqe resonablement, qar avant sez houres ils soleyount prendre forsqe deux sould ou dusze deners et ore ils prenount qaraunt sould et dis livers ou plus a lour volunte, a grant distruccioun et oppressioun du poeuple.

4. Plese auxi a nostre seignur le Roy de ordeyner pur certeyn ceo qe viscounts prenderount pur suete de prisounes, qar ore ils prenount si grant summes pur suete de prisounes qe le poeuple est grantment destrut et enpovre. Dount le commune prie remedie pur le amour de Dieu.

Note

This petition was originally in a series of chancery files which, according to a note on the guard, were firmly datable to the period 1409–1410, presumably meaning the regnal year 11 Henry IV (September 1409–September 1410). The parliament held in this year, in January–May 1410, was dominated by the political crisis that led the king's eldest son to take effective control of the government, and by the bill presented by the commons (not on the parliament roll) calling for the disendowment of the Church (*PROME*, VIII, 449–453, 509). The matters raised in this petition fit with the general concerns of the enrolled common petitions of this year, which are preoccupied with fiscal, economic, and legal issues of a practical nature (*RP*, III, 635–646 = *PROME*, VIII, 483–508). There are, however, no other reasons for associating this petition specifically with the parliament of January–May 1410, and it has been dated here more impressionistically, on the basis of the form and hand, to the early fifteenth century.

Item 1 cites the Statute of Marlborough of 1267, referring to its clause 35 (clause 22 in modern readings of the statute) on the requirement that lords could not distrain tenants to answer for their tenements against their will (*SR*, I, 24; Brand 2003: 479; the Anglo-Norman text here effectively translates some key phrases of the Latin statute); the main emphasis of the petition is on the abuses of associated powers by the ministers of liberties of franchises. Item 2 is linked to a common petition of the late fourteenth century complaining of the excessive fees taken by collectors of taxes to issue letters of acquittance to their sub-collectors (no. 122). Items 3 and 4, on the fees taken for proving wills and the large sums demanded for release of prisoners on bail, represent matters of perennial concern in the fourteenth and fifteenth centuries. There was a series of common petitions made in parliament during the 1370s about the adverse effects of high fees charged by ecclesiastical officials for granting probate (*RP*, II, 305, 313; III, 25, 43 = *PROME*, V, 241, 266; VI, 56, 92), and the matter came up again in a long and detailed common petition in the first parliament of Henry V, in May–June 1413 (*RP*, IV, 8–9 = *PROME*, IX, 16–17). The royal responses to all these petitions made it clear that the crown was severely constrained in its ability to legislate and control on matters that concerned the ecclesiastical courts, and it was not until 1529 that parliament took decisive action to regulate these and other fees taken by the Church (Lehmberg 1970: 76–94). An ostensibly more surprising case is the crown's apparent reluctance, over a long period of time, to attempt to regulate the amounts of money that sheriffs and others levied when releasing prisoners on bail. The confusion seems to have arisen because of the formal distinction between the mainprise or surety itself, which was assessed on the case according to the means of the prisoner, and the fee taken by the sheriff or other for conducting this assessment, which was finally fixed at 4d by a statute of 1445 (*SR*, II, 335; Pugh 1968: 169–177). The petition draws attention to the fact that the officials could relatively easily inflate the mainprise to include a disguised bribe.

There is no recorded response to the four items set out in this schedule, and it therefore remains unclear whether the decision to abandon its contents was made by the commons, by the clerk of parliament, or by the king and council.

APPENDIX
CHRONOLOGICAL LIST OF KNOWN COMMON PETITIONS, 1290–1340

The table that follows attempts to summarize all known instances of extant common petitions, either in original form, in enrolments on the parliament rolls, or in transcriptions made elsewhere in the public records and in other archives, between the earliest known common petition (of 1290) and the year 1340. After 1343 the clerks of parliament normally included on the parliament roll a transcript of the schedule of common petitions submitted in the assembly, often in conjunction with grants of taxation; although there remain a significant number of unenrolled common petitions dating from after 1340, the overall chronology of the records is therefore rather more straightforward.

The list includes all petitions edited in the present collection that have been dated before 1340, including those dated only impressionistically to the early fourteenth century; those categorized as mid fourteenth century have not been included, but it is apparent that a number of these could date from before 1340. The overall numbers represented here are clearly an underestimate. (The unnumbered petitions are those which have not been included in this volume.)

As explained in the Introduction, we have used 'commonalty' to translate *communitas* and *commune* as 'commonalty' for the period before 1340; that convention is observed in the 'Petitioner' column of this table. Note that it was common practice for 'commonalty', 'people', 'land', 'realm', and 'kingdom' to be followed by the qualifier 'of England' in the naming of the petitioners: this qualifier has been omitted in this table for the sake of economy.

Date	Original/ enrolment/ transcript	Petitioners	Single/ multiple clause	TNA reference	Previously published	Edition in this volume
1290[1]	Enrolment	Many of the people	Single	SC 9/2, m. 1d	*RP*, I, 47 = *PROME*, I, 297	no. 19
c.1300–c.1335	Original	Lieges of the commonalty	Single	SC 8/79/3944		no. 53
Early 14th century	Original	Commonalty of the land	Single	C 49/8/22		no. 31
Early 14th century	Original	The people	Single	SC 8/79/3906		no. 32
Early 14th century	Original	[None]	Single	SC 8/79/3920		no. 5
Early 14th century	Original	The common people	Single	SC 8/80/3952		
1301[2]	Transcript[3]	People of the commonalty of the land	Multiple		*Parl. Writs*, I, 104–105; *EHD*, III, 510–512	
1302[4]	Original	The people	Single	SC 8/316/E216	Haskins 1937: 316	no. 1
1303–1309	Original	[None]	Single	SC 8/202/10065		no. 71

[1] Parliament at Westminster, April–July 1290.
[2] Parliament at Lincoln, January–February/March 1301.
[3] The schedule of petitions survives in a transcript in the archives of the Dean and Chapter of Canterbury Cathedral: see *PROME*, I, 100 and n. 32.
[4] Parliament at Westminster, July–August 1302.

1305[5]	Enrolment	Poor men of the land	Multiple	SC 9/12, m. 19d	*Mem. de Parliamento*, p. 306 = *PROME*, II, 195
1305	Enrolment	The commonalty[6]	Single	SC 9/12, m. 3d	*Mem. de Parliamento*, p. 54 = *PROME*, II, 74
1305	Enrolment	The commonalty	Single	SC 9/12, m. 7	*Mem. de Parliamento*, pp. 122–123 = *PROME*, II, 104–105
1305	Enrolment	The commonalty	Single	SC 9/12, m. 7	*Mem. de Parliamento*, pp. 126–127 = *PROME*, II, 106
1305	Enrolment	The commonalty	Single	SC 9/12, m. 20d	*Mem. de Parliamento*, pp. 313 = *PROME*, II, 200–201
c.1305–c.1331	Original	[None]	Multiple	SC 8/155/7740	no. 109

[5] This and the next four entries all date from the parliament at Westminster, February–April 1305.

[6] This and the next three petitions each give a different combination of petitioners but the marginal annotations in SC 9/12 (or, in the first case, the *Vetus Codex*) claim that the petitions are from 'the commonalty of England': *RP*, I, 161–162, 166, 178; *Memoranda de Parliamento*, pp. 54, 122–123, 126–127, 313; Rayner 1941: 550 n. 2. The *Vetus Codex* (C 153/1) is a later transcription from the parliament rolls recording the petitions presented in a sequence of parliaments between 1290 and 1307, plus that of 1320. See *PROME*, II, 430–431.

Date	Original/ enrolment/ transcript	Petitioners	Single/ multiple clause	TNA reference	Previously published	Edition in this volume
1307[7]	Original	Good people of the realm	Single	SC 8/79/3936	Haskins 1937: 315–316	no. 73
1307	Original	Good people of the land	Single	SC 8/77/3808	Haskins 1937: 316–317; *Crisis of 1297–1298*, p. 198	no. 72
1307	Original	Good people of the realm	Single	SC 8/79/3936	Haskins 1937: 315–316	no. 73
1307	Transcript[8]	Commonalty of the realm	Multiple	C 153/1, ff. 148v–150v	*RP*, I, 219–221 = *PROME*, II, 528–531	
1307	Transcript	[Commonalty of the realm][9]	Single	C 153/1, ff. 136v–137r;	*RP*, I, 201 = *PROME*, II, 491–492	
1307–1327	Original	Commonalty of the land	Single	C 49/5/18		no. 2
1307–1327	Original	[None]	Single	SC 8/73/3615		no. 74
c.1307–c.1320	Original	People of the realm	Single	SC 8/ 334/E1149		no. 3
c.1307–c.1327	Original	Commonalty of the people of the realm	Single	C 49/5/23		no. 75

[7] This and the next four entries date from the parliament at Carlisle, January–April 1307.
[8] This and the next entry come from the *Vetus Codex*: see above, n. 5.
[9] The transcribed summary of this petition refers to it as having been made by 'those who have been in the king's service before the justices of trailbaston', but a subsequent order to the trailbaston justices in Devon refers to it explicitly as having been made by the 'commonalty of the realm': *CCR, 1302–1307*, p. 531.

Date	Original & enrolment[11]		Single/Multiple	SC ref	Other ref
1309[10]	Original & enrolment[11]	Commonalty of the realm	Multiple	SC 8/294/14698; C 54/127, m. 22	CCR, *1307–1313*, p. 225; *RP*, I, 443–445; *Select Documents*, pp. 6–8 no. 110
c.1309–c.1318	Original	Knights of the counties and good people of the cities	Multiple	SC 8/156/7796	no. 111
1311–1331	Original	Prelates, earls, and barons and all the commonalty of the realm	Single	SC 8/136/6751	no. 4
1315[12]	Enrolment	Commonalty of the people	Multiple	SC 9/18, m. 3	*RP*, I, 290 = *PROME*, III, 56–57
1315	Enrolment	The commonalty	Single	SC 9/18, mm. 2, 8	*RP*, I, 289, 299 = *PROME*, III, 53, 76–77
1315	Enrolment	The commonalty	Single	SC 9/18, mm. 4, 18	*RP*, I, 291, 319 = *PROME*, III, 58, 126
1315	Enrolment	The commonalty	Single	SC 9/18, mm. 4, 20	*RP*, I, 291, 324 = *PROME*, III, 58, 139
1317–1327	Original	Commonalty of the land	Single	SC 8/80/3957	no. 76

[10] Petitions submitted in the parliament at Westminster, April–May 1309, and answered in the parliament at Stamford, July–August 1309.
[11] In this case the enrolment is not on the parliament roll (which is not extant for either of the two relevant parliaments), but on the dorse of the close roll.
[12] This and the next three entries come from the parliament roll of the parliament at Westminster, January–March 1315. For further evidence of the answering of common petitions in this assembly, see Sayles 1988: 319.

Date	Original/ enrolment/ transcript	Petitioners	Single/ multiple clause	TNA reference	Previously published	Edition in this volume
1318[13]	Enrolment	Baronage with the commonalty of the realm[14]	Multiple	SC 9/21, m. 2	*Documents English History*, pp. 6–7 = *PROME*, III, 257–259	
1318	Enrolment	The commonalty	Single	SC 9/21, m. 4d	*Documents English History*, p. 16 = *PROME*, III, 272	
1318	Enrolment	The commonalty	Single	SC 9/21, m. 9	*Documents English History*, p. 36 = *PROME*, III, 301	
c.1318–c.1322	Original	The commonalty	Single	C 49/4/20	Davies 1918: 582	no. 5
1319[15]	Enrolment	Commonalty of the realm	Single	SC 9/22, m. 2d	*Documents English History*, p. 54 = *PROME*, III, 356	
1319	Original	Commonalty of the realm	Single	SC 8/79/3948		no. 7
1319	Original	Commonalty of the realm	Single	SC 8/109/5435		no. 78
1319–1325	Original	The commonalty	Multiple	SC 8/80/3951		no. 112

[13]This and the next two entries date from the parliament at York, October–December 1318.
[14]There are four petitions given in continuous sequence on this roll, the first and last addressed by the 'baronage with the commonalty of the realm', the middle two by the 'prelates, earls and barons'; see Rayner 1941: 549 n. 4.
[15]Parliament at York, May 1319. The next two entries likely date from the same assembly.

1320[16]	Original & enrolment	The commonalty[17]	Single	SC 8/3/129; SC 9/23, mm. 9, 9d	RP, I, 372, 374 = PROME, III, 410, 412–413	no. 6
1320	Enrolment	Commonalty of the realm[18]	Single	SC 9/23, m. 4d	RP, I, 371 = PROME, III, 381	
1320	Enrolment	Commonalty of the realm	Single	SC 9/23, m. 6	RP, I, 375–376 = PROME, III, 389	
1321–1327	Original	[None]	Single	SC 8/123/6119		no. 54
1322[19]	Original	[None]	Multiple	C 49/66/29	Ormrod 1990a: 27–31	no. 113
1322	Original	Knights of the shires and all the commonalty of the land	Single	SC 8/80/3955	Davies 1918: 597	no. 94
1322	Original	Good people and the common people in parliament	Single	S C8/203/10148		no. 79
c.1322	Original	Poor people of the land	Single	SC 8/144/7193		no. 95

[16]Parliament at Westminster, October 1320. The next two entries date from the same assembly. For further evidence of the presentation of a (now lost) schedule of petitions in the name of the 'commonalty of the realm' at this parliament, see Sayles 1988: 51–52.
[17]The original does not specify a petitioner; but the enrolled Latin summary cites it as coming from 'the commonalty'.
[18]The parliament roll specifies that this petition was delivered by 'the knights, citizens and burgesses present on behalf of the counties, cities and boroughs of [the king's] realm': see Rayner 1941: 550–551.
[19]Parliament at York, May 1322. The next two entries date from the same assembly.

Date	Original/ enrolment/ transcript	Petitioners	Single/ multiple clause	TNA reference	Previously published	Edition in this volume
1324[20]	Original	The commonalty	Multiple	SC 8/108/5398	Buck 1983b: 176; Ormrod 1990a: 6 n. 3; 20 n. 1	no. 114
1324[21]	Original	The people	Multiple	C 49/5/25	Ormrod 1990a: 31–33	no. 115
1324–1325	Original	Archbishops, bishops, prelates earls, barons, and others of the commonalty	Single	SC 8/257/12802		no. 33
1325[22]	Original & enrolment[23]	The king's liege people	Multiple	SC 8/8/392	*RP*, I, 430 = *CCR*, 1323–1327, pp. 539–540	no. 116
1327[24]	Enrolment[25]	Good people of the commonalty	Multiple	C 65/1	*RP*, II, 7–12 = *PROME*, IV, 11–26	

[20] Parliament at Westminster, February–March 1324.
[21] Parliament at Westminster, October–November 1324.
[22] Parliament at Westminster, November–December 1325.
[23] The enrolment is not on the parliament roll (which is not extant for the relevant parliament), but on the dorse of the close roll.
[24] Parliament at Westminster, February–March 1327. The next two entries dates from the same assembly.
[25] There is continuing debate as to whether an alternative version of the common petitions of this parliament found in C 49/83 (published in *RPHI*, pp. 116–126 = *PROME*, IV, 27–35) represents something closer to the base text of the enrolled version in C 65/1, as argued in *RPHI*, pp. 100–102, or is a defective transcript of it, as argued in *PROME*, IV, 2. C 65/1. Although this document is classified here as an enrolled version of the relevant set of common petitions, the argument for such a designation is not completely straightforward, since the responses, written on the dorse, have additions in different hands/inks that make it appear rather more like a 'work in progress' towards a final version. Note the existence of another version of the common petitions of this parliament among the records of the borough of Bridport: Maddicott 1981: 81.

Date	Type	Petitioners	Single/Multiple	Reference	Additional Reference	Number
1327[26]	Enrolment	Knights and the commonalty[27]	Multiple	C 54/145, m. 23d	RP, II, 5–6 = CCR, 1327–1330, pp. 101–102	
1327	Original &	People of the realm transcript[28]	Single	SC 8/167/8336	RPHI, p. 284; RPHI, p. 150 = PROME, IV, 63	no. 34
1327–1328[29]	Original	Good people of the commonalty	Single	SC 8/261/13018	SCCKB, V, pp. cxxxii–cxxxiii	no. 55
1327–1330	Original	Good people	Single	SC 8/159/7909		no. 20
1327–c.1350	Original	[None]	Single	SC 8/168/8399		no. 80
c.1327–c.1337	Original	[None]	Multiple	C 49/8/23	SCCKB, V, p. cxliii	no. 117
c.1327–c.1350	Original	[None]	Single	SC 8/154/7666		no. 7
c.1329–c.1341	Original	Commonalty of the land	Multiple	SC 8/80/3959		no. 118
c.1330	Original	Good people	Single	SC 8/79/3938		no. 21
c.1330	Original	People of the commonalty	Single	SC 8/165/8223		no. 35
1331	Original	[None]	Multiple	C 49/33/22		no. 119
1333[30]	Enrolment	The commonalty	Multiple	C 49/6/20	RPHI, pp. 224–230 = PROME, IV, 190–194	

[26] The enrolment of this group of petitions is not on one of the rolls of proceedings of this parliament, but on the dorse of the close roll.

[27] The preamble refers to the petitioners as the 'knights and commonalty of the quarrel of the earl of Lancaster', but the text that follows is wide-ranging in its application and suggests that this group of petitions, though recorded separately from other business of the same assembly, should be treated as common petitions. See discussion in *PROME*, 11 n. 31.

[28] The transcript comes from a British Library manuscript and is part of a seventeenth-century abstract made from an original (but now lost) roll of petitions dating from this parliament: see *RPHI*, pp. 104–105.

[29] This petition, submitted to the council at Pontefract in November 1327, cites verbatim an earlier common petition submitted in the parliament at Lincoln in September 1327, the original of which is not extant.

[30] Parliament at York, January 1333.

Date	Original/ enrolment/ transcript	Petitioners	Single/ multiple clause	TNA reference	Previously published	Edition in this volume
1334[31]	Enrolment[32]	People of the commonalty	Multiple	C 65/4	*RPHI*, pp. 232–239 = *PROME*, IV, 197–203	
1334–1335	Original	Common people of the realm	Single	SC 8/79/3945		no. 22
1337[33]	Original	The commonalty	Multiple	SC 8/272/13584, SC 8/272/13587	*RPHI*, pp. 268–270	no. 120
1340[34]	Transcript[35]	Commonalty of the realm	Multiple		Harriss 1975: 518–520	

[31] Parliament at York, February–March 1334.
[32] The preamble to the list of petitions specifies that these are the common petitions identified in this parliament 'to be enrolled, with the answers given to them, to remain in chancery'.
[33] Parliament at Westminster, March 1337.
[34] Parliament at Westminster, March–May 1340.
[35] The schedule of petitions survives in a transcript in the archives of the Dean and Chapter of Winchester Cathedral: see *PROME*, IV, 275–276.

BIBLIOGRAPHY

Unpublished Primary Sources

Kew: The National Archives

C 47	Chancery: Miscellanea.
C 49	Chancery: Council and Parliament Proceedings.
C 54	Chancery: Close Rolls.
C 65	Chancery: Parliament Rolls.
C 81	Chancery: Warrants for the Great Seal, Series I.
C 153	Chancery: Vetus Codex.
C 254	Chancery: Files, Tower and Rolls Chapel Series, *Dedimus potestatem*.
E 175	Exchequer: Parliament and Council Proceedings.
PRO 31/7	Record Commission Transcripts, Series I: Parliamentary Petitions, Miscellaneous.
SC 8	Special Collections: Ancient Petitions.
SC 9	Special Collections: Parliament Rolls, Exchequer Series.

Published Primary Sources

AP Northumberland	*Ancient Petitions Relating to Northumberland*, ed. C.M. Fraser, Surtees Society, 176 (1966).
Anonimalle Chronicle	*The Anonimalle Chronicle, 1333 to 1381*, ed. V.H. Galbraith (Manchester, 1927).
Baronial Movement	*Documents of the Baronial Movement of Reform and Rebellion, 1258–1267*, ed. R.F. Treharne and I.J. Sanders (Oxford, 1973).
CChR	*Calendar of Charter Rolls*.
CCR	*Calendar of Close Rolls*.
CFR	*Calendar of Fine Rolls*.
CIM	*Calendar of Inquisitions Miscellaneous*.
CLBL	*Calendar of the Letter Books of the City of London*, ed. R.R. Sharpe, 11 vols (London, 1899–1912).

CMR	*Calendar of Memoranda Rolls (Exchequer), Michaelmas 1327–Michaelmas 1328* (London, 1968).
CPL	*Calendar of Papal Registers Relating to Great Britain and Ireland, 1198–1404*, ed. W.H. Bliss and J.A. Twemlow, 4 vols (London, 1893–1902).
CPR	*Calendar of Patent Rolls.*
Crisis of 1297–1298	*Documents Illustrating the Crisis of 1297–98 in England*, ed. M. Prestwich, Camden Society, 4th ser., 24 (London, 1980).
Dialogus	Richard FitzNigel, *Dialogus de Scaccario: The Dialogue of the Exchequer*, ed. and trans. E. Amt, and *Constitutio Domus Regis: Disposition of the King's Household*, ed. and trans. S.D. Church (Oxford, 2007).
Documents English History	*Documents Illustrative of English History in the Thirteenth and Fourteenth Centuries*, ed. H. Cole (London, 1844).
EHD	*English Historical Documents*, ed. D.C. Douglas, 12 vols (London, 1953–1977).
English Wycliffite Writings	*Selections from English Wycliffite Writings*, ed. A. Hudson (Cambridge, 1978).
Eyre of London	*The Year Books of Edward II: The Eyre of London, 14 Edward II, A.D. 1321*, ed. H.M. Cam, 2 vols, Selden Society 85–86 (London, 1968–1969).
Foedera	*Foedera, conventiones, literae et cujuscunque generis acta publica*, ed. T. Rymer, 3 vols in 6 parts (London, 1816–1830).
Hansische Urkundenbuch	*Hansische Urkundenbuch*, ed. K. Höhlbaum, K. Kunze, H.-G. von Rundstedt, and W. Stein, 11 vols (Halle, 1876–1939).
Mem. de Parliamento	*Memoranda de Parliamento 1305*, ed. F.W. Maitland, Rolls Series, 98 (London, 1893).
Northern Petitions	*Northern Petitions Illustrative of Life in Berwick, Cumbria and Durham in the Fourteenth Century*, ed. C.M. Fraser, Surtees Society 194 (1982).
'Oxford Petitions'	'Parliamentary petitions relating to Oxford', ed. L. Toulmin Smith, in *Collectanea*, 3rd ser., Oxford Historical Society Publications, 32 (1896).
Parl. Writs	*The Parliamentary Writs and Writs of Military Summons*, ed. F. Palgrave, 2 vols in 4 parts (London, 1827–1834).

Petitions Religious Houses	Petitions to the Crown from English Religious Houses, c.1272–c.1485, ed. G. Dodd, A.K. McHardy, and L. Liddy, Canterbury and York Society, 100 (2010).
PROME	The Parliament Rolls of Medieval England, ed. P. Brand, [J.R.]S. Phillips, [W.]M. Ormrod, G.[H.] Martin, C. Given-Wilson, A. Curry, and R. Horrox, 16 vols (Woodridge, 2005).
RP	Rotuli Parliamentorum, 6 vols (London, 1783).
RPHI	Rotuli Parliamentorum Anglie hactenus inediti, ed. H.G. Richardson and G.O. Sayles, Camden Society, 3rd ser., 51 (1935).
Select Charters	Select Charters and Other Illustrations of English Constitutional History, ed. W. Stubbs, 9th edn (Oxford, 1913).
Select Documents	Select Documents of English Constitutional History, 1307–1485, ed. S.B. Chrimes and A.L. Brown (London, 1961).
St Albans Chronicle	The St Albans Chronicle: The Chronica Maiora of Thomas Walsingham, ed. J. Taylor, W.R. Childs, and L. Watkiss, 2 vols (Oxford, 2003–2011).
SCCKB	Select Cases in the Court of King's Bench, ed. G.O. Sayles, 7 vols, Selden Society, 55, 57, 58, 74, 76, 82, 88 (London, 1936–1971).
SR	Statutes of the Realm, 11 vols (London, 1810–1828).
VCH	Victoria County History.
Visitations	Visitations of Religious Houses in the Diocese of Lincoln, ed. A.H. Thompson, 2 vols in 3 parts, Canterbury and York Society, 17, 24, 33 (London, 1915–1927).
War of Saint-Sardos	The War of Saint-Sardos (1323–1325), ed. P. Chaplais, Camden Society, 3rd ser., 87 (1954).
Westminster Chronicle	The Westminster Chronicle, 1381–1394, ed. L.C. Hector and B.F. Harvey (Oxford, 1982).
Year Books Edward I	Years Books of the Reign of King Edward the First, ed. A.J. Horwood, 5 vols, Rolls Series, 31 (London, 1863–1879).

Secondary Sources

Aberth, J., 1996, *Criminal Churchmen in the Age of Edward III: The Case of Bishop Thomas de Lisle* (University Park, PA).

Adams, N., 1936, 'The writ of prohibition to court Christian', *Minnesota Law Review*, 20: 272–293.

Adams, N., 1937, 'The judicial conflict over tithes', *English Historical Review*, 52: 1–22.
Adams, N., 1946, '*Nullus filius*: A study of the exception of bastardy in the law courts of medieval England', *University of Toronto Law Journal*, 6: 361–384.
Allen, M., 2012, *Mints and Money in Medieval England* (Cambridge).
Ambühl, R., 2013, *Prisoners of War in the Hundred Years War: Ransom Culture in the Late Middle Ages* (Cambridge).
Amor, N.R., 2011, *Late Medieval Ipswich: Trade and Industry* (Woodbridge).
Bailey, M., 1988, 'The rabbit and the medieval East Anglian economy', *Agricultural History Review*, 36: 1–20.
Bailey, M., 1991, ' "Per impetum maris": Natural disaster and economic decline in eastern England, 1275–1350', in *Before the Black Death: Studies in the 'Crisis' of the Early Fourteenth Century*, ed. B.M.S. Campbell (Manchester), 184–208.
Bailey, M., 2014, *The Decline of Serfdom in Late Medieval England: From Bondage to Freedom* (Woodbridge).
Baker, R.L., 1961, *The English Customs Service, 1307–1343: A Study of Medieval Administration*, Transactions of the American Philosophical Society, NS 51, 6 (Philadelphia, PA).
Baldwin, J.F., 1913, *The King's Council in England during the Middle Ages* (Oxford).
Barnie, J., 1974, *War in Medieval Society: Social Values and the Hundred Years War 1337–99* (London).
Barrell, A.D.M., 1991, 'The Ordinance of Provisors of 1343', *Historical Research*, 64: 264–277.
Barron, C.M., 2004, *London in the Later Middle Ages: Government and People, 1200–1500* (Oxford).
Bazeley, M.L., 1921, 'The extent of the English forest in the thirteenth century', *Transactions of the Royal Historical Society*, 4th ser., 4: 140–172.
Bean, J.M.W., 1968, *The Decline of English Feudalism, 1215–1540* (Manchester).
Bean, J.M.W., 1989, *From Lord to Patron: Lordship in Late Medieval England* (Manchester).
Bell, A., and Sutcliffe, C., 2009, *Valuing Medieval Annuities: Were Corrodies Underpriced?*, ICMA Discussion Papers in Finance DP2007-15, rev. edn (Reading).
Bellamy, J.G., 1989, *Bastard Feudalism and the Law* (Portland, OR).
Bevan, K., 2013, 'Clerks and scriveners: Legal literacy and access to justice in late medieval England', PhD thesis, University of Exeter.
Birrell, J., 1982, 'Who poached the king's deer? A study in thirteenth-century crime', *Midland History*, 7: 9–25.
Blatcher, M., 1936, 'Distress infinite and the contumacious sheriff', *Bulletin of the Institute of Historical Research*, 13: 146–150.
Bolton, J.L., 1980, *The Medieval English Economy 1150–1500* (London).
Bradford, P.J., 2007, 'Parliament and political culture in early fourteenth-century England', PhD thesis, University of York.
Bradford, P.[J.], 2011, 'A silent presence: The English king in parliament in the fourteenth century', *Historical Research*, 84: 189–211.
Brand, P., 2001, 'Lawyers' time in the later middle ages', in *Time in the Medieval World*, ed. C. Humphrey and W.M. Ormrod (York), 73–104.
Brand, P., 2003, *Kings, Barons and Justices: The Making and Enforcement of Legislation in Thirteenth-Century England* (Cambridge).
Brand, P., 2004a, 'The mortmain licensing system, 1280–1307', in *English Government in the Thirteenth Century*, ed. A. Jobson (Woodbridge), 87–96.

Brand, P., 2004b, 'Petitions and parliament in the reign of Edward I', *Parliamentary History*, 23: 14–38.
Brand, P., 2009, 'Understanding early petitions: An analysis of the content of petitions to parliament in the reign of Edward I', in *Medieval Petitions: Grace and Grievance*, ed. W.M. Ormrod, G. Dodd, and A. Musson (York), 99–119.
Bridbury, A.R., 1982, *Medieval English Clothmaking: An Economic Survey* (London).
Briggs, C., 2005, 'Taxation, warfare and the early fourteenth-century "crisis" in the north: Cumberland lay subsidies, 1332–1348', *Economic History Review*, NS 58: 639–672.
Britnell, R.H., 1987, 'Forstall, forestalling and the Statute of Forestallers', *English Historical Review*, 102: 89–102.
Britton, C.E., 1937, *A Meteorological Chronology to A.D. 1450* (London).
Brown, A.L., 1989, *The Governance of Late Medieval England 1272–1461* (London).
Buck, M., 1983a, 'The reform of the exchequer, 1316–1326', *English Historical Review*, 98: 241–260.
Buck, M., 1983b, *Politics, Finance and the Church in the Reign of Edward II: Walter Stapeldon, Treasurer of England* (Cambridge).
Cam, H.M, 1950, 'Shire officials: Coroners, constables and bailiffs', in *The English Government at Work, 1327–1336*, Vol. III: *Local Administration and Justice*, ed. J.F. Willard, W.A. Morris, and W.H. Dunham (Cambridge, MA), 143–183.
Cam, H.M., 1963, *Liberties and Communities in Medieval England* (London).
Campbell, J., 1965, 'England, Scotland and the Hundred Years War in the fourteenth century', in *Europe in the Late Middle Ages*, ed. J.R. Hale, J.R.L. Highfield, and B. Smalley (London), 184–216.
Chaplais, P., 1971, *English Royal Documents, King John–Henry VI, 1199–1461* (Oxford).
Cheyette, F., 1963, 'Kings, courts and sinecures: The Statute of Provisors and the common law', *Traditio*, 19: 295–349.
Childs, W., 1990, 'Finance and trade under Edward II', in *Politics and Crisis in Fourteenth-Century England*, ed. J. Taylor and W. Childs (Gloucester), 19–37.
Clanchy, M.T., 1985, 'Magna Carta and the common pleas', in *Studies in Medieval History Presented to R.H.C. Davis*, ed. H. Mayr-Harting and R.I. Moore (London), 219–232.
Clarke, M.V., 1936, *Medieval Representation and Consent* (London).
Crook, D., 1982, 'The later eyres', *English Historical Review*, 97: 241–268.
Cullum, P.H., 1991, *Cremetts and Corrodies: Care of the Poor and Sick at St Leonard's Hospital, York in the Middle Ages*, Borthwick Paper 79 (York).
Davies, J.C., 1918, *The Baronial Opposition to Edward II: Its Character and Policy* (Cambridge).
Davis, J., 2012, *Medieval Market Morality: Life, Law and Ethics in the English Marketplace, 1200–1500* (Cambridge).
Dobson, R.B., 1983, *The Peasants' Revolt of 1381*, 2nd edn (London).
Dodd, G., 2000, 'Richard II and the transformation of parliament', in G. Dodd (ed.), *The Reign of Richard II* (Stroud), 71–84.
Dodd, G., 2001, 'The hidden presence: Parliament and the private petition in the fourteenth century', in *Expectations of the Law in the Middle Ages*, ed. A. Musson (Woodbridge), 135–149.
Dodd, G., 2002, 'The Calais Staple and the parliament of May 1382', *English Historical Review*, 117: 94–103.

Dodd, G., 2007, *Justice and Grace: Private Petitioning and the English Parliament in the Late Middle Ages* (Oxford).
Dodd, G., 2009, 'Parliamentary petitions? The origins and provenance of the "Ancient Petitions" (SC 8) in the National Archives', in *Medieval Petitions: Grace and Grievance*, ed. W.M. Ormrod, G. Dodd, and A. Musson (York), 12–46.
Dodd, G., 2011a, 'Was Thomas Favent a political pamphleteer? Faction and politics in later fourteenth-century London', *Journal of Medieval History*, 37: 397–418.
Dodd, G., 2011b, 'The rise of English, the decline of French: Supplications to the English Crown, c.1420–1450', *Speculum*, 86: 117–150.
Dodd, G., 2014, 'Kingship, parliament and the court: The emergence of "high style" in petitions to the English crown, c.1350–1405', *English Historical Review*, 129: 515–548.
Dodd, G., and Petit-Renaud, S., 2015, 'Grace and favour: The petition and its mechanisms', in *Government and Political Life in England and France, c.1300–c.1500*, ed. C. Fletcher, J.-P. Genet, and J. Watts (Cambridge), 240–278.
Dodd, G., Phillips, M., and Killick, H., 2014, 'Multiple-clause petitions: Instruments of pragmatism or persuasion?', *Journal of Medieval History*, 40: 176–194.
Dunn, C., 2007, 'Damsels in distress or partners in crime? The abduction of women in medieval England', PhD dissertation, Fordham University.
Dunn, C., 2013, *Stolen Women in Medieval England: Rape, Abduction and Adultery, 1100–1500* (Cambridge).
Edwards, J.G., 1925, 'The parliamentary committee of 1398', *English Historical Review*, 40: 321–333.
Edwards, J.G., 1979, *The Second Century of the English Parliament* (Oxford).
Faith, R., 1984, 'The "great rumour" of 1377 and peasant ideology', in *The English Rising of 1381*, ed. R.H. Hilton and T.H. Aston (Cambridge), 43–73.
Flahiff, G.B., 1944 and 1945, 'The writ of prohibition to court Christian in the thirteenth century', *Medieval Studies*, 6: 261–313 and 7: 229–290.
Fratcher, W.F., 1969, 'Uses of uses', *Missouri Law Review*, 34: 39–66.
Fryde, E.B., 1951, 'Hugh Despenser the Younger's deposits with Italian bankers', *Economic History Review*, NS 3: 344–362.
Fryde, E.B., 1969, 'Parliament and the French war, 1336–40', in *Essays in Medieval History Presented to Bertie Wilkinson*, ed. T.A. Sandquist and M.R. Powicke (Toronto), 250–269.
Fryde, N.M., 1975, 'Edward III's removal of his ministers and judges, 1340–1', *Bulletin of the Institute of Historical Research*, 48: 149–161.
Fryde, N.[M.], 1979, *The Tyranny and Fall of Edward II, 1321–1326* (Cambridge).
Gemmill, E., and Mayhew, N., 1995, *Changing Values in Medieval Scotland: A Study of Prices, Money, and Weights and Measures* (Cambridge).
Given-Wilson, C., 1978a, 'The merger of Edward III's and Queen Philippa's households, 1360–9', *Bulletin of the Institute of Historical Research*, 51: 183–187.
Given-Wilson, C., 1978b, 'Richard II and his grandfather's will', *English Historical Review*, 93: 320–337.
Given-Wilson, C., 1983, 'Purveyance for the royal household, 1362–1413', *Bulletin of the Institute of Historical Research*, 56: 145–163.
Given-Wilson, C., 1986, *The Royal Household and the King's Affinity: Service, Politics and Finance in England, 1360–1413* (London).
Given-Wilson, C., 2004, 'The rolls of parliament, 1399–1421', *Parliamentary History*, 23: 57–72.

Given-Wilson, C., 2016, *Henry IV* (London).
Goffin, R.J.R., 1901, *The Testamentary Executor in England and Elsewhere* (London).
Gorski, R., 2003, *The Fourteenth-Century Sheriff: English Local Administration in the Late Middle Ages* (Woodbridge).
Grant, A., 1984, *Independence and Nationhood: Scotland 1306–1469* (London).
Green, R.F., 2002, *A Crisis of Truth: Literature and Law in Ricardian England* (Philadelphia, PA).
Hamilton, J.S., 2010, 'King Edward II of England and the Templars', in *The Debate on the Trial of the Templars*, ed. J. Burgtorf, P.F. Crawford, and H. Nicholson (Farnham), 215–224.
Hanawalt, B.A., 1979, *Crime and Conflict in English Communities, 1300–1348* (Cambridge, MA).
Harding, A., 1975, 'Plaints and bills in the history of English law, mainly in the period 1250–1350', in *Legal History Studies 1972*, ed. D. Jenkins (Cardiff), 65–86.
Harding, A., 1978, 'Early trailbaston proceedings from the Lincoln roll of 1305', in *Medieval Legal Records Edited in Memory of C.A.F. Meekings*, ed. R.F. Hunnisett and J.B. Post (London), 143–168.
Harding, A., 1983, 'The origins of the crime of conspiracy', *Transactions of the Royal Historical Society*, 5th ser., 33: 89–108.
Harding, A., 2002, *Medieval Law and the Foundations of the State* (Oxford).
Harris, S.J., 2009, 'Taking your chances: Petitioning in the last years of Edward II and the first years of Edward III', in *Medieval Petitions: Grace and Grievance*, ed. W.M. Ormrod, G. Dodd, and A. Musson (Woodbridge), 173–192.
Harriss, G.L., 1963, 'The commons' petitions of 1340', *English Historical Review*, 78: 625–654.
Harriss, G.L., 1975, *King, Parliament and Public Finance in Medieval England to 1369* (Oxford).
Harriss, G.L., 1981, 'The formation of parliament, 1272–1377', in *The English Parliament in the Middle Ages*, ed. R.G. Davies and J.H. Denton (Manchester), 29–60.
Harriss, G.L., 2005, *Shaping the Nation: England, 1360–1461* (Oxford).
Haskins, G.L., 1937, 'Three early petitions of the commonalty', *Speculum*, 12: 314–318.
Haskins, G.L., 1938, 'The petitions of representatives in the parliaments of Edward I', *English Historical Review*, 53: 1–20.
Hatcher, J., and Bailey, M., 2001, *Modelling the Middle Ages: The History and Theory of England's Economic Development* (Oxford).
Hector, L.C., 1966, *The Handwriting of English Documents*, 2nd edn (London).
Helmholz, R.H., 1969, 'Bastardy litigation in medieval England', *American Journal of Legal History*, 13: 360–383.
Helmholz, R.H., 1975, 'Writs of prohibition and ecclesiastical sanction in the English courts Christian', *Minnesota Law Review*, 60: 1011–1033.
Helmholz, R.H., 1981, 'The writ of prohibition to courts Christian before 1500', *Medieval Studies*, 43: 297–314.
Hewitt, H.J., 1966, *The Organization of War under Edward III* (Manchester).
Hilton, R.H., 1973, *Bond Men Made Free: Medieval Peasant Movements and the English Rising of 1381* (London).
Hilton, R.H., 1983, *The Decline of Serfdom in Medieval England*, 2nd edn (London).
Holford, M.L., and Stringer, K.J., 2010, *Border Liberties and Loyalties: North-East England, c.1200–c.1400* (Edinburgh).

Holmes, G.A., 1957, *The Estates of the Higher Nobility in Fourteenth-Century England* (Cambridge).
Holmes, G., 1975, *The Good Parliament* (Oxford).
Housley, N., 1982, *The Italian Crusades* (Oxford).
Housley, N., 1996, *Documents on the Later Crusades* (Basingstoke).
Hunnisett, R.F., 1977, *Editing Records for Publication* (London).
James, M.K., 1951, 'The fluctuations of the Anglo-Gascon wine trade during the fourteenth century', *Economic History Review*, NS 4: 170–196.
Johnson, C., and Jenkinson, H., 1915, *English Court Hand A.D. 1066 to 1500*, 2 vols (Oxford).
Johnstone, H., 1940, 'The queen's household', in *The English Government at Work, 1327–1336*, Vol. I: *Central and Prerogative Administration*, ed. J.F. Willard and W.A. Morris (Cambridge, MA), 250–299.
Jones, M. 2004, 'Gournay, Sir Matthew, d.1406', in *Oxford Dictionary of National Biography*, ed. H.C.G. Matthew and B.H. Harrison, 60 vols (Oxford), XXIII, 86–87.
Jones, W.R., 1966, 'Bishops, politics and the two laws: The *gravamina* of the English clergy, 1237–1399', *Speculum*, 41: 209–245.
Jones, W.R., 1973, '*Rex et ministri*: English local government and the crisis of 1341', *Journal of British Studies*, 13: 1–20.
Jones, W.R., 1974, 'Keeping the peace: English society, local government, and the commissions of 1341–44', *American Journal of Legal History*, 18: 307–320.
Jones, W.R., 1975, 'Purveyance for war and the community of the realm in late medieval England', *Albion*, 7: 300–316.
Jordan, W.C., 1996, *The Great Famine: Northern Europe in the Early Fourteenth Century* (Princeton).
Kaeuper, R.W., 1979, 'Law and order in fourteenth-century England: The evidence of special commissions of oyer and terminer', *Speculum*, 54: 734–784.
Killick, H., 2011, 'Thomas Hoccleve as poet and clerk', PhD thesis, University of York.
Killick, H., 2016, 'Treason, felony and Lollardy: A common petition in the hand of Richard Osbarn, clerk of the chamber of the Guildhall 1400–*c*.1437', *Historical Research*, 89: 227–245.
Lacey, H., 2009, *The Royal Pardon: Access to Mercy in Fourteenth-Century England* (York).
Lambert, B., and Ormrod, W.M., 2015, 'Friendly foreigners: International warfare, resident aliens and the early history of denization in England, *c*.1250–*c*.1400', *English Historical Review*, 130: 1–24.
Latham, L.C., 1933, 'The collection of wages of knights of the shire in the fourteenth century', *English Historical Review*, 67: 455–464.
Lehmberg, S.E., 1970, *The Reformation Parliament, 1529–1536* (Cambridge).
Lewis, N.B., 1933, 'Re-election to parliament in the reign of Richard II', *English Historical Review*, 48: 364–394.
Liddy, C.D., 2001, 'The estate of merchants in the parliament of 1381', *Historical Research*, 74: 331–345.
Liddy, C.D., 2005, *War, Politics and Finance in Late Medieval English Towns: Bristol, York and the Crown, 1350–1400* (Woodbridge).
Lloyd, T.H., 1977, *The English Wool Trade in the Middle Ages* (Cambridge).
Lloyd, T.H., 1982, *Alien Merchants in England in the High Middle Ages* (Brighton).
Lloyd, T.H., 1991, *England and the German Hanse, 1157–1611* (Cambridge).
Lunt, W.E., 1934, *Papal Revenues in the Middle Ages* (New York).

Lunt, W.E., 1939, *Financial Relations of the Papacy with England to 1327* (Cambridge, MA).
Lunt, W.E., 1962, *Financial Relations of the Papacy with England, 1327–1534* (Cambridge, MA).
McDougall, S., 2009, 'The punishment of bigamy in late-medieval Troyes', *Imago Temporis: Medium Aevum*, 3: 189–204.
McFarlane, K.B., 1973, *The Nobility of Later Medieval England* (Oxford).
McHardy, A.K., 1975, 'The alien priories and the expulsion of aliens from England in 1378', *Studies in Church History* 12: 133–141.
McHardy, A.K., 1989, 'The effects of war on the church: The case of the alien priories in the fourteenth century', in *England and her Neighbours 1066–1453: Essays in Honour of Pierre Chaplais*, ed. M. Jones and M. Vale (London), 277–295.
McNall, C., 2002, 'Some aspects of the business of statutory debt registries, 1283–1307', in *Credit and Debt in Medieval England, c.1180–1350*, ed. P.R. Schofield and N.J. Mayhew (Oxford), 68–88.
Maddicott, J.R., 1970, *Thomas of Lancaster 1307–1322: A Study in the Reign of Edward II* (Oxford).
Maddicott, J.R., 1975, *The English Peasantry and the Demands of the Crown, 1294–1341*, Past and Present Supplement 1 (Cambridge).
Maddicott, J.R., 1978, 'The county community and the making of public opinion in fourteenth-century England', *Transactions of the Royal Historical Society*, 5th ser., 28: 27–43.
Maddicott, J.R., 1981, 'Parliament and the constituencies, 1272–1377', in *The English Parliament in the Middle Ages*, ed. R.G. Davies and J.H. Denton (Manchester), 61–87.
Maddicott, J.R., 1984, 'Magna Carta and the local community', *Past & Present*, 102: 25–65.
Maddicott, J.R., 2010, *The Origins of the English Parliament, 924–1327* (Oxford).
Mate, M., 1972, 'Monetary policies in England, 1272–1307', *British Numismatic Journal*, 41: 34–74.
Mate, M., 1975, 'High prices in early fourteenth-century England: Causes and consequences', *Economic History Review*, 2nd ser., 28: 1–16.
Matheson, L.M., 1986, review of J.H. Fisher, M. Richardson, and J.L. Fisher, *An Anthology of Chancery English* (Knoxville, TN, 1984), in *Speculum*, 61: 646–650.
Morgan, M.M., 1941, 'The suppression of the alien priories', *History*, 26: 204–212.
Morris, W.A., 1943, 'Magnates and community of the realm in parliament, 1264–1327', *Medievalia et Humanistica*, 1: 58–94.
Morris, W.A., 1947, 'The sheriff', in *The English Government at Work, 1327–1336*, Vol. II: *Fiscal Administration*, ed. W.A. Morris and J.R. Strayer (Cambridge, MA), 41–108.
Musson, A., 1996, *Public Order and Law Enforcement: The Local Administration of Criminal Justice, 1294–1350* (Woodbridge).
Musson, A., 1997, 'Twelve good men and true? The character of early fourteenth-century juries', *Law and History Review*, 15: 115–144.
Musson, A., 2001, 'Second "English Justinian" or pragmatic opportunist? A re-examination of the legal legislation of Edward III's reign', in *The Age of Edward III*, ed. J.S. Bothwell (York), 69–88.
Musson, A., and Ormrod, W.M., 1999, *The Evolution of English Justice: Law, Politics and Society in the Fourteenth Century* (Basingstoke).
Musson, A., and Powell, E., 2009, *Crime and Society in the Later Middle Ages* (Manchester).

Myers, A.R., 1937, 'Parliamentary petitions in the fifteenth century', *English Historical Review*, 52: 385–404, 590–613.
Myers, A.R., 1985, *Crown, Household and Parliament in Fifteenth-Century England* (London).
Neilson, N., 1940, 'The forests', in *The English Government at Work, 1327–1336*, Vol. I: *Central and Prerogative Administration*, ed. J.F. Willard and W.A. Morris (Cambridge, MA), 394–467.
Nightingale, P., 1995, *A Medieval Mercantile Community: The Grocers' Company of London, 1000–1485* (London).
Ormrod, W.M., 1984, 'Edward III's government of England, c.1346–1356', DPhil thesis, University of Oxford.
Ormrod, W.M., 1990a, 'Agenda for legislation, 1322–c.1340', *English Historical Review*, 105: 1–33.
Ormrod, W.M., 1990b, *The Reign of Edward III: Crown and Political Society in England, 1327–1377* (London).
Ormrod, W.M., 1991, 'Political theory in practice: The forced loan on English overseas trade of 1317–18', *Historical Research*, 64: 204–215.
Ormrod, W.M., 1995, *Political Life in Medieval England, 1300–1450* (Basingstoke).
Ormrod, W.M., 2000, 'Competing capitals? York and London in the fourteenth century', in *Courts and Regions in Medieval Europe*, ed. S. Rees Jones, R. Marks, and A.J. Minnis (Woodbridge), 75–98.
Ormrod, W.M., 2004, 'On – and off – the record: The rolls of parliament, 1337–1377', *Parliamentary History*, 23: 39–56.
Ormrod, W.M., 2008a, 'The road to Boroughbridge: The civil war of 1321–2 in the Ancient Petitions', in *Foundations of Medieval Scholarship: Records Edited in Honour of David Crook*, ed. P. Brand and S. Cunningham (York), 77–88.
Ormrod, W.M., 2008b, 'The Trials of Alice Perrers', *Speculum*, 83 (2008), 366–396.
Ormrod, W.M., 2009a, 'Introduction: Medieval petitions in context', in *Medieval Petitions: Grace and Grievance*, ed. W.M. Ormrod, G. Dodd, and A. Musson (York), 1–11.
Ormrod, W.M., 2009b, 'The language of complaint: Multilingualism and petitioning in later medieval England', in *Language and Culture in Medieval Britain: The French of England, c.1100–c.1500*, ed. J. Wogan-Browne with C. Collette, M. Kowaleski, L. Mooney, A. Putter, and D. Trotter (York), 31–43.
Ormrod, W.M., 2009c, 'The origins of tunnage and poundage: Parliament and the estate of merchants in the fourteenth century', *Parliamentary History*, 28: 209–227.
Ormrod, W.M., 2010, 'Parliament, political economy and state formation in later medieval England', in *Power and Persuasion: Essays on the Art of State Building in Honour of W.P. Blockmans*, ed. P. Hoppenbrouwers, A. Janse, and R. Stein (Turnhout), 123–140.
Ormrod, W.M., 2011, *Edward III* (London).
Ormrod, W.M., 2013a, 'Henry V and the English taxpayer', in *Henry V: New Interpretations*, ed. G. Dodd (York), 187–216.
Ormrod, W.M., 2013b, 'Parliamentary scrutiny of royal ministers and courtiers in fourteenth-century England: The disgrace of Sir John atte Lee (1368)', in *Law, Governance and Justice: New Views on Medieval Constitutionalism*, ed. R.W. Kaeuper (Leiden), 161–188.

Ormrod, W.M., 2015, ' "Common profit" and "the profit of the king and kingdom": Parliament and the development of political language in England, 1250–1450', *Viator*, 46: 219–252.
Parkes, M.B., 1969, *English Cursive Book Hands 1250–1500* (Oxford).
Perkins, C., 1910, 'The wealth of the Knights Templars in England and the disposition of it after their dissolution', *American Historical Review*, 15: 252–263.
Perkins, C., 1930, 'The Knights Hospitallers in England after the fall of the Order of the Temple', *English Historical Review*, 45: 285–289.
Phelan, A., 2000, 'Trailbaston and attempts to control violence in the reign of Edward I', in *Violence in Medieval Society*, ed. R.W. Kaeuper (Woodbridge), 129–140.
Phillips, J.R.S., 1972, *Aymer de Valence: Earl of Pembroke 1307–1324: Baronial Politics in the Reign of Edward II* (Oxford).
Phillips, [J.R.]S., 2010, *Edward II* (London).
Phillips, M., 2013, 'Church, crown and complaint: Petitions from bishops to the English crown in the fourteenth century', PhD thesis, University of Nottingham.
Phillips, S., 2009, *The Prior of the Knights Hospitaller in Late Medieval England* (Woodbridge).
Phillips, S., 2010, 'The Hospitallers' acquisition of the Templar lands in England', in *The Debate on the Trial of the Templars*, ed. J. Burgtorf, P.F. Crawford, and H. Nicholson (Farnham), 237–242.
Plucknett, T.F.T., 1940, 'Parliament', in *The English Government at Work, 1327–1336*, Vol. I: *Central and Prerogative Administration*, ed. J.F. Willard and W.A. Morris (Cambridge, MA), 82–128.
Plucknett, T.F.T., 1956, *A Concise History of the Common Law*, 5th edn (London).
Post, J.B., 1976, 'The peace commissions of 1382', *English Historical Review*, 91: 98–101.
Post, J.B., 1980, 'Sir Thomas West and the Statute of Rapes, 1382', *Bulletin of the Institute of Historical Research*, 53: 24–30.
Powell, E., 1987, 'The administration of criminal justice in late medieval England: Peace sessions and assizes', in *The Political Context of Law: Proceedings of the Seventh British Legal History Conference*, ed. R. Eales and D. Sullivan (London), 48–59.
Prestwich, M., 1972, *War, Politics and Finance under Edward I* (London).
Prestwich, M., 1983, 'Parliament and the community of the realm in fourteenth-century England', in *Parliament and Community*, ed. A. Cosgrove and J.I. McGuire (Belfast), 5–24.
Prestwich, M., 1988, *Edward I* (London).
Prestwich, M., 1990a, *English Politics in the Thirteenth Century* (Basingstoke).
Prestwich, M., 1990b, 'The Ordinances of 1311 and the politics of the early fourteenth century', in *Politics and Crisis in Fourteenth-Century England*, ed. J. Taylor and W. Childs (Gloucester), 1–18.
Prestwich, M., 1996, *Armies and Warfare in the Middle Ages* (New Haven, CT).
Prince, A.E., 1940, 'The army and navy', in *The English Government at Work, 1327–1336*, Vol. I: *Central and Prerogative Administration*, ed. J.F. Willard and W.A. Morris (Cambridge, MA), 332–393.
Pugh, R.B., 1968, *Imprisonment in Medieval England* (Cambridge).
Putnam, B.H., 1929, 'The transformation of the keepers of the peace into the justices of the peace, 1327–1380', *Transactions of the Royal Historical Society*, 4th ser., 12: 19–48.
Putnam, B.H., 1950, *The Place in Legal History of Sir William Shareshull* (Cambridge).
Raban, S., 1974, 'Mortmain in medieval England', *Past and Present*, 62: 3–26.
Raban, S., 1982, *Mortmain Legislation and the English Church* (Cambridge).

Rayner, D., 1941, 'The forms and machinery of the "commune petition" in the fourteenth century', *English Historical Review*, 56: 198–233, 549–570.
Richardson, H.G., 1922, 'Year books and plea rolls as sources of historical information', *Transactions of the Royal Historical Society*, 4th ser., 5: 28–70.
Richardson, H.G., and Sayles, G.O., 1981, *The English Parliament in the Middle Ages* (London).
Rodger, N.A.M., 1996, 'The naval service of the cinque ports', *English Historical Review*, 111: 636–651.
Rollison, D., 2010, *A Commonwealth of the People: Popular Politics and England's Long Social Revolution, 1066–1649* (Cambridge).
Roskell, J.S., Clark, L., and Rawcliffe, C., 1992, *The House of Commons, 1386–1421*, 4 vols (Stroud).
Ross, C.D., 1956, 'Forfeiture for treason in the reign of Richard II', *English Historical Review*, 71: 560–575.
Rosser, G., 1989, *Medieval Westminster, 1200–1540* (Oxford).
Saul, N., 1981, *Knights and Esquires: The Gloucestershire Gentry in the Fourteenth Century* (Oxford).
Saul, N., 1984, 'The Despensers and the downfall of Edward II', *English Historical Review*, 94: 1–33.
Saul, N., 1986, *Scenes from Provincial Life: Knightly Families in Sussex, 1280–1400* (Oxford).
Saul, N., 1990, 'The commons and the abolition of badges', *Parliamentary History*, 9: 302–315.
Saul, N., 1997, *Richard II* (New Haven, CT).
Sayles, G.O., 1952, 'The seizure of wool at Easter 1297', *English Historical Review*, 67: 543–547.
Sayles, G.O., 1975, *The King's Parliament of England* (London).
Sayles, G.O., 1988, *The Functions of the Medieval Parliament of England* (London).
Seabourne, G., 2003, *Royal Regulation of Loans and Sales in Medieval England: 'Monkish Superstition and Civil Tyranny'* (Woodbridge).
Sergeant, F., 1918, 'The wine trade with Gascony', in *Finance and Trade under Edward III*, ed. G. Unwin (Manchester), 257–311.
Sherborne, J., 1994, *War, Politics and Culture in Fourteenth-Century England* (London).
Sneddon, S.A., 2009, 'Words and realities: The language and dating of petitions, 1326–7', in *Medieval Petitions: Grace and Grievance*, ed. W.M. Ormrod, G. Dodd, and A. Musson (York), 193–205.
Steel, A., 1941, *Richard II* (Cambridge).
Stevenson, E.R., 1947, 'The escheator', in *The English Government at Work, 1327–1336*, Vol. II: *Fiscal Administration*, ed. W.A. Morris and J.R. Strayer (Cambridge, MA), 109–167.
Stubbs, W., 1896, *The Constitutional History of England in Its Origin and Development*, 4th edn (Oxford).
Sutherland, D.W., 1973, *The Assize of Novel Disseisin* (Oxford).
Thompson, B., 1994, 'The laity, the alien priories and the redistribution of ecclesiastical property', in *England in the Fifteenth Century: Proceedings of the 1992 Harlaxton Symposium*, ed. N. Rogers (Stamford), 19–41.
Tout, T.F., 1920–1933, *Chapters in the Administrative History of Mediaeval England*, 6 vols (Manchester).

Trueman, J.H., 1956, 'The privy seal and the English Ordinances of 1311', *Speculum*, 31: 611–625.
Tuck, J.A., 1969, 'The Cambridge Parliament of 1388', *English Historical Review*, 84: 225–243.
Tuck, J.A., 1984, 'Nobles, commons and the Great Revolt of 1381', in *The English Rising of 1381*, ed. R.H. Hilton and T.H. Aston (Cambridge), 194–212.
Veale, E.M., 1957, 'The rabbit in England', *Agricultural History Review*, 5: 85–90.
Veale, E.M., 2003, *The English Fur Trade in the Later Middle Ages*, 2nd edn (London).
Verduyn, A.J., 1991, 'The attitude of the parliamentary commons to law and order under Edward III', DPhil thesis, University of Oxford.
Verduyn, A., 1993, 'The politics of law and order during the early years of Edward III', *English Historical Review*, 108: 842–867.
Verduyn, A., 1995, 'The selection and appointment of justices of the peace in 1338', *Historical Research*, 68: 1–25.
Walker, S., 1990, *The Lancastrian Affinity, 1361–1399* (Oxford).
Warren, W.L., 1973, *Henry II* (London).
Watts, J., 2007, 'Public or plebs: The changing meaning of "the commons", 1381–1549', in *Power and Identity in the Middle Ages: Essays in Memory of Rees Davies*, ed. H. Pryce and J. Watts (Oxford), 242–260.
Watts, J., 2015, 'The commons in medieval England', in *La legitimité implicite: Actes des conférences organisées à Rome en 2010 et 2011 par SAS en collaboration avec l'École française de Rome*, ed. J.-P. Genet, 2 vols (Paris), II, 207–222.
Waugh, S.L., 1975, 'The confiscated lands of the Contrariants in Gloucestershire and Herefordshire in 1322: An economic and social study', PhD thesis, University of London.
Waugh, S.L., 1988, *The Lordship of England: Royal Wardships and Marriages in English Society and Politics, 1217–1327* (Princeton).
Waugh, S.L., 1991, *England in the Reign of Edward III* (Cambridge).
Weske, D.B., 1937, *Convocation of the Clergy: A Study of Its Antecedents and Its Role with Special Emphasis upon Its Growth and Activities in the Thirteenth and Fourteenth Centuries* (London).
Wilkinson, B., 1924, 'The authorisation of chancery writs under Edward III', *Bulletin of the John Rylands Library*, 8: 107–139.
Willard, J.F., 1907, 'The English Church and the lay taxes of the fourteenth century', *University of Colorado Studies*, 4: 217–225.
Williard, J.F., 1908, 'The Scotch raids and the fourteenth-century taxation of northern England', *University of Colorado Studies*, 5: 237–242.
Willard, J.F., 1934, *Parliamentary Taxes on Personal Property, 1290–1334* (Cambridge, MA).
Willard, J.F., 1947, 'The collectors of lay taxes', in *The English Government at Work, 1327–1336*, Vol. II: *Fiscal Administration*, ed. W.A. Morris and J.R. Strayer (Cambridge, MA), 201–226.
Williams, G.A., 1963, *Medieval London: From Commune to Capital* (London).
Wood, D., 1989, *Clement VI: The Pontificate and Ideas of an Avignon Pope* (Cambridge).
Young, C.R., 1979, *The Royal Forests of Medieval England* (Philadelphia, PA).

INDEX

Statutes are indexed by year of issue, with names where they are commonly attached; the use of the calendar year helps to link statutes to the list of parliaments elsewhere in the index. For sessions of parliament, dates have been restricted to the year, with the months given where necessary. Dates of death are included only where there are several persons in the same family of the same name during the period covered by this volume. English place names are given with historic county, when needed.

abduction of women 192, 193, 196
Aberdeen 138
actions: *capias* 171–172; champerty 53, 212, 216; distraint 103–104, 199, 203, 269–270, 271; essoin 210–211; felony 99–100, 106, 112, 199, 202–203, 245, 246, 247, 249; homicide and murder 191, 192, 199, 202, 208, 245, 247–248; *nisi prius* 106–107; *novel disseisin* 260, 261; replevin 171–172; statute merchant 116–118; trespass 192, 193, 215, 219, 239–241, 242; *see also* writs
ale, price of 136–137
aliens: expulsion of 61; right to trade 257; *see also* priories
alnager 135–136, 146–147
Ammanati company 130–133
Anne of Bohemia, queen (d.1394) 94
annuities, royal 44–45
Antwerp 258
assize: justices of 107, 124, 240–242; *see also* bread and ale, cloth, writs
attaint, writ of 107–109
Avignon 56

badges and liveries 125–127
bailiffs, return of money by 212, 215
Baldock, Robert, chancellor 238
bastards: and tenancy 246, 249; legitimization of 55–56
Bedfordshire 155–156
Bereford, William, chief justice of common pleas 139–140

Berkeley (Glos.): castle 102
Berwick-upon-Tweed 138–139; keeper of 174
Beverley (Yorks.) 76–77
bigamy 53–55
Black Death 12, 170, 172, 178, 242
Blencanhop, Thomas de 173
Bohun, Humphrey, earl of Hereford (d.1322) 71
Bolingbroke, Henry, duke of Lancaster 91; *see also* Henry IV
Boniface VIII, pope 132
boroughs, *see* cities and boroughs
Boroughbridge, Battle of 8, 71, 165, 220
Boulogne, Declaration of (1308) 7
bread and ale, assize of 192–193, 196
Brembre, Nicholas, mayor of London 123
Bridport (Dorset) 280n
Brittany 176
Bury St Edmunds 76–77; abbey of 77
butler, king's 129–130

Calais, staple at 8
Cambridge, parliament at, 1388 10, 263
Cambridgeshire 155–156, 176–179
Canterbury, cathedral archives of 10, 275n
capias, see actions
caps, manufacture and sale of 139–140
Carlisle, parliament at, 1307, *see* parliament
Castile 185
chamber, king's 32–33, 71–72; receiver of 33
champerty, *see* actions

298 INDEX

chancellor 24, 198, 199, 202, 203, 205, 235, 236, 238, 245, 247, 250; *see also* Baldock
chancery 21, 31, 57, 75, 76, 133, 139, 140, 194, 198, 199, 201, 202, 205, 212, 216, 221, 222, 225, 229, 233, 235, 237, 245, 247, 252, 256, 270; clerks of 3, 15, 102; petitioning in 221, 222; *see also* chancellor, writs
Cheshire, palatinate of 10
chirographers, fees of 41–42, 263–265
Cinque Ports 167–169, 246, 247–248
cities and boroughs: curfews in 191, 193; false verdicts in 88–89; franchises and customs of 252, 256; mayors, bailiffs, and aldermen of 224, 228; parliamentary petitions of 198, 201–202
civil war (1321–1322) 138, 196, 239
Clarendon, Constitutions of (1164) 48
Clement V, pope 49, 224
Clement VI, pope 57
clergy: benefit of 53–55; *gravamina* of 48; marriage of 53–55
Cleydon, William 22
cloth, assize of 135–136, 146–147
coinage: counterfeit 192, 194, 196; exchange 150–151; value of 197, 201, 204–205
Colchester 245, 248
commissions of the peace, *see* peace
common pleas, court of 31, 142, 199, 203; chief justice and justices of 31–32; *see also* Bereford, Herle, Staunton
Commons, House of, *see* parliament, commons in
constable of England: and debts and contracts 267; and marshal of England, court of 267–68; *see also* marshal of England
constables: and keeping the peace 191, 193; of castles 199, 203
Contrariants 70–71, 165–166
Cornwall, Piers Gaveston, earl of 204
coroner, office of 192, 193
council, king's 2, 3–5, 7, 13, 14, 19, 20, 24, 25, 26, 29, 32, 49, 50, 57, 58, 60, 67, 68, 69, 74, 98, 99, 100, 101, 103, 111, 113, 114, 115, 119, 122, 123, 126, 134, 136, 137, 138, 142, 143, 155, 158, 159, 161, 165, 172, 173, 176, 177, 180, 181, 186, 188, 190, 198, 202, 204, 208, 209, 220, 224, 227, 232–233, 241, 250, 265, 266, 268, 271; 1317 session 209; 1327 session 102–103; 1384 session 123; 1353 session of great council 58; 1381 session of great council (Reading) 185
crusade against Flanders (1383) 185–187
Cumberland 188–189; sheriff of 30
currency, *see* coinage
customs system 130–131, 142–144, 161–163, 197, 200, 207; new custom (1303) 205, 208

debt: repayment of from estates of deceased 98–99; *see also* writs
debtors: imprisonment of 119–122; restoration of lands to 116–118
dedimus potestatem, writ of 31–32
Denmark, Hanse towns in 154
Derbyshire 155–156
Despenser, Henry, bishop of Norwich 179, 185–186
Despenser, Hugh the elder, earl of Winchester (d.1326) 49–50, 165, 233, 239
Despenser, Hugh the younger (d.1326) 22, 49–51, 165, 233, 239
Devon 48; justices of trailbaston in 98
disseisin, *see* writs
distraint, *see* actions
Doddington (Cambs.) 115
Dounbrigge, William 122
Dunbar (Scotland): castle 173
Dunbar, George, earl of Dunbar and March (d.1420) 173–174
Durham, palatinate of 169

ecclesiastical courts, jurisdiction of 47–48, 53–58
Edward I, king 1, 4, 7, 9, 20, 21, 22, 23, 36, 39, 53, 54, 75, 79, 81, 82, 87, 88, 131, 143, 154, 168, 195, 199, 202, 205, 209, 233
Edward II, king 4, 7, 8, 17, 21, 22, 23, 26, 27, 49, 70, 71, 72, 93, 102, 110, 134, 136, 137, 154, 165, 195, 196, 206, 208, 209, 211, 220, 223, 232, 233
Edward III, king 4, 7, 8, 17, 21, 22, 23, 24, 27, 30, 31, 33, 36, 37, 38, 39, 42, 60, 72, 73, 74, 80, 81, 82, 87, 93, 100, 108, 110, 119, 134, 143, 144, 149, 154, 169, 174, 176, 185, 195, 197, 208, 220, 233, 234, 239, 244, 264, 266; debts of 151–153, 160–161
Edward, prince of Wales (d.1376) 185

INDEX

Ely, Thomas de Lisle, bishop of 115–116
enfeoffment 118–119
escheats 215, 217, 245–246, 259
escheators 199, 203, 235, 237, 243, 259–260; oaths of 31
Essex 177–179
essoin, *see* actions
exchequer 19, 20, 45, 102, 121–122, 130, 131, 135, 136, 142, 149, 150–151, 161, 189, 213, 216, 221, 223, 226, 231, 234, 235, 236, 260, 261, 262; accounting at 71–72; and ancient increment 262; barons of 19, 100–101, 225, 226, 230, 231; *Dialogue of the Exchequer* 93; justices filing documents at 213, 216; and queen's gold 93; *see also* treasurer of the exchequer, writs
executors 116–117, 214, 218, 244–245, 247, 267
Exton, Nicholas, mayor of London 123, 159
eyre 30, 213, 217, 220, 226, 231, 233–234, 245, 246, 248, 251, 254

fairs 198, 202, 225, 229–230, 233
famine and harvest failure 137
fee farms, leasing of 68–69
felons: chattels of 213–214, 217, 226, 231, 233, 245, 248; enlisting in Scottish wars 251, 253–254; evasion of due process by 199, 202–203, 206–207; fugitive 251, 254; imprisonment of 239–241
felony, *see* actions
Felton, Mary 185
Felton, Robert 185
Felton, Thomas, seneschal of Gascony 183–185
fines, abuse of 82–83
firewood, sale of 147–148
Flanders 138
Florence 131–133
Fogg, Thomas 176, 185
forests: courts in 30; election of officials in 29–30; jurisdiction of officials in 20–22, 86–88; keepers or justices of 20–22; perambulations of 21–22; regards and regarders in 29–30; verderers in 29–30
forestalling and forestallers 133–135, 141–142
France 131, 232, 239; Philip IV, king of 49
franchises, bailiffs of 40–41
freeholders, rights of 182–183
Fresney, Gerard de 132–133

Friskney, Walter 141
furs, wearing of 214, 218

gaol delivery, commissions and justices of 124, 212, 216, 240–242, 245, 247
Gascony 74, 213, 216; Thomas Felton, seneschal of 183–185
Gaunt, John of, duke of Lancaster 123, 185
Gaveston, Piers, earl of Cornwall 204
Gerard, Henry 122
Germany, English merchants trading in 133–135
Gisors, John, mayor of London 100
Gloucester 75; parliament at, 1378, *see* parliament
Gournay, Matthew 174–176
Gravesend, Stephen, bishop of London 235, 236, 238
Great Yarmouth (Norfolk) 165
Gregory X, pope 54
Gregory XI, pope 59

Hale, Sir Mathew 51, 70, 73, 115
Hanchach, John 177–179
Hanse, company and merchants of 153–155
Harley, Richard de 20
Henry I, king 74
Henry II, king 21, 48, 74
Henry III, king 7, 21, 74–75, 213, 216, 221, 243; debts of 221–222
Henry IV, king 45, 66, 93, 96, 126, 162, 190, 262, 270; *see also* Bolingbroke
Henry V, king 190, 270, 271
Henry VI, king 6
Henry VII, king 1
Hereford, Humphrey Bohun, earl of (d.1322) 71
Herle, William de, justice of common pleas 235, 236, 238
Heselden, Thomas 179
highways, maintenance of 144–145
Hoccleve, Thomas 15n
homicide, *see* actions
honors, forfeited by rebels 235, 237, 239
Hospitallers, *see* St John of Jerusalem, order of
household, king's 33, 37–38, 76, 126, 142, 143, 149, 161, 195, 196, 205, 251, 253; marshal of 205; steward of 205; *see also* Lee
household, queen's 148–150, 196, 251, 253
Hundred Years War 59, 61

300   INDEX

hundreds: bailiffs of 39–40; courts of 38–40
Huntingdonshire 155–156, 177–178

Ilsington (Norfolk) 155–156
imprisonment, after false accusations 235, 236–237
indictments, false 52–53, 180–181
inheritance 67–68, 209–211, 212, 215, 233, 268
inquests 97–98, 199, 203, 243, 246, 249
inquisitions post mortem 68
Ipswich (Suffolk), customs service at 161–163
Isabella of France, queen (d.1409) 94
Italy, merchant companies of 131–133

John, king (d.1216) 22, 243
juries and jurors: bribery of 246, 248; perjury by 109; review of verdicts by 88–89
justices of the peace, *see* peace

Kent 169, 177–178
king's bench: chief justice and justices of 31–32; court of 106, 111–114, 142; marshal of 27–29; marshalsea of 29; *see also* Mablethorpe, Scrope
Kings Langley (Herts.) 205
King's Lynn, *see* Lynn

Lancashire 185
Lancaster, duke of, *see* Bolingbroke, Gaunt
Lancaster, Thomas of, earl of Lancaster (d.1322) 71, 165–167, 220, 239, 281n; ministers of 166–167
lands, illegal alienation of 209–211, 212, 215
Larcher, Thomas, prior of the order of St John of Jerusalem in England 49–50
leases 85–86
Lee, John atte 76
legal memory, limit of 74–75, 81–82
legal system, abuse of 79, 239–242, 265–266; by lords 265–266
legislation, *see* statutes
Leicestershire 155–156
Lesnes (Kent), abbot of 66
liberties, justice in 72–74, 76–78
Lincoln: diocese of 65; parliaments at, *see* parliament, 1301, 1316, 1327
Lisle, Thomas de, bishop of Ely 115–116
liveries and badges 125–127

loan, forced (1317) 209
Lollards 10
London 45–45, 74, 99–100, 133, 139–40, 141–142, 158–160, 224, 228, 257; absence of courts and exchequer from 142; bail in 99–100; cappers of 139–140; eyre of 100; fishmongers and victuallers of 158–160; Fleet prison 119–120; Fleet Street 139–140; mayor and aldermen of 8, 158–160; mayor and sheriffs of 139–140; regraters in 141–142; Tower of 146, 174–175
London, bishop of, *see* Gravesend
Lords, House of, *see* parliament, lords in
Lynn (Norfolk) 138–139, 156, 162
Lyons, Council of, II (1272–1274) 54

Mablethorpe, Robert, justice of king's bench 141
Male, Louis, count of Flanders (d.1384) 186
March, earl of, *see* Mortimer
Markeley, Robert de 44–45
marshal of England: and debts and contracts 267–268; suits of pleas 198, 201–202; *see also* constable of England
Melrose (Scotland) 174
Mercer, Andrew 173
Mercer, John 173
military service 192, 193
ministers, royal, misconduct by 22–23, 103–104, 197, 199, 235, 237, 242–243
minors, land rights of 82–83
mints, royal 196
monastic houses, sale of benefits by 65–66
money, *see* coinage
mort d'ancestor, writ of 84–85
Mortimer, Roger, earl of March (d.1330) 50, 73
mortmain 63–65
Mowbray, Thomas, duke of Norfolk (d.1399) 91
murage 224, 228
murder, *see* actions
Musgrave, Thomas de 173–174
Musgrave, Thomas de, the younger 173–174

Newcastle upon Tyne 188–189
nisi prius, *see* actions
Norfolk 162; ancient increment of 260–263; flooding in 155–157; knights of the shire for 262; and Suffolk, shrievalty of 262

INDEX

Norfolk, Thomas Mowbray, duke of (d.1399) 91
Northampton, John, mayor of London 122–124, 159–160
Northamptonshire 155–156
Northumberland 188–190; sheriff of 26
Northumberland, Henry Percy, earl of (d.1408) 173
Norway, Hanse towns in 154
Norwich, bishop of, *see* Despenser
Nottingham: commissions of oyer and terminer at 251, 253, 257; council at 209
novel disseisin, *see* actions, writs

ordinances: 1305 (trailbaston) 194–195; 1306 (of the forest) 21; 1311 (New Ordinances) 21, 24, 195, 206, 208, 220, 249; 1317 136–137; 1343 (of Provisors) 57; 1373 150–151; *see also* statutes
Oxford, University of 62–63
oyer and terminer, commissions and justices of 23, 34–35, 194, 213, 217, 251, 253; *see also* writs

papacy: cases at curia of 56–58, 224; income from benefices for 58–60; provisions by 57 58; taxation by 59
pardons 199, 202–203, 205, 206–207, 208, 242–243, 251, 254, 257
parliament:
  clerks of 5, 6, 9, 15–16, 76, 110, 120, 123, 157, 233, 239, 241, 258, 265, 271; commission (1398) 91
  commons in 2–9, 12–13, 15–16, 37, 40, 41, 42, 43, 45, 49, 53, 54, 57–58, 59, 61, 63, 64–65, 75, 76, 77, 78, 80, 81, 88, 89, 91, 105, 107, 109, 110, 112–113, 115, 118, 122, 123, 126–127, 144, 151, 155, 158, 162, 169, 171, 175–176, 177, 179, 181, 190, 205, 208, 209, 220, 238–239, 241, 242, 250, 257, 258, 260, 265, 267–268, 270, 271; knights of the shires 7, 181, 208, 220; knights of the shires and burgesses 2, 4, 7, 8, 53, 208; speaker of, *see* Savage
  lords in 8, 13, 105–106, 108, 115, 159, 181, 188
  common petitions 1–16; enrolment of 2, 5–6, 9–10, 16; form 12–16; language 12–13; not answered 252–253, 256, 258; scribes of 14–16

private petitions 2–5, 6, 10–15, 33, 37, 77, 90–92, 205–206, 209, 211, 223, 239, 250, 258; not answered 198, 201–202, 205–206, 221–223, 258
rolls 1, 5, 6, 9–10, 11, 12, 17, 22, 26, 28, 31, 33, 39, 40, 43, 48, 50, 53, 54, 56, 69, 61, 64, 66, 68, 69, 79, 80, 81, 83, 84, 85, 86, 88, 89, 91, 92, 94, 95, 105, 109, 113, 116, 119, 120, 121, 122, 123, 126, 131, 139, 144, 146, 148, 151, 155, 157, 159, 163, 167, 168, 172, 185, 186, 190, 195, 204, 205, 211, 223, 250, 258, 260, 264, 265, 268, 270
sessions of:
  1290 (Westminster) 274n
  1301 (Lincoln) 10, 274n
  1302 (Westminster) 20, 274n
  1305 (Westminster) 48, 275n
  1307 (Carlisle) 97–98, 131, 133, 275n
  1309, Apr.–May (Westminster) 197, 199, 204, 208, 277n
  1309, July–Aug. (Stamford) 197, 200, 204, 208, 277n
  1313 (Westminster) 48
  1315 (Westminster) 85, 134, 277n
  1316 (Lincoln) 211
  1318 (York) 25, 26, 139–140, 209, 211, 278n
  1319, May (York) 28, 139–140, 211, 278n
  1320, Jan. (York) 28, 211
  1320, Oct. (Westminster) 28, 279n
  1321 (Westminster) 100, 219
  1322, May (York) 26, 72, 75, 142, 166, 167, 206, 211, 219, 249, 279n
  1322, Nov. (York) 167, 211
  1324, Feb.–Mar. (Westminster) 27, 223, 280n
  1324, Oct.–Nov. (Westminster) 70, 220, 232, 234, 280n
  1325, June (Westminster) 70
  1325, Oct.–Dec. (Westminster) 238, 280n
  1327, Jan.–Mar. (Westminster) 22, 30, 49, 54, 72, 166, 280n
  1327, Sept. (Lincoln) 102, 211, 281n
  1330, Mar. (Winchester) 73
  1330, Nov.–Dec. (Westminster) 50, 73, 196
  1331 (Westminster) 195, 196, 249, 250
  1332–1333 (York) 258, 281n
  1334, Feb.–Mar. (York) 52–53, 54, 242, 282n

1334, Sept. (Westminster) 53
1335 (York) 53
1336 (Westminster) 53
1337, Mar. (Westminster) 257, 258, 282n
1339, Feb. (Westminster) 257–258
1339, Oct. (Westminster) 144–145
1340, Mar.–May (Westminster) 235, 282n
1341 (Westminster) 112
1343 (Westminster) 58, 112
1344 (Westminster) 54, 58, 112–113
1346 (Westminster) 58, 59, 113
1348, Jan–Feb. (Westminster) 56, 58, 77, 113, 115, 117
1348, Mar.–Apr. (Westminster) 77–78, 117
1351 (Westminster) 58, 59
1352 (Westminster) 171
1354 (Westminster) 109
1361 (Westminster) 109
1362 (Westminster) 80, 148
1363 (Westminster) 37, 38, 80
1365 (Westminster) 37
1368 (Westminster) 76
1369 (Westminster) 61, 81
1371 (Westminster) 37, 91, 263, 264
1372 (Westminster) 80, 81
1373 (Westminster) 59, 61, 170, 188, 264
1376 (Westminster), the 'Good Parliament' 39, 40, 54, 60, 61, 80, 81–82, 83, 91, 149, 151, 168, 175, 185, 242, 262, 264
1377, Jan.–Mar. (Westminster), the 'Bad Parliament' 42, 80, 88, 119, 149
1377, Oct.–Nov. (Westminster) 61, 84, 88, 92, 119, 120, 121, 150, 151–152, 173, 183, 265, 266
1378 (Gloucester) 92–93, 151, 153, 154
1379 (Westminster) 91, 153, 156, 161
1380, Jan.–Mar. (Westminster) 154, 156
1380, Nov.–Dec. 1380 (Westminster) 158, 161
1381–1382 (Westminster) 64, 85, 158, 177, 179, 181, 185, 186
1382 (Westminster) 159
1383, Feb.–Mar. (Westminster) 159, 179, 187
1383, Oct.–Nov. (Westminster) 94
1384 (Westminster) 268

1385 (Westminster) 155, 170–171, 179, 162
1386 (Westminster), the 'Wonderful Parliament' 43
1388 (Westminster), the 'Merciless Parliament' 10, 91, 94–96, 123, 161
1388 (Cambridge) 262
1390 (Westminster) 43, 63, 123, 268, 000
1391 (Westminster) 123, 171, 188
1394 (Westminster) 64
1397, Jan.–Feb. (Westminster) 188
1397, Sept. (Westminster) 95
1398 (Shrewsbury) 91
1399 (Westminster) 95, 126, 188
1401 (Westminster) 66, 96, 126–127, 268
1402 (Westminster) 45, 66, 93, 188, 189–190
1404 (Westminster) 126
1404 (Coventry) 162
1406 (Westminster) 162–163
1410 (Westminster) 10, 268, 270
1413 (Westminster) 271
1429 (Westminster) 268
pavage 224, 228
peace, commissions and justices of 29, 36–37, 111–113, 124, 242
Peasants' Revolt 176–183, 186, 188
Pecche, John 141
Pembroke, Aymer de Valence, earl of 22
Percy, Henry, earl of Northumberland (d.1408) 173
Perrers, Alice 148–149
petitions, *see* parliament
Philip IV, king of France 49
Philippa, queen 94; debts of 148–150
Phippe, Robert 177–178
Pistoia (Italy) 131–132
Poitou 174
pontage 224, 228
Pontefract (Yorks.), council at 100–103
Pontvallain (Maine, now Sarthe), Battle of 185
priories, alien 60–62
prisage, receivers of 198, 202, 205
prisoners: bail and release of 27–29; of war 173–174
privy seal 205; *see also* writs
prohibition, writ of 48
Prussia, Hanse towns in 144
Pulci company 131–133
Pulle, Thomas 183–185

INDEX   303

purveyance and prises 35–38, 191, 192, 195–196, 197, 200, 204–205, 220, 251, 253, 257; *see also* victualling

queen's gold 93–94

rabbit warrens, destruction of 89–90
rape 192, 193, 196
Reading (Berks.), *see* council, king's
regraters 133–135, 141–142
Remertini company 133
Remonstrances of 1297 7
replevin, *see* actions
Richard I, king 21, 74, 81
Richard II, king 6, 17, 37, 42, 43, 44, 45, 54, 61, 85, 87, 88, 91, 93, 94–95, 119, 126, 149, 151, 161, 154, 169, 174, 176, 181, 186, 190, 266
right, *see* writs

St John of Jerusalem, order of (Hospitallers) 49–51, 221–224; prior of, *see* Larcher; Tibertis
St Loo, John 175–176
Saint-Sardos, War of 233, 239
Sandwich (Kent) 168
Savage, Arnold, speaker of the commons 126
scire facias, writ of 117
Scotland: money of 150–151; prisoners of war from 173–174; raids from 188–190; war with 204, 251, 254
Scrope, Geoffrey le, chief justice of king's bench 235, 236, 238
Scrope, Henry, chief justice of king's bench 27–28
Segrave, Stephen 141
serjeants at law, king's 235, 236
sheriffs 192, 193, 195, 226, 230, 233, 243; castles attached to office of 42–43; clerks of 226, 230; delivery of gaols by 212, 216, 239–241, 245, 247; and fugitive felons 251, 254; misconduct by 19–20, 23, 25–27, 29–30, 221, 222, 223, 225–226, 229–231, 233, 234, 240, 241, 242–243, 244, 245, 247, 259; oaths of 30; replacement of 24–25, 26, 260; return of money by 212, 215; rights of 24–25; sureties for prisoners 269, 270, 271; suspension of 25; tourns of 38–40
Shrewsbury (Salop), parliament at, 1398 91

Shropshire and Staffordshire, sheriff of 19–20; Richard de Harley 20
Shudy Camps (Cambs.) 179
soldiers 252, 255
Somerset 175
Southampton, tronager of 144
Spink, Richard 115–116
Stamford (Lincs.), parliament at, 1309 197, 200, 204, 208
Stamford Articles (1309) 195, 197–206, 208, 239
Stapeldon, Walter, treasurer of the exchequer 72
statutes:
  enrolment of 79–81
  1215 (Magna Carta) 7, 135–136, 145, 107, 200, 213, 216, 217, 225, 229, 235, 237, 250, 253
  1216 (Magna Carta) 219–220
  1217 (Charter of the Forest) 21, 22, 30, 234, 236, 250, 253
  1217 (Magna Carta) 220
  1225 (Magna Carta) 39, 195, 220
  1267 (Marlborough) 225, 229, 233, 269, 270–271
  1275 (Westminster I) 74, 104, 220
  1276 54
  1278 (Gloucester) 209–211, 212, 216, 219
  1279 63–65
  1283 (Acton Burnell) 117
  1285 (*de donis*) 244
  1285 (Merchants) 118, 213, 217
  1285 (Westminster II) 42, 173, 210, 211, 212, 215, 219, 264
  1285 (Winchester) 191, 193, 195
  1297 (Magna Carta) 39, 195
  1300 (*Articuli Super Cartas*) 20, 25, 36, 195, 205, 220
  1309 (Stamford) 205–206
  1316 (Lincoln) 25–26, 221, 222, 223, 225, 226, 229, 230, 233
  1322 (York) 25
  1324 223–224
  1327 87–88, 108
  1328 (Northampton) 25, 136, 244
  1330 36, 53, 244
  1331 28–29, 107, 108, 195, 244
  1335 (York) 252, 256, 257
  1336 43
  1337 257
  1340 43, 234
  1351 (Provisors) 58, 59

304　INDEX

1352　145–146
1353 (Praemunire I)　58, 59
1353　147
1357　39
1361　109
1362 (Purveyors)　35–38
1362　80
1371　264
1377　80–81, 119
1382　158–160
1383　179
1384　268
1388 (Cambridge)　263
1390　268
1391　64
1392　37
1399　126, 262–263, 268
1445　271
statute merchant: clerks of recognizances of 33–34; *see also* actions
Staunton, Hervey, justice of common pleas 139–140
stewards, courts of 32–33, 269–270; false presentments 212, 216; fines taken by 261, 262; suits of pleas 198, 201
Stirkland, William de　173
Stirwyth, Roger　173
storm of 1362　147–148
Straw, Jack　177–179
Suffolk 155–156, 162; ancient increment of 260, 261, 262; knights of the shire for 262
Suffolk, William Ufford, earl of　157
Sussex　133–134, 169

tallage　234, 236
taxation: assessment of clergy 62–63; collectors of 207, 260, 261, 263, 269, 270, 271 illegal 251–252, 254–255; parliamentary grants of, 1309 (twenty-fifth) 204; 1332 (tenth and fifteenth) 252, 255; 1334 (tenth and fifteenth) 252, 255; *see also* papacy
Templars, lands of　48–51, 221, 222, 223–224
tenements, ejection from　92–93
testaments, fees for　269, 270, 271
Tibertis, Leonard of, prior of the order of St John of Jerusalem in England　50
tithe of *silva cedua*　263–264
Toutheby, Gilbert, king's sergeant at law 139–140
towns, disturbances of the peace in　224, 228

trailbaston, commissions and justices of 36, 98, 111–113, 191, 192, 194–195, 197, 257; *see also* ordinances
treasurer of the exchequer 24–26, 71, 72, 93, 100–101, 103, 135, 150, 160, 226, 231; *see also* Stapeldon
trespass, *see* actions, writs
trials, conspiracy in　53
tronager　142–144
Tyler, Walter (Wat)　177–178

Ufford, William, earl of Suffolk　157
Urban VI, pope　187
usury　227, 232

Valence, Aymer de, earl of Pembroke　22
victualling 123, 158–160; by great lords 214–215, 218–219; *see also* purveyance
Vienne, Council of (1312)　50
villeinage, exception of　113–116
villeins, fugitive　169–173, 185–188

Wales　168
Walsingham, Thomas　174
warranty, vouchers of　78–79
Warwickshire　155–156
waste land, leasing of　69–71
waterways　155–157
Watling Street　144
weights and measures　145–146, 214, 217, 220, 225, 232, 228–229
Westminster: absence of courts and exchequer from 142; parliaments at, *see* parliament
Westmorland　190
Wiggenhall (Norfolk)　155–156
wills, executors of　214, 218, 244–245, 247, 267
Wiltshire, sheriff of　30
Winchester: cathedral cartulary of 10, 282n; parliament at, March 1330 104
Winchester, earl of, *see* Despenser
wine: gauge of 157–158; prisage of 129–130
woodland, hunting rights in　86–88
wool: custom of 207, 208–209; prise (1297) 130–131, 209; staple 214, 218; tronage 142–144, 161–162
Workesley, Geoffrey　176, 183–185
writs:　assize 84–85;　attaint 108–109; chancery 27–28, 114–115, 182; debt

219, 244, 247; *dedimus potestatem* 31–32; disseisin 212, 215; exchequer 22–23; mort d'ancestor 84–85; *novel disseisin* 74, 84–85; oyer and terminer 251, 254; privy seal 198–199, 202, 223, 268; prohibition 48; right 74, 213, 216; *scire facias* 117; trespass 213, 214, 217, 218; *see also* actions

Wykeham, Willam 176

York: courts and exchequer at 102, 141; parliaments at, *see* parliament, regraters 141–142
Yorkshire, sheriff of 30

Zwin Estuary, naval battle in (1385) 155